Contemporary France

Contemporary France
Politics and society
since 1945

D. L. Hanley, A. P. Kerr
and N. H. Waites

Routledge
London and New York

First published in 1979
Revised edition published in 1984 by
Routledge & Kegan Paul Ltd
Reprinted 1988 by Routledge

11 New Fetter Lane, London EC4P 4EE

Printed in the USA by
Routledge
a division of Routledge, Chapman and Hall, Inc.
29 West 35th Street, New York, NY 10001

Set in IBM Press Roman
by Hope Services, Abingdon
and printed in Great Britain by
The Guernsey Press Co. Ltd., Guernsey, Channel Islands.

Reprinted 1986 and 1988

Library of Congress Cataloging in Publication Data

Hanley, D. L. (David L.), 1944-

Contemporary France.
Bibliography: p.
Includes index
1. France—Politics and government—1958- .
2. France—Social conditions—1945- .   3. France—
Economic conditions—1945- .   I. Kerr, A. P.
II. Waites, N. H. (Neville H.)   III. Title
UN2594.2.H35 1984   944.082   84-6895

British Library Cataloguing in Publication Data available

ISBN 0 415 02522 2 (pbk.)

Contents

Figures

Tables

Preface and acknowledgments

This textbook is designed mainly for use by students in departments of French Studies or European Studies, i.e. those who in addition to learning the French language are studying the social and political structure of modern France. We also hope, however, that it will be of interest to students in politics departments, perhaps by dint of its rather different approach. Our book aims to analyse the working of the French political system and set this into its social and economic context. We give considerable attention to the latter, in fact, and spend less time than some authors on the formal mechanisms of government decision-making; in our view, these are more than adequately analysed in much recent work on French politics (see bibliography) which fits into the 'government and politics' tradition, rather than into the 'politics and society' approach undertaken here.

A second feature of the book is that its approach is historical. This reflects not simply the fact that its authors all teach modern French history, but also a methodological belief common to them all, viz. that a social system can only be understood in any of its constituent parts – political, cultural or whatever – if analysed in terms of its historical development. For this reason we begin with a general historical outline of developments in key sectors – social and economic structures, domestic politics, foreign relations – since 1945. After this, specific aspects of the social and political system are then analysed in turn, again from a historical point of view.

It is hoped that thus equipped students will be able to engage in further exploration of French politics and society. Our book therefore embodies a third distinctive feature, a critical bibliography. At the risk of sacrificing quantity for quality, we have tried to give some idea of what various secondary works involve (degree of difficulty, type of analysis, etc.), rather than giving the undifferentiated list in alphabetical order that some textbooks use. As we assume that any serious student of contemporary France will have a reading knowledge of the language, no special effort has been made to single out material in English.

So far as possible we have tried to avoid jargon and to explain fully our terminology. This may involve being over-explicit in places; but we feel that this is a risk worth taking in a work which aims above all to initiate. Although there was clearly a division of labour among the authors (D.L. Hanley was responsible for chapters 1(1), 1(4), 1(5), 2, 3(3) and 4: A.P. Kerr for 1(3), 3(1), 3(2) and 6: and N.H. Waites for 1(2) and 5), this work is to some extent a joint effort, in that it represents several years of dialogue and shared experience. None the less, readers will notice clear differences of emphasis or approach in some parts of the book. There are no apologies to be made for this: it simply reflects the fact that in the social sciences there are in the end no definite answers, particularly in the study of a society like contemporary France, which is clearly in a period of dynamic change. But this does not mean that the book fails to express any opinions; the authors have made their viewpoints and conclusions clear at each stage of the book rather than impose a formal conclusion at the very end. Their intention is to encourage argument and discussion among readers who can formulate judgments of their own on the basis of the text, followed up by the recommended reading.

Our thanks are due to the staffs of several institutions, who helped us greatly with documentation – the Centre de documentation of the Ministère de l'éducation and the former Ministère des universités: the Institut d'études politiques: the Institut national de la statistique et des études économiques (rue de Bercy, Paris): the French Embassy, London: the Royal Institute of International Affairs: the Service de traitement de l'information et de la statistique industrielle. We are also grateful to the Research Board of Reading University for the provision of money to facilitate our research and to Reading University Library for helping to provide resources in books and periodicals despite severe financial cuts.

Many individuals helped particularly in the preparation of this book, by giving expert advice or technical assistance, or answering questions. Our thanks are offered to them in alphabetical order - J. Boisson, C. Calvez, S. Cann, G. de Carmoy, P. Collet, A. Duguet, M. Fowkes, D. Hay, P.M. Jones, V. Laloy, F. Loncle, J. Ouvrier, K. Sainsbury, F. de la Serre, A. Shlaim, M. Vaïsse and P. Woodward. For the second edition we are additionally grateful to J.-A. Arnéodo, D. Breillat, H. and J. Chuquet, A. Gardrat, B. Hughes, T. Lyne, Y. Madiot, M. Paillard, M.-C. Smouts, C. Verley, and P. Wass. Valerie Andrews was a marvel of efficiency and helpfulness in producing the final typescript. As always, there were many others, too numerous to mention, who helped in many different ways; our thanks are offered to them also. Responsibility for errors remains of course with us.

The authors and publishers are grateful to the following for permission to reproduce copyright material: the French Embassy, London, for Fig. 5.2; Librairie Armand Colin for Table 1.1; *Le Nouvel Observateur* for Table 2.8; La Documentation française for Tables 2.9 and 2.10; OECD for Table 2.11; Professor Thompson and Butterworths for Table 2.13; Hodder & Stoughton Ltd for Table 2.14.

D.L. Hanley, A.P. Kerr, N.H. Waites

Abbreviations

APLE	Association parlementaire pour la liberté de l'enseignement
BEP	Brevet d'études professionnelles
CAP	Certificat d'aptitude professionnelle
CAPCEG (or CAPEGC)	Certificat d'aptitude au professorat d'enseignement général de collège
CAPES	Certificat d'aptitude au professorat du second degré
CD	Centre démocrate
CDS	Centre des démocrates sociaux
CEG	Collège d'enseignement général
CEP	Certificat d'éducation professionnelle *or* Certificat d'études primaires
CERES	Centre d'études, de recherches et d'éducation socialistes
CES	Collège d'enseignement secondaire *or* Commission d'établissement et de spécialistes
CFDT	Confédération française démocratique du travail
CFTC	Confédération française des travailleurs chrétiens
CGC	Confédération générale des cadres
CGPME	Confédération générale des petites et moyennes entreprises
CGT	Confédération générale du travail
CIASI	Comité interministériel d'ampenagement des structures industrielles
CIDUNATI	Comité d'information et de défense – Union nationale des artisans et travailleurs indépendants
CIR	Convention des institutions républicaines
CNAL	Comité national d'action laïque
CNDP	Centre national de documentation pédagogique
CNEC	Centre national de l'enseignement catholique
CNES	Conseil national de l'enseignement supérieur
CNESER	Conseil national de l'enseignement supérieur et de la recherche
CNIP	Centre national des indépendants et paysans
CNJA	Centre national des jeunes agriculteurs
CNPF	Conseil national du patronat français

CODENE	Comité pour le désarmement nucléaire en Europe
CPDM	Centre pour le progrès et la démocratie moderne
CPG	Common programme of government
CPPN	Classe pré-professionnelle de niveau
CSCU	Conseil supérieur des corps universitaires
CSEN	Conseil supérieur de l'éducation nationale
CSP	Catégorie socio-professionnelle
CSU	Conseil supérieur des universitaires
CSPU	Conseil supérieur provisoire des universités
DATAR	Délégation à l'aménagement du territoire et à l'action régionale
DEA	Diplôme d'études approfondies
DESS	Diplôme d'études supérieures spécialisées
DEUG	Diplôme d'études universitaires générales
DGF	Dotation globale de fonctionnement
DOM-TOM	Départements et territoires d'outre-mer
DUEL	Diplôme universitaire d'études littéraires
DUES	Diplôme universitaire d'études scientifiques
DUT	Diplôme universitaire de technologie
EIP	Etablissement d'intérêt public
ENA	Ecole nationale d'administration
FCPE	Fédération des conseils de parents d'élèves des écoles publiques
FEN	Fédération de l'éducation nationale
FER	Fédération des étudiants révolutionnaires
FFA	Fédération française de l'agriculture
FGDS	Fédération de la gauche démocrate et socialiste
FLNC	Front de libération nationale corse
FNSEA	Fédération nationale des syndicats d'exploitants agricoles
FO	Force ouvrière
INSEE	Institut nationale de la statistique et des études économiques
IUT	Institut universitaire de technologie
JCR	Jeunesses communistes révolutionnaires
LEP	Lycée d'enseignement professionnel
LT	Lycée technique
MAU	Mouvement d'action universitaire
M22M	Mouvement du 22 mars
MDSF	Mouvement démocrate socialiste de France
MIAGE	Maîtrise d'informatique appliquée à la gestion
MODEF	Mouvement pour la coordination et la défense de l'exploitation familale
MRG	Mouvement des radicaux de gauche
MRP	Mouvement républicain populaire

MSG	Maîtrise de sciences de gestion
MST	Maîtrise de sciences et techniques
ONISEP	Office national d'information sur les enseignements et les professions
OP	Ouvrier professionnel
OQ	Ouvrier qualifié
ORTF	Office de la radiodiffusion-télévision française
OS	Ouvrier spécialisé
PCF	Parti communiste français
PEGC	Professeur d'enseignement général de collège
PEEP	Parents d'élèves de l'enseignement public
PME	Petites et moyennes entreprises
PR	Parti républicain
PS	Parti socialiste
PSU	Parti socialiste unifié
RI	Républicains indépendants
RPF	Rassemblement du peuple français
RPR	Rassemblement pour la république
RTL	Radio-télévision Luxembourg
SFIO	Section française de l'internationale ouvrière
SGEN	Syndicat général de l'Education nationale
SMAG	Salaire minimum agricole garanti
SMIG	Salaire minimum interprofessionnel garanti
SNALC	Syndicat national des lycées et des collèges
SNC	Syndicat national des collèges
SNES	Syndicat national de l'enseignement secondaire
SNESup	Syndicat national de l'enseignement supérieur
SNI	Syndicat national des instituteurs
SNPMI	Syndicat national des petites et moyennes industries
UCC	Union confédérale des cadres
UDF	Union pour la démocratie française
UDR	Union des démocrates pour la république
UDT	Union démocratique du travail
UDVᵉR	Union des démocrates pour la cinquième république
UER	Unité d'enseignement et de recherche
UFR	Unité de formation et de recherche
UGITC	Union générale des ingénieurs techniciens et cadres
UNEF	Union nationale des étudiants de France
UNR	Union pour la nouvelle république

Chapter 1

The French experience since 1944

(1) The liberation era and the Fourth Republic, 1944–58

The years 1944–58 are decisive ones for the development of modern France. During them France experienced major change in all her main structures — economic, social, political and diplomatic. In many ways the France of 1944 was more like that of 1900 than that of 1958; but by 1958 France was already clearly moving towards the rank she enjoys today — that of a foremost second-rank power. The following pages will outline some of these changes.

Our analysis must begin, however, with some attempt, brief though it may be, to evoke the peculiar atmosphere of liberation France — a moral and political climate which it is quite difficult to understand a generation later. In 1944 France was emerging from a foreign occupation, following on the humiliating defeat of 1940; her economy lay in ruins. Her status as an international power, taken for granted before 1939, was now open to question: the very liberation of French territory had been achieved largely by the force of Allied arms, with the Free French forces and various resistance groups playing an ancillary role. Above all, the field of domestic politics was one of bitter strife, with in the latter stages of the war a virtual civil war being waged between the various groups who collaborated with the Nazi occupier and the resistance, pledged to overthrow the occupier and his supporters. Paradoxically, though, the climate of the liberation was one of exhilaration, almost of lightheartedness, despite the enormous tasks confronting France. The newly emerged élites and many of the great mass of French people seemed to feel that as the country had reached a nadir, it could only set a new and better course. The different resistance groups which provided the forcing-ground, as it were, of the new generation of political and economic élites had already caught the mood of optimism in their various pronouncements which called for a radical shake-up of the whole of the French social structure.

Changes there were to be, of course, and they would be many and far reaching. On the whole, though, they would fall short of what many of the élites and many ordinary Frenchmen expected. In many ways, then, the years after 1944 are a long, slow descent from the

1

peaks of optimism. We shall now try to seize the most important changes as they occurred in the fields of economic and social life, domestic politics and international relations.

At the liberation in 1944 the economy lay in ruins after the defeat of 1940, a Nazi occupation which pillaged French resources systematically and the effects of Allied bombing and invasion. Much infrastructure (ports, roads, rail) was destroyed or unusable; there was a chronic housing shortage: energy and industrial output were below the level of 1938 and much industrial plant was in any case antiquated, due to pre-war failure to invest in new equipment. There was insufficient food available to feed a population which had lost 600,000 killed or missing and a further half million of whom were still in German prisons – a grave loss to a country whose population decline had been a source of worry even before 1939. Finally, France faced acute inflationary problems connected with money supply. Given these accumulated difficulties, the economic and political leaders of 1944 had very much the feeling that they were starting from zero – which helps perhaps to explain the bold nature of some of their reconstruction policies.

Their strategy had two axes: first, structural reforms of certain areas of the economy and second, use of limited economic planning. As regards structural reforms, nationalizations were to play a key role. The Renault car company was the first, in January 1945 (its owner had collaborated with the Nazis, which made the operation more acceptable politically). It was followed by the major part of the aerospace industry, the coalmines and Air France: in January 1946 came gas, electricity and the four main deposit banks, plus a large part of the insurance sector. The state now employed directly one-tenth of the workforce and was responsible for one-quarter of all investment: indeed thanks to its control of banking it was in effect directly influencing some 47 per cent of all investment by 1949.

The state could not rebuild the economy on its own, however; clearly, the co-operation of the working classes and of employers was crucial. To enlist the aid of the former, the post-war governments created, like their counterparts in much of western Europe, the nucleus of a welfare state. By April 1946 a system of social security had been extended to all wage-earners, replacing the previous rather patchy system of private or co-operative schemes and giving protection against the major hazards of sickness, accident and old age. It was supported by a generous system of family allowances, aimed at raising the birthrate, which was crucial if France were to have a labour force capable of expanding production. The policy would pay off handsomely, with population rising by 5.6 per cent by 1954 and by 8.8 per cent in the eight years following. Inside the workplace, the decree of February 1945 set up the *comités d'entreprise* and the *délégué syndical* was given official recognition. The latter's task was to transmit workers' grievances to management; the former body, where labour and management sat together, was supposed to discuss the general workings of the firm (it was restricted to large firms). In practice its powers would turn out to extend no further than organizing social activities within the firm; and the hope that workers would participate in the running of industry remained no more than a hope.

To secure the help of private industry, governments adopted the system of five-year plans advocated by J. Monnet, who would be the first Planning Commissioner. Unlike the Soviet plans, which set compulsory targets for industry, French plans were indicative. They brought together in committee employers, state experts and in the early stages at least, representatives of organized labour. The committees were to assess the resources and possibilities of their sector of the economy and propose targets which might realistically be achieved given the co-operation of all partners, especially government. The latter had, in fact, extensive statutory powers at its disposal, whereby it could requisition goods and services from firms if required; but these were never used. Collaboration was forthcoming, because the plans were modest in their aims and suited a wide spectrum of interests. The first (1947–53) aimed to rebuild the infrastructure vital for basic economic activity – coal, electricity, transport, agricultural equipment. The second (1954–7) continued on the same lines, but branched out more into housing and regional development.

It is important to point out that although during the decisive period of reforms from 1944–6 socialist and communist influence was strong both in government and administration, the reforms described did not mean that France was embarking upon a socialist economy, with control of the means of production in the hands of workers. The presence of General de Gaulle at the head of the provisional government until January 1946 and of the strong christian democrat party MRP in the governing coalition were insurance against that. Rather the reforms of 1944–6 are symptomatic of a desire for renewal arising in the resistance organizations which had fought against the occupiers and had hoped for a new republic after the war. The charter of the main resistance organization CNR (*conseil national de la résistance*) had spoken in 1943 of 'une véritable démocratie économique et sociale, impliquant l'éviction des grandes féodalités économiques et financières de la direction de l'économie'. But such a project requires that power be firmly in the hands of socialist forces with unambiguous aims, and this was not the case in 1944. Post-war economic reconstruction is really the prolongation of an old French tradition of *dirigisme* (the state giving clear and precise leadership to the private sector), to revive a moribund capitalism. But as such the operation succeeded very well.

Table 1.1 shows the steady rise of French GDP (and within it, of industrial production) during the Fourth Republic. It is a rapid growth of around 5 per cent per annum and a fairly even one overall. Unfortunately it was marred for some years by monetary problems.

Table 1.1   Growth of French production, 1947–58 (indices)*

Year	Total GDP	Industrial production
1947	109.9	113.4
1948	113.2	118
1949	107.5	106.5
1950	107.9	108.7
1951	106.4	109.6
1952	102.3	102
1953	103.1	102.4
1954	105.4	104.7
1955	106	106
1956	105.1	109.1
1957	106.3	105.8
1958	102.6	103.8

* Each index takes the previous year as 100.
Source: M. Parodi, *L'Economie et la société française de 1945 à 1970*,
        Colin, 1971, p. 64.

At the root of the inflation lay the fact that too much money was in circulation at the liberation; in the run-down economy of the period, with less goods available, this inevitably meant higher prices. Governments were reluctant to grasp the nettle, either by reducing the value of the currency or by soaking up the excess with stiff taxation; either of these measures would have upset some of the better-off, though they would have prevented an inflationary spiral. As it was, wage-earners could only press for higher wages to cover higher costs of living, and so the spiral began. All sectors of the population lost confidence in the value of money. The only actions taken by government were attempts at wage and price freezes, which were unsuccessful and only aroused the hostility of capital and labour alike.

The loss of confidence was compounded by another related problem, the inadequacy of government finance. As well as the usual state debts, the post-war liberation governments inherited the legacy of reparations paid to the occupant, the cost of maintaining a war effort through 1945 and a major share of reconstruction investment. As economic activity was at a low ebb and it was in any case difficult to evaluate resources available, the government could never raise

enough by taxation. Moreover, French governments had long preferred indirect tax to direct; in other words they had taxed the poorer
end of the population proportionally more heavily than the rich. There
was little real change in this policy for several years after 1944, with
the result that the budget was in constant deficit — a factor which
hardly encouraged non-inflationary behaviour in the population at
large.

To bring down the spiral it took the injection of Marshall Aid
from the USA[1] and some classic deflationary policies applied after
1948 by governments of more conservative hue (in particular reducing
expenditure, raising rents and costs of some public services and selective taxation). By 1949 these measures, together with the effects of
post-war investment that were beginning to show through, meant
that prices could remain fairly stable while real expansion got under
way. Although this situation would be perturbed in the 1950s (especially as a result of the Korean war), it did mean that the economy
had turned a corner. But the modernization had been achieved by
inflation, and this meant that the wage-earners had carried a major
share of the burden.

There is no doubt either that the nature of the economy was now
changed. Before 1939 it was often described as 'Malthusian': the
family firm predominated, modest in scale (though there were exceptions, notably in steel and motors), fearful of expansion, and prone
to hiding behind tariff barriers. Instead of profits being ploughed
back into expanded production, they were often immobilized in
safe but unproductive outlets, like government stock. The modern-
izers aimed to break this structure, and part of their strategy was to
encourage mergers so as to give bigger units of production. This process was well under way by 1958: Parodi shows that for limited companies in the period 1950–60 there was an average of eighty-five
mergers per year.[2] The other axis of the modernizing strategy was
to open up the economy to international competition, with the aim
of forcing it into greater rationalization and efficiency. Thus it was
that in 1950 France joined the European Coal and Steel Community
and in 1957 a much wider trade area, the European Economic Community.

This streamlining and directing outwards of the economy had
inevitable repercussions on social structure. Growth implies always
a move away from the primary sector (agriculture and fisheries) into
the secondary (manufacturing) and tertiary (commerce, services,
administration). France was typical of this after 1945. Before 1939
the peasantry had been the largest and most inert class in France;
after 1945 it declined by 1 or 2 per cent annually. By 1958 the percentage of workforce on the land had fallen from 35 to 23, and
300,000 farmers had disappeared. In 1947 agriculture still took 25.4

per cent of the national income; after 1951 it would take between 11 and 14 per cent.[3] Post-war growth told against the farmer. There were limits to how much produce he could sell (families spent progressively less of their income on food) and at the same time the price of machinery (tractors, etc.) rose faster than the prices he received. Modernization meant in fact that only the bigger farmers using advanced techniques could be assured of survival; many of the smaller ones could linger on for a few years at the level of subsistence farming (G. Wright estimates that half of them were in these straits by 1958), or else leave the land and go to work in one of the new factories springing up, perhaps selling off their land to a bigger operator. Thus agriculture underwent concentration of productive units as did industry. The process was resisted by farmers, sometimes violently; but the rural exodus went on, with governments reluctant to tackle the problem of agricultural structures till the 1960s.

The other main victims of modernization were also old social groups, the *artisans* or craftsmen (especially those in the older trades, whose skills were made obsolete by mechanization) and the small shopkeepers, squeezed by the growth of co-operatives and supermarkets, and finding taxes difficult to pay once inflation had slowed down. Like the peasants, such categories were too numerous for a developed economy, and a certain thinning-out was bound to occur. A shopkeeper from the Lot, P. Poujade, organized resistance to tax inspectors, which developed into a political movement. Battening on the discontent of the self-employed and of the poor farmers, especially in the centre and south-west, Poujadism was the violent and anarchic protest movement *par excellence*. Although it had over fifty deputies elected to the 1956 parliament, they were able to do little about the structural problem which explained their presence there, viz. that of obsolescent economic groups, squeezed out by a developing economy.

Other social changes included the emergence of new managerial strata (*cadres*), whose numbers rose sharply and whose self-awareness was reflected in the creation of their own professional organization, the CGC. Beside them there emerged, in the advanced industries, highly skilled types of worker, whose knowledge and sophistication seemed to contrast increasingly with the subaltern roles assigned them in the productive process. By the end of the 1950s, observers were wondering if they might not be the beginnings of a 'new working class'.

The social and economic changes of the period were not accompanied, however, by a similar renovation in the field of politics.

Politically, liberation France was in a vacuum. The Third Republic had committed suicide in July 1940, when most of the deputies and senators, panicked by the French collapse, voted the abolition of the republic and passed over full powers to Marshal Pétain. The latter ruled over the *état français* (the part of France not occupied by the Nazis); this was a régime of personal power, based largely on the prestige and moral authority of the Marshal. It collaborated fairly willingly with Nazism in all domains, even to the extent of helping the Nazis implement their policies of genocide. Its own domestic policies were an odd mixture of cultural archaism and economic dynamism, with an increasingly fascist influence predominating in the later stages. By 1943 the Vichy régime, as it was called (Vichy being its capital), was engaged in virtual civil war with the resistance, those who had decided to oppose the occupant and his allies by armed force. This explains the savagery with which collaborationists were punished when France was liberated.[4] When the Nazis withdrew in 1944, Vichy collapsed. In its place was installed a provisional government, based on personalities and groups from the resistance and the Free French forces which had fought outside France; this included representatives of the political left as well as followers of de Gaulle, widely recognized as head of the resistance. De Gaulle was head of the provisional governments (until he resigned in January 1946) but his authority was moral. To obtain the legitimacy conferred by universal suffrage the government had to organize elections for a constituent assembly, which would devise a constitution and submit it to the French people in a referendum for approval or rejection. In this way regular political life could restart.

In fact it proved hard to devise an acceptable constitution. A constituent assembly was duly elected in October 1945, but its draft constitution was rejected in May 1946 by 10.5 million to 9.5 million votes, mainly because it had no provision for an upper chamber. A second constituent assembly elected in June 1946 produced another draft, which was voted on in October. This time it scraped the barest measure of popular approval with 9 million for, 8 million against and 8.5 million abstaining. But France now had a constitution and elections for a national assembly (lower house) were held in November 1946. Thus was the Fourth Republic born with grudging approval; it is perhaps unsurprising that it was only to last twelve years.

Its politics fall into several phases. First there is *tripartisme*, with government shared between socialists, communists and MRP. This is a period of social and economic reform and inflation; it ends in May 1947 when the socialists evict the communists from government as the Cold War begins. Governments now need an alternative basis, which means that Radicals and conservatives now enter ruling coalitions; their influence helps bring some financial stability. We are now in the period of the 'third force', i.e. groups supporting the republic and opposed both to communism and a new challenger, Gaullism. The 1951 elections give the right a majority, and governments are now based mainly on conservatives and radicals; economic growth continues, but problems of foreign policy loom larger, as France adjusts traumatically to its new role as a second-rank power. Social discontent from the victims of modernization takes the shape of farmers' revolts and Poujadism. The 1956 elections give a majority to the socialists and their allies in the 'republican front'; but by now the dominant problem is the colonial war in Algeria. This will tax both the economic resources of governments and their political authority to a point where in 1958 the republic will emulate its predecessor and call in a saviour, de Gaulle. We shall now explore in detail the political failure of the republic.

Discerning observers had seen that the new constitution promised to be very like that of the late Third Republic, which many still blamed for the collapse of 1940. It had been characterized by a clear lack of governmental authority, which was due to several factors. One was cultural. It was widely felt among republican politicians that firm government was only one step away from the authoritarianism (*césarisme*) which has often marked French political life. Weakness or at least pliability was almost a civic virtue: energetic personalities with strong ideas about policy were kept carefully away from office, unless needed in times of crisis. But behind this lay a more structural factor. French society, economically underdeveloped and with deep cultural divisions, had spawned a great variety of political opinions and sectional interests, which all found their expression in political movements. In other words, the chamber of deputies was never dominated by one or two parties, as in Anglo-Saxon systems; it was a place where several groups of roughly equal strength confronted each other. Governments were always coalitions, which meant compromises between their members (and these were often hard to achieve) or plain immobilism (by doing nothing, one offended nobody). Premiers were weak, hostages of their party colleagues, of deputies from other groups and ultimately of the pressure groups outside parliament, who pushed their demands vigorously. The parties themselves were mostly undisciplined and unstructured, having little contact with their supporters outside election time. Now, such a system can last a long time, provided that (a) social change proceeds slowly, so that there is no unmanageable discontent from displaced groups and (b) there is no external threat. The Third Republic lasted seventy years on this basis, though it did have periodic recourse to heroic leadership, the deputies scenting trouble and passing their prerogatives briefly to a strong premier. But the economic crisis of the thirties, followed by the Nazi invasion, found the Republic too weak to riposte. *Gouvernement d'assemblée* stood condemned: hence the anxiety when the Fourth Republic seemed likely to develop on similar lines to its predecessor.

To begin with, the occupation and resistance had had little effect on the fragmentation of political opinion. No united left-wing party emerged, and the right was still as untidy as ever. The centre was occupied by an apparently new force, the MRP. Later on, new movements such as Gaullism or Poujadism would mushroom in response to various grievances. Even the change in the electoral system from the old single-member system (which favoured local dignitaries and thus encouraged fragmentation) to proportional representation had little effect: there were still some six major groups in the parliaments. Their demands were as conflicting as ever, at least on paper. Communists and socialists could agree about nationalizations, but not on wage controls or foreign policy. Socialists and MRP both favoured European political and economic integration, but could be split on a question like state aid to catholic schools. Radicals might agree with socialists about schools, but would quarrel with them bitterly over how to deal with nationalist movements inside the empire. Parties were often split internally on these and other questions. In short, no durable consensus was possible.

In addition, the president of the republic was still a figurehead without authority; at most he could be an 'honest broker' between party leaders. A premier wishing to confirm his authority dare not follow an option open to his British equivalent, i.e. dissolve parliament and call elections, even though he had the constitutional right to do so. The one premier who did dissolve, Faure, never became prime minister again. A premier could not, incredibly, plan his legislation by controlling the parliamentary timetable; this was the prerogative of party leaders. If he wanted too much authority in some matters, deputies might delay voting the budget and eke out money supply to the government in monthly *douzièmes provisoires*. And there was still a last obstacle before bills got on the statute book – the senate. Dominated by rural interests, it had a long tradition of obstructing and occasionally overthrowing upstart governments. In short, the deputy still ruled, and behind him the pressure groups were as active as ever, urging him to obtain concessions and favours: the North African lobby and the wine and alcohol producers are the classical ones, but there were a host of others. Scandals involving greedy or corrupt parliamentarians continued, as they had done under the previous republic.

The result was that by the mid-1950s the 'system', as many now called it, seemed to work in a vacuum, cut off from the voters and very much the preserve of the professionals from the political class. Attempts were made to give governments some authority but they came to little; increasingly canvassed was a presidential solution, whereby the clear focus of authority would be a president with some sort of electoral mandate and power to dissolve the lower house if need be.

De Gaulle suggested this as early as 1946, and his RPF challenged the republic on this basis. Increasingly, then, the republic seemed unable to deal with the urgent problems of France – less her economic ones, perhaps, than her political ones. And foremost among the latter were those of foreign and colonial policy.

The domestic politics of the Fourth Republic were always over-shadowed by foreign questions in fact, which compounded differences already existing between parties. These questions come under two headings: relations with (a) Europe and the USA, and (b) the empire.

The Yalta treaty of 1945 effectively split Europe into two spheres of influence, the east falling under Soviet hegemony, the west under American. Some time was necessary for both politicians and public to realize that a new map of the world had been drawn and that for the older powers, especially Britain and France, their role was now reduced. They could at best aspire to that of second-rank powers behind the two super-powers, the USA and the USSR. Tension grew between the latter after 1945, as the extent of Soviet influence over the new com-munist-dominated governments in the East became clear. Marshall Aid and the Prague coup of February 1948 (when Czech communists seized full power in an insurrection) confirmed that the wartime alliance had broken down and that capitalist and Soviet blocks con-fronted each other in a 'cold war'. French governments recognized this by their decision in 1949 to join NATO, the alliance of western states under US leadership, formed to confront what seemed to be a threat of Soviet expansionism. Within NATO lay a delicate problem for French governments, though – that of Germany. When West Germany was admitted to statehood by the Allies in 1949, the question of adding its military and economic potential to the Western alliance was clearly acute. It became even more so the following year when the cold war became a hot one. In Korea, the USA and its allies inter-vened to save the régime in the south from a Soviet-backed invasion by the communist north. One consequence of this was that Western governments felt obliged to re-arm, thus putting an unwanted strain on the new resources that post-war growth was beginning to produce; but the other was political. How could Germany be admitted into NATO? French foreign policy had, for obvious reasons, always seen Germany as a major threat: and this was still so after 1945 (cf. French demands for the dismemberment of Germany at the end of the war). This clearly made the admission of Germany into the alliance very hard to swallow, despite the fact that the balance of forces in Europe had now been changed drastically.

An ingenious way around the problem was proposed by R. Pleven, premier in October 1950. This was the European Defence Community (EDC) – a sort of European army into which would be incorporated soldiers from all NATO countries, along with Germans, under a centralized, multi-national command. German soldiers would thus be disguised as European ones, as it were, and the spectre of German rearmament somehow concealed. The Pinay government signed the EDC treaty in 1952, but it needed parliamentary ratification. For two years governments procrastinated, because opinion in country and parliament was extremely divided. Eventually in 1954 the energetic Mendès-France forced the deputies to a vote, and ratification was refused. It made little difference to France, because eventually the USA was able to force acceptance of German rearmament and admission into NATO as a full member. But it did make for further division inside French politics, giving a boost to those who were increasingly dissatisfied with what seemed to be lack of independence from outside (read US) pressure and who were anxious about France's status in the world.

Similar feelings were bred in the other crisis area, that of colonial policy. In 1945 the French empire was second only to the British, covering much of North, West and sub-Saharan Africa and including, in Asia, Laos, Cambodia and Vietnam. Like other colonial powers, France soon faced demands for autonomy or independence from nationalist forces inside her empire. Her reply was negative: the Brazzaville conference of 1944, called by the Gaullists to discuss the future of the empire, spoke of economic development for colonies, but eschewed any idea of independence. The reasons for this attitude are complex: certainly the idea of assimilation is important (according to this official philosophy, in time all indigenous populations were supposed to develop into French men and women). So too are the activities of various colonial lobbies. Whatever the reasons, though, France was the slowest of all imperial powers, Portugal apart, to learn that decolonization must be carried out in the end. The two main arenas of decolonization were Indo-China and North Africa.

At the end of the war Vietnam was mostly under the control of the nationalist Vietminh.[5] The Japanese occupation during wartime had displaced the former colonial officials, and the Vietminh had filled the vacuum left by the Japanese surrender. France had thus a choice: either to find an arrangement with the Vietminh or begin what was in effect a war of reconquest. Although the Vietminh was led by Ho Chi Minh, head of the Vietnamese communist party, it was by no means exclusively communist, grouping together other types of nationalists under a common umbrella. Moreover, its demands were modest — recognition by France of a unified Vietnamese state inside the French union (as the empire had been prudently rebaptized) but with its own government, parliament, defence and finances. Ho and Sainteny, the French negotiator, agreed on the above terms in March 1946, and the agreement was to be submitted to government and parliament for approval; the nature of Vietnam's diplomatic relations and her future status (whether the agreement was a stepping-stone to total independence or not) was left vague. But what had been agreed was a useful basis. It was never to be incorporated into a formal treaty, though: the ill-will and cowardice of governments in Paris and the provocative actions of local administrative and military chiefs saw to that. In the summer of 1946 Thierry d'Argenlieu, whom de Gaulle had appointed Commissioner for Vietnam, proclaimed — quite illegally — a separate republic of Cochin-China. This was a deliberate attempt to split off the Catholic south from the rest of Vietnam. In November the French fleet shelled Haiphong, killing several thousand people, on the slimmest of provocations. Neither action was countermanded from Paris, and war became inevitable. The Vietminh began an armed struggle that would last seven years, and in which France would pay dearly for the missed opportunity of 1946.

The war of reconquest meant increasing expenditure and heavy commitment of men and material, despite an influx of US aid after 1950 as part of their wider anti-communist strategy. It also brought military and diplomatic defeat: even by 1950 large tracts of territory had been abandoned to the Vietminh and were run by them as 'liberated zones'. In their search for support inside Vietnam, the French were forced to offer first autonomy and then total independence to alternative nationalist forces, based on the wealthier sections of Vietnamese society and headed by the hereditary monarch Bao Dai. But even this, which was more than Ho ever received, proved too little. New techniques of rural guerilla warfare, perfected by General Giap and combined with skilful building of political support among the local population were crucial. Eventually in May 1954 a large part of the French forces was trapped and defeated, despite its superior equipment, in the base at Dien Bien Phu. The war was lost, and in the resultant peace conference at Geneva during July it took the energy and lucidity of Mendès-France to secure reasonable terms for French withdrawal. Vietnam was cut in two, with the north left to the Vietminh, by now much more communist and dependent on Soviet aid. The south was left to clients of the USA; one imperialism replaced another, with results known to all. France escaped cheaply in fact. Vietnam was far from home and there were few settlers to repatriate. Conscript troops had never been used. Even the drain on the economy had been palliated by US aid, and Mendès-France's skill at Geneva had avoided excessive diplomatic humiliation. Unfortunately, then, the real lessons were never learned. Few saw the danger of abandoning policy initiatives to local officials or the trauma that the army had experienced. Many soldiers, captured by the Vietminh and admiring their tactical and political skills, could still never understand how they had lost: the temptation to blame others — 'the politicians' — was strong. In these circumstances France faced her next colonial ordeal in Africa.

France was able to disengage with relative ease from her protectorates of Morocco and Tunisia, with their small settler populations, in 1955 and 1956. The outline-law of G. Defferre in 1956 also set decolonization in motion in Black Africa: it would result in the creation of a series of new states, most of them clients of France, which would become first members of the French union, then fully independent by 1960. If there was comparatively little opposition to this strategy, then Algeria was a different matter. It was legally part of France, under the jurisdiction of the interior minister. Its nine million people included a million white settlers, *colons* or *pieds-noirs*, of French nationality (most of whose parents had in fact come from parts of the Mediterranean other than France). The other eight million, Arab Muslims in the main, enjoyed few political or civic rights, the commanding heights of the Algerian economy being firmly in white hands. The *colons* had the ear of local officials sent from France and powerful friends in parliament. They were thus easily able to stifle attempts to improve the political and economic lot of Arabs, such as the 1947 statute (parts of which were simply never applied and parts of which were adapted, by devices such as intimidation and electoral fraud, so as to preserve the status quo). In November 1954 the nationalist FLN (*Front de libération nationale*) began an armed rising that would lead to Algerian independence in 1962.

Few French politicians were inclined to concede anything to the FLN. Most favoured a military solution, i.e. defeat of the FLN by force of arms; though some, notably the left and some MRP, would follow this up with a package of political and economic reforms. No one, not even the communists, admitted independence. The consequences of this attitude would be fatal for Algeria and for the Fourth Republic.

First, France had to mount massive repression: by 1957 some 400,000 troops, including conscripts, were needed to maintain order in Algeria. Military service was extended. From 1954 to 1960 the cost of the war was reckoned to amount to some 28 per cent of the budget. There were nasty side-effects: hundreds of thousands of Arabs were herded into internment camps: urban civilian life was subjected to sophisticated and degrading techniques of military surveillance: torture and murder of Algerian nationalists and European sympathizers went unchecked. In France itself, governments suppressed opposition papers and jailed suspected FLN sympathizers arbitrarily. These tendencies reached their peak in 1956–7 when government was dominated by socialists and Radicals, who were drawn, despite good intentions, into the implacable logic of colonialist nationalism. Observers coined the phrase 'national molletism' (after G. Mollet, the socialist premier) to describe the feeling of national decline and frustrated impotence which seemed by now to be widespread in France, and which found expression in the Suez expedition of November 1956. Here French and British combined to invade Egypt in a classic piece of gunboat-diplomacy, the French because of alleged Egyptian support for the FLN and the British because Egypt had nationalized the Suez canal (where the majority of the share capital was British). The warnings of the two super-powers and the condemnation of the United Nations were necessary before the expeditionary forces withdrew in humiliation and it was realized where real power lay in the modern world.

The crucial effects of Algeria were on domestic French politics, however. Increasingly governments in Paris shut their eyes to events in Algeria, leaving policy to local forces – a collusion of settlers' leaders, pro-settler administrators (of whom the socialist minister-resident, R. Lacoste, was to become particularly notorious) and above all the army, desperate to retrieve honour lost in Vietnam. Orders from Paris were disobeyed or disregarded. In 1956 the FLN leader Ahmed Ben Bella was illegally abducted from a Moroccan aircraft. Presented with the *fait accompli* by his secret services, Mollet merely gave his approval. In February 1958 the airforce bombed illegally a village in Tunisia, Sakhiet (allegedly a shelter for FLN troops) and killed sixty-nine civilians. The premier Gaillard by now did not dare to condemn this. When he resigned soon after over Algerian policy, no one could form a government for thirty-eight days – the longest ministerial crisis in a republic that had known plenty of them. The system was grinding to a halt. When P. Pflimlin, leader of a liberal tendency in the MRP who was reputed to be less severe on Algerian nationalism than some, was eventually appointed prime minister, the pent-up forces in Algiers exploded.

On 13 May 1958 *colons* and soldiers staged an open insurrection in Algiers, setting up para-governmental bodies called, with appropriate nostalgia for earlier centuries, committees of public safety. Corsica was already under the control of insurgent troops: there were rumours of an invasion of Paris. The Fourth Republic had lost control, and the only alternative to civil war seemed to the political class to be an appeal to a figure whom they believed capable of placating all sides (and whose supporters had certainly been hard at work amid the Algiers insurrectionists) – de Gaulle. The General accepted office as prime minister, but only on the understanding that he could devise a new constitution. This would be drafted and approved by referendum at the end of the summer. Civil war was thus averted, but the Fourth Republic was dead.

Its unfortunate end might make us forget its achievements. It had an impressive record in economic and social modernization, and in foreign policy it took the NATO and EEC options clearly and decisively. Later governments would benefit from its work – much more than they ever admit. Its failure was political, with its lack of authority being cruelly exposed by the colonial crisis. Some explanations have been suggested for this, mainly of a structural order; though as Julliard says, the cowardice and weakness of the political class, and its failure to bring party politics closer to the public, are also important. It remained to be seen whether the new republic would deal any better with the major problems still facing France.

(2) The Fifth Republic: establishment and consolidation, 1958-68

The crisis of 13 May became the matrix for the birth of the Fifth Republic. On 1 June General de Gaulle was voted the last prime minister of the Fourth Republic by 329 to 224 deputies in the national assembly. His coalition government containing SFIO socialists and conservatives was handed a basket of special powers for six months, mainly to restore public order and resolve the Algerian problem but also, on de Gaulle's insistence, to propose changes to the constitution so as to get rid of what he saw as weaknesses in the public powers in France. Thus the deputies were induced to issue a death sentence for the Fourth Republic in their anxiety to end the Algerian crisis. Nevertheless, the basic socio-economic structures developing in France since 1945 were not likely to be revolutionized by a formal change of régime in 1958; nor were the issues at stake in the Algerian war.[6]

Although legal power could be conferred by the national assembly in Paris, real power lay in Algeria. The army had joined with *colons* to form the committees of public safety, in Algiers and other large cities, which continued to rule local affairs for several months. Colonels in the parachute regiments were particularly determined to recover military pride and to keep Algeria French by winning the war. Older generals, however, feared army disunity if civil war broke out in France; their caution opened the minds of Massu and Salan to persuasion that perhaps de Gaulle would guarantee a French Algeria. The loyalties of General Salan hung in the balance for he was military commander and head of the civil administration in Algeria while at the same time acting as nominal leader of the rebellion.

De Gaulle had no ready-made Algerian policy any more than his predecessors.[7] But he was careful during several flying visits to Algeria to maintain his acceptability to the rebels by making vague but sympathetic speeches such as the one at the Forum in Algiers on 4 June which began 'Je vous ai compris!'; at Mostaganem on 7 June he even cried for the first and last time 'Vive l'Algérie française!' Moreover, he reaffirmed the authority of General Salan. But he usually preferred to adopt sphinx-like attitudes while appointing new and trusted administrators. By the middle of October, army officers were withdrawn from the committees of public safety which were finding themselves increasingly by-passed by administrators from Paris. Thus was quietly severed the umbilical cord attaching de Gaulle to the rebellion of 13 May; but his survival would remain precarious for another four years.

The search for a solution to the Algerian problem went through four stages. Initially, between June 1958 and September 1959, de Gaulle's policy was to float trial balloons to test public opinion while also introducing reforms to improve the climate for a settlement without making any commitments on the future status of Algeria. At Constantine early in October he outlined a plan to spend 100,000 million francs per annum over five years on a programme of social and economic reform to benefit Moslems and enable them to participate in Algerian administration. That this was not enough in itself to win Moslem confidence was apparent when de Gaulle's appeal for a *paix des braves* in his first press conference on 23 October was rejected by the FLN who regarded it as merely a cease-fire without guarantees. Just as the army and *colons* in Algeria waited anxiously for reassurance, so did Moslem doubts persist. Even if they achieved military success, the Algerian nationalists feared that the French might resort to partitioning the coastal area and the oil-producing regions of the Sahara. Such fears were justified, for de Gaulle's first prime minister, M. Debré, was suggesting a partition policy as late as June 1961.

The search for a settlement entered a second phase on 16 September 1959, when de Gaulle admitted the right of all Algerians to eventual self-determination, while clearly hoping that they would choose to retain close links with France. A storm of protest culminated in a revolt in Algiers in January 1960 by *colons* aided by some army officers. De Gaulle survived this crisis with a successful broadcast appeal for army loyalty and then moved some dangerous officers to metropolitan France. Having restored order, de Gaulle made secret preparations leading to negotiations with FLN leaders at Melun in June 1960. The talks soon broke down, but having now recognized the FLN as a representative Algerian organization, de Gaulle put his plan to prepare for self-determination in Algeria before the French people in the form of a referendum, in January 1961. He was encouraged by the 75 per cent vote in favour of his plan, but the result provoked another revolt in Algeria in April led this time by four generals whom de Gaulle had recently retired. Generals Challe, Jouhaud, Salan and Zeller won support from only part of the army, and after only four days their insurrection collapsed in confusion. Secure once more, de Gaulle had further abortive negotiations with the FLN between May and July, this time held at Evian, a French spa town on Lake Geneva.

There followed a third phase during the summer of 1961, a period of reappraisal when there were serious doubts whether de Gaulle was capable of solving the Algerian problem, which was the task for which he had been given power. Public opinion had become increasingly critical of the war and its brutalities, and the previous September a *déclaration des 121* signed by well-known intellectuals had even proclaimed the right of national servicemen to refuse to fight in Algeria. Meanwhile on the extreme right the *Organisation de l'armée secrète* (OAS) mounted a campaign of assassinations and plastic bomb attacks intended to break down law and order by terrorism and thereby prevent a settlement in Algeria. To meet the challenge the FLN tightened its organization and redefined its aims to combine socialist revolution with the fight for independence.

The way was cleared for the final phase of the crisis when de Gaulle renounced the possibility of partition at his press conference on 5 September 1961 and thereby based his hopes on association between France and a unified Algeria. The FLN responded on 24 October by suggesting provisions to serve the interests of France and *colons* remaining in Algeria after independence. Secret preparations led to more negotiations at Evian which resulted in a cease-fire agreement on 18 March 1962, accompanied by a complex settlement labelled 'independence in co-operation with France', which was approved by 91 per cent of French voters in a referendum on 8 April and by almost 100 per cent of Algerians on 1 July. The settlement provided for minority rights for *colons* if they chose to stay; it provided for French interests in Saharan oil, atomic tests and the Mers-el-Kebir naval base, but only for a limited period; it provided for a major role by the FLN in organizing the referendum; and most important it provided for absolute sovereignty in internal and external affairs for an independent Algeria. By means of an aid programme on a similar scale to the Constantine Plan the French hoped to keep a special relationship with Algeria, but after eight years of war and in view of differences of ideology and national interest, it was unlikely that a spirit of co-operation would prevail. Both before and after the settlement of 1962 most of the million *colons* in Algeria moved to metropolitan France. Last desperate efforts at sabotage by the OAS merely made the break more complete, their bomb attacks driving *colons* out and their assassination attempts against de Gaulle enabling him to win support to entrench himself in power.

Apart from returning to power to restore order and solve the Algerian problem, de Gaulle and his coalition government were empowered to draft a new constitution according to five principles embodied in a constitutional act passed on 3 June 1958. To meet de Gaulle's wishes, the executive should be strengthened and separated from the legislature. To meet the wishes of the leading Fourth Republic politicians both legislature and executive should be based on universal suffrage, the government should be responsible to the legislature, an independent judiciary should be maintained, and relations between France and her overseas territories should be reformed. Accordingly, de Gaulle's legal advisor, Debré, drafted a text that was slightly amended by a committee formed by both government and parliament before being published on 4 September and submitted to a referendum.

The subsequent campaign paid little attention to constitutional details because most French people feared that a rejection of the constitution would cause de Gaulle to resign, leaving them with little hope of peace in Algeria and the strong possibility of civil war in France. In any case, the absence of clear proposals for an alternative constitution left the opposition weak and disunited. It was in these circumstances that the referendum on 28 September 1958 resulted in 79 per cent of the vote in metropolitan France being cast in favour of the constitution. The opposition vote of mainly four million communists was much lower than anticipated. For the overseas territories the constitution offered a choice between secession and co-operation that would involve devolution of power; only Guinea voted for secession, but when the snags involved in the terms of co-operation with France became clear during the following year, most of the other territories followed the path towards independence, so that the world-wide French empire had largely disappeared by 1962.

The most significant features of the new constitution were the presidential powers to dissolve the national assembly (but not more than once a year), to hold a referendum under certain conditions, to appoint the prime minister and other ministers, and to assume full powers when he deemed that there was a state of emergency; for its part the government had power to extend legislation by means of decrees and ordinances, and could control parliamentary agendas during the relatively short sessions of the national assembly; finally parliament had power to refuse a vote of confidence in a new government and to pass a motion of censure to force an existing government to resign. There was considerable debate at the time as to whether it was a presidential or a parliamentary régime, but in reality the 1958 constitution had to be hybrid to satisfy de Gaulle and the politicians in his coalition government.

Following provisions in the new constitution, national assembly elections were held in November to fill 532 seats (including 67 in Algeria) by means of single-member constituencies decided by two ballots failing an overall majority in the first ballot; this reverted to a Third Republic practice, instead of the proportional representation of the Fourth Republic. The Gaullists formed a new organization, the *Union pour la nouvelle république* (UNR), and surprised everyone by increasing their seats from 20 to 189; with the dependable support of 132 conservative deputies in the *Centre national des indépendants et paysans* (CNIP) the Gaullists would be able to form a reliable majority. Likely to be in opposition on the other hand were thirty-four radicals and other centre groups, fifty-seven MRP, forty SFIO, two other socialists and ten communists. Apart from the communists, who polled over a million votes less than in 1956, the opposition parties maintained their vote; but they all suffered from a disproportion between votes and seats, partly due to new constituency boundaries but mainly due to fragmented strategies exposed by safety-first voting for the UNR and CNIP in the second ballot. Three-quarters of former deputies had not been returned to the national assembly which was therefore revolutionized, though many former deputies subsequently managed to win seats in elections to the senate.[8]

Encouraged by this evidence of public support, de Gaulle proceeded to contest the presidential election held on 21 December with an electorate of 81,764 deputies, senators, local mayors and councillors. He duly won 79 per cent of the poll against 8 per cent for a centrist and 13 per cent for a communist. Now securely in power, de Gaulle announced drastic financial and economic reforms including a 17 per cent devaluation of the currency; the gradual introduction of a new franc worth 100 old francs; a major reduction in tariffs on foreign imports, particularly from countries in the new European Economic Community (EEC); increased budgetary expenditure for military and other purposes; reduced subsidies on public services and family allowances, and finally new taxes that would meet about half the increase in expenditure. De Gaulle could now afford to dispense with the socialists, who refused to serve in the new government in protest against his economic policies, though promising to continue to vote for his Algerian policy. Confident of a safe majority in the national assembly, de Gaulle could appoint Debré prime minister in January 1959, together with the conservative Pinay as finance minister, in terms that emphasized presidential power while paying scant regard to the need for the government to win a vote of parliamentary confidence.

Now president instead of prime minister, de Gaulle nevertheless wished to keep personal direction of government policy in Algeria and foreign affairs to an extent that exceeded the presidential role of arbiter according to the constitution. The Gaullist party congress in 1959 justified the creation of a *domaine réservé*, a presidential sector of policy; but the extent and nature of the sector was not defined by de Gaulle and was likely to vary according to the president's interests. Moreover, de Gaulle assumed special powers in 1961, when he declared a state of emergency from 23 April to 30 September, even though the generals' revolt lasted only four days. He was aware of considerable speculation that he might be manoeuvred out of power when the Algerian war ended and that the OAS were attempting to bring his rule to a rather more sudden end, and his greatest concern was that the essentials of presidential power in France should be upheld beyond his term of office. He therefore decided that election by universal suffrage would be the best means to give the president a national authority at least as great as that of the national assembly. Fears of political instability were widespread due to persistent OAS terrorism, particularly following de Gaulle's narrow escape from assassination at Petit-Clamart in August 1962. De Gaulle chose this opportunity to propose, by means of a referendum, that the presidential electoral system be changed from a restricted to a universal suffrage. The politicians in the national assembly objected that it was constitutionally unjustifiable to make such a change by referendum and they passed a motion of censure against the government on 4 October. In the referendum on 28 October, of the 77 per cent who went to the polls, only 62 per cent voted to support the government's proposal; but rather than change his government to suit the national assembly, de Gaulle chose a dissolution. In the elections in November 1962 the Gaullist UNR, with its left-wing *Union démocratique du travail* (UDT), won 230 seats out of 482 and could rely on support from 35 Independent Republicans plus a few other conservative allies. Indications of doubt and opposition among the electorate were that only 69 per cent voted in the first ballot and that the parties campaigning for a 'no' vote in the October referendum raised their votes from eight to eleven millions, against seven millions for the Gaullists and their allies. But incoherent programmes and strategies resulted in the opposition groups occupying only 189 seats, of which the SFIO had 66 and the communists had 41.

Thus de Gaulle had not only strengthened the presidency through success in the referendum, but even more by the unexpected triumph of the UNR in the elections. He had replaced Debré in March, partly due to differences over Algerian policy, and appointed a new prime minister, G. Pompidou, who was regarded as a nonentity and who lost a vote of censure within six months. But after the elections had returned a safe majority, Pompidou was reappointed for the next six years to become the longest serving prime minister in French republican history. Freed from the Algerian incubus and with a firm power base, de Gaulle was able not only to pursue his foreign policy ambitions to the full but even to win re-election to the presidency in December 1965, in spite of opposition efforts to combine more effectively against him in the meantime.

In his speeches and writings de Gaulle had always attached the greatest importance to French influence and independence in world affairs.

On his return to power in 1958 he proceeded to interpret articles 5 and 15 of the new constitution, which made the president guarantor of national independence, territorial integrity, and respect for treaties, as well as commander-in-chief of the armed forces, as authority for him to take control of all aspects of foreign affairs and defence policy.[9] But he shared the same problems that handicapped his predecessors, whatever the formal powers he assumed; the constraints arising from the cold war and preoccupations with the Algerian problem also affected him during his first four years in power. This was anticipated by allied powers who tended to disregard French interests. De Gaulle's ambitions were largely ignored in June 1958 when American and British troops moved into Jordan and the Lebanon, a traditional French sphere of interest, and again in September when his request for a French share in the direction of NATO met with no reply from Washington. His one moderate achievement during these early years was to develop French participation and influence in the EEC. By devaluing the franc he cushioned the French balance of trade against the scheduled tariff cuts laid down by the 1957 treaty of Rome; and by exchanging friendly visits with Chancellor Adenauer, beginning in July 1960, he cultivated West German support in order to create a political base from which he could prepare to launch an attack on the existing international power structure.

Nevertheless, it was not until 1962 that developments at home and abroad significantly increased French freedom of action in world affairs. In France de Gaulle's power was strengthened by the ending of the Algerian war and by the election of a stable majority to the national assembly. Abroad there was a cold war crisis in October 1962 when the United States refused to allow the siting of Soviet missiles on the island of Cuba; although they came close to war, the two super-powers resolved the crisis peacefully in a way that indicated their agreement to co-exist. Friction was reduced by a clearer demarcation of interests. The Soviet Union withdrew its missiles from Cuba, but it had proceeded from August 1961 to build a wall to divide East and West Berlin, the area of greatest tension in Europe. Co-existence instead of conflict brought a sigh of relief from the world, followed by the dawning recognition that *détente* between the super-powers might provide scope for lesser powers to take initiatives in their own interest, rather than lining up automatically with Moscow or Washington. This view was most clearly articulated in France where traditions of great power status made cold war constraints particularly objectionable.

De Gaulle broke the conventions of American leadership at a press conference on 14 January 1963. A recent Anglo-American meeting in the Bahamas had reaffirmed their long-standing co-operation in producing nuclear weapons, while perfunctorily suggesting that France might buy some sea-to-air Polaris rockets. Now de Gaulle rejected the offer, pointing out that France had neither the submarines nor the warheads to use such rockets; he also rejected American proposals for a multilateral Atlantic nuclear force, which he believed might undermine French plans for a nuclear force of their own. At the same press conference he indicated that he considered it impossible for Britain to enter the EEC, his veto thus bringing to an abrupt end negotiations begun in October 1961. He did not refer directly to Anglo-American military agreements, but by expressing concern that their economic links might adversely affect the EEC if Britain joined, he indicated his belief that Britain was an American 'Trojan horse'. Thus de Gaulle declared a war of independence from 'Anglo-Saxon' overlordship. C. Delmas points out (*Défense nationale*, January 1983) that apart from personal motives the General's decision arose from concern in France about Anglo-American policies dating back to the Fourth Republic in 1957.

At the same time he strengthened his power base in Europe by signing a treaty on Franco-German co-operation on 22 January, which involved links in foreign affairs, defence and education by means of regular meetings between heads of state and relevant ministers. Close West German relations with Washington meant that the timing of the treaty with France was an embarrassment to the Germans; Adenauer's visit to Paris to sign the treaty had been arranged before the 14 January press conference and he decided to go through with it, though the subsequent terms of ratification by the *Bundestag* set limits to co-operation with de Gaulle. Suspicion of his personal friendship with Adenauer lay beneath the surface in German politics, until the latter's retirement in March 1966 allowed an open assertion of German interests diverging from those of France.

The decision taken under the Fourth Republic in 1954 to develop a French nuclear weapon system was upheld enthusiastically by de Gaulle, who greeted the first successful atomic test in the Sahara in February 1960 with the acclamation 'Hourra pour la France!' But his ambition would not be satisfied until there was a nuclear striking force under independent French command. This became official policy in spite of the great expense involved, and it survived a motion of censure which had the support of more than two hundred deputies in the national assembly on 25 October 1960. De Gaulle also resisted constraints from abroad by refusing, in July 1963, to sign a nuclear test ban treaty sponsored by the United States, the Soviet Union and Britain; he regarded it as an attempt to protect their existing privileges to the detriment of China and France, the newest nuclear powers.

De Gaulle was convinced that an independent French foreign policy was restricted by the integrated military command structure of NATO. As early as March 1959 he withdrew the French navy from NATO command, though the decision was interpreted as mainly serving special French security needs in the Mediterranean during the Algerian war. In spite of de Gaulle's efforts to develop friendly relations with communist powers, firstly by recognizing the Chinese People's Republic in 1964, and then by negotiating several commercial and diplomatic agreements with the Soviet Union in 1965, many Frenchmen remained convinced that national security required the firmest possible alliance with the United States. Therefore it was only after being safely re-elected to the presidency in December 1965 that de Gaulle announced in February 1966 his decision to leave the NATO military system, while remaining in the Atlantic Alliance as a purely diplomatic agreement. The decision meant that American forces had to leave French soil within twelve months, together with NATO headquarters which had to be transferred from Paris to Brussels. De Gaulle then visited the Soviet Union in June 1966 and agreed to consult regularly and to construct a direct telephone link between the Kremlin and the Elysée. He insisted, however, that his aim was not neutrality but rather to make France an independent power within the western alliance.

Contacts with the Soviet Union and subsequently with other states in eastern Europe were part of a European policy not confined to the six members of the EEC but geared rather to a Europe stretching from the Atlantic to the Urals. De Gaulle appreciated the economic benefits of the EEC, particularly those derived from the Common Agricultural Policy which solved the problem of French farming surpluses; but he objected to supranational integration, as proposed in the treaty of Rome. Between 1960 and 1962 he presented plans to the EEC through Fouchet, his ambassador in Copenhagen, which purported to strengthen political co-operation in the Common Market but were rejected because they ruled out genuine integration by leaving full sovereignty with each member state. A loosely-knit political co-operation was the kind which de Gaulle hoped would be ultimately acceptable to eastern European states. As he was attempting to bridge east and west, the other five EEC members proposed to go ahead with integration by means of qualified majority voting procedures on the council of ministers which were laid down in agreements under the treaty of Rome. For seven months there was deadlock while French delegates boycotted EEC meetings, until the Luxembourg agreements in January 1966 enabled France to keep a veto on issues involving her vital interests. The French veto was exercised yet again, in spite of opposition from the other five members, when a second British application for membership was blocked in May 1967.

During his presidency de Gaulle travelled to most parts of the world. He offered his creed of national independence to the developing countries, particularly those subjected to neo-colonialism at the hands of the United States. He was bitterly critical of American policy in the Vietnam war. Convinced that American influence in the world was artificially maintained by privileges derived from the Bretton Woods monetary system created at the end of the Second World War, the gold exchange standard which gave the dollar equal status to gold, de Gaulle recommended at a press conference on 4 February 1965 a return to a straightforward gold standard without privileged currencies. The subsequent French practice of converting dollars into gold amounted to a 'gold war' that proved an irritant to the United States though not actually defeating their policies. Nevertheless, at the cost of considerable isolation, de Gaulle had succeeded in creating world-wide awareness of a distinctive French policy and influence. Its durability would depend, however, on how long conditions at home and abroad continued to allow scope for French freedom of action.

De Gaulle's electoral successes and general popularity were partly due to the prosperity of the influential sectors of French society derived from economic growth since the Second World War.[10] An average 5 per cent per annum growth rate meant that by 1965 the French gross national product was twice that of 1950. The régime in power benefited politically from the general feeling of prosperity. Inflationary tendencies, however, were as endemic under the Fifth as under the Fourth Republic. The 1958 devaluation eased the problem for a time, but unlike his predecessors de Gaulle attached pride and prestige to maintaining the value of the new franc. In September 1963 the finance minister, Giscard d'Estaing, leader of the independent republicans supporting de Gaulle, introduced a deflationary *plan de stabilisation* involving cuts in public spending and tighter controls on credit which lasted well beyond 1965. This coincided with the Fourth Plan (1962–5), whose social investment priorities for items such as schools and hospitals were jeopardized; the priorities remained, but corners were cut by means such as jerry-building. The planning commissariat was overridden by the ministry of finance with its short-term budgetary priorities, and this continued to be so under the Fifth Plan (1966–70). The pursuit of economic growth was maintained by giving tax-rebate incentives to business corporations. But, if inflation was to be controlled while high industrial investment was accompanied by high social investment, then the sole remaining target for a credit squeeze had to be consumer spending. In these circumstances it was hardly surprising that the trade unions objected to planning discussions that tended to focus on wage controls, or that they were impelled to produce a counter-plan of their own in 1965. Expectations of full employment and increasing incomes were now shaken by pressure on wages and a significant rise in the unemployment figures by 1968. It was against this background that the government decided to rule by ordinance in the economic sphere for six months from April 1967.

Harsh measures such as price increases in the public services became the focus of attack from the increasingly combative French left.

From 1964 the opposition to de Gaulle became more coherent and effective. Undoubtedly his foreign policy was generally popular; his ability to score points off the United States contrasted with the insecurity and ignominy of the war and post-war years. But his economic and social policies on the other hand met with increasing criticism, particularly as de Gaulle clearly regarded foreign and defence policies as being vastly more important. His paternalistic declarations at press conferences and in appearances on state-controlled television provoked all the more resentment because the attenuated role of the national assembly left public opinion with few outlets.

In May 1964 the French communist party decided on various changes in organization and strategy that would facilitate co-operation with other parties of the left in the period leading to the presidential election in December 1965. Disorganization in the non-communist left, however, was not resolved until Mitterrand emerged as the leader capable of creating a framework to meet the interests of diverse tendencies. He became the candidate of a united left on 9 September, having won communist backing and at the same time organized the SFIO, the Radicals and socialist clubs, into a new *Fédération de la gauche démocrate et socialiste* (FGDS). Although this achievement came rather late, it did enable Mitterrand to force de Gaulle into a second ballot before he won with a 55 per cent to 45 per cent majority on 19 December 1965. It was a lively campaign in which access to state television for the first time enabled Mitterrand, and the centrist candidate Lecanuet, to rival de Gaulle briefly as public personalities. Moreover debates on the economy such as one between Mendès-France and Debré in November revealed attractive possible alternatives to government policies. Public interest resulted in an 85 per cent poll.

Preparations soon followed for the national assembly elections due in March 1967. The structure of the non-communist left was maintained and the FGDS published its election programme by July 1966; its critique of government social and economic policies lost some of its impact, however, when attention was diverted during the campaign towards constitutional conflicts between president and parliament. Rivalries on the left resulted in the five million communist and four million FGDS voters only forming an alliance in the second ballot on 12 March 1967. Nevertheless the eight million Gaullist voters needed to recuperate all possible support from centrists and independent republicans, whose leader Giscard d'Estaing had only grudgingly offered qualified support, before they could emerge with a knife-edge majority − 244 seats in an assembly numbering 485. Faced with opposition from 73 communist and 116 FGDS deputies, apart from possible defections among the 43 independent republicans, the government chose to rule by ordinance in economic and financial affairs from April to October and thereby exacerbated a tense and potentially unstable political situation.

De Gaulle had to cope with problems abroad in 1967 as well as in France. Although he had emerged from EEC disputes in 1966 with the French veto intact and the Common Agricultural Policy firmly established, opposition from other members was increasing. He became particularly isolated after March 1966 when Adenauer's successors in West Germany pursued policies less sympathetic to French interests; with a considerable growth of economic power behind them, they felt able to adopt more independent policies such as negotiating directly with the Soviet Union and eastern Europe, and maintaining the value of the mark to preserve their favourable trade balance. It was not merely that de Gaulle resented being upstaged in international diplomacy, but also that West German economic and financial strength placed competitive pressure on France.

At this difficult time 'perfidious Albion' increased the isolation of France within the EEC by submitting a second application for membership in 1967. Although de Gaulle promptly issued a veto in May, the British left their application on the table. This meant that the issue remained on the agenda of subsequent EEC meetings and provided a focus for anti-French criticism and resulted in deadlock in all important Common Market negotiating.

De Gaulle continued to cultivate support in the developing countries of the third world, partly to extend the *rayonnement* of French civilization. But his travels abroad showed an increasing tendency to play to the gallery, so much so that foreign governments became wary of offering him invitations. During a visit to Canada in July 1967 he was asked to leave after proclaiming 'Vive le Québec libre!', and a subsequent visit to Poland gave rise to anxiety that he might ignite Russo-Polish relations. The French public, too, were increasingly critical of his fascination for the world stage at the expense of French problems at home.

Of all the problems facing French society in the aftermath of the 1967 elections, the most deep-seated and intractable arose from a massive increase in population over twenty years, together with a huge migration from country to town. France needed to give high priority to resolving attendant socio-economic problems such as shortages in housing, hospitals, schools and recreational facilities. Action had been delayed until the Fourth Plan in the early 1960s which in any case had been undermined by changes in government policy. It was not surprising, therefore, that a challenge to de Gaulle's régime in 1968 should come from young people, particularly school-children and students.

(3) The events of May 1968

Student unrest since the war had been concerned with practical considerations, unless stirred by political events such as the Algerian and Vietnam wars. The unrest which immediately sparked off the events was generated at Nanterre, one of several university institutions built in the 1960s to cope with the ever increasing student population; in this case specifically to take up some of the overspill from the Sorbonne. Although of modern design, there seemed to have been little thought as to the suitability of the site (it had originally belonged to the defence ministry), nor had any provision been made for cultural facilities – the building of the library was only begun in 1968.[11]

Yet students at Nanterre enjoyed better material conditions for their work, and from an academic standpoint the situation should have been easier than at the Sorbonne. A number of teachers were attracted by the new complex and by the possibilities that it offered of a new approach to teaching, and to staff-student relations. They were encouraged in this attitude by the dean, P. Grappin, whose efforts had succeeded in creating a more human and liberal atmosphere. Why did things go wrong? One cause was the growth of student numbers which at Nanterre had been phenomenal (1964 (opening year) – 2,000; 1967 – over 11,000), with the inevitable over-straining of the academic facilities; but all university institutions were in a similar position. Two other factors, specific to Nanterre, added to the unrest.

First, there was a strong sociology department, with between 600 and 700 students mainly in their first and second years. Sociology students have always played a central role in student protest movements, whether in France or elsewhere. They study society, which gives rise to a critical attitude to their own society. In practical terms also, students of sociology had reason to be dissatisfied with contemporary society, since it offered little in the way of jobs to sociology graduates, who were thus particularly vulnerable at what was then regarded as a time of general unemployment.

The second factor was the comparatively liberal climate of Nanterre; it was at once too extensive and too limited. 'Le libéralisme de la faculté fut assez grand pour tolérer certains actes, mais trop limité pour remettre activement en cause une situation universitaire qui empêchait des initiatives autonomes.'[12] The liberalism of Nanterre can thus be viewed as a provocation in that it promised but could not perform, given the centralized organization of higher education in France.

Unrest had broken out in Nanterre in autumn 1967. This was caused by the Fouchet reforms of 1965 which were then due to come into effect. There was uncertainty about how these were to operate – which was particularly worrying for students who had begun their studies under the old dispensation, and had now to change over to the new. It was enough to cause a ten-day strike of about 10,000 students, under moderate leadership. The demands at this stage were moderate, dealing with size of classes, examination standards and student representation in university councils. The last of these demands was perhaps the most significant. A committee composed of both staff and students was indeed set up to propose changes which would be put to the ministry of education. However, since it had no powers itself to make changes, it achieved very little. Students were thus made to realize that partisans of mere reform were likely to get nowhere, and moderate demands were therefore fruitless. The more moderate student leadership thus lost its following to those of more radical persuasions (such as Daniel Cohn-Bendit, a second-year sociology student), whose criticisms went far beyond the French university system and who wished to see an entirely new form of society established in France and elsewhere.

After the notorious exchange between F. Missoffe, minister of youth and sports, and Cohn-Bendit on 8 January, when the swimming-pool at Nanterre was opened, the rumour became current that the student – a German national – was likely to be expelled by order of the ministry of the interior.[13] Another rumour, never proved, about the existence of a 'black list' of militant students, served to poison the atmosphere yet further, and P. Grappin, the dean, became the object of personal attacks. On 6 January, a number of militants demonstrated in the sociology building. Strictly speaking, political activity on the campus was forbidden, and when members of the administration asked the students to stop they were roughly handled. Grappin called for police assistance to restore order. A fight took place between police and students and the former were chased off the campus.

In common with other faculties throughout France, Nanterre was involved in protests over visiting hours in student residences in 1968 – a protest symbolic of the students' desire not to be kept in a kind of artificial minority by the authorities, but to be treated as adults with all the liberties which that implies. An issue of more immediate significance was that of American involvement in south Vietnam.

The war in Vietnam aroused not only the political consciousness of students, but also that of the *lycéens*, via the organization of the *Comité Vietnam national* in 1966 by the JCR and the PSU. Many CVN committees were formed in the *lycées* and these were to form the basis of the *comités d'action lycéens* (CAL), which were to be very active during May, bringing many *lycéens* out on to the streets in support of the students. The Tet offensive in spring 1968 caused demonstrations in Paris which became more violent in mid-March.

Members of the CVN (among them one Nanterre student) were arrested after bombs were exploded outside some buildings which housed American organizations. On 22 March a meeting was held at Nanterre to protest against these arrests, which were regarded as repressive action by the police. After the meeting, Cohn-Bendit led a move to take over the conference chamber in the administration building, where lengthy discussions were held late into the night. Thus was born the *mouvement du 22 mars* (M22M). A teach-in on the struggle against imperialism was proposed for 29 March, but when this news became known to the administration, Grappin closed Nanterre from 28 March to 1 April.

During April, it became increasingly clear that the administration could not control the campus at Nanterre — in part, at least, because it could not decide what tactics to adopt. It seems to have been neither authoritarian enough to take up a hard line and stick to it, nor liberal (or independent) enough to make concessions; and the student militants, gauging this to a nicety, knew very well how to prey upon it.

> The originality of Nanterre lay not in the environmental conditions of the students there, but in the tactical sense of Daniel Cohn-Bendit and some of his fellow-students. Their genius lay in drawing the conclusions from the failure of traditional forms of protest. Their answer lay in taking, and keeping, what they demanded, and so forcing the authorities to choose between total surrender or forceful repression. (J. Gretton, *Students and Workers*, p. 77)

Later on, similar tactics were to be equally effective on a much grander scale.

The short Easter vacation was punctuated by the news that selection was to be introduced at university entrance (instead of the 'open door' policy hitherto practised) and of the attempted murder in West Berlin of Rudi Dutschke, the socialist student leader, which provoked left-wing student protest in France. At the end of April, fear of reprisals by the right-wing commando groups, principally *Occident* (an up-dated version of the pre-war *Action française*), caused a further heightening of tension at Nanterre, and on the night of 1–2 May, preparations of a quasi-military nature were made by students in case of attack. Matters were not improved by the knowledge that eight students — all members of M22M — had been ordered to appear before a disciplinary committee at the Sorbonne on 6 May. Further disorders occurred, and on 3 May all teaching was suspended at Nanterre.[14]

The focal point of activity was now the Sorbonne, where, on the morning of 3 May, a demonstration took place to protest against the closure of Nanterre and the possibility of disciplinary action to be taken against the eight students. The main student organizations were represented: UNEF (vice president/acting president: J. Sauvageot), JCR (founded and led by A. Krivine), FER, MAU (formed by Sorbonne graduates in March 1968) and M22M, led by D. Cohn-Bendit. These people, together with A. Geismar, leader of SNESup (part of the FEN), were to be the most prominent amongst the leaders of protest during the May events. A similar meeting was held in the afternoon, but there were again fears of a clash with the right-wing groups. The Sorbonne authorities were consequently very anxious for the demonstrators to leave, but initially they declined to do so. The *Occident* forces did try to reach the Sorbonne, but were repulsed by the police, who were present in force outside. Since the danger of a left–right clash had been averted, it might have been thought that no further police action was necessary. The *recteur*, J. Roche, possibly under pressure from the education minister, A. Peyrefitte, seems to have felt the need to have the police evacuate the Sorbonne, which was done only after written instructions had been given to that effect. The police entered the Sorbonne, and after discussions with the student leaders, it was agreed that the students would leave quietly. However, on quitting the courtyard, they found that they were all (over 500) put into police vans and driven away to have their papers verified.[15] Outside was a crowd of about two thousand, comprised partly of militant students, partly of others who had left the Sorbonne earlier, on the suspension of their classes. At the sight of their comrades herded into police vans, there were jeers and shouts, and anger soon turned to action — paving stones were thrown at the police who responded with tear gas and truncheons. Several hundred people were injured, of whom 80 were policemen, and 590 people were arrested.

It seems clear from all accounts that not only was the student reaction spontaneous, but it was also very violent (it took 1,500 policemen a long time to bring 2,000 students under control). This violence caused the police to over-react, which was to assist in bringing the forces of law and order into disrepute. Moreover, the police had had to enter the Sorbonne, which was seen as a violation of the academic freedom of France's most ancient university. Previously uncommitted students had consequently become very partisan. This would not perhaps have affected the non-student population at all, but it was the police 'mopping-up' operations which did the most harm in terms of public opinion. Many innocent passers-by suffered from police attack and arrest, and these arbitrary actions inevitably gave the impression that the students were the victims of police oppression. There seems little doubt that the police were at a later stage guilty of violent and at times sadistic attacks on demonstrators. However, the point must in fairness be made that, for a few weeks following 3 May, the police would have been guilty in the eyes of the public, whatever they had done.[16] By 8 May, 80 per cent of the Parisian population was pro-student.

On the afternoon of 6 May there was another violent clash between police and students who were pressing for the release of four students sentenced by the courts over the weekend to two months' imprisonment for their actions on 3 May. The fighting lasted for twelve hours; 422 arrests were made, with several hundred people injured on each side. Further protest demonstrations against the violence occurred on 7 and 8 May.

At this stage the student demands were simple enough: the reopening of the Sorbonne, the withdrawal of the police from the Latin Quarter and the release of students sentenced by the courts.

Hitherto the students had been regarded as 'faux révolutionnaires', guilty of 'aventurisme gauchiste', who would without fail bring disrepute on the genuine revolutionary movement pursued by the working class (see *L'Humanité*, 3 May 1968). On 8 May, communist attacks switched from the students to the government, not only in *L'Humanité*, but also in the *assemblée nationale*.

For the government, too, 8 May was a significant moment. The politicians were in difficulties; G. Pompidou, the prime minister, was on an official visit to Iran and Afghanistan from 2 to 11 May. Interim authority was in the hands of L. Joxe (justice minister and acting prime minister), A. Peyrefitte (education) and C. Fouchet (formerly education, now interior minister). Such a divided authority was difficult to exercise, since the essential power lay with the president of the republic. Furthermore, the triumvirate appear to have had differing views on what should be done. Fouchet seems to have taken a hard line throughout, whereas Peyrefitte, possibly less consistent, seems to have been more flexible in his approach. During the debate in the *assemblée nationale* he let it be known that if calm were restored, both the Sorbonne and Nanterre could soon be re-opened. While not complying with all the student demands, Peyrefitte's statement was vaguely conciliatory; but on 9 May a tougher line was imposed on him by de Gaulle himself, and the minister was forced to announce that the Sorbonne would remain closed, much to the dismay of many liberal-minded university teachers, whose hopes had been raised by his earlier pronouncement.[17] An opportunity to defuse the situation was lost, causing a hardening of the students' attitude, not without significance in view of the violence to come on the night of 10–11 May.

The fighting on 10–11 May in the Latin Quarter was by all accounts savage, particularly in the rue Gay-Lussac (see Gretton, op. cit., pp. 110–12). Prior to it, there had been vain attempts at negotiation and much hesitation on the government's part which, incidentally, gave time for the building of barricades. The order to clear the area was not given until early on 11 May; fighting began around 2.30 am and went on until about 6 am. CS gas and tear-gas were used by the police and hand-to-hand fighting occurred in an endeavour to take over the barricades. Many of these were set on fire before their defenders retreated; 367 people were wounded, 460 arrested and 188 cars were either damaged or destroyed.

It was inevitable that excessive violence would occur in such a situation, with the students trying to repel police attacks with paving-stones and molotov cocktails. What caused greater shock were the police attacks on Red Cross volunteers, on people already wounded, on spectators looking on from their flat windows (some were dragged from their homes). Certainly some onlookers did render assistance to the students, taking them in to avoid arrest, providing food and generally giving moral and practical support. M. Grimaud asserts[18] that objects were thrown at the police from flat windows; this may explain, if not justify, certain actions, but the police were the object of virtually universal blame.

This was the situation confronting Pompidou on his return to France; but he, unlike his ministers, was able to persuade de Gaulle that a policy of conciliation might work. In his television broadcast of 11 May, he announced that student demands would be met (including the release of students after an appeal court hearing). The worst seemed to be over, but the change of policy had come too late. There was to be a twenty-four-hour general strike and demonstration, called by the CGT, CFDT and FEN on 13 May to protest against police brutality. Circumstances had forced the communists to adopt a more positive attitude to the students, but the student-worker alliance was never an easy one. Negotiations over the organization of the demonstration were difficult.[19] The atmosphere of distrust and resentment was not lessened when, after the joint demonstration, a reference was made by Cohn-Bendit, whom the CGT had wished to exclude, to 'Stalinist filth'. Such a gross insult to the communist leadership may account for the continued hostility with which he was regarded.

The demonstration was massive; calculations range from half a million to a million. Student protest could no longer be brushed aside as the work of a few trouble-makers. There were also echoes in the provinces, where similar demonstrations were held – notably in Marseille, Toulouse, Lyon and Nantes.

After the demonstration the Sorbonne, re-opened as promised, was occupied and an occupation committee elected. Thus was born the 'commune étudiante' of the Sorbonne (and its extension in the Odéon theatre, taken over on 15 May), which lasted until 16 June. This was certainly the most picturesque of the May events, if perhaps less than wholly positive. All power stemmed in theory from the daily general assembly, but it was the occupation committee (in theory re-elected each day) which held effective power and dealt with the logistics and organization, while debates on every conceivable issue went on incessantly. The 'commune' was an immense talking-shop, with an aura of festival about it. It was also perhaps a kind of *défoulement*, where each individual re-discovers the pleasure of communication, of escaping from society's strait-jacket, of the freedom to speak, to work out ideas without any constraint. 'Everywhere spirits were unmuzzled, and intellectual dykes burst in a splendidly wasteful release of youthful energy.'[20] Splendid it may have been, but there was a negative side to it. Up till then, there had been virtual unity among the students, moulded by what was viewed as state repression; once the Sorbonne was occupied, the luxury of disagreement was again possible. *Groupuscules* apart, there were two main currents of thought, one concerned principally with university problems and the other which viewed university reform as of secondary importance, when compared with the need to bring about a total revolution in state and society.

After 13 May begins the second phase of events, when the emphasis shifts from students to workers. De Gaulle left France on 14 May for a state visit to Romania, leaving Pompidou in charge, but announcing that he would address the nation on 24 May. In the few days of his absence, drastic changes occurred. Young workers were attracted to the ideas of worker participation or control, and all had seen that forceful action had compelled the authorities to react. It was clearly a good opportunity to obtain redress of grievances, of which there were many. Between 13 and 20 May, factory after factory was occupied until, by about 23 May, many millions of workers were on strike.[21] Even then the unity which the students sought so eagerly between themselves and the working class was not assured. Attempts made by the students on 16 and 17 May to link up with the workers occupying the Renault factory at Boulogne-Billancourt were frustrated by the watchful and suspicious shop stewards of the CGT, anxious to prevent any ideological 'infection'.

One of the most interesting aspects of the strike was the involvement of professional people (usually assumed to be essentially middle-class and consequently conservative). In many cases they showed themselves to be more radical than the workers in their demands for the structural reform of their professional activity, for a greater degree of autonomy. Demands of this kind were made throughout France in areas such as the cinema, medicine, teaching and the arts. One strike which was particularly serious for the government was that of the ORTF, where a complete reorganization of the media was demanded, to make it independent of the state and safeguard freedom of expression.

With the country virtually at a standstill, de Gaulle decided to return from Romania earlier than planned. Exceedingly angry with his government for having let matters get out of hand, he was only persuaded with difficulty from having the Sorbonne and the Odéon forcibly evacuated. Meanwhile Pompidou was preparing for negotiations with the CNPF.

On 21–22 May the government faced and survived a censure motion in the *assemblée nationale*. For over a week there had been little street fighting, but the news that Cohn-Bendit, then in Germany, was forbidden to return to France, provoked an upsurge on 23 May and again on 24 May (which the student leadership tried vainly to prevent), with the inevitable score of wounded; 110 demonstrators, 78 policemen. On 24 May also, de Gaulle addressed the nation on television, promising a referendum: 'la voie la plus directe et la plus démocratique possible' (see *Le Monde*, 26 May 1968). It would be centred on renovation of the education system and of the economy. He made it clear that if the referendum went against him, he would resign. The address was, unusually for de Gaulle, who is said to have recognized the fact, a 'flop'; reaction to it was at best lukewarm. It was now up to Pompidou to see what negotiations with the unions and the employers could achieve. These lasted from 25 until 27 May; the outcome was the following package, known as the *accords de Grenelle*: a 35 per cent increase in both SMIG and SMAG (now 3 NF per hour – a monthly increase on a theoretical forty-hour week from 384 NF to 520 NF, and on an actual working week of forty-five hours, nearly 600 NF per month); a general wage increase of 10 per cent (7 per cent immediately and 3 per cent in October); an agreement in principle on a shorter working week; the proportion of medical expenses not reimbursed by social security reduced from 30 to 25 per cent; strike pay at 50 per cent of normal wages; a government promise to introduce legislation giving greater rights to unions on the shop floor. Not all union demands had been met, but the CGT, with its emphasis on practical improvements, was probably better pleased than the CFDT which was more interested in the reform of structures via participation or workers' control. Substantial gains had however been extracted from the employers, and it was thought that the strike would soon end. With the rejection of the package by workers at Boulogne-Billancourt when it was presented to them, G. Séguy, the CGT leader, had no option but to accept, and to make his own, the decision to continue the strike. Other large factories followed suit, and it seemed as if nothing could save the Fifth Republic from the fate of its predecessors.

Inevitably, members of the opposition considered the possibility of stepping into the apparent power vacuum, which would have required the existence of a united left; and it seemed, with the rally at the Charléty stadium on the evening of 27 May, organized by UNEF, the FEN and the PSU, as if a new left-wing revolutionary, but non-communist, movement had been born. Although no clear strategy was formulated, the meeting was critical of the CGT's attitude: there were calls for Séguy's resignation, and an enthusiastic welcome for A. Barjonet, an ex-CGT official who had resigned in protest at what he viewed as betrayal of the socialist cause by the CGT. The link between the 'new left' and the conventional political world was provided by P. Mendès-France, one of the few real statesmen of the Fourth Republic, and a member of the PSU. He declined to speak at the rally, but received a considerable ovation.[22] At a press conference on 28 May, F. Mitterrand, leader of the FGDS, proposed the formation of a provisional government headed by Mendès-France, in the event of the government's fall. He would himself be a candidate at the presidential elections which would ensue if de Gaulle resigned. This did not suit the communists, always suspicious of Mendès-France's atlantic sympathies, and now outraged by his presence at Charléty on the previous evening.

All this came to nothing with the news, on 29 May, of de Gaulle's 'disappearance'. Ostensibly wishing to spend a quiet day at his home in Colombey-les-deux-Eglises, he in fact went to Baden-Baden to confer with General Massu, commander of the French armed forces there. It seems reasonably certain that de Gaulle did, in various ways, assure himself of military support (which was later paid for by the release of General Salan and his associates), but also that his disappearance was merely a tactical manoeuvre, designed to turn attention away from events in Paris. On his return on 30 May he made an energetic radio broadcast to the nation. He would not resign, nor change his prime minister. The referendum was deferred, the *assemblée nationale* dissolved, and elections would be held (this last decision included at Pompidou's specific request). That evening, a vast anti-communist demonstration (300 or 400 thousand people) organized in advance by leaders of the Gaullist party and the various Gaullist organizations took place. This show of strength was perhaps less important than the disarray of the left in the face of a government which had regained its confidence. For differing reasons, the unions were, on the whole, opposed to any demonstration against de Gaulle's policy as revealed in the 30 May address. UNEF therefore, supported by the PSU, decided to go it alone, in the teeth of a round condemnation by the CGT, now only interested in the elections. The split between students and unions was now self-evident, a factor which would be of weight during the electoral campaign. The UNEF demonstration of 1 June was a large one — 35,000 people — but there was now a feeling of lassitude and defeat.

The workers' strike, too, began to fade during June, although some did not return to work until the second half of the month. Strikes ended through lack of money, or a feeling that public opinion was no longer sympathetic, which allowed various types of pressure to be used. Force was used against strikers in two car factories, at Flins (Renault), where a *lycéen*, Gilles Tautin, was drowned on 10 June while trying to escape from the police, and at Sochaux (Peugeot), where two workers died on 11 June. These deaths brought one final protest demonstration on 11 June, in which the street fighting was very violent; but this time the students, not the police, were blamed. A frightened public opinion had become hostile to the students, and this in turn allowed the government to act decisively. On 1 June it banned demonstrations until the elections, and outlawed a number of extreme left-wing groups. On 14 and 16 June respectively, the Sorbonne and the Odéon were cleared of their last occupants.

It is perhaps in its electoral campaign that the government showed clearly its move to the right, in spite of the presence in Pompidou's revamped administration of several left-wing Gaullists. Taking its tone from de Gaulle's broadcast of 30 May, it was dominated by the theme of law and order, and the threat of a communist dictatorship. All the parties of the left were lumped together by the Gaullists for electoral purposes. This was an effective strategy, but was unfair not only on the PCF and the CGT (which could, in Gaullist terms, have taken advantage of an apparently crumbling Fifth Republic, and did not do so), but also on Mitterrand (and the FGDS) who had acted in a perfectly legal manner.

From a Gaullist standpoint the calling of elections was a masterstroke. It gave a scared electorate the chance to express an opinion, at the same time doing away with the justification of revolutionary action, since the elections could not be viewed as anything but democratic. While the students did their best to persuade the electorate that it should boycott the elections, rather than accept a bourgeois form of legality, i.e. the existing political framework and its mechanisms, the electorate did not accept such a view, as the election results proved. After the second ballot, it was clear that the Gaullists and their allies had won 358 seats out of 485, a victory which paradoxically owed its existence to the events which had almost destroyed the régime a month earlier.

The causes of the May events, though complex, may be looked at from two main standpoints — educational and social. If we look first at the educational aspect, one cause is clearly a long-standing dissatisfaction with inadequate facilities: overcrowding caused by rising student numbers (136,700 in 1949; 508,199 in 1967 — of which 153,865 were students of literature); the inadequacy of the grant system which forced students to pay their own way through university, and the inevitable wastage that ensued.[23] Education, which provided qualifications, was increasingly viewed as a passport to financial and social advance, but the system was defective. In 1967, for example, 57 per cent of the children of top management and the liberal professions attended university, whereas only 3.4 per cent of working-class children did so.[24] There thus seemed to be a self-perpetuating upper-class élite, maintained by the educational system, which was therefore considered socially unjust. Unemployment, which had risen to almost 400,000 in 1967, was also a factor.[25] The post-war population explosion was in part responsible, with many young people, graduates amongst them, seeking work. These problems caused students to think deeply about the purposes of education, which seemed on the one hand to keep a small class of people perpetually in power, and on the other to be governed solely by market forces.

Yet, had student unrest encountered no echoes in the rest of French society, it seems unlikely that the events could have taken hold of the country as they did; and here, students and other workers had similar grievances. That society was suffering from a malaise is demonstrated by the reaction, not only of students, but of numerous categories of professional people as well as some of the younger industrial workers (those not yet 'set in their ways'), against the hierarchical structures of their own professional activities. It was suggested, shortly before the events began, that France was bored (P. Viansson-Ponté in *Le Monde*, 15 March 1968). This can well be accounted for by the centralization of French society, administratively and, to a lesser extent, politically. 'The constitution created and interpreted by General de Gaulle has done much to exclude the citizen from government. He has downgraded the Assembly, which at least offered the voter a share in public affairs by proxy, and has bypassed it with the referendum which offers the citizen only the primitive choice of saying "yes" or "no" to loaded questions' (C. Serpell, 'Participation', *Listener*, 27 June 1968). This may help to explain the significance of a number of key words for people in very differing walks of life – *participation, autogestion, autonomie, contestation*. The use of these words reveals a thirst for responsibility, for personal involvement, and for communication and discussion, which France's institutions did not provide, and which was not satisfied by de Gaulle's alternatives of national independence and policy of 'grandeur'.

It might perhaps be thought that the May events achieved nothing, in view of de Gaulle's devastating come-back. In the short term, they brought about an attempt to change the higher education system (*Loi d'Orientation*, November 1968). They also hastened the radicalization of the CFDT, with its emphasis on total change of industrial structures via workers' control and hence of the whole of society. They also brought about a change of leadership and changes in policy. De Gaulle's promised referendum on participation (regional reform and reform of the senate) was rejected in April 1969, and his resignation followed immediately. Some changes had already taken place; although the *accords de Grenelle* had not been accepted overall, they had formed the basis for subsequent agreements in numerous industries. This, together with the effects of the long general strike, put France in a weaker economic position, forced her to abandon her monetary policy (the *étalon-or*), and brought her within a hairsbreadth of devaluation, while de Gaulle was still president. De Gaulle's policy of national independence also, based as it was on co-existence between east and west, seemed less credible in view of the Russian invasion of Czechoslovakia in August 1968 and the Brezhnev doctrine of 'limited sovereignty'.

In the long term, its effects are not easy to define. It cannot be said that the structures of French society have as yet been seriously altered. Yet some changes of approach can be discerned. There have been some small-scale attempts to work out different forms of education, the *écoles nouvelles*, *écoles parallèles*, where an attempt has been made to bring up children according to a different set of values – the basis for an alternative culture (for more details see *Autrement*, no. 13, April 1978, and *Le Monde de l'Education*, May 1978, pp. 8–13).[26]

The political world too has not escaped the effects of the events of May. 'Il faut voir qu'aujourd'hui toutes les formations politiques s'occupent des questions qui, auparavant, étaient tabou. Les jeunes, les femmes, les immigrés, les prisonniers, l'écologie: ce sont les produits de Mai 68. . . . Mai 68 a imprégné profondément tous ceux qui ont eu une responsabilité dans ce pays' (P. Mendès-France in *Le Nouvel Observateur* no. 695, 4 March 1978). In the first decade after 1968, there was perhaps a greater concern with social justice, particularly in the early years of Giscard's presidency, shown in the Haby reform of 1975, as well as in the reduction of the age of majority to eighteen, more liberal legislation on abortion, divorce, radio and television.

If May 1968 had a perceptible effect on the parties of the right and centre when in power, it was inevitable that there should have been an even greater one on the parties of the left. While they were still in opposition, there had to be some ideological adjustment (the CGT, for example was forced to adopt the concepts of participation and *autogestion*). Since coming to power, the left is in the process of introducing legislation which, if not showing signs of direct influence, indicates a desire to prevent a repetition of the events. One example is the Savary higher education law of 21 December 1983, whose purpose is essentially to improve upon the *loi d'orientation* of 1968. The most telling example, however, must be the decentralization laws of 2 March 1982, 7 January and 22 July 1983, which purport to bring about a fundamental change away from administrative centralization. If this legislation proves to be efficacious, in terms of genuine participation, it might well be that similar disturbances would be less likely to occur.

At this stage, it is perhaps appropriate to ask how the events of May should be described. From what has already been said, two interpretations are possible, namely that they were the outcome (a) of a crisis in higher education, and (b) of a crisis in the institutions of the Fifth Republic. Further interpretations include the consequence of subversion with massive resources, undertaken by the left. This has been adequately refuted by M. Grimaud,[27] as far as foreign subsidies were concerned. The economic crisis has also been indicated as the source of the troubles, as in the case of earlier revolutions. It has been further suggested that the events constitute a kind of mass liberation, a psycho-drama, where students acted out a revolution.[28] This interpretation aroused some hostility at the time, but it must be admitted that, in the past, a certain revolutionary mythology has influenced the leaders, even although on this occasion the influences were perhaps not wholly French in origin. For Alain Touraine, the May events present the first example of a new kind of class struggle, against the technological society, undertaken not only by the working class, but by the students and the professional classes. One, however, which may embrace all of these interpretations (all of which undoubtedly contain some element of truth) is that which sees the May events as one example of a crisis of our civilization. It could well be suggested that, with the decline of organized religion, which lies at the basis of Western civilization, the values which it imposed became somewhat eroded and were replaced by an indiscriminate materialism and a consumer society, so strongly condemned in May '68.

Yet the view has also been put forward that the passage of time and an economic crisis, in comparison with which that of 1968 pales into insignificance, have brought about a different attitude to those things which the student leaders of '68 regarded as worthy of so much blame.

La France de '83 a d'autres soucis en tête: le chômage, la diminution du niveau de vie, la peur des voleurs et celle de la guerre. Elle n'est pas loin d'avoir la nostalgie non seulement de cette société de consommation dont elle se croyait, il y a quinze ans, dégoûtée, mais de tabous sociaux et moraux que '68 a durablement mis à mal.
(A. Fontaine, *Le Monde*, 2 May, 1983)

Paradoxically, therefore, May '68 is at once both more and less significant in French society. Some of the values it condemned are regarded differently in the present economic climate, but at the same time May '68 certainly represents a watershed in terms of a change in social values. A recent poll makes it clear that the French nation in general still regards May '68 as significant in a number of areas, but more on a social than on a political level.[29]

In political terms, however, May '68 has assumed its place as a landmark, albeit a recent one, to which all political parties refer, for good or ill, depending on the ideological viewpoint. Certainly prophecies of a return to May '68 tend to be made often, either on the anniversary of the events (e.g. M. Jobert in *Le Monde*, 6 May 1978), or when violent demonstrations over a specific grievance conjure up yet again the possibility that the violence may once again spill over into other groups and provoke a nation-wide response.

Yet there is a specific sense in which May '68 may be said to have a greater possibility of triumphing than it has ever had before. If it is true to say that the legislation enacted by the present government may prevent a return of May '68, it could equally be true to suggest, more positively, that this is because some of the aspirations so much desired fifteen years ago have now some chance of being met.

(4) From Gaullism to Giscardism: 1968–81

1968 had ended in apparent triumph for Gaullism. The Grenelle agreements, the electoral victory and the intelligent concessions of Faure's education law seemed to have brought the régime out of danger. But in the spring of 1969 de Gaulle made an attempt to confirm his authority that was to misfire and to open up a new era in French politics: this was the April referendum. In it the General offered voters a package deal: they were asked to approve a regional law providing for some small measure of decentralization away from Paris and, in the same vote, to approve changes in the composition and powers of the senate, long a thorn in de Gaulle's side (especially since its opposition to the 1962 referendum on presidential elections). The senate was now to lose its legislative powers, and henceforth only half of it would be elected – the other half being nominated by interest groups. The stick was thus combined with the carrot, and the French asked to give a single yes or no to two quite different proposals, which in any case contained several dozen sub-clauses. Opinion polls and de Gaulle's advisers suggested that there were limits to how far the public's arm could be twisted, but he went ahead with the referendum, making a 'yes' vote the condition of his staying in office. Whether this reflected his belief that he could coerce the electorate or whether, as some have claimed, it was a kind of deliberate political suicide, the General lost his referendum by 53.2 per cent to 46.8. Decisive in his defeat were not merely votes from the left, but also those of the centrists and most of all, the Independent Republicans of V. Giscard d'Estaing who were allied with Gaullism, but whose leader had been dropped from government in 1966. On 24 April de Gaulle resigned, to die the following year. A new chapter in politics had been opened.

The June presidential election saw the Gaullists present G. Pompidou as their candidate – a clear admission that the victor of 1968 was heir-apparent. He faced opposition from A. Poher, centrist senator and acting president of the republic until elections could be held. There were also two challengers from the left, as socialists and communists were still feuding. The former ran G. Defferre, considered one of their more moderate figures, and the latter presented the veteran J. Duclos. On the first ballot Defferre was beaten badly and Duclos did well, pulling in all the available communist votes. Poher did better than expected for such a mild gentleman with a Fourth Republic image, and Pompidou came first. The second ballot was thus between him and Poher, and he won easily (57.5 per cent to 42.5), as not many left supporters were ready to vote Poher rather than Pompidou (it was, as Duclos put it, a choice between 'blanc bonnet et bonnet blanc'). Pompidou thus began a presidency that would last till his untimely death in April 1974: this period forms a whole to some extent, so we shall deal with it as such, leaving the presidency of Giscard d'Estaing till later.

Pompidou's presidency was no period of dramatic social and economic change. By now the broad lines of French development were clearly fixed and Pompidou continued the course set in the 1960s. France aimed to become a major economic power, which meant greater efficiency and productivity, plus a heavier commitment to exports. It also meant more French investment abroad and greater penetration into France of foreign investment (by 1971 there would be more of this in France than in Germany). Inside France the number of industrial mergers would continue: the number of self-employed, especially in agriculture, would decline and that of wage-earners rise steadily. Pompidou's reign saw no great change in foreign policy, either: if there was slightly less frigidity with regard to the USA, then France still maintained privileged links with Eastern Europe. And if Britain was admitted to the EEC, then traditional French hostility to supranational initiatives remained strong. What is interesting about Pompidou's presidency is domestic political development and we shall concentrate heavily on this.

Pompidou had two premiers – J. Chaban-Delmas from June 1969 to July 1972 and P. Messmer until his death. Chaban saw himself as the progressive type of Gaullist, eager to innovate and broaden the bases of governmental support; the dour Messmer believed that what France needed was order and stability. That Pompidou used both is significant.

Any examination of his policies should begin, however, with an attempt to situate him in the context of Gaullism. Clearly Pompidou could never have the charismatic authority of de Gaulle: he admitted as much by his careful cultivation of the image of a shrewd Auvergnat, dependable and undramatic. While the Gaullist barons (Debré, Foccart, etc.) had been closely involved in all the heroic periods of Gaullism, as well as in the 'traversée du désert' (the long years when de Gaulle was out of power), Pompidou had been working quietly in banking, occasionally giving the General financial advice. If he had risen in the hierarchy after 1962 thanks to his political skills, this did not mean that he was popular with historic Gaullists, or indeed with the General, who had in the end sacked him for being right in 1968 against the General's own point of view. But these personal and historical differences were compounded by a more serious one, namely the differing analyses of French society which Pompidou and the older Gaullists had. The latter had a dynamic view of the state: it was to give leadership and drive in the modernization of France, and make her a great power again. It has been shown how the 'technocrats' of the Fifth Republic pursued vigorous industrial policies, encouraging the private sector to expand – to such an extent that some analysts have spoken in terms of a state capitalism, animated by aims of national grandeur. Now, such policies have their social costs: modernization hit at large sectors of the peasantry, as well as shopkeepers, craftsmen and small businessmen. De Gaulle and his associates believed that these categories could be carried along on a tide of economic growth and nationalist rhetoric; but Pompidou was clever enough to see the extent of their hardship (manifest in the emergence of militant organizations such as CIDUNATI) and to try and placate them. For their electoral weight (worth up to four million votes, according to how one calculates) was clearly vital to Gaullism and arguably to the régime. In 1968 Pompidou had appealed pretty directly to the fears of such categories: increasingly his presidency could be seen as an attempt to steer between concessions to them and modernizing imperatives.

There was another twist to Pompidou's Gaullism, however, which involved an attempt to broaden its support in another direction. At its peak in the 1960s when the economy was booming, the UDR had pulled in an increasing number of working-class and lower white-collar votes, many of which the left might normally expect to claim. It seemed possible to Pompidou to try and reconcile them more durably to the régime, however, even though their claims might differ radically from those of the categories just described. This thinking probably lay behind the appointment of Chaban-Delmas, with his project for a 'new society'. Chaban was as keen a modernizer as Pompidou, and he believed it possible to build a very wide consensus inside French society on the basis of economic growth and political stability (both of which could be attributed to the Fifth Republic). Such a consensus could be found by a series of reforms, thought Chaban; if it did not already exist, then this was because (a) the administration was out-dated and arbitrary in its practices, and (b) too many people had an ideological (therefore wrong) view of social relations, which stressed conflict at the expense of consensus. In fact this mixture of pious hope and shrewd political calculation proved hard to translate into practice. In industrial relations, Chaban achieved some small changes: manual workers began to be paid increasingly on a monthly, not weekly basis; the guaranteed minimum wage, SMIG (dating from 1952), was indexed to the cost of living and became SMIC (the C standing for 'croissant'). In the Renault works, a small percentage of dividends was redistributed to workers (Pompidou's version of de Gaulle's participation involved turning workers into small capitalists). More importantly, in the public sector Chaban was able to sign *contrats de progrès* with unions (detailed agreements covering wages and prices). Whether these measures would suffice to rally more lower-class support to the régime without frightening off some of its more comfortable supporters remained to be seen.

Certainly in other areas of policy where he might appeal to a more progressive audience, Chaban was less successful. The regional law of 1972 created bodies with no power, hence incapable of dealing with grave problems of economic imbalance faced by regions like Alsace-Lorraine, with its declining coal and steel industries, the Vosges, with its obsolescent textile production, or the south-west with its industrial under-development and inefficient farming. In the field of civic liberties, Chaban's attempts to liberalize the notoriously pro-government news broadcasts were killed at birth by Pompidou's private office. All this suggested that part at least of the Pompidolian majority was not in favour of trying to broaden the régime's appeal towards more popular or more progressive groups.

Pompidou's modernizing tendencies were seen in his use of the state as industrial spearhead. The building of the Fos port and industrial complex near Marseille used government funds to cover the first one-sixth of the costs: the two steel giants of Usinor and Wendel were then persuaded to amalgamate and the remaining cost was covered by a 25 per cent participation by foreign capital. This is a good example of heroic state leadership to the private sector. On another level, the acceptance of British entry into the EEC served notice that Pompidou was fully committed to the ultimate logic of economic expansion, exposure to foreign competition.

Yet such policies had their counterpart: if Pompidolism favoured the development of big capital, it had also to make concessions to small. Thus in agriculture, although the Common Agricultural Policy, with its guaranteed prices and insurance against market risks, was especially favourable to the big farmers of northern France, it also slowed down the exodus of the smaller farmers, because of both the price supports and the structural reforms agreed by the EEC on the basis of the Mansholt Plan. Thus Pompidou did not run the risk of too rapid a rural exodus and the alienation of farmers' support. Similar steps were taken in commerce, where the small shopkeepers were struggling against competition from larger units by the early 1970s.

To keep the support of this numerous and vocal category, J. Royer, minister of commerce, passed in December 1973 a law which effectively gave small shopkeepers blocking power over the granting of building permits for commercial premises — this despite the claims of finance minister Giscard d'Estaing that the whole of the commercial structure still needed considerable modernization.

Another category favoured by Pompidolism was property-development. Developers enjoyed something of a golden age in the early 1970s, when Paris and many other towns were covered in concrete, which was lucrative for them, if less pleasant for those who had to live in or look at their buildings. Given the extent of the housing crisis, it was perhaps inevitable that there should be a property boom. What was more surprising was the extent to which the Gaullist machine became involved in it, even though certain developers were known to be enthusiastic contributors to UDR funds. Gaullist favouritism extended from granting developers planning permission in green belts to involvement by a number of deputies in schemes where house-buyers were the victims of distinctly sharp practice. Some of these deputies resigned or were expelled from the UDR. This helped to spread an atmosphere of scandal, redolent of previous republics, which did no good to the general reputation of the UDR: nor did the publication in 1972 of documents showing Chaban's skill at tax avoidance.

By this time indeed 'le système Pompidou', as hostile observers called it, was beginning to creak. The crisis with which all are familiar since 1974 had not yet fully broken, but there were disturbing signs. Unemployment was over half a million; prices were rising steadily; some regions and sectors stood out in sharp decline; housing was inadequate. Pompidou's 1972 referendum on British entry to the EEC turned out to be a very damp squib, with 46.6 per cent of the electorate abstaining. To prepare for the 1973 elections, Pompidou replaced Chaban with Messmer. In so doing he had almost certainly been swayed by his private advisers — P. Juillet and M. -F. Garaud — who wanted to move Gaullism on to an increasingly conservative course. They believed that reformism of the Chaban type (anodine as it might seem to outsiders) was already a concession to the opposition left. As such, it would never win wider support but merely antagonize 'la France des profondeurs' — the rural, the aged, the religious, the reactionary pure and simple, many of whom fitted into the declining economic categories described above and whose votes were increasingly necessary to Gaullism. Such people wanted not dynamic change, but preservation of their own status; not workers' participation in industry, but measures against trade unions and communists; not liberalization of media or mores, but rather 'law and order'. Whether Pompidou could satisfy their demands is dubious: but the dismissal of Chaban signified a step to the right and set the tone for the 1973 parliamentary elections.

Pompidou and his allies fought these defensively, on a platform of anti-left, and especially anti-communist, feeling. There was a reason for this. Since 1969 the socialist party had renewed its organization, its leaders and its policies. It had also moved closer to the communists after the freeze of 1968. In 1972 the two signed, for the first time, a common programme of government (CPG), which committed them, if victorious at the polls, to making certain changes within precise deadlines. In the constitutional field, they were pledged to abolition of the special presidential powers and creation of a supreme court; in economic policy, as well as a large give-away element (wage rises and improved benefits), the programme promised higher growth and looked to more intensive planning, based on a number of strategic nationalizations, as the means of achieving this. Differences in foreign and defence policy (e.g. over NATO and the EEC) and in economic policy (how to run nationalized industry) were disguised with reasonable skill.

The attractions of this package, plus discontent with long years of 'l'Etat UDR', were likely to mean a swing towards the opposition. Hence the defensive campaign of the government and Pompidou's special appeal on the media just before polling – both of them on the themes of the dangers to France implied by the 'adventurist' and 'irresponsible' economic strategy of the left and the fundamental incompatibility of socialists and communists. The mixture worked well enough for the UDR to remain the leading party, though the socialists gained considerably. But the three years of peace to which Pompidou had looked forward before the 1976 presidential elections were not to be. He looked increasingly ill and seemed progressively less in command of government; thus few were surprised when, after a painful illness, he died in April 1974. Once again, there was turmoil at the prospect of unexpected presidential elections.

In the May election, three major candidates stood at the first ballot, along with a wide spectrum of others, from the feminist and Trotskyist candidate A. Laguiller to ex-minister Royer, whose appeal was very much to 'la France des profondeurs'. F. Mitterrand was again candidate of the united left (though not pledged to implement the common programme in its entirety); V. Giscard d'Estaing, with his long experience as finance minister, competed with the ex-premier Chaban-Delmas for the votes of the right. The latter pair were rated fairly evenly by opinion polls until there occurred an event which had more implications than many realized. Forty-three UDR deputies, led by J. Chirac, had doubts about whether Chaban (a 'fragile' candidate because of his recent sacking and the publicity about his tax affairs) could beat Mitterrand in the run-off at the second ballot. They therefore declared publicly in favour of Giscard (a non-Gaullist). Chaban's rating in the polls collapsed drastically, once it was known that some of his own party considered him a loser. At the same time Giscard secured the support of the opposition centrists of Lecanuet (worth, as the latter boasted on BBC television, some three million votes). This effectively meant a second-round duel between Giscard and Mitterrand, with the former scraping home by 50.6 per cent to 49.4. The left could lament the missed opportunity, and Giscard now had to govern with a majority (in parliamentary terms) which was broadly sympathetic, but whose dominant party was not his own. This fact he recognized by making Chirac his premier. Gaullism had paid dearly for not having a successor to Pompidou ready in the wings.

Giscard had placed his campaign under the sign of 'change without risk': he promised voters an 'advanced liberal society'. His approach, then, was more along the lines of Chaban-Delmas than the conservative course lately set by Pompidou. It implied broadening the power-base of the government – a task doubly necessary given the slimness of Giscard's victory. But as with Chaban-Delmas, there were limits to how far Giscard could go. Nothing in his background or that of his party suggested any radical disagreement with the workings of French capitalist society in the seventies. It would rather be a question of making this society work less conflictually, by reconciling as many social groups to it as possible. This would involve reforms, but not far-reaching ones: it might also involve a good deal of publicity, to suggest that more was being changed than was actually the case. We shall now examine some of the policies of the advanced liberal society.

Giscard clearly intended his presidency to be a reforming one. His book *Démocratie française* (1976) gives a theoretical justification of his politics. Like most developed countries France is, he writes, losing those features of class antagonism characteristic of early phases of industrialization. Society today consists of a vast middle group, white- and blue-collar alike, which has known political stability and steady economic growth: this has brought rising living standards, increased property ownership and indeed a similar culture and aspirations. What modern Frenchmen want then is more of the same – steady material progress in an atmosphere of political and social consensus. This is best guaranteed in a pluralistic, democratic society under the aegis of enlightened leaders who know when and how to reform and who can 'plan the twenty-first century'. There is no need for revolution nor for the type of peaceful but far-reaching structural changes proposed by the left: the existing framework of French capitalism is adequate for such progress. Such is the essential of Giscardian philosophy: it is descended, as its author proudly claims, from a long tradition of nineteenth-century liberalism albeit suffused here with a number of humanistic and fraternal glosses which the founding fathers would probably have disliked.

Unfortunately for Giscard, whatever the sincerity of his intentions, it was always likely to be hard to turn them into effective policies. As he won office the effects of the first oil crisis struck at the industrial world, with the depressive results that have since become familiar. In international relations, the era of détente between East and West rapidly subsided into what some have called the second Cold War. More seriously, it was doubtful if within France herself there were the social or cultural bases to sustain such a vision. Divisions within France were and are deeper than Giscard cared to admit: so too — and this is more important — are the ideological ways in which people see such differences. Politically, half the country had just voted against Giscard and even within his own camp, the right, there would soon emerge opposition to the man and his policies that would prove fatal. Retrospectively it seems that the dice were loaded against Giscard before he begun: but even so, his presidency seemed to develop an increasing reluctance to attempt any sort of change and an obsession with survival. Reformism became *attentisme*. We shall now examine some aspects of the presidency in detail.

So far as decision-making goes, Giscard accentuated the trend towards presidential power incarnate in the Fifth Republic.[30] His style reinforced this impression, with his six-monthly open letters to the government laying down the next policy objectives to be followed, his interventions in electoral campaigns to urge 'le bon choix' upon the public and his heavy use of the pedagogical fireside chat to explain policy to the nation. More concrete evidence can be seen in the steady expansion of his private office to cover the increasing number of areas in which he took a direct interest and his systematic packing of key posts in the state apparatus, especially the media, so as to ensure better execution of his decisions.[31] The Etat-UDR was fast becoming l'Etat-UDF; and this seemed especially true after the first prime minister, J. Chirac, was forced to resign in September 1976.

It is true that Giscard never used those devices in the constitution such as ordinances, referenda or special powers which enable government to bypass parliament. Yet it would be hard to say that the latter's influence increased during his term, despite his known enthusiasm for strengthening it. Giscard made it easier for parliamentarians to seize the *conseil constitutionnel* (see chapter 3) as to the legality of government bills: but many saw this less as an assertion of parliament than as a *garde-fou* against the actions of a possible left government.[32] His proposal after the 1978 parliamentary elections to involve the opposition more, by dint of giving it the chairmanship of two of the six standing committees in the National Assembly, was effectively crushed by Chirac. As time went on his relations with this body, where in theory he had an easy majority — provided that Chirac's supporters voted with his own — became sourer. Chirac stepped up a series of niggling campaigns against his ex-ally, and the left stood by. At the end of 1980 Giscard and his prime minister R. Barre were forced to use Article 49-iii (heavy artillery in parliamentary terms), to get their budget through the lower house. Long before 1981 it was clear that hopes of a parliamentary consensus were dead.

Turning from the institutional sphere to the economic we find that again the passage was less than smooth. The early phase particularly was very much one of 'stop-go' — encouraging periods of strong expansion then, when these caused problems in areas such as balance of payments, cracking down with a harsh deflationary package. Thus Chirac began by encouraging a frenetic phase of expansion, the government running a big deficit to pay for public sector infrastructure in the hope of stimulating private industry. The higher growth obtained was however accompanied by an increasing deficit on the balance of payments and with an inflation rate still much higher than that of competitors. The economy was over-heated; to cool it down Giscard replaced Chirac (with whom he also had more political disagreements) with R. Barre, who would serve out the rest of the presidency. He would implement a more conservative economic policy in the series of plans named after him, with the aim of laying foundations for a long-term recovery of the economy.

'Barrism' was a series of macro-economic measures aimed at clearing the problems left by previous governments. If successful it would re-create conditions in which the normal workings of the market could resume and, so the theory has it, lead to growth and prosperity. In its underlying logic of restoring priority to market forces it is close to those monetarist policies now widely used in Western countries.

Barre aimed to reduce the trade deficit, cut inflation, and maintain the value of the franc. The means to this end were to be balanced budgets and control of money supply: he also counted on discreet pressure on wage settlements (a formal prices and incomes policy was out of the question) and, after the 1978 election win, freeing price controls and making higher charges for public services. These latter measures would in effect transfer resources from labour towards capital, in the form of increased profits for firms. Some of this should then return in the form of job-creating investment, though as Barre said, to provide this was not the task of the state, but rather of the employers; 'c'est leur affaire'.

As regards industry Barre wanted to end the overmanning and feather-bedding which he believed widespread in France. Henceforth lame ducks (Edward Heath's phrase became very popular in Giscardian France) were not to be baled out by the state but rely on their own efforts. If the firms could not make sufficient profits to continue they must face the consequences. In practice, as Green shows, a less harsh attitude prevailed.[33] The CIASI (*Comité interministériel d'aménagement des structures industrielles*) continued to act as an 'infirmary' for ailing firms, often with local political considerations in mind. At the same time, market rhetoric apart, the Barrists carried on the Gaullist strategy of 'national champions', encouraging well-placed firms to increase their shares of key export markets. This drew from the left charges that the government had submitted to a new 'international division of labour', dictated by the USA, whereby France was led to abandon some types of industry and specialize in others, usually not the most advanced ones. The left suggested that it would both protect the older industries which Barre was allowing to decline and make sure that enough investment occurred to ensure that France would be well involved in the new 'sunrise industries'. Barre's strategy was further diverted by his having to intervene in areas where previous governments had long put off awkward decisions. Thus a Vosges plan (1979) had to be hastily put together to save the disintegrating textile industry, and a special steel plan virtually national-ized what remained of the French steel industry, the state paying out huge sums in redundancy money and alternative job creation.

In the end the results of Barrism were bound to fall below expec-tations. If exports were rising by 1979, the second 'hike' of oil prices following the Iranian revolution cancelled that out at a stroke. If industry had to some extent been slimmed down, then it was at high cost. Green estimates that by 1979 bankruptcies were running at 1,300 per month, with rising unemployment partially concealed by temporary job-schemes for school-leavers not unlike the British YOPS. Increased profitability was still not being translated quickly enough into job-creating investment. The government borrowing deficit remained high and the reaction was to print more money (money supply was rising at 14 per cent per annum instead of the anticipated 11 per cent). Barre would doubtless argue that the monetarist medicine was beginning to work and that without it things would be worse; but on the right as well as on the left alternative strategies were advocated.

One long-term aspect of Giscardian economics was the systematic development of civil nuclear energy. By 1981 France had some 3 dozen such power stations in operation, being built or projected. The aim was clearly to reduce dependence on imported oil and with it balance of payments deficits. The potential hazards of such a choice also became clearer after incidents like the accident at Three Mile Island in the USA in 1979. As Barre left office it emerged that France was in fact over-endowed with energy;[34] but by then the nuclear choice was well-nigh irreversible, despite the protests of the growing ecological movement (see chapter 4).

In non-economic policy Giscard showed evidence of a reforming zeal which was never taken too far. In local government he was known to favour increased decentralization of power and resources, if not some kind of regional power. Yet he did little. Doubtless under Gaullist pressure he soon abandoned any moves towards regionalism. If he allowed com-munes (see chapter 3) greater freedom to spend government money and to vary their local tax base, he was not ready to go further in challenging either local habits or the mistrust of his Gaullist partner. In 1975 he did reform the statute of the city of Paris, allowing it to elect its own mayor in line with other communes. This in fact led to a bitter battle in the 1977 municipal directions, when Chirac beat a Giscardian nominee to take the town hall.

The field of civil liberties showed similar traits. The septennate began enthusiastically with laws liberalizing divorce and abortion, and lowering the majority to eighteen, even if the help of the parliamentary left was required to pass them against the wishes of some Giscardians! This first impulse waned, though, as economic and social tension grew. Giscard's first interior minister, M. Poniatowski, took from the first a tough line: his use of police dogs to clear strikers out of occupied workplaces and his media denunciations of 'soft' magistrates never did blend particularly well with the liberal tones of his leader. The independence of judges was, in the view of many, weakened by a series of disciplinary measures against magistrates who had stood up visibly to pressure from above. At the end of the septennate justice minister A. Peyrefitte, responding to a widespread psychosis about law and order which the government had in no small measure helped to create, would present the bill *Sécurité et liberté*, which sharply increased repressive powers.[35] And as Frears shows, nothing was done about those aspects of the legal system which seem to privilege the state against the individual, such as the excessive custodial powers (*garde à vue*) or the existence of special tribunals outside the normal hierarchy of courts and on which the military sat; these were used to try regional autonomists.[36]

In this context we should mention immigration policy. Throughout the years of post-war expansion, France encouraged immigration, but tried to shut the door once the recession set in. No work permits were issued after 1976 and the minister, L. Stoléru, offered 10,000-franc lump-sums to immigrants willing to return home — an offer later deemed illegal by the constitutional council. From then on the government sought to round up and expel illegal immigrants (hundreds of thousands of whom had been encouraged to enter during the boom, for the simple reason that an illegal immigrant is far more docile to employ than one who has some rights). Indeed it is hard to avoid the feeling that the government was less active than it might have been in discouraging those xenophobic and racialist feelings which arise in times of crisis. Scapegoats have their uses.

One large group that might feel disappointed with Giscardian social policy was women. It is true that at times the government contained more women than any other European one, including a junior minister for women's affairs. But it is hard to see more substantial results. Women's earnings remained systematically lower than men's and they suffered most from unemployment. On the credit side, maternity leave provisions were improved as were financial arrangements for widows, and the government did pass a law (later repealed by the constitutional council) which imposed a quota of 20 per cent women on lists for municipal elections. Feminists would find this a rather modest record.

In education Giscard began with the Haby reform of 1975 (see chapter 6). It aimed to increase equality of opportunity for school-children and to adapt schooling to the needs of a modern economy. Overambitious in terms of the resources available and never popular with teachers, the new reform seemed like its innumerable predecessors to be unlikely to change very much. In higher education after 1976 Alice Saunier-Séité led a more open attack, in her highly personal style. Proclaiming the need to make university syllabuses 'relevant', she cut numerous programmes, especially in establishments reputed hostile to the government. She also increased pressure on younger staff and tried to reverse some of the effects of the Faure Act by concentrating more power in the hands of senior professors. Clearly reformism had its limits in the colleges.

One area in which there was again little movement was industrial relations. If the 1976 Sudreau report recommended involving workers in the running of firms, albeit on a consultative rather than a decision-making basis, these proposals were promptly shelved. Stoléru made a number of gestures towards workers, including savings schemes for those wanting to set up their own businesses and early retirement for some categories, but these actions and their accompanying rhetoric ('valoriser le travail manuel') remained peripheral and rather cosmetic. Giscardism was not interested in integrating the working class by institutional or legal means. It simply relied on its overall economic performamce to secure enough working-class votes for re-election.

It is now possible to assess roughly who, in sociological terms, benefited from Giscard's running of the economy. At the bottom of the scale, old age pensioners' buying power increased by some 65 per cent, albeit from a very low base in 1974; average workers' buying power rose by 29 per cent and that of *smicards* (minimum wage earners) by some 28 per cent.[37] Lower white-collars did slightly better and the upper part of the working class (supervisors, etc.) slightly worse. In other words Giscardism assured some redistribution of income, in a way that we expect more from social-democratic types of régime. Generally few lost out overall in terms of income (agriculture being perhaps the major exception), even though by the end income levels were beginning to taper off rather than rise steadily as had been the case previously. Against this achievement must be set the fact that unemployment rose by 320 per cent (from 2.3 per cent to 7.3 per cent of the workforce) up to 1981: the young people, women and those who generally lived in declining regions, all of whom were the worst-affected categories, clearly fell behind the overall level of prosperity. Giscard himself favoured reducing income differentials, as shown by his 1976 proposal for a capital gains tax; but his own conservative majority in parliament saddled it with a series of exemptions that made it worthless. There were obviously limits to how far economic egalitarianism could be extended. Yet Giscard was careful not to disturb the established system of welfare benefits (family allowances, social security, etc.) even though the funds which finance these were in chronic deficit by 1981 ('le trou de la Sécu'). Health Minister J. Barrot attempted to introduce a two-tier system of medical charges which would have forced some patients to pay more for their treatment,[38] and there was the one-off tax on pensions already mentioned. But the unpopularity of such measures led Giscard to reflect that reform of the system of benefits, urgent though it was (commentators spoke of 'la crise de l'Etat-providence') could best be left to a future government.

Foreign policy was as Frears remarks, heavily tied to economic (see chapter 5). In Europe, while increasing inter-governmental co-operation through the regular summit meetings of EEC heads of state and government, Giscard prized Franco-German co-operation above all. He saw the Paris/Bonn axis as the motor of Europe and made considerable financial sacrifices to put the franc into the new EMS (European Monetary System) in 1979 as proof of his goodwill. He saw a division of labour, as it were, between German economic power and French diplomatic and military strength, whereby the two could give leadership to the rest of Europe. As regards the USA, he kept his distance from NATO, refusing to rejoin the integrated command structure or to offer the French nuclear arsenal in disarmament negotiations. French conventional and nuclear forces were kept at a high level, with defence spending increasing threefold in seven years. Sensitive to accusations of pro-Americanism, Giscard also improved links with the USSR; his 1980 trip to Warsaw to meet Brezhnev after the Soviet invasion of Afghanistan was considered by many to be overindulgent towards the USSR (Mitterrand called him 'le petit télégraphiste').

With regard to the third world, Giscard talked of a new economic order to bridge the gap between developed and underdeveloped countries, calling the North-South conferences from 1975–9 and appealing for a 'trialogue' between the Arab world, the EEC and the Organization for African Unity. These initiatives were prompted by the belief that exchanges between North and South could be adjusted to the advantage of both without making major structural changes. Hardly surprisingly there has been little tangible follow-up.

In the Middle East, pragmatism prevailed. Whatever Giscard's personal sympathy for Israel, France remains a heavy importer of Gulf oil. Thus he maintained strong economic and political ties with Gulf oil producers, notably Saudi Arabia and Iraq (to whom he sold arms and nuclear power facilities), as well as recognizing officially the PLO (Palestine Liberation Organization).

Africa revealed much of the nature of Giscardian foreign policy. The quasi-imperial links, economic, diplomatic and military, which France had forged with her ex-colonies in the de Gaulle era were kept intact.

African policy was still decided by the President himself and his Africa specialist in the Elysée and conducted in a highly personal and sometimes spectacular manner. The basic pattern was that sympathetic African élites were nurtured by France in return for economic and other benefits which she derived (see chapter 2). At times such help could take the form of military intervention, as in 1978 to rescue the Mobutu régime in Zaire from an internal rebellion, or with the numerous and complex interventions in Chad. Sometimes when the élites became embarrassing, as with the Central African dictator Bokassa, who committed some particularly foul atrocities on his subjects, they were replaced by alternative leaders ushered in by French arms. African policy had changed little since the time of de Gaulle and Foccart.

All in all, Giscardian foreign policy showed a heavy pragmatism and an awareness of the economic bases of such policy. It also showed up the weight of the Gaullian legacy of independence. As such it could not be said to have innovated much.

In party politics, the new president deplored the division of France into two and called for a relaxing of the hostility between left and right. *Décrispation* was a slogan much used in the media; but how it was to be translated into practice was not clear. Giscard would have liked some arrangement with the socialists, detaching them from their communist partners and at the same time allowing his own supporters to escape from the Gaullists. This was never likely to be forthcoming, though, and Giscard would probably have been happy with the kind of polite relationship that prevails in Britain between government and opposition, with regular exchanges of views between party leaders. Despite his numerous overtures in this direction, all he had managed to achieve by the summer of 1978 was to win over one or two personalities from the fringe of the opposition (with the prospect of some others to follow, no doubt) and to have had talks at the Elysée with the trade-union and opposition leaders, following the left's defeat in the election of March 1978. Later he persuaded R. Fabre, the MRG leader, to accept a special mission on unemployment and then to become the *médiateur* (roughly the equivalent of the British parliamentary commissioner or ombudsman). Doubtless Fabre regretted his decision when he saw the election results in 1981, for he would have enjoyed high office under Mitterand. Apart from that Giscard's attempt to change the political culture of France met with little success.

The oppositions in French politics run deeper perhaps than Giscard or some commentators realize. Perhaps the comment of the veteran Gaullist Sanguinetti is appropriate in this context: 'Qu'est-ce que Giscard? C'est Guizot, c'est la grande bourgeoisie libérale d'émanation protestante, quant à la mentalité, même si elle est en pays catholique. On veut gouverner ce pays comme s'il était anglais ou allemand. C'est une erreur, qui peut coûter cher à la France'.[39]

In fact as we shall see Giscard had increasing difficulty in keeping harmony within his own camp, never mind that of the opposition.

(5) A socialist France? The Mitterrand years, 1981-

As 1981 dawned Giscard could perhaps feel fairly satisfied with his term of office. In the economy things could have been much worse: growth was higher than in the rest of Europe and if unemployment was rising it was still well below that of the UK or West Germany. Inflation was still high, and the balance of payments deficit was beginning to look permanent, but most people's living standards were still holding steady if not creeping upwards. Investment was just beginning to accelerate and Barre, feeling that recovery was coming, resisted fairly successfully the temptation of a give-away budget before the election, preferring to appear consistent with his stated aims. In foreign policy consistency had been shown, and in the area of social reform there had been some small achievements even if, as we saw, there was often a tendency to back away from reforms which needed to be done and could have been with more commitment – taxation, industrial relations, social security, local government. On the debit side, the increasingly aloof and almost monarchical style of the president was becoming tiresome and the régime was slowly becoming engulfed in an air of scandal. The diamonds which Bokassa offered his 'cher parent', the suicide of Labour Minister R. Boulin in mysterious circumstances and what looked like a parliamentary cover-up of possible government foreknowledge of the murder of de Broglie, a Giscardian deputy – all these were publicized assiduously by the opposition press and must have weakened the régime's image.

At the same time Chirac's RPR party increased its *coups de canif*, sniping at Giscard's foreign policy (now too pro-American, now too pro-Soviet) or his economic management (deriding Barre for his failure to generate higher growth) and obstructing him in parliament. But many thought this mere ritual. As for the left, communists (PCF) and socialists (PS) remained polemically divided. Since the signing of the CPG in 1972 the alliance had prospered, picking up increasing numbers of votes in local and national elections, until it seemed sure to win the 1978 élections to the national assembly. Then in September 1977 the partners split, largely through PCF intransigence (see chapter 4), and the right won against the odds in 1978. Subsequent PCF behaviour confirmed that it preferred to see the right in office rather than help elect a left government where it would only have a junior rôle. The PS itself was badly divided after 1978, some claiming that the old style of state socialism incarnated by the CPG needed replacing by a modern, liberal-tinged version aimed at the new middle classes. This clash of beliefs, symbolized by the clash between Mitterrand and M. Rocard for the party's presidential nomination, caused clashes within the PS as bitter as those which have rent the British Labour party of late, threatening to damage electoral credibility beyond repair. The left electorate at large, however, continued to vote in a unitary way in by-elections, showing its desire for change irrespective of the quarrels of party élites. Nevertheless as the two-round presidential contest of 26 April and 10 May neared, few believed that the weaknesses of the Giscard camp were less than those of its opponents. The re-election of Giscard II, as one newspaper gloomily called him, seemed inevitable.

All four major parties fielded candidates, as did the centre-left MRG, far left PSU and the Trotskyites (this was Arlette Laguiller who stood in 1974). B. Lalonde represented the ecologists and there were two independent right-wingers in M. Debré and Marie-France Garaud. All the small candidates displayed some ingenuity in finding the required 500 signatures from local officials to be present on the ballot.[40] The PCF campaign had begun before the end of 1980 and the candidate G. Marchais made every effort to mobilize both the party and the trade-union CGT (see chapter 4). His main aim was clearly to stop Mitterrand, whose 'virage à droite' he regularly denounced, predicting austerity for the French if he were elected. This the PCF pledged itself to combat, and to give the public a foretaste of its likely tactics, PCF and CGT activists indulged in such operations as breaking up a live election debate in the TV studios. Another tactic used was the openly racist, anti-immigrant campaign undertaken in several PCF-controlled suburbs; here the party was trying to kill two birds with one stone. On the one hand it was after the sort of votes that normally go to the far right, on the other it was frightening off, by such irresponsible behaviour, floating voters from the middle of the political spectrum who might be thinking of voting for its notional ally, Mitterrand.

Mitterrand had eventually been endorsed as the PS candidate after Rocard withdrew. His campaign was based on his '110 propositions', considerably less radical than the official PS line. He promised economic reflation, based on a number of key nationalizations, criticized Giscard's monarchical style and modest record on civil liberties and above all was clever enough to avoid promising to have PCF ministers in his government. He used all factions of his party, especially Rocard who was so popular with the media, to help with the campaign, and his publicity, run by J. Séguéla, a professional advertiser, was incomparably better than in 1974.

Giscard started his campaign late, relying on his media skill and his control of the state apparatus. He seemed much less enthusiastic than in 1974 and was perhaps overconfident that the PCF would take care of Mitterrand for him. After much speculation, Chirac declared his own candidacy in February; his organization was superb, his publicity skilful and his confidence abundant. Immediately — perhaps with the help of a little manipulation of opinion polls – he suggested that he was catching up with Giscard.

As the campaign progressed the polls showed a latish swing to Mitterrand, while Giscard stagnated, as did Marchais.[41] Sensing that its spoiling tactics were not paying off and that its supporters were drifting towards Mitterrand, the PCF changed tack. Attacks on Mitterrand became demands for places in the now inevitable 'government of popular unity'. The results of the first ballot showed Mitterrand close enough to Giscard to be able to beat him on the second.

The lessons of the vote were eloquent. A quarter of PCF support had gone straight to Mitterrand on the first ballot; this was tactical voting (*le vote utile*). Chirac and the dissident right-wingers Debré and Garaud had taken enough votes off Giscard to weaken him fatally. In the middle Lalonde with his surprising million votes virtually held the balance (see Table 1.2).

The fortnight between ballots sealed Giscard's fate. Having failed to beat Mitterrand the PCF could only join him, and it urged support for him with few conditions (though in PCF-run towns, voters were sometimes given different recommendations). Mitterrand went some small way towards ecologist demands on nuclear energy and thereby got two-thirds of Lalonde's votes on the second ballot, even though the latter made no recommendation to his supporters. Finally Chirac, in a much-awaited speech, declared that he personally felt obliged to vote for Giscard, but made no recommendation to his supporters . . .

On 10 May the results were thus: Mitterrand 15.7 million votes (51.75 per cent of votes cast), Giscard 14.6 million (48.25 per cent). A furious Giscard denounced the 'premeditated treason' which had led to his defeat. Chirac could reflect that as in 1974 he had been kingmaker;

Table 1.2   Presidential election 26 April 1981, first ballot

Candidate	Votes (millions)	% Votes cast	% Registered electorate
V. Giscard d'Estaing (UDF)	8.22	28.3	22.6
F. Mitterrand (PS)	7.51	25.8	20.6
J. Chirac (RPR)	5.23	18	14.3
G. Marchais (PCF)	4.47	15.3	12.2
B. Lalonde (Ecol.)	1.13	3.9	3.1
A. Laguiller (Trotskyist)	0.67	2.3	1.8
M. Crépeau (MRG)	0.64	2.2	1.8
M. Debré (Independent)	0.48	1.7	1.3
M. F. Garaud (Independent)	0.39	1.3	1.1
H. Bouchardeau (PSU)	0.32	1.1	0.9

but now there was a real chance of his own coronation in 1988. Meanwhile the Fifth Republic had its first socialist president. He rapidly made P. Mauroy head of a caretaker government, which passed some hasty reforms by decree, and then as he had promised to do dissolved the national assembly. The voters knew what they had to do if they were to be consistent with their vote of 10 May, and with Mitterrand visibly not owing much to the PCF, felt free to give him a parliamentary majority.

The second round turned into a landslide, with the PS winning a huge majority over all the others combined for the first time ever. The final allocation of the 491 seats was as follows (gains or losses from 1978 in brackets):

PCF	44	(− 42)
PS	269	(+ 162)
MRG	14	(+ 4)
other left	6	(+ 5)
UDF	65	(− 55)
RPR	86	(− 69)
other right	7	(− 5)

The government now had a firm majority as it set out to implement Mitterrand's brand of socialism. But the Mitterrand experiment was constrained by even graver limits than Giscard had faced in 1974. The recession had now deepened everywhere in the West, with declining production and rising unemployment. Most of the governments who are France's main trading partners sought to fight these trends not by Keynesian policies of expansion but by harsh monetarist remedies, cutting expenditure and money supply in order to 'purge' their economies. France was now more 'locked in' to the international economy as her foreign trade had increased, and hence that much more dependent on international fluctuations. The steady worsening of East-West relations scarcely needs comment. Moreover, in France itself Mitterrand's power base was narrow: the victories of 1981 were not massive mandates for a 'break with capitalism', but more a desire for some moderate change without destabilization of habits or institutions. They were also the culmination of a slowly maturing discontent with twenty-five years of rule by the right and the expression of readiness by previously conservative categories to vote for the moderate left (to put it briefly, I am referring culturally to certain Catholic voters and sociologically to parts of the salaried middle classes − see chapter 2). And finally the socialists knew that some of their latter support was due not to the unitary alliance with the PCF but to the fact that many voters perceived them as dominating the latter and reducing it to impotence! Thus, high as the stakes were, the room for manoeuvre was very narrow.

Mitterrand's early governments were characterized by high numbers and relatively high consistency of personnel. The two major reshuffles in mid-1982 and after the municipal election reverses of March 1983 did not amount to structural change. Throughout this period the premiership remained in the hands of P. Mauroy, leader of the socialists of Northern France, considered a moderate pragmatist. The economy was entrusted to J. Delors, a former adviser to Chaban-Delmas, again considered reassuring to business. Foreign affairs remained the province of C. Cheysson, career diplomat and long-time Mitterrand supporter. Justice was entrusted, boldly, to another old friend of Mitterrand, R. Badinter, a lawyer famous for his libertarian views. The delicate post of Interior Minister, responsible for local government as well as law and order, went to the veteran mayor of Marseille, G. Defferre, again from the reformist wing of the party. Four PCF ministers were squeezed into relatively minor posts, so as to mollify that party and also so as to make it more difficult for it to cause obstruction. The only big post to go to a left socialist was Research (later merged with Industry) which was given to J.-P. Chevènement, leader of the CERES fraction (see chapter 4). His resignation in March 1983 at what he saw as the excessively deflationary policies of Delors was compensated by the promotion of L. Fabius, a clever young leader of the new generation of Mitterrandists. Earlier P. Bérégovoy, a Mitterrand camp-follower of long standing, had replaced the CERES activist Nicole Questiaux at Social Affairs, when she protested at spending cuts. Thus if any pattern can be discerned, it is in the sense of a weakening of the socialist left to the advantage of the more pragmatic wing of the party.

By late 1983 it was possible to see how the Mitterrand experiment was working. We shall consider succinctly the main policy areas, starting with the one by which the rest stand or fall, economic policy. The socialists aimed by a mixture of Keynesian techniques (basically increasing domestic demand) and *dirigisme* (deliberate structural intervention by the state) to provoke a steady expansion of the economy which should cut unemployment, maintain or improve living standards and firms' profits, without leading to high inflation or a big foreign trade deficit.

To increase demand (i.e. give households more to spend), the government increased the wages of *smicards*, whose purchasing power rose by over 11 per cent in two years,[42] shortened the working week by one hour without loss of pay (this after some haggling), gave an extra week's paid holiday per year and stepped up welfare benefits, especially family allowances and pensions. The pump was thus primed and the new money would be spent, it was hoped, on French goods and services: firms should thus make more profits and be able to reinvest, taking on more staff. They would also be able to afford to pay higher taxes which would enable the government to recoup its initial outlay, which of course it had financed by deficit. The circle would thus be squared and a whole virtuous cycle of economic growth begin. Such is the hope of Keynesian economists.

In addition there were the structural changes. The main commercial banks were nationalized, as were several major industrial groups and the two big finance companies Suez and Paribas;[43] the groups were deemed to have a strategic importance for the French economy, either because they had monopolistic positions on the market, were vital for defence purposes or were in any case living off public subsidies or contracts. The public sector now comprized 29.4 per cent of all industrial activity and 22.2 per cent of the industrial workforce; it represented 29.9 per cent of value-added and 51.9 per cent of industrial investment. The figures before 1981 were respectively: 17.2 per cent, 11 per cent, 17.3 per cent and 43.5 per cent. This reinforced public sector, plus control of the financial circuits, gave the socialists a strong economic weapon for which they had prepared a detailed strategy. It is this graft of a bold *dirigisme* on to a traditional Keynesian type of reflation that had led some analysts to describe French socialism as being of a 'third type', different from classic social-democracy and from what passes for socialism in Eastern Europe.[44]

The new public sector was to play a central rôle in the economy. Reorganized and suitably fuelled by the national banks, it should remain competitive in those *créneaux* (key positions) which France had already won on export markets; thus the strategy of 'national champions' continues. In the longer term, the state would guarantee a high rate of investment, especially into the research budget of the groups (sadly neglected by the previous management). Thus when world recovery occurred France would be in a position, financially and technologically, to take advantage of it. The public sector would also serve as a tow-rope for the rest of the economy, in which by now smaller firms (PME) were in the majority: by subcontracting, purchasing and selling it would stimulate these smaller firms, releasing their full potential for productivity gains and above all job creation. It should also be possible to fulfil a strategic objective, viz. to attain independence in some sectors by creating *filières* (complete industrial systems in which virtually every input from the raw materials to the end product is made largely or wholly in one country). And lastly it should prove possible to renew and deepen the type of indicative planning so successful after 1945, preferably by making it a more decentralized process with more inputs from local authorities and firms.

Two final pieces completed the socialist economic design. One was a classic programme of job-creation out of public funds (over 100,000 jobs in the public services in the first eighteen months), and the other was more political. The Auroux Acts (named after the labour minister) of August and December 1982, increased workers' rights in firms. They provided greater benefits and protection for recognized union representatives, more stringent observation of health and safety norms and an obligation for firms above a certain size to provide more information and to negotiate annually on pay and conditions (though not of course to award increases). These acts aimed not so much at generalized workers' control of the type which the PS had been advocating as at involving workers more in their firms, hoping to reduce conflict and stimulate productivity. It is significant that these acts did not give the workforce any say in matters such as forward planning or redundancies. In this context too should be placed the law of December 1982 which restored to workers their right to elect administrators to the social security funds — a practice broken by de Gaulle in 1967.

Such was the policy for revitalizing the economy. Success would prove elusive but after two years it could not be said that Mitterrand had failed either. Taking the negative aspects first, one major consequence of reflation was a balance of payments deficit, as the French spent their new money not on home-produced goods but on imports. This put pressure on the franc which would eventually have to be three times devalued (autumn 1981, June 1982, March 1983).[45] As the expected growth did not materialize fully, the government debt, aggravated by the cost of the nationalizations and the huge cash needs of the new public sector, also swelled: this meant heavy borrowing abroad and increased pressure on the franc. British observers who remembered Labour governments of the 1960s being 'blown off course' by balance-of-payments and sterling problems had a sense of *déjà vu*. Moreover too little private investment was forthcoming, whether through lack of confidence in the government on the part of capital owners, employers' dislike of the Auroux acts or the timidity of the banks in lending. All of this meant that there was no chance of developing a new type of planning; *ad hoc* plans for each sector remained the rule.[46] Even the current Ninth Plan is, as Estrin and Holmes point out (*Guardian*, 28 September 1983) reluctant to give mid-term forecasts, so depressed is the international environment. And as these authors show, the lack of internal co-ordination and of corporate planning within large firms, even publicly owned ones, does not make planning any easier. Finally inflation remained high, as it must when increased money wages are not bolstered by higher productivity.

By mid-1982 the government was obliged to change tack sharply; after the 'go' came the 'stop'. The by-word was now *la rigueur*, as Delors strove to peg inflation. Early measures included a five-month wages-and-prices freeze, expenditure cuts and higher social security contributions. Firms' overheads were reduced with a mixture of tax deferments and exemptions, and the shifting of some employer-paid benefits on to employees. In general the state tried to transfer resources from consumption towards investment, that is from households towards firms. But despite this compressing of living standards, private investment trickled steadily downwards and employers demanded more concessions, including greater freedom to make workers redundant. When the government raised firms' contributions (along with employees') to the UNEDIC unemployment funds, the employers walked out of this jointly run institution. A further austerity package followed in 1983, with increased health charges and higher public service charges; there was a 1 per cent across-the-board tax increase and a compulsory savings scheme (over three years) for higher incomes. A foreign exchange limit of £200 per head per year was also imposed; though temporary, it caused an exasperation which made some wonder if politically it was worth the currency saved.

If the strategy had run into problems, it was not wholly unsuccessful. Growth for 1981–2 was around 2 per cent higher than in rival countries, even if government borrowing was high and the balance on foreign trade depressingly poor. Unemployment had been stabilized around two millions, whereas it rose steadily elsewhere. Inflation was falling slowly but still likely to be over 9 per cent in 1983. And ground had been laid for the future with the invisible but vital heavy investment in the new public sector.

Other policy areas showed an almost frenetic desire to make changes. In local government the 1982 act (see chapter 3) began a break with centuries-old habits as it decentralized power away from Paris. On the liberties front, Peyrefitte's act was abrogated, as was the death penalty. The state security courts and army tribunals disappeared, their functions reverting to the normal courts. The very repressive high security wings in prisons were closed and the *loi anti-casseurs* (a conspiracy law) was abolished. As well as providing extra redress for the victims of crime, Badinter sought to make the penal system more supple. For all these efforts he was denounced, predictably, by the right as being 'soft on criminals'. More seriously in June 1983, policemen in Paris staged some highly political demonstrations, largely inspired by hostility to Badinter. Though Defferre reacted promptly by sacking the ringleaders, this episode was disturbingly reminiscent of the latter days of the Fourth Republic. As regards immigration, an area where the right continued to exploit fears about jobs and housing, the socialists retreated from their proposal to allow immigrants the vote in local elections and stepped up their pursuit of illegal entrants.

In communications, the Filioud Act of 1982 tried to make broadcasting more independent by creating a High Authority for audiovisual matters (see chapter 3), which would give licences to radio networks and appoint senior officials. The principle of the state monopoly of broadcasting was not infringed. In housing, the Quilliot Act increased tenants' rights in such areas as rent and tenure. The short-term effect may well have been to reduce the supply of rented accommodation, as property owners resisted this curtailment of their prerogatives. British Labour governments had faced similar difficulties with their housing acts, and clearly this is an area where vested interests are particularly hard to tackle.

In education (see chapter 6), Mitterrand avoided grasping the nettle as long as he dared. Eventually Savary's higher education act tried to rationalize access to overcrowded faculties and to increase the workloads of staff; the summer of 1983 was thus marked yet again by teacher and student demonstrations. In secondary education, the government was pushed by its anti-clerical supporters into outlining proposals for the 'integration' of private (mainly catholic) schools into the state system. The catholic education lobby was, understandably, not keen and 1984 seemed likely to see ideological struggles from the Third Republic coming back to the centre of the political stage. More relevant was the reform of the top training school for civil service élites, ENA, where a 'third way' of entry was opened up to cater for those in full-time employment, especially in local government trade unions or voluntary associations. Former *énarques* promptly denounced this modest democratization as 'lowering of standards' and 'giving presents to the communist CGT'.

Foreign policy and defence were areas where continuity was stronger than change (see chapter 5). If Mitterrand spoke of new relationships with the Third World and made supportive gestures towards the Sandinistas and other progressive movements in Latin America, the overall line of policy was faithful to Gaullian orthodoxy. As international tensions increased, so did Mitterrand move closer to the USA, as de Gaulle had had to do on occasions. This is seen in his generally more anti-Soviet line than his predecessor, notably in his support for the installation of Cruise and Pershing missiles in Europe – though not of course in France. There was still no question of France's returning to NATO, however, and she continued to modernize her nuclear capacity. One newer note was the hint, frequently made by leading socialists and later by other party leaders, that the Atlantic Alliance would prove less and less reliable, placing thus an onus on Europeans to make alternative collaborative arrangements for their defence, nuclear and conventional.

Orthodoxy prevailed in African policy and it was discreetly criticized by the minister in charge J.-P. Cot, who resigned in November 1982. The reasons were that the policy was still run from the Elysée over the minister's head and that French succour for sympathetic clients sometimes went beyond the bounds of the acceptable, as when Mitterrand invited to Paris the Guinean dictator Sékou Touré, whose record on human rights was sadly wanting. In European affairs, it is clear that Mitterrand sought much greater EEC cohesion, particularly against US monetary and commercial hegemony. But the dominant right-wing and monetarist orientation in most of the rest of Europe, combined with strong national perceptions of self-interest, meant that this would be hard to find.

Politically, Mitterrand encountered relatively few difficulties in governing. Despite cries from supporters that 'heads should roll' (e.g. at the PS congress in 1981), the socialists did not purge the state apparatus extensively so as to insert their own men into key positions. If one or two media administrators were removed and some familiar faces disappeared, temporarily, from the TV screen, there were virtually no changes at the top of the armed forces or in the prefectoral corps; in the ministries of justice, interior or foreign affairs, senior officials left in post outnumbered those removed.[47] In education some sixteen *recteurs* out of twenty-eight were removed. None of this suggests systematic packing of the type practised by Giscard. In terms of his social basis of support, the president again had relatively little hardship. The trade unions supported his economic policies with more solidarity than British Labour governments usually experience, with the exception of the major white-collar unions who represent, it is true, many of the sorts of people who had swung to Mitterrand in 1981.[48] The PCF with its four ministers kept its criticisms fairly muted; its departure from government was predicted frequently but still seems unlikely in the near future (see chapter 4). In the PS itself factionalism remained resolutely subterranean, as is often the case when socialist parties are in government rather than opposition. To some extent quiet was guaranteed by a skilful distribution of government posts among factions and by regular consultation between Mitterrand and his loyal henchman in charge of the party, L. Jospin.[49] Little changed in the presidential nature of government decision-making: clearly the machinery of the Fifth Republic suited the socialists well as a means of getting policy decided and executed. One obstacle which did prove hard to circumvent was the constitutional council, which on the nationalizations and other matters held up the government considerably and fully justified its reputation as a last refuge for ageing sexists.

As 1983 ended, electoral losses, slipping opinion-poll ratings and discontent from white-collar groups suggested that the government was struggling. The right-wing parties felt confident as they fanned the flames of discontent. Political commentators went back to their favourite game of guessing what would happen when a left president has to deal with a right parliamentary majority, supposing that the latter would win in 1986. Against this the socialists might feel that their economic strategy was working slowly (the foreign trade figures moved briefly into surplus in September) and that the qualitative, non-economic reforms might show their effect before long.

The popular verdict on the socialist experiment is anything but cut and dried, in fact. It is not the intention here to guess what the voters will say, but rather to take a longer-term look. The historians of the future may well see in the Mitterrand years a second great wave of modernization, comparable to that undertaken by de Gaulle. France has been prodded into updating herself in many areas where she had begun to slip behind — economic policy certainly, but also local government, justice, civil liberties and industrial relations. These efforts may not have been an unqualified success, any more than they were under

Gaullism;[50] and it is true that foreign affairs do not seem to have undergone the same dynamic impulse as domestic. None the less a resolute attempt at modernization has been made and in the long run it is hard to believe that it will have been worse for France than the morose years of Giscardian *attentisme*.

Chapter 2

The structures of contemporary France

(1) The economy

The process of industrialization in France was long and relatively complex, compared with that of other developed countries. Economic historians have some difficulty in singling out any one period of 'take-off', such as is held to have occurred in, say, Britain or Germany, i.e. a relatively short time during which, from being agriculture-based, the economy moved decisively towards domination by industry. In France it seems that from the early nineteenth century onwards the pattern was one of slow but steady industrial advances (especially in the Second Empire, early Third Republic and 1920s) without there ever having been a dramatic industrializing surge. Such industrial growth varied greatly between sectors and regions, and the reasons for the slowness are too complex to be discussed here.[1] A good index of this slowness is to look at the high percentage of the workforce employed on the land, in comparison with other countries. Clearly this high density of peasantry is important not just in explaining France's industrial lag, but also some aspects of her politics; we shall have to refer to this phenomenon later (see Figure 2.1).

Since 1945, though, industrial expansion has been spectacular, and France today is one of the foremost industrial powers. Table 2.1 shows the growth of the French GDP *per capita* over the past years, in comparison with other developed economies. Of the French GDP in 1981, a mere 8.6 per cent was accounted for by agriculture, with industry representing 31.9 per cent. The full measure of French industrial dynamism is given by looking at the growth of the GDP since the full effects of the world recession began to be felt after 1974.

In the past ten years French GDP has still grown at an average of 2.6 per cent p.a. If this compares unfavourably with the average of 5.2 per cent between 1952 and 1973, it is still better than the average growth in similar countries over the last decade (UK 1.9 per cent p.a., USA 2.3 per cent, W. Germany 2.4 per cent).

Another index of industrial strength is exports; France has developed rapidly here. In 1981 she ranked fifth among world exporters, some 22 per cent of GDP going in exports, compared with 18 per cent in 1973.

Table 2.1 GDP per head of developed nations since 1960 (dollars)

	1960	1970	1975	1979	1982
W. Germany	1,301	3,055	6,798	12,419	10,650
Belgium	1,232	2,652	6,417	11,260	8,400
France	1,315	2,775	6,419	10,720	9,937
Italy	690	1,875	3,440	5,686	6,100
U.K.	1,360	2,702	4,140	7,192	8,379
EEC	1,160	2,310	5,060	8,670	8,719
USA	2,757	4,851	7,205	10,777	13,100
Japan	462	1,969	4,470	8,627	8,900

Source: UN, Yearbook of National Account Statistics, 1980, vol. 2. Nouvel Observateur, Atlaséco 1983

This sum amounted to 5.2 per cent of total world trade.[2] The jobs of some six million people depend, directly or indirectly, on exports. Particular export strengths include agricultural products (only the USA exports more), where France has 9 per cent of world markets. Industrial exports include particularly electrical and mechanical engineering, arms, telecommunications, air and land transport and nuclear energy facilities (plants often being built abroad by French firms and delivered 'clé en mains' to purchasing governments. Earnings from invisibles (export of services, tourism etc.) are also rising. Yet French imports have also risen from 17.6 per cent of GDP in 1973 to 24.4 per cent today. The ratio of exports to imports has dropped from 105 to 90 — as sure an index as any of the growing internationalization of the economy and a source of potential problems.

At this point we might pause briefly to consider the reasons behind this exceptional economic performance. Clearly the seeds were sown in the immediate postwar years, but historians are divided in their explanations of the ultimate causes. While most admit that the plans were of some importance (especially, perhaps, British commentators trying to explain why the French economy has forged far ahead of its British counterpart), many are reluctant to ascribe overmuch influence to what was after all only a flexible, indicative type of planning. Thus for C. Kindleberger the plans were important only insofar as

Table 2.2   Value of French exports since 1962 (millions of francs)

	1962	1965	1968	1974	1975	1977	1979	1981
Value	36,345	49,619	62,576	217,181	220,751	311,550	414,675	550,363
Index*	294	387	506	1754	1785	2520	3354	4452

* The indices take 1949 as 100.
Source: INSEE, Annuaire statistique, 1968–1982.

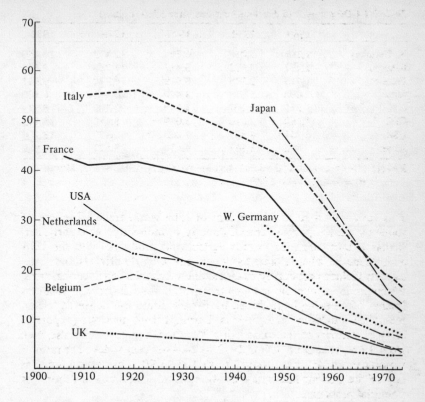

Figure 2.1   Agricultural workers as percentage of total workforce per country, 1900–74
Source: INSEE, *Les Agriculteurs*, 1977, p.25.

they helped foster or spread new attitudes among the public; if growth took place it was because the public wanted to consume more and because entrepreneurs were now on hand who were willing to invest more so as to satisfy the new demand.[3] Perhaps the spread of such attitudes is part of a wider revulsion towards the whole ethos of the 1930s, with its economic and political stagnation, which postwar Frenchmen could now see as responsible for the disasters of 1940–4. Kindleberger also draws attention to the role of 'new men' with dynamic ideas, both in the state apparatus and in business. R. Paxton has shown that some of them were not entirely new, in fact; for even under the Vichy régime there were areas where men of an expansionist, 'technocratic' outlook came to the fore, and some of them would still be influential after 1945.[4] Another vital input came from the civil service élites emerging from *grandes écoles* such as the *Ecole Nationale d'Administration* and *Polytechnique*. These highly trained administrators, generalists and specialists alike, would find themselves increasingly involved in work outside the ministries, running public and semi-public companies and later private ones. Their competence, dynamism and their excellent relations with the state that had trained them made a major contribution to the resurgence of French business. M. Parodi insists more on another cause of growth, viz. the role of the state.[5] It provided both the infra-structural improvement necessary for expansion and also strong competition for an ailing private sector, the new nationalized sector serving as a spur to the latter. More crucial was its role as a direct investor, referred to in chapter 1, and its creation of the various social institutions of the liberation era. These were surely vital in creating among wage-earners that climate of security and confidence necessary to any phase of demand-led growth. In more recent years government policy has again been important in streamlining French industry and agriculture, with the express aim of orienting the economy increasingly towards export, i.e. towards competition with other advanced industrial states. Whatever the underlying reasons for three decades and more of economic growth, though, that growth has been impressive, and France's future as an industrial power looks more secure than that of some of her neighbours.

The most dynamic sectors of French industry today are probably chemicals and certain areas of the metal-working industries, notably motor vehicles and armaments; all of these figure prominently among French exports. Sectors in decline include textiles, especially of the cheaper varieties, shipbuilding and steel. All these industries, which are quite long established, have suffered, like their counterparts in OECD countries, from the competition of emergent, more efficient rivals (Taiwan, south Korea, etc.).

A potential weakness of industry in France is its high dependence on imported energy; 'la France n'a pas de pétrole', as government advertising slogans put it. Despite her domestic production of coal, natural gas and hydroelectric energy, reinforced of late by nuclear power, France has seen a steady widening of the gap between the energy she produces and that which she consumes (see Table 2.3).

Table 2.3   French energy consumption

	1970	1972	1974	1977	1978	1980
Home produced energy as percentage of total domestic consumption	35.2	29.1	25.4	25.3	24.9	26.2

Source: STISI (Ministry of Industry Statistical Office)

Strenuous government efforts to reduce firms' and households' consumption and to substitute nuclear energy for other sources have of late begun to bear fruit. Thus the equivalent of 78 kg. of oil was needed to produce a thousand francs worth of GDP in 1973, compared with only 70 today. Similarly whereas nuclear energy represented only 1.5 per cent of energy consumed in 1973, it now represents over 12 per cent and should be nearer to 30 per cent by 1990. As most inputs into nuclear power are home-produced, this will reduce energy dependence sharply; it is predicted that the amount of home-produced energy used in 1983 will be as high as 37 per cent.

Let us now look more closely into the structures of French industry, however. Figure 2.2 shows the location of industrial activity according to the number of workers employed; in so doing, it clearly reveals some long-standing regional disparities. The heaviest industrial concentrations are clearly in the Paris region, Nord/Pas-de-Calais, the north-east and the Rhône valley; these were the original industrial areas, based on mining, metal-working and textiles. To the west of the Caen–Marseille line, there is much less industry, especially in the south-west (even here the apparently industrialized regions of Aquitaine and Midi-Pyrénées are accounted for largely by the success of two towns, Bordeaux and Toulouse, home of much of France's aerospace industry).

Regional imbalances are paralleled by imbalances in the size of firms. In general, the more developed an economy is, the higher will be the degree of concentration. By this term is meant not just mergers, whereby one firm acquires a controlling interest in another, but any arrangement whereby two or more firms pool their resources in an attempt to obtain greater efficiency and a bigger share of the market. Concentration thus includes such practices as the creation of subsidiary companies (*filiales*), by one firm or by several acting together, the grouping of numerous firms in different conglomerates or under the aegis of financial groups, the creation of networks of sub-contractors, and so on. In all such operations the aim is to corner a bigger share of the market; hence it is a tendency that is potentially monopolistic. The extent to which concentration has been taken in France shows how far economic structures have changed since 1945; its industrial structure today is a far cry from the 'Malthusian' structure of the 1930s, dominated by the small family firm, largely self-financing and unadventurous.

This means that to some extent France has a dual industrial structure. On the one hand a small number of vast groups, public and private, increasingly dominant in their sector of the economy; on the other a host of small and medium-sized firms, *les petites et moyennes entreprises* (PME).[6] Table 2.4 gives the position in 1981.

In 1981, out of the top 500 companies outside the USA, forty-two

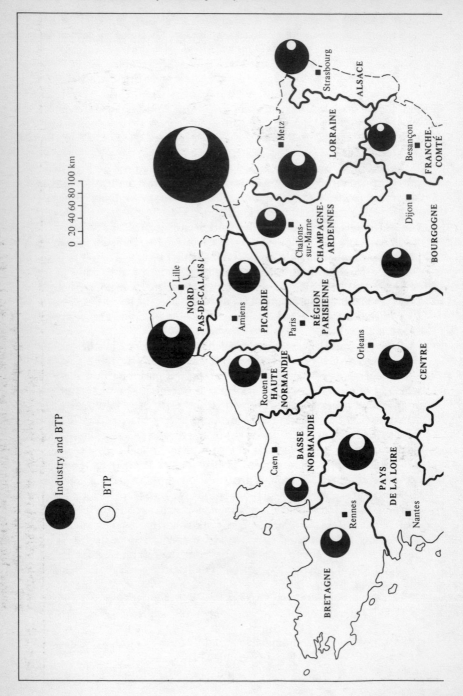

Strasbourg
ALSACE

Metz
LORRAINE

Besançon
FRANCHE-
COMTÉ

Chalons-
sur-Marne
CHAMPAGNE-
ARDENNES

Dijon
BOURGOGNE

Lille
NORD
PAS-DE-CALAIS

PICARDIE
Amiens
Paris
RÉGION
PARISIENNE

Orleans
CENTRE

Rouen
HAUTE
NORMANDIE

Caen
BASSE
NORMANDIE

PAYS
DE LA LOIRE

Rennes
Nantes

BRETAGNE

0 20 40 60 80 100 km

Industry and BTP

BTP

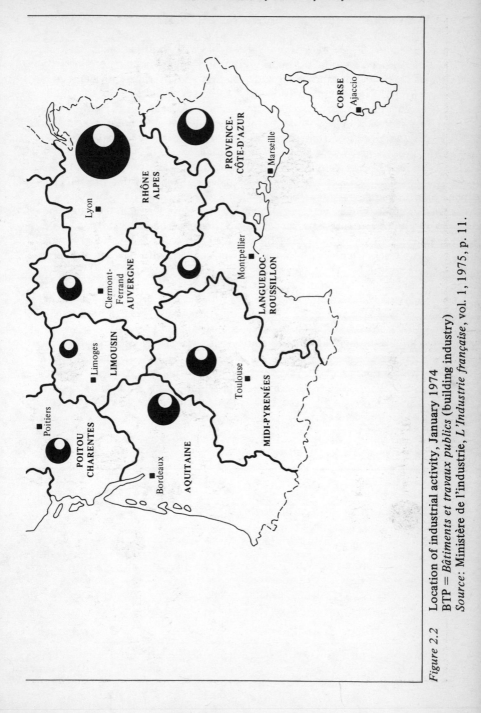

Figure 2.2   Location of industrial activity, January 1974
BTP = *Bâtiments et travaux publics* (building industry)
Source: Ministère de l'industrie, *L'Industrie française*, vol. 1, 1975, p. 11.

were French (eighty-eight British and 121 Japanese); fourteen of these figured in the top hundred and eight were publicly owned.[7]

Many of the largest French firms are now multinationals, realizing increasing amounts of their production abroad, where productivity gains are higher (and wages and social protection usually lower) than in Europe. This is especially true of the recent additions to the public sector (e.g. 55 per cent of the production of the chemical giant Rhône-Poulenc takes place abroad). Their weight in the economy – and that of the groups of firms immediately below them in terms of size – is considerable. G. Mathieu demonstrated in 1972 that some 1,100 firms (0.7 per cent of the total) accounted for over 33 per cent of turnover. At the other end of the scale, 1.5 million firms (93 per cent of the total) accounted for a mere 15.9 per cent of total turnover. To put it another way, 1.300 small firms achieve less than one huge one. Recent years have however seen a certain sluggishness on the part of the big groups. Whereas in 1981 the top 500 French firms showed an overall loss, their counterparts elsewhere were moving into healthy profit (an average of 15 per cent in the USA and 10 per cent in Japan). In other words such dynamism as French business was still capable of coming increasingly from the PME. In 1981 this sector created a net 15,000 jobs and averaged a rate of profit of 7.5 per cent; clearly productivity here was much higher than among the big market leaders.[8]

Concentration has gone furthest in heavy industry (steel, engineering, chemicals) and in the newer industries (oil, electronics, cars); it is relatively weak in such areas as precision engineering, furniture and clothing – in other words, hardly the leading sectors of an advanced economy. Mining, energy, transport and communications are also fairly highly concentrated.

Table 2.4   French firms by size, 1981

Size	No. of firms	(%)	Employees (%) thousands		Sales (bn. francs)	(%)	% of national exports
Nos. of workers employed per firm							
10–19	10,149	(29.9)	150	(3.5)	38	(1.9)	13.0
20–49	12,665	(37.3)	418	(9.7)	120	(6.2)	10.5
50–99	4,591	(13.5)	328	(7.6)	96	(4.9)	13.5
100–199	2,839	(8.4)	396	(9.2)	131	(6.7)	18.2
200–499	1,955	(5.8)	603	(13.9)	206	(10.6)	20.7
500 +	1,126	(3.3)	2,410	(55.7)	1,334	(68.4)	24.1
Total	33,956	(100)	4,323	(100)	1,950	(100)	100

Source: Ministère de la recherche et de l'industrie, *Les chiffres-clé: industrie*, 1983
N.B.: Firms employing below ten are now considered statistically as part of the artisanat.

With its growing degree of concentration, the French economy is like that of other developed capitalist systems. It resembles these in another way also – the extent of its internationalization. There are two measures of this. One is the growth of foreign trade, to which reference has already been made; the other is the penetration of foreign capital into French industry and the export of similar French capital abroad.

An increasing number of French workers are working for foreign capital within France. In 1979 it was estimated at 13.5 per cent of the workforce. Figure 2.3 shows where such capital goes; the further to the right the horizontal lines, the more that sector is controlled by non-French capital. Foreign capital favours, logically, areas where profits will be highest, i.e. industry which is, as INSEE put it, 'qualitativement concentrée, dynamique, moderne'. Until 1968 most of such capital came from the USA. Since then, with the growth of the EEC (and perhaps, to a small extent, Gaullist anti-Americanism?) the percentage of US capital in France has tended to decline in favour of EEC investment.

The countervailing tendency is for French capital to be exported overseas; like Britain, France has had, historically, great expertise in this field. Interestingly, most French capital today goes not so much to the USA or the EEC, but to under-developed capitalist countries, especially former French colonies in Africa. Thus in 1970 some 63.5 per cent of direct French investment overseas went outside the EEC and North America, most of it towards the under-developed world, where it was absorbed mainly in oil and other extractive industry. This economic link that France retains with her former possessions is reinforced by the panoply of military and political agreements which the Fifth Republic has concluded with most of its former dependencies, and the arrangement works very much to France's advantage.

This assertion is borne out when we consider France's trade balance with these countries. In 1981 French trade with the developing world accounted for some 28 per cent of exports, of which some 10 per cent went to OPEC countries; but in return some 28 per cent of French imports came from these countries, of which 18 per cent came from OPEC (i.e. oil). In other words, French industry needs to import from the under-developed world most of its energy, considerable amounts of raw materials (including some food) and indeed, when the economic situation requires it, quantities of immigrant labour; in return France exports to such countries manufactures (both consumer goods and some capital goods). Such a neo-colonialist or imperialist arrangement is, then, crucial to the running of the French industrial system, as of course are similar deals to virtually every developed economy (see Table 2.5).

Agriculture has long occupied a privileged place in French life.

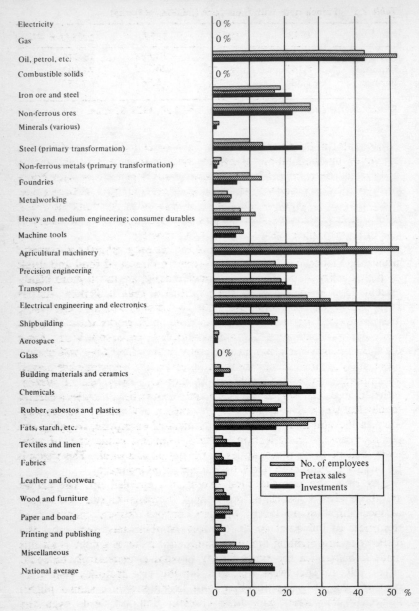

Electricity — 0 %
Gas — 0 %
Oil, petrol, etc.
Combustible solids — 0 %
Iron ore and steel
Non-ferrous ores
Minerals (various)
Steel (primary transformation)
Non-ferrous metals (primary transformation)
Foundries
Metalworking
Heavy and medium engineering; consumer durables
Machine tools
Agricultural machinery
Precision engineering
Transport
Electrical engineering and electronics
Shipbuilding
Aerospace
Glass — 0 %
Building materials and ceramics
Chemicals
Rubber, asbestos and plastics
Fats, starch, etc.
Textiles and linen
Fabrics
Leather and footwear
Wood and furniture
Paper and board
Printing and publishing
Miscellaneous
National average

No. of employees
Pretax sales
Investments

0   10   20   30   40   50   %

Figure 2.3   Penetration of French industry by foreign capital, 1970
Source: INSEE, *La Mutation industrielle en France*, vol. 1,
1975, p. 82.

Table 2.5   French trade with franc zone (millions of francs)

	1973	1977	1979	1981 (Jan.–Nov.)
Imports	5,841	12,018	13,823	16,946
Exports	8,145	16,259	20,790	24,102
Balance	+2,304	+4,241	+6,967	+7,157

Source: *Statistiques et études financières*, nos. 338, 1982–3, p. 84.

For people in Britain where only 2.3 per cent of the workforce is employed on the land and where for two centuries a large proportion of food has been imported from cheap primary producers, with prices cushioned by government subsidies, agriculture is by and large something that one takes for granted. In France it is different, however; some understanding of French agricultural structures is necessary if one is to grasp some aspects of politics and society.

Exceptionally suited to agriculture by her geographical and climatic situation, France has long been a surplus producer of food and drink of high quality — both of which, incidentally, are much more highly esteemed, in every sector of the population, than in Britain. As has been explained, the exodus from the land was slower than elsewhere; even today 9.3 per cent of the workforce still works there (7.6 per cent are owner-farmers, 1.7 are agricultural labourers). Many town dwellers still have relatives in the country to whom they will go (or, more likely, send their children) for holidays. The peasantry has played an important role in French history (albeit usually one of inertia, rather than dynamism) and it has acquired over the centuries a certain ideological stock. There is in French opinion a vision of the country-man as the epitome of hard work, individual enterprise, frugality and common-sense — a reflection perhaps, even if a crude one, of what many believe to be the qualities of the nation as a whole. This vision is by no means dead, even if it is based on a shrinking reality.

For since the war the rural exodus has speeded up. The causes are those always associated with rapid industrialization. The spread of mechanization on farms, the gap between farmers' incomes and the prices of industrial goods (tractors, combine-harvesters, etc.), the difficulties in obtaining credit to cope with increasing debt — all this made it harder for the small farmer to survive. Increasingly he could either sell up and leave the land for the new factories that were springing up, or group together with neighbours in a similar plight. For only the bigger and more efficient units survived. Even the Common Agricultural Policy and measures based on the Mansholt Plan (designed precisely to humanize this relentless weeding-out of the small man) have not changed this basic fact. Farming is becoming increasingly capital-intensive and industrialized; there will be less and less room for the small producer, as Giscard d'Estaing himself has made plain.[9]

Where does this leave French agriculture today? In 1981 the activity of French farmers could be broken down as in Table 2.6.

Turning from type of production to size of farms, one finds some interesting discrepancies: other figures reveal a steady disappearance of farms at the rate of 1.9 per cent per annum over the last twenty years (see Table 2.7).

As with French industry one notices a dualistic tendency; there are indeed 'two agricultures' in France. If we take farms of less than 20 hectares as 'small', then we see that they account for 55 per cent of the total of farms but cover only 18 per cent of the arable surface. At the other end of the scale, large farms (50 hectares and above) account for a mere 13.5 per cent of the total of farms, but cover over 44 per cent of the arable surface. On the one hand, the tendency is towards the family farm ill-equipped, technically, financially and organizationally; on the other, the industrial farm, run impersonally and efficiently, like a large corporation. There is a world of difference

Table 2.6   French agricultural production, 1981

Type of product	% of national agricultural product
Cereals	16.8
Fruit and vegetables, incl. vines	28
Livestock	27
Poultry	7.3
Dairy and miscellaneous	20.9
Total	100

Source: adapted from INSEE, *Les Comptes de l'agriculture en 1981*, 1982c, p. 35.

Table 2.7   French farm sizes, 1979*

Size of farm (ha.)	% of total farms	% of total arable surface
1- 5	19.4	1.8
5–10	14.9	4.1
10–20	21.2	11.9
20–50	31.0	37.8
50+	13.5	44.4
	100	100

Source: INSEE, *Tableaux de l'economie française*, 1982.
*1 hectare = $2\frac{1}{2}$ acres (approx.). The number of farms in 1979 was some 1,103,000

between, say, the ageing melon-grower of Lot-et-Garonne, working long hours on his 20 hectares to make a bare and hazardous living and the cereal-grower of the Paris basin, producing massively for the export market.

The geography of French agriculture brings this out even more cruelly. Figure 2.4 shows the strong areas with the big farms: the northern departments, Paris basin, Normandy and some of Brittany (though the latter area has many poor farms also). Equally the south-west, Auvergne, Limousin and the east in general, are all areas, not on the whole favoured by their geography, where the further decline of agriculture seems inevitable.

It remains briefly to set French agriculture in an international context. France is the leading agricultural producer of the EEC, producing 27.1 per cent of the total value added therein.[10] In Table 2.8 the high percentage of GDP accounted for by agriculture in Greece and Ireland should not mislead the reader, for in both cases the total value added is well *below* that of France. In other words, the agricultural sectors of both these countries are too large and too inefficient, compared with the French.

In terms of international trade, France is probably now second to the USA as an exporter of agricultural products; as an exporter of the key commodity cereals she ranks third in the world.

We must also consider the 'tertiary' sector of the French economy. This accounts for an increasing part of the workforce (currently some 55 per cent) and covers such activities as transport, education, banking and insurance as well as the more classical activity, commerce. Table 2.9 shows the variety of branches in which people are increasingly finding employment. The tertiary sector employed 55 per cent of the workforce in 1978 compared with 44 per cent in 1962.[11] In terms of job

Table 2.8   The weight of agriculture in the European economies, 1982

Country	Agriculture as % of GNP	% of work force in agriculture
Belgium	3	3
Denmark	8	7.4
France	5	8.6
W. Germany	2.5	5.5
Greece	16	31
Ireland	12	18
Italy	6	11.4
Luxembourg	3	5.6
Netherlands	6	5
UK	3	2.6

Source: *Nouvel Observateur*, Atlaseco, 1983 (adapted)

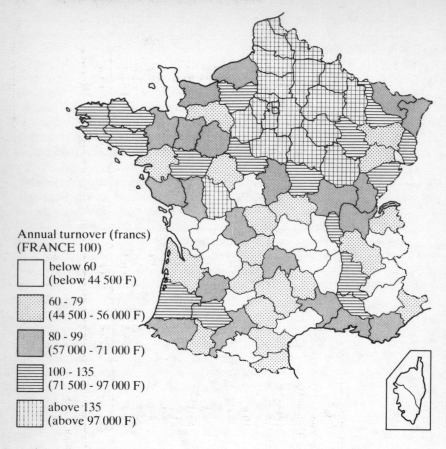

Annual turnover (francs)
(FRANCE 100)

below 60
(below 44 500 F)

60 - 79
(44 500 - 56 000 F)

80 - 99
(57 000 - 71 000 F)

100 - 135
(71 500 - 97 000 F)

above 135
(above 97 000 F)

Figure 2.4   Average productivity per farm, 1982 – comparison
                between departments
Source: INSEE, *Les Comptes de l'agriculture française en 1982*, p. 124.

creation it is the liveliest sector of the economy and has been called 'un refuge de main d'oeuvre', thanks to its alleged sensitivity towards new demands for services as they emerge, responding easily and quickly to these. We shall concentrate particularly on commerce here, because of its rather special place in the economic and political structures of the country.

Commerce in France bears witness in many ways to the late economic development of that country; it has many features that seem archaic in a system that in so many other ways is ultra-modern. The first of these is undoubtedly the very high proportion of self-employed shopkeepers or *indépendants*, as they like to call themselves. Anyone who has spent much time in France knows that the French use these

Table 2.9   Employment in tertiary sector, 1962–78

| | (a) annual average of jobs created (thousands) | | | (b) (a) as % increase p.a. | | | |
	1962–8	1968–73	1973–8	1962–8	1968–73	1973–8	1962–78
Commerce	40.4	29.0	18.6	+1.8	+1.2	+0.7	+1.3
Vehicle repairs etc.	14.9	10.8	4.5	+5.4	+3.1	+1.1	+3.3
Hotel and Catering	2.6	6.5	3.7	+0.5	+1.2	+0.7	+0.8
Transport	10.3	4.0	5.0	+1.3	+0.5	+0.6	+0.8
Posts and Telecom	9.8	7.2	12.9	+3.1	+2.0	+3.1	+2.8
Services to firms	33.8	30.7	23.7	+6.8	+4.5	+2.9	+4.8
Services to individuals	33.4	56.7	86.5	+3.5	+4.7	+5.6	+4.5
Property, estate agents etc.	1.8	4.2	2.1	+8.5	+12.3	+4.1	+8.2
Insurance	2.2	4.7	3.0	+2.7	+4.8	+2.6	+3.3
Finance	10.0	20.9	11.0	+5.0	+7.6	+3.0	+5.2
Non-commercial services	11.0	66.4	28.9	+0.3	+1.9	+0.8	+1.0
Total tertiary	170.1	241.1	200.0	+1.9	+2.4	+1.8	+2.0

Source: INSEE, *Rapport sur les comptes de la nation, 1978.*

small and often quite specialized shops (*boulangerie, crèmerie, cordon-nerie*, etc.) much more than do the British. Why this should be so is hard to say. It has certainly something to do with a culture which still places a high value on well-made things, as opposed to mass-produced but less aesthetically appealing ones, and in which stress is placed on rather formal personal relationships (cf. the mystique of 'personal service' which surrounds the shopkeeper/customer relation-ship). Whatever the reasons for its survival, though, *le petit commerce* has proved remarkably long-lived, even though the percentage of owners is going down steadily and that of wage-earners increasing. That this shrinkage still takes place relatively slowly is due as much as anything to the obstinacy of the *petit commerçant*, who, tightly organized in his professional associations and pressure groups and using his political muscle to the maximum, manages to delay his lingering decline: how this happens will be discussed below in chapter 4. In com-merce as elsewhere in the economy, the struggle of big and small goes on; here perhaps the small seem to have put up a more effective resistance. In 1980 they could still claim 60 per cent of the retail trade against bigger competitors. One could say that it is harder to classify commerce under the headings of *grand, petit* and *moyen*, as is done for industry. The essential polarity, though, is still between the big chain on the one hand and the family business on the other, between giant and 'indepen-dent' (see Table 2.10).

Small commerce is in fact a very volatile sector, where many still feel confident enough to set up in business 'se mettre à leur compte'. If a surprising 9,000 small enterprises per year were appearing at the end of the 1970s (mainly in the non-food branches) and if economists were looking to commerce to create 20,000 jobs a year (albeit many of them part-time), this does mask the underlying trend to some extent. That trend is towards reduction of the number of self-employed (a net

Table 2.10   Workforce in commerce (thousands)

	1974 all	1980 all	1980 employees only
Wholesale	842.2	873.4	812.8
(Food)	(273.2)	(269.1)	(242.3)
(Other)	(569.0)	(604.3)	(570.5)
Retail	1,539.6	1,614.1	1,107.2
(Food)	(566.6)	(595.9)	(406.3)
(Other)	(973.3)	(1.018.2)	(700.9)
Total commerce	2,381.8	2,487.5	1,920.0

Source: INSEE, *Tableaux de l'économie française*, 1982, p. 127.

loss of 15,000 from 1968 to 1974) and also of the number of establishments. The *petit commerçant* remains an obstinate but shrinking breed.

Thus far we have concentrated on those in employment. Of late however these have been a rapidly diminishing species, in France as elsewhere. In August 1983 the government admitted to some 2,035,400 unemployed.[12] There is always controversy about unemployment figures, which governments understandbly try to minimize, usually by expedients such as omitting certain categories (males over fifty-five, say, or housewives seeking work) from the registers. Thus International Labour Office or trade-union figures will usually be higher than official ones. That said, the French figures are much less depressing than those for the UK or West Germany. Whichever figure one takes, though, it is clear that unemployment is high, and shows no sign of diminishing substantially. Unemployment hits at the young and the less qualified (white-collar rather than manual). But even the managerial strata (*cadres*) are sufficiently affected for their unions to be worried (see Tables 2.11 and 2.12).

The situation in 1984

It is clear that France increasingly faces the same structural problems as other developed states; thus these general concluding remarks will have a deliberately international scope. The slump in the world economy is no transitory phenomenon, which can be ascribed simplistically to the greed of Arab oil magnates or trade unions pushing up wage rates. The crisis is as much a mutation of a mode of production as anything else, and the solutions to it, if such there be, are more political than economic, however much this may displease those who blame the crisis on increasing state intervention in the economy.[13]

The 'trente glorieuses' − three decades of post-war economic growth − combined high productivity with high wages and high consumption, this balance being buttressed by a well-developed system of social benefits: marxist economists sometimes refer to this mode of production as 'fordism'. Yet by the early 1970s the fordist model was reaching the point of exhaustion. As the economies of developed states became more and more internationalized, the subtle link between high productivity, high wages and high profits became distended: rising inflation and

Table 2.11   Unemployment trends in France since 1965 (thousands)

	1965	1967	1968	1970	1974	1975	1976	1979	1982
Unemployed	142	196	254	262	498	840	934	1350	1902
Unfilled vacancies	30	32	36	93	205	109	124	88	148

Source: OECD, Economic Surveys, INSEE, *Bulletin mensuel de statistique*

Table 2.12   (a) Unemployment in France by socio-economic group (CSP), 1981.

	Absolute number (thousands)	As percentage of CSP
agriculteurs	1.3	0.1
salariés agricole	22.1	7.6
patrons de l'industrie	24.2	1.4
professions: cad. sup.	41.7	2.2
cadres moyens	113.2	3.5
employes	317.4	7.8
ouvriers	653.7	8.1
personnel de service	156.2	10.1
first job seekers	256.0	–

(b) Unemployment by age and sex, 1981

	Men		Women	
	no. (thousands)	% of total unemployed	no. (thousands)	% of total unemployed
under 25	264	15.9	398	24.0
25–49	188	21.2	331	20.0
50+	188	11.3	126	7.6
Total	803	48.4	855	51.1

Source: INSEE, *Tableaux de l'économie française*, 1982, p. 65

currency instability were symptoms of this. As productivity gains faltered, profits fell with consequent effect on investment, jobs and output. The standard remedy to this situation in the West has been monetarism, which seeks to restore profitability at the expense of wages and those social benefits financed out of state expenditure. The level of this latter, amounting in France to some 44 per cent of GDP, is denounced as excessive, whereas in Sweden it is around 60 per cent. This strategy has certainly cut inflation, but at the cost of a steady decline in investment, output and of course, employment. Investors can hardly be expected to finance the manufacture of products when they know that potential buyers of these are having their purchasing power cut in different ways. And at the same time the burden on state finance which the strategy was supposed to reduce has been increased, as there are more unemployed to maintain. The horse-medicine may have cured the patient's symptoms but at the cost of bleeding him to death.

At the same time technology has made huge strides; the microchip is the symbol of possible productivity gains. Depending on how they are used, however, such technologies may well lead to what some have called the 'collapse of work', i.e. mass unemployment on an even greater scale. Some economists prophesy the rise of a 'dual economy' of which Japan might be a forerunner. Here one part of the workforce works hard and earns well in the advanced, export-oriented part of the economy; the rest, poorly paid and ill-protected, toil on in the declining or older industries (often subcontracting to the market leaders) and in the public services (or such of them as monetarism allows to survive). Alternatively, if introduced intelligently with a measure of worksharing and income redistribution, these technologies could lead to much greater freedom for the mass of working people. Yet the European economies must somehow integrate these technologies if they are to remain competitive, for the USA and Japan have built up a big lead. And this problem only compounds that of existing but declining industries (steel, textiles, ship-building) where France and Europe have lost out in competitive terms to the 'new industrial states' of South-east Asia.

It is hard to imagine that these problems of reconversion and invest-ment in the high technology industries of the future will be solved by purely national strategies. We have seen that even the modest degree of economic reflation which the socialist government tried was very prob-lematic; the type of problem to be faced here is much tougher. Action at European level is required if France and her European neighbours are to continue to exist as relatively autonomous industrial states, without subsiding into near-total dependency on the USA and Japan. Such action must aim at the development of increasingly transnational economic policies, pivoting on issues such as: the type and speed of economic reflation, industrial restructuring and the type of protective measures needed to ensure it, research and development particularly with regard to new technologies, concerted reduction of working hours and a monet-ary policy that might counteract the worse effects of the dollar on international exchanges.

Logically the EEC for all its weaknesses is the forum where such initiatives might be begun, and thus the Athens summit at the end of 1983 took on unusual importance. The failure of this meeting and the apparent impossibility of overcoming the incubus of the Common Agri-cultural Policy, left little ground for optimism. The immediate future for France and her neighbours seemed likely to be one of slow but steady strangulation.

(2) Social stratification

Who are the people, then, who carry out economic activity in France? France has always had a distinctive population structure, compared with her neighbours; in particular, observers have been struck by the very slow rate of population growth through the nineteenth and twentieth centuries. Demographers cannot agree as to why this should have been so; among the many and highly varied explanations adduced are the effect of military service in delaying marriages, the inhibiting

Table 2.13   Comparative trends in fertility in Europe, 1861–1939*

	1861–70	1881–90	1901–10	1930–4	1935–9
France	26.4	23.9	20.6	17.0	14.8
Germany	37.2	36.8	32.9	16.3	19.4
England	35.2	32.5	27.2	15.8	15.3
Italy	36.9	37.8	32.7	24.5	23.2

* Birth-rate taken per 1,000, approximately.
Source: I. Thompson, *Modern France: a Social and Economic Geography*,
     Butterworths, 1970, p. 4.

effects of an agriculture-dominated economy, the desire to limit
property-fragmentation among heirs, or even the generally timorous
nature of élites; whatever the reason, the French were for a century
and a half 'Malthusian', not wishing to procreate. The First World War
compounded an already serious demographic weakness, and it has been
calculated that if the French population increased at all between
1801 and 1939, then this was only because (a) people lived longer
and (b) immigration was encouraged (see Table 2.13).

The turn-round began after 1945. Encouraged by the pro-natality
policies of post-liberation governments, especially family allowances
first promoted systematically by Vichy, the French procreated rapidly
for some twenty years in the famous 'baby boom'. At the same time,
as years would elapse before the new babies could join the workforce,
and as expanding industry needed rapid supplies of labour, the
traditional policy of immigration was continued. Now immigrants
came increasingly, not from Italy or eastern Europe as before 1939,
but from the Iberian peninsula, North Africa and later on, Black
Africa. Immigration accounted for roughly one-third of the post-
war population increase. Over the last few years, the fertility boom
has slackened off, and the French seem to be returning to a level of
procreation near to that of the thirties. INSEE has calculated that
by the year 2000 the population of France would still be below 60
millions (see Table 2.14).

The last census was taken in 1975.[14] It estimated the French population to be 52,599,430 — an increase of 5.8 per cent on the 1968
figure. Distribution by age and sex, together with the proportion of
working population within either of those categories, is shown in
Table 2.15. Of the total population in 1975, some 48 millions (93.5
per cent) were French; of the 6.5 per cent of foreigners, 1.4 were
Algerian, 1.4 Portuguese and 0.9 Spanish. These foreigners represented
some 7.3 per cent of the working population (and only 6.5 per cent
of the total population), proving that France, like other countries,
admits immigrants basically because the economy needs labour.

Table 2.14   Average number of births per annum in France, 1945–62

	Total	per 1,000 population
1945	643,000	16.2
1946–9	860,650	21.1
1950–3	825,150	19.6
1954–7	806,300	18.5
1958–62	822,840	18.0

Source: C. Dyer, *Population and Society in Twentieth-Century France,* Hodder & Stoughton, 1978, p. 134.

Since 1968, some long-term trends are confirmed. Inhabitants of rural communes continue to diminish as a percentage of the population; they tend also to become older, as younger country people migrate to the towns and their suburbs. This phenomenon seems most marked in the Massif Central and the south-west, where departments like Gers and Lozère lose population steadily (see Table 2.16).

Turning to the economic activities of the population, we find the classification given in Table 2.17 (the figures from the 1954 census are given so as to show up the rapid change in the socio-economic structure). These figures are in fact based on the socio-economic grouping CSP (*catégorie socio-professionnelle*). The CSP was developed by INSEE as a standard measure of social stratification, and it is advisable for any student of French politics and society to become familiar with it, as it is the basis of most surveys, opinion polls and the like. But the CSP does have its shortcomings as a means of social analysis, for it clearly privileges economic status or the nature of one's employment as a determinant. In so doing, it avoids what is in our view a much more crucial social determinant, class.

Although a much less visible or measurable structure than the CSP, class exists in France, as it does anywhere else. Much of what happens to an individual will in the last analysis be decided by the class into which he/she is born or might move, thanks to various mechanisms of social mobility. This is not to imply that class is a cast-iron framework which produces immediate and visible effects on individuals; rather, the whole process by which people's lives are structured by their class-position is a much more subtle and complex one than rather caricatural views of the above kind would suggest.

We shall attempt in the brief space available to try and hint at the importance and the complexity of social class. Classes arise, historically, with economic development. In any mode of production (a structure in which men, tools and materials are brought together so as to transform by their labour natural objects into objects that satisfy needs),

Table 2.15   French population by age and sex, 1975

Year of birth	Age at 1.1.76	Total population Both sexes			Males			Females		
		Total	%	No. working	Total	No. working	% (o)	Total	No. working	% (o)
1971-5	0-4	3,424,210	6.5		1,752,645			1,671,565		
1966-70	5-9	4,185,945	8.0		2,138,455			2,047,490		
1961-5	10-14	4,299,265	8.2		2,196,590			2,102,675		
1956-60	15-19	4,242,255	8.1	1,012,235	2,162,380	571,255	26.4	2,079,875	440,980	21.2
1951-5	20-24	4,211,185	8.0	2,884,400	2,127,530	1,508,555	70.9	2,083,655	1,375,845	66.0
1946-50	25-29	4,390,285	8.3	3,465,035	2,264,060	2,132,150	94.2	2,126,225	1,332,885	62.7
1941-5	30-34	3,060,575	5.8	2,350,895	1,594,795	1,550,085	97.2	1,465,780	800,810	54.6
1936-40	35-39	3,022,335	5.7	2,255,620	1,553,940	1,512,070	97.3	1,468,395	743,550	50.6
1931-5	40-44	3,270,555	6.2	2,402,875	1,657,915	1,605,670	96.8	1,612,640	797,205	49.4
1926-30	45-49	3,312,455	6.3	2,409,000	1,663,055	1,586,255	95.4	1,649,360	822,745	49.9
1921-5	50-54	3,203,030	6.1	2,231,685	1,567,415	1,445,380	92.2	1,635,615	786,305	48.1
1916-20	55-59	2,011,740	3.8	1,230,845	971,880	794,625	81.8	1,039,860	436,220	41.9
1911-15	60-64	2,466,590	4.7	990,900	1,148,250	623,945	54.3	1,318,340	366,955	27.8
1906-10	65-69	2,442,120	4.6	343,275	1,093,285	208,040	19.0	1,348,835	135,235	10.0
1901-05	70-74	2,096,545	4.0	118,595	882,345	67,615	7.7	1,214,200	50,980	4.2
1900 or before	75 or over	2,960,340	5.6	79,500	969,895	37,030	3.8	1,990,445	42,470	2.1
Total		52,599,430	100.0	21,774,860	25,744,475	13,642,675	53.0	26,854,955	8,132,185	30.3
1956-75	0-19	16,151,675	30.7	1,012,235	8,250,070	571,255		7,901,605	440,980	
1911-55	20-64	28,948,750	55.0	20,221,255	14,548,880	12,758,735	87.7	4,399,870	7,462,520	51.8
1910 or before	65 or over	7,499,005	14.3	541,370	2,945,525	312,685		4,553,480	228,685	

% (o) = percentage of same sex or age-group.
Source: INSEE, *Recensement de la population de 1975* (1 in 5 sample).

Table 2.16   Population decline in rural departments, 1968–75

	Population 1975	1968	Absolute loss	Loss as percentage
Gers (total)	175,366	181,577	−6,211	−3.4
Urban communes	61,223	58,156	+3,067	+5.3
Rural communes	114,143	123,421	−9,278	−7.5
Lozère (total)	74,825	77,258	−2,433	−3.1
Urban communes	24,131	23,315	+ 816	+3.5
Rural communes	50,694	53,943	−3,249	−6.0

Source: INSEE, *Principaux Résultats du recensement de 1975*, 1977, p. 48.

there is no 'pure' economic activity, with production taking place in some neutral, technical vacuum; production always involves social relations between those engaged in it. Such relations involve domination by some, and subordination on the part of others; here is where classes have their origin. It is important to realize that they arise, and remain, in antagonism. Now, social relations pivot on the control of the means of production (land, labour, materials and, as development proceeds, capital – which represents the accumulated labour of previous workers). In the capitalist mode of production, currently dominant in the world, the dominant class will be that which possesses or effectively controls the major means of production, i.e. it is essentially a capital-owning bourgeoisie. This contrasts with a working class which owns neither capital nor any other means of production, but sells its labour-power to the bourgeoisie in return for wages. The latter never fully cover the labour input which the worker has contributed to the productive process, however; and it is this extra unpaid labour (taking concrete form as money or capital) that enables the original capital invested to reproduce or to expand itself. Workers and bourgeois are the two fundamental classes of any developed social formation, and all other social groups need situating with reference to them.

But if ownership (or not) of the means of production is the prime determinant of social class, there are others also. Crucial in our view is ideology. As classes emerge, they secrete an ideology, i.e. a certain view of society and of their relation to it; such ideology can go very deep and have wide ramifications. Often, many members of a class will endorse a whole ideology, or large parts of it, without ever realizing it; many aspects of their lives (moral beliefs, work situations, personal relationships even) they will interpret quite spontaneously in ideological terms. Ideologies exist, and although they vary from one social

Table 2.17   Population by economic activity, 1975 and 1954

CSP	1975 Number	Percentage
Agriculteurs exploitants	1,605,865	7.6
Salariés agricoles	375,480	1.7
industriels	59,845	0.3
artisans	533,635	2.5
maîtres pecheurs	15,835	0.1
gros commerçants	186,915	0.9
petits commerçants	912,695	4.2
Patrons de l'industrie et du commerce	1,708,925	7.8
professions libérales	172,025	0.8
professeurs, professions littéraires et scientifiques	377,215	1.7
ingénieurs	256,290	1.2
cadres administratifs supérieurs	653,755	3.0
Professions libérales, cadres supérieurs	1,459,285	6.7
instituteurs, profs. intellectuelles	737,420	3.4
services médicaux et sociaux	298,455	1.4
techniciens	758,890	3.5
cadres administratifs moyens	970,185	4.5
Cadres moyens	2,764,950	12.7
employés de bureau	3,104,105	14.3
employés de commerce	736,595	3.4
Employés	3,840,700	17,6
contremaîtres	443,305	2.0
ouvriers qualifiés	2,985,865	13.7
ouvriers spécialisés	2,946,860	13.5
mineurs	73,444	0.3
marins et pecheurs	38,280	0.2
apprentis ouvriers	106,690	0.5
manoeuvres	1,612,725	7.4
Ouvriers	8,207,165	37.2
gens de maison	234,355	1.1
femmes de ménage	154,100	0.7
autres personnels de service	855,035	3.9
Personnels de service	1,243,490	5.7
artistes	59,075	0.3
clergé	116,945	0.5
armée et police	347,980	1.6
Autres catégories d'actifs	524,000	2.4

CSP	1954 Number	Percentage
Agriculteurs exploitants	3,983,840	20.8
Salariés agricoles	1,151,520	6.0
Patrons de l'industrie et du commerce	2,295,840	12.0
Professions libérales, cadres supérieurs	554,240	2.9
Cadres moyens	1,139,540	5.9
Employés	2,078,480	10.9
Ouvriers	6,465,100	33.8
Personnels de service	983,870	5.1
Autres actifs	499,040	2.6
Total	19,151,470	100%

Sources: INSEE, *Recensement de la population de 1975* (1 in 5 sample);
Recensement de 1954, pp. 58–9.

formation to another, their core can usually be identified. They help to give stability and cohesion to classes and class-fractions.

Ideology as a basis of class seems to us more crucial than other factors sometimes adduced, e.g. income level, life-style, access to various desiderata. Such factors can, however, be useful adjuncts to class consciousness in that they help to reinforce basic feelings of belonging (or not). We shall therefore discuss them briefly later; the ideologies of different classes are probably best left to the chapter on political forces.

Finally it should be stressed that classes are not massively homogeneous. On the contrary, they are differentiated within themselves, probably increasingly so. A century ago 'the capitalists' seemed much easier to identify as a social group; so did the workers and the peasantry. The growing complexity of capitalist development obliges the analyst to be more nuanced, though, and to locate within each class layers or fractions, whose relationships are often quite conflictual, as they contend for overall hegemony. Indeed as new types of economic activity emerge, it can be quite difficult to place those who practice them firmly in one class.

Given these reservations, then, we can perhaps reinterpret the French CSPs of 1975 in terms of social class. This analysis will deal with the working population only.

The pivot of French society is clearly the most numerous class, the working class, some nine million strong in 1975. It includes all those engaged *directly* in the production of material goods and in the auxiliary activities vital to such production. It is located essentially, then, in agriculture, industry, transport, public works and construction and its work is largely manual (though one must beware of over-facile distinctions between 'manual' and 'intellectual' work, as will be seen). Three layers are often distinguished within the class; the top bracket consists of three million OP (*ouvriers professionnels*), or OQ (*ouvriers qualifiés*), as they are often called. These are skilled workers who have served an apprenticeship, and they command higher wages and prestige. Below them come the OS (*ouvriers spécialisés*) — a misleading term, since such workers are specialized in nothing except the execution of one narrow, repetitive task, usually on the assembly-line. For this they require little training; the English term 'semi-skilled' would be a very loose equivalent. Today there are some three million OS located mainly in the key industries (two-thirds of the total work-force in cars and electronics, over one-half in steel). Many of them are immigrants.[15] At the bottom are the *manoeuvres* — over one and a half million totally unskilled labourers.

The working class is a class that largely reproduces itself. Table 2.18 shows the origins of workers in 1964; over one-half had worker fathers. The remainder came mostly from agriculture, and the traditional

Table 2.18   Origins of workers' fathers by CSP, 1964 (percentages)

Ouvriers	51.6	
Agriculteurs	19.1	
Petits commerçants, artisans	9.8	
Employés	9.8	
Salariés agricoles	6.7	
Cadres moyens	1.7 ⎫	
Industriels, gros commerçants	0.7 ⎬ 2.9	
Cadres supérieurs	0.5 ⎭	
Total	100	

Source: INSEE, *Economie et statistique*, February 1970.

petty-bourgeoisie, reflecting thereby the decline of those sectors. Very few (some 3 per cent) had fathers from the upper reaches of society.

Increasingly, the working class is female, with a high concentration of women in *manoeuvre* and OS jobs – a reflection of the demand for cheap labour by new, often provincial, industry. Thus in 1975, women represented 26.8 per cent of the total of OS, and 38.1 per cent of unskilled labourers.

Such then is the French working class; its hard core is in the established industrial areas, probably in factories with large numbers of employees. This core tends to provide the union and political élites of the class. But the diversity of the class and the fact that it is continually evolving, should not be forgotten.

If it is easy to identify the working class, then this is not true of its counter-pole, the bourgeoisie. Who does control the major means of production and exchange in France, and how numerous are such people? The census lists some 60,000 industrialists and over 180,000 *commerçants*. Many of these will, however, be in a fairly small way of business and cannot really be counted at the top end of the bourgeoisie. On the other hand, many of the upper reaches of the *professions libérales/cadres supérieurs* could be, either because of their level of capital ownership, their economic decision-power or their expertise, which is necessary to the continuation of the social system. Such professionals (who need of course to be distinguished from the rest of their CSP) would include senior experts (technical, legal, etc.), senior managers (in public and private sectors alike) and certainly the top echelons of the different parts of the state apparatus, whether repressive (police, army, judiciary) or ideological (media, education). These figures are sometimes referred to as 'faux salariés', i.e. although notionally wage-earners, as with managing directors, say, they in fact derive most of their income from surplus produced by others. In addition there are still a number of the more traditional type of capitalists, who live simply off dividends from shareholdings; these would appear in terms of CSPs as part of the non-working population! At any rate, in so far as it is possible to identify a ruling class in France, then it is comprised of these groups. They would probably amount to some 300–500,000 people.

Such a class is by no means monolithic, of course. There seems to be one very obvious split between the big and medium-sized bourgeoisie. The latter comprises the owners of medium-sized capital, whether industrial, financial or commercial; to it would be assimilated part of what Gramsci called the 'intellectuals': those from the middle ranks of the professions and state apparatus, as described above, whose activities are cultural or administrative and who are so necessary for maintaining the hegemony of a class or class-fraction within civil society (i.e. the process whereby such groups secure, by non-violent means, the consent of the mass of the population to their rule). By antithesis, the big bourgeoisie comprises the representatives of the biggest forms of capital, plus the very summit of the state apparatus, consisting of a few tens of thousands at most. It is distinguished from the medium-sized bourgeoisie primarily by the extent of the capital that it controls;[16] within its ranks the dominant force is that of finance capital. In the view of theorists such as Quin and Morin, there are some twenty financial groups which effectively control the major part of French industry and commerce; and this phenomenon is at the heart of what the PCF calls monopoly capitalism.

According to this analysis, the tendency within any one sector of economic activity is towards concentration of capital-ownership. This will eventually entail monopolistic domination of that particular sector of the market, for this is seen as the only way in which capital, once invested, can reproduce itself with sufficient profit. One can identify some 200 monopolistic groups in France, and within their ranks, finance capital (banks, finance houses, etc.) has increased its penetration. It should be pointed out that formal ownership is not the only means of assuring effective control over the operations of a concern; thus while monopoly capital has made little direct penetration into such fields as agriculture or construction, it often exercises decisive control here by influencing, say, the supply of materials or the marketing of eventual products. F. Morin has shown[17] the hold of finance capital over many sectors of the French economy. Penetration by foreign capital extends naturally into the monopolistic sector. Thus Quin claims that in 1971 fifty-six of the top hundred companies in France were effectively controlled by non-French big capital. Here lies clearly a major source of potential conflict.

Theorists of monopoly capitalism see this tendency as a long-standing and inevitable one within capitalism; they give the theory another dimension when they speak of state monopoly capitalism. We shall discuss the full implications of this theory later, in connection with the PCF, but briefly, such theorists see the state as a ready and willing tool of monopoly groups. By direct aid (contracts, subsidies, etc.), by economic policy (prices and incomes, taxation), by use of its own economic power (using the public sector as a 'crutch' for private capital) the state is seen as helping the drive towards concentration of capital and monopoly. Clearly such a theory takes no account of any measure of autonomy that the state might develop with regard to capital.

Such, then, is the bourgeoisie in France. What of the groups between it and the workers? These are not easy to classify. The 3.8 million *employés* (white-collar wage-earners, in industry and commerce, performing mostly subaltern tasks with little power of initiative or decision) and the 1.2 million service workers are unhesitatingly counted as 'proletarians', along with the working class, by sociologists like Baudelot and Establet. Although they do not enable capital to expand itself, as do workers (rather, their function is to transfer or distribute such capital), they are none the less exploited in their work, as are workers, and often their working conditions are similar. This seems to us however to ignore the cultural or ideological difference between white-collar and productive workers, predicated largely, as Poulantzas has shown, on the distinction between 'manual' and 'intellectual' work. Although this distinction is less and less relevant in reality, it is always likely to induce white-collars to see themselves as distinct from workers.[18] Hence it is advisable to see them as part of the petty-bourgeoisie. With them would need to be counted the bottom end of the professions, the *cadres moyens* and most of the engineers and technicians; these latter categories are mostly wage earners, even if their income and conditions of work are usually superior to those of the lower white-collars. Baudelot and Establet believe that there is a tendency for petty-bourgeois working in the public sector (teachers, lower civil servants, etc.) to develop a different mentality from that of their equivalents in the private sector; but this hypothesis should be treated with some caution.

If such categories comprise the new petty-bourgeoisie, resulting from a development of production that demands more and more auxiliary services, then they still coexist with the old petty-bourgeoisie. This consists of the artisans, the small businessmen and the shopkeepers described above. Although they own their means of production or exchange (shop, small business, etc., usually family-run and employing less than five workers), they are effectively subordinated to bigger capital which allots them their modest place in the economy, usually by controlling either their supplies or their outlets. Clearly there is a parallel between their class-situation and that of the numerous small farmers. And like its newer variants, the traditional petty-bourgeoisie occupies a sandwich position between the capitalist class and the workers.

If we were to redraw the map of French society in terms of class, rather than of CSPs, we would probably get something like this:

bourgeoisie	— *industriels*	
	grands commerçants	
	cadres supérieurs	
	top of *professions libérales* and *agriculteurs*	
petty-bourgeoisie	— rest of *professions libérales; petits commerçants; artisans; (agriculteurs)*	old petty-bourgeoisie
	— *cadres moyens;* top technicians; *employés;* most *personnel de service;* most *autres actifs*	new petty-bourgeoisie
working class	— *salariés agricoles*	
	ouvriers	
	most technicians	
	some *personnel de service*	

If any definition of social class must start with production relations, there are many other factors involved outside the workplace which can help in different ways to reinforce feelings of class. How much one earns: what sort of life-style one can afford as a result: what access to culture or education one has: where one lives. These factors are important in anyone's life and can always impinge on his/her way of looking at themselves and their relation to society. Without claiming that all members of a class experience reality in the same way, it does seem to us that there is a fair degree of similarity in the conditions that most members of a class are likely to experience in their everyday lives, and that this similarity can be measured; in other words there is a material foundation to class present in everyday life, even if individual members of a class perceive it to different degrees, if at all.

At the risk of simplification, one can single out several factors that help solidify French society into classes. Taken on their own, they would not necessarily prove anything. Taken together, though, they show up a consistent pattern which suggests that the famous social 'inequalities' about which so much debate rages in France are not the effects of accident or economic misjudgment, but necessary symptoms of a deep-lying structure whereby the productive system reproduces itself from one generation to the next, allotting individuals places in the classes and fractions that compose society. By way of illustration we shall look at income, education and (in the widest sense) patterns of consumption.

The following figures are of necessity crude: they are averaged out per CSP on the basis of households rather than individuals. Clearly such aggregates contain innumerable individual cases ranging far above or below the mean. As measures of inequality they thus need treating with caution[19] even leaving aside such questions as to how much equality is necessary or desirable between social groups. None the less, these figures do show a clear hierarchy, which when taken alongside the other differentiations discussed here, can plausibly be seen as helping to structure the class-position of groups and individuals.

It is a commonplace to point out that economic growth has led to a steady increase in purchasing power *per capita* for all sections of the population (roughly 3.3 per cent per annum in 1960–1980). This overall increase conceals a big hierarchy, however. Just looking at wage-earners, the average yearly wages per CSP in 1975 were as in Table 2.19. For the self-employed, the figures were as stated in the same table (though they are not fully accurate, because less is known about them than about the income of wage-earners. In particular, the members of families of farmers and shopkeepers, the *aides familiaux*, contribute large amounts of notionally unpaid labour).

It will be objected that the modern welfare state irons out these discrepancies by taxation, allowances and the like. Even after such transfer payments have been completed, though, and despite a small

Table 2.19   Household income by CSP, 1975 (francs)

(a) *wage earners*	*pretax*	*disposable* (after tax and transfers)
Cadres supérieurs	106,191	96,632
Cadres moyens	62,109	59,134
Employés	46,481	45,872
Ouvriers qualifiés	40,565	41,874
Ouvriers non qualifiés	34,652	32,421
(b) *self-employed*		
exploitants agricoles	22,303	23,377
salaries agricoles	29,710	33,309
artisans/petits commerçants	57,307	49,461
industriels/gros commerçants	132,847	100,121
professions liberales	127,613	95,610
national average	48,690	46,169

Source: INSEE, *Données statistiques sur les familles*, 1981, p. 109; 146

narrowing of differentials between groups and within any one group over the past ten years, the overall hierarchy of income is still clear enough (see Table 2.20).

A significant point here is the high incomes not just of the self-employed but also of *cadres supérieurs*, most of whom belong, as we saw, to the top bourgeois stratum. If we take the average wage of the top 10 per cent of non-working-class wage-earners (mainly *cadres supérieurs*, in fact) and the bottom 10 per cent (*employés*), we will find that the ratio between the two is 5 to 1 in France, compared with 2.8 to 1 in the UK or 2.3 to 1 in West Germany.[20] So even on the level of income the bourgeoisie, or part of it, stands out. The same is true of the petty-bourgeoisie (e.g. *cadres moyens*), as compared with workers; the difference between the average wage of each group being 63 per cent higher than that in the UK and 57 per cent higher than that in West Germany.[21]

Similar hints are provided by examination of French taxation. A tax system usually provides insights into the political and social structures of a country. The most striking thing about France is that a high proportion of tax receipts comes from *indirect* tax (mainly VAT); this percentage was calculated at 65.6 in 1972, as against 33.5 per cent from direct taxes on incomes (in Germany the figures were 50.9 and 48.7 per cent respectively[22]). As indirect tax, unlike a progressive tax on incomes, covers most basic items such as food and clothing, it hits all social categories equally. In other words the French state

Table 2.20   Index of disparity for household incomes by CSP, 1975
(100 = national average for each column)

CSP of head of household	Gross income	Gross income and family allowances	Gross income less tax	Net income
Exploitants agricoles	45.8	48.9	47.2	50.6
Salariés agricoles	61.0	67.3	65.5	72.1
Artisans, petits commerçants	117.7	115.5	109.1	107.1
Industriels, gros commerçants	272.8	263.1	225.2	216.9
Professions libérales	262.1	253.1	214.6	207.1
Cadres supérieurs	218.1	211.6	207.3	200.6
Cadres moyens	127.6	126.1	129.8	128.1
Employés	95.5	96.1	98.9	99.4
Ouvriers qualifiés	83.3	86.2	87.7	90.7
Ouvriers non qualifiés	71.2	76.2	75.7	81.1
Inactifs	68.8	66.4	70.4	67.6
Ensemble	100.0	100.0	100.0	100.0

Source: *ibid*. p. 151

has always preferred to raise its revenue by penalizing the lower classes more than the higher.

Even within the income tax hierarchy, there are some striking discrepancies. One could cite those of the spectacular kind that can probably be found in most developed countries, though perhaps not quite to the same extent as in France, e.g. the ratio of 1 to 105 between the income of an old age pensioner (479 francs per month in 1974) and one of the top 10,000 taxpayers. (The real gap is probably bigger for it is universally admitted that opportunities both for legal evasion and actual fraud are high at the top end of the tax scale.) But more significant perhaps is the fact that the bottom 42.4 per cent of taxpayers (representing some 21.5 per cent of the total population) held 21.1 per cent of taxable income in 1975; what they paid in tax represented 8.7 per cent of government receipts. At the other end of the scale some 4.43 per cent of taxpayers, representing 2.23 per cent of the population, held 19.1 per cent of taxable income; but what they paid in tax came to 43.5 per cent of total receipts. To put it another way, some 470,000 households (the core of the bourgeoisie, surely) accounted for over half the receipts, whereas 22.8 million others (working class and different *petit-bourgeois* fractions) paid in only one-third. Of the latter, 10.7 millions did not in fact earn enough to be taxed.[23]

So the fiscal system again sheds light on class structure, both by the way in which it privileges indirect tax and by the hierarchy within taxpayers. But if this suggests a certain material basis to class, what can we learn from other areas of everyday life?

We might start by considering the availability of a commodity that most people consume at some time in their lives, viz. education. The intention here is not to give a detailed breakdown of the education system in France (this will be done in chapter 6) but to show how education contributes to the reproduction of social classes across the generations. Inspired by the euphoria of rapid growth, some observers assumed that this growth would necessarily increase social mobility, i.e. people would be able to rise more or less freely out of the class or CSP of their parents, thanks to the 'equality of opportunity' afforded by an expanding education system. The higher your qualifications, the better your job; all you had to do was obtain these qualifications. But that would happen if you were good enough to deserve them. Recent theorists have argued, however, that although a few people might rise socially in accord with this meritocratic vision, they tend rather to be the exception that reinforces the rule. Parkin suggests that much social mobility in western Europe takes place on the margin of the lower petty-bourgeoisie and the upper reaches of the working class, often between generations; moves from very high up the social ladder to very low down are rare.[24] By and large it emerges that in

France, as elsewhere in the developed world, education is mainly a process whereby, in Poulantzas's phrase, individuals are assigned places in the relations of production, or if one prefers to put it thus, are prepared for insertion into one class or another.

It has long been realized that upper-class children are abnormally highly represented in higher education, with a corresponding under-representation of the children of lower groups, notably workers and farmers. But we know now that this process has its roots in the second-ary school. This is the place where future careers are effectively chosen and where, for all the apparent egalitarianism of the CES, bourgeois children will mainly tend to get into the academic streams, leading to university and better jobs; most working-class and white-collar children will gravitate towards the technical streams, which lead mainly to work in industry and services at the age of sixteen. Various explanations were initially given for this (pressure from teachers, ignorance of parents about the relationship between qualifications and employ-ment, etc.) but increasingly these came to be fitted into a deeper sort of analysis. Theorists such as Baudelot and Establet realized that the process of guidance (or selection?) of children was much more systematic; the school was seen as the place where the productive system allotted roles to the rising generations, where the future bour-geois, petty-bourgeois, workers (and unemployed?) were to be shaped. They claimed that there were really two education systems, running in parallel – PP (*primaire/professionnel*) and SS (*secondaire/supérieur*) – and that most children would be firmly embarked on one or the other by the last year of primary school. PP led through the technical stream to worker or low-white-collar jobs; SS led on to university and a position of *cadre* or above. Although there were exceptions, most lower-class children tended to be PP, most upper-class ones SS. In between the two main streams it was possible to discern a third stream, producing mainly *petits-bourgeois*; in it one found most of those working-class children who did better, and the less successful bourgeois children. In other words, this was the place where such limited social mobility as existed would occur. At any rate, in 1966 a working-class child had a 54 per cent chance of being PP and only a 14 per cent one of being SS; for a bourgeois child the odds were almost the exact reverse.

The Bourdieu school laid emphasis on the hidden constraints within education, showing how much success is not a matter of mastering a neutral body of knowledge, thanks to one's innate ability, but more of an ideological matter, involving implicit skills. They stressed the acquisition of what they called 'cultural capital', i.e. a whole series of codes, social and linguistic, which teachers and, later on, others in authority will expect 'good' pupils to know. To put it crudely, success in education is not so much what one knows as how one expresses it. What teachers call 'gifted' pupils are really ones who have an articulate mastery of these codes, which of course are transmitted mainly through family mechanisms. Thus bourgeois children are obviously best placed to inherit this cultural capital, essential if one is to climb to a high place within society, because only their families possess it in the first place.

Even the few who make their way out of the lower classes to university are not guaranteed a brilliant social future. For the job market steadily demands new qualifications, which only those in the know will be aware of. Thus for some years degrees in arts and pure science have been losing value, whereas economics degrees seem to lead to good jobs. Yet of the lower-class children in university, a high percentage are to be found precisely in arts faculties. Moreover, as access to the best economics courses depends on having the maths *baccalauréat* C, the competition to get into this stream is acute; indeed for Alain Touraine this is one of the key points where social reproduction takes place. It is legitimate to suppose that lower-class children are by and large not preponderant in the C stream.

One is led to conclude then that the education system is a place where classes compete for the life-chances of their children but where, *pace* the ideologists of social mobility, the privileged position of the dominant class and its ability to reproduce itself are not greatly threatened.

Where people live can often influence their view of their place in society, as can their ownership (or not) of their home. Table 2.21

Table 2.21   French households, 1978: owners and occupiers (percentages)

| CSP | Renting accommodation | | Housed free | Owners | Owner-occupiers |
	Total	Incl. HLM* tenants			
Agriculteurs exploitants	3.1	–	24.3	51.9	20.7
Patrons	34.6	(3.3)	5.2	32.1	27.1
Inactifs	34.2	(8.5)	13.5	47.5	4.8
Salariés agricoles	33.2	(1.8)	29	18.3	19.5
Personnel de service	58.4	(20)	14.7	16.9	10
Autres actifs	54.6	(19.3)	25.3	3.9	16.3
Professions libérales, cadres supérieurs	37.5	(4.7)	7.5	16.3	38.7
Cadres moyens	49.4	(13.9)	7.8	9.1	33.7
Employés	55	(20.3)	6.2	13	25.8
Ouvriers	55.5	(22.7)	5.9	13.1	25.5
Moyenne nationale	43	(13.3)	10.3	26.8	19.9

*Habitations à loyer modéré: corresponds roughly to British council housing.
Source: INSEE, *Données sociales*, 1981, p. 251

shows that property ownership does tend still to be the preserve of the upper groups in society, though the number of owner-occupiers among workers and the newer *petits-bourgeois* is growing, as France develops the mortgage system familiar in the English-speaking countries. Again, these figures say little about the different quality of housing available to social groups, or the fact that for the upper groups a second home is increasingly prevalent. Table 2.22 shows figures that do bring out the hierarchy that exists in this domain.

Recent research has also confirmed that the area in which people live has much to do with social class.[25] The authors distinguish several possible ways in which the areas of a town can be divided among bourgeois, petty-bourgeois and workers, and indeed among the sub-groups thereof; what is always certain, though, is that towns are divided along these class lines, and measurably so, with differential access to various amenities for social groupings.

There are many other factors of life-style that point up the way in which social classes are structured and structure their members. Let us consider access to medical services (cf. Table 2.23). As well as enjoying unequal access to medicine, social classes are unequal before death (cf. Table 2.24).

Patterns of cultural consumption show a similar hierarchy, even if one refers to things as anodine as visits to the theatre or reading newspapers (Table 2.25).

What emerges from all this is that social classes are quite clearly structured in France; there is a clear hierarchy within and between classes. J. Marceau sums up well the ways in which class structures people's lives when she says of the workers, small farmers and white collars that they earn least (but contribute most to social transfer

Table 2.22   Characteristics of accommodation by CSP, 1978 (%)

	% of households housed uncomfortably	overcrowded
agriculteurs	47.2	13.9
salariés agric.	43.9	31.1
patrons	18.1	12.5
cad. sup et prof. libérales	2.6	6.8
cad. moyens	6.2	12.9
employés	13.9	19.9
ouvriers	23.1	24.3
personnels de service	28.1	30.3
inactifs	44.2	13.9
nat. average	26.9	17.1

Source: INSEE, *Données sociales, 1981*, p. 249

Table 2.23   Annual access to health facilities by CSP, 1973

	No. of visits to doctor per head per year		
	Men	Women	Both
agriculteurs	2.28	3.62	2.75
patrons	2.91	3.84	3.27
professions et cad. sup.	2.36	5.52	3.04
employés et cad. moyens	4.51	5.84	5.20
ouvriers	2.29	2.75	2.40
personnel de service	3.14	2.94	2.98
inactifs	3.12	3.50	3.36
national average	3.22	4.09	3.70

Source: INSEE, *Données sociales 1981*, p. 76

Table 2.24   **Life expectancy by CSP, 1971**

CSP	No. of survivors at 75 years for every 1,000 at 35 years	Life expectancy at 35 years
Instituteurs	574	40.9
Professions libérales, cadres supérieurs	551	40.5
Clergé catholique	524	39.5
Cadres moyens (public)	518	39.3
Techniciens	507	39.0
Cadres moyens (privé)	489	38.5
Agriculteurs exploitants	473	38.0
Contremaîtres	472	37.8
Ouvriers qualifiés (public)	446	37.3
Employés (public)	448	37.2
Artisans et commerçants	460	37.6
Employés (privé)	448	37.4
Ouvriers spécialisés (public)	406	36.0
Ouvriers qualifiés (privé)	380	35.6
Salariés agricoles	356	34.8
Ouvriers spécialisés (privé)	362	34.7
Manoeuvres	310	32.9
National average	412	36.1

Source: G. Desplanches, *La Mortalité des adultes suivant le milieu social*, INSEE, 1976, p. 13.

Table 2.25   Cultural activity by CSP, December 1974 (%)

	(a)	(b)	(c)	(d)
Agriculteur	61.2	21.1	8.7	1.5
Patron de l'industrie ou de commerce	60.2	17.2	20.8	14.6
Professions libérales, cadres supérieurs	61.1	57.2	65.3	35.8
Cadres moyens	57.9	34.6	48.9	33.5
Employé	60.4	18.8	36.3	12.0
Ouvrier qualifié/contremaître	54.3	10.7	24.7	7.4
OS/manoeuvre/personnel de service	50.0	12.2	26.3	6.0
Femme inactive de moins de 60 ans	41.5	9.0	28.9	13.1
Inactif de 60 ans et plus	66.3	14.1	19.9	8.6
National average	55.1	16.6	28.4	12.1

(a) reading a daily newspaper; (b) reading a social or political periodical;
(c) reading twenty books per annum on average; (d) having visited theatre
once in past year.
Source: INSEE, *Données sociales, 1978*, p. 310.

payments), have least income security (and the highest risk of unemployment), have the least capital, the fewest consumer goods and
the shortest holidays. They participate least in leisure and cultural
activities, and above all they know very little about their position
of deprivation compared with other social groups.[26] Of such realities
is class, in France and elsewhere, made.

(3) Political culture

In any social system, we can identify what is often called a political
culture. By this is understood a set of political values (beliefs about the
nature of that particular society and the ways in which it runs – or
should run – its affairs). Such a culture is an historical product and
depends on the classes and fractions that make up the society in
question; it is in fact a distillation of different ideologies that has
taken place over a period of time.[27] Hence it is more appropriate to
speak of a series of sub-cultures in any one society, rather than to
imply the existence of one uniform, national political culture. Amid
these contending sub-cultures, however, one can see a number of
common threads running. A bourgeois may have a concept of the
nation, say, that is different from that of a worker; but both do have
a concept of nation. It is this common core of concern that we shall
try to identify in this section.

Such an exercise is essential if one is to have an understanding of
French political behaviour; there is after all a strong connection between what people feel about politics and how they are likely to act

in the political system. Indeed we would say that for France the political culture is doubly important. In most areas of French life, not just in politics, discussion and argument are more prominent than in Britain; the French are less ready to concede a point and can usually defend their ideas articulately. Often too the level of such debate is different from that of Anglo-Saxon countries in that people are much readier to conceptualize and to analyse – and this is valid for many sectors of the population, not simply for intellectuals. In short, much French political debate takes place at a higher level of explicitness and self-consciousness than in Britain. Thus the outsider needs to become familiar with the assumptions and values of those conducting the debate.

Given this, we can now try to identify some of the constants of French political culture – all of which are refracted in different ways and for different purposes, by the ideologies of the different groups and classes of French society. Most of these constants have their origin, logically enough, in the period that saw the birth of modern France – the Revolution of 1789. This affected the social and economic structures of France, her political system and her ideological structures. Socially, the Revolution confirmed the loss of hegemony within civil society by a declining nobility, to the advantage of what one is obliged to call a bourgeoisie of property-owners, timid and fragmented though it was; at the same time, the peasantry, acquiring noble and church lands, emerged as a class in its own right, the most numerous and the most inert in France. In the later stages of the Revolution, the movements of the *sans-culottes* and *babouvistes* showed that the urban population of small traders, artisans and manual workers was beginning to emerge as a social force to be reckoned with. Politically, the Revolution saw the change from the *Ancien Régime* (personal power of a monarch, based on divine right) to something approaching a constitutional monarchy, and then to a republic with an attempt at parliamentary government. This gave way, under the pressure of foreign invasions, to the 'patriotic dictatorship' of Jacobinism (highly centralized rule by a small élite, supposedly incarnating the national will). Later, when the emergent bourgeois fractions could not reconcile their differences by any of these systems, Bonapartism arrived to guarantee order. Based on personal power and the creation of a powerful and efficient type of state machinery, it combined in a unique mixture the support of the new propertied élite and the peasant mass. Although its duration was brief it gave France a series of basic institutions – administrative, legal, educational – that would prove remarkably long-lived.

In short, in the quarter-century after 1789, France saw the emergence of a socio-economic structure that would change only slowly over the next 150 years (although the struggle between social classes was unrelenting and often more violent than elsewhere in Europe), and of a series of political régimes (republic/constitutional monarchy/ Bonapartism) that would alternate with regularity. Needless to say, at the level of ideology or value-systems, similar bases were laid. The Revolution saw the emergence of a number of ideologies which express the aspirations of different classes or fractions. Leaving aside the *ultra* theories (total opposition to the Revolution and return to a divine-right monarchy), which were steadily losing influence from the early nineteenth century onwards, the two main ones could be clearly seen to be liberalism (for economic freedom, based on property: for political and civil liberties and political participation, though by no means extended to all), and, in a crude but recognizable form, socialism (opposition to a régime based on property and demands that individual welfare be taken in hand by the collectivity). Of course these value systems would undergo modification throughout the succeeding centuries, in the light of social and economic change, as well as of political experience. None the less the Revolution is the fountain-head of these value systems which are still very vigorous (as witness their bitter clash in the 1981 elections).

As well as changing social and political structures and secreting these value systems, the Revolution also raised two other issues which seem to cut across class cleavages. One is the question of the Catholic church and its role in the French social and political system; the other is the problem of the nation. What is the nation? What values does it stand for? Who incarnates these? On both the religious and the national questions, the Revolution began a debate that is still going on.

Let us now look in detail, then, at these problems which the Revolution raised and which have become constants of French political culture. First, the question of the régime. Textbooks on French politics, especially those written by Anglo-Saxons, delight in pointing out the number of régimes France has enjoyed since 1789 (fourteen, not counting the provisional governments in between régimes) and contrasting this lack of political consensus unfavourably with the solid basis enjoyed by the monarchy in the UK or the presidency in the USA. Why is there this lack of agreement about the régime?

Discounting the racial or cultural type of explanation that one sometimes still hears (i.e. the French, like other Latins, are volatile and unstable by temperament, and this inevitably comes out in their political behaviour), it seems to us that there are sound historical reasons for this uncertainty. Ideally, each change of régime would need a full analysis of all the short- and long-term factors that contributed to its demise, but in the brief space available, some general hypotheses can be put forward. The first of these concerns the type of bourgeoisie that emerged from the Revolution: composed of professionals, administrators, commercial and financial elements, which had increased their strength under the *Ancien Régime*, it had been above all an acquirer of land. Gains realized in commerce and various forms of speculation during the revolutionary period were promptly immobilized in landed property, which became the key to political influence (access to the electoral register was proportionate to the amount of property owned until 1848). What did *not* emerge was a dynamic, industrializing bourgeoisie. Frightened by the chaos of the revolutionary years, content with the comfort and power it had acquired, this 'Malthusian' bourgeoisie wanted not further change but stability. Having taken power illegally itself, it felt insecure and was always looking over its shoulder, as it were, to see if there were other social forces ready to supplant it in its turn. This bourgeoisie was also divided as to the nature of the régime. If most of the July Monarchy *notables* favoured the constitutional monarchy with restricted suffrage, others favoured the republic based on universal (male) suffrage; it would take until 1870 for the latter view to prevail.[28] These internal differences were of course subordinated to what the various bourgeois fractions had in common, viz. defence of property; hence their readiness to accept a *régime d'exception* (Bonapartism) when threatened from below. But on occasions (notably 1848) their differences could be serious enough to endanger the régime and their own class-domination for a while.

It is probably this timidity that explains the reluctance to broaden the political basis of the early régimes (in 1848 there were only 250,000 electors from a population of 36 million). It also explains why any economic or political demands from lower classes, such as those of the emergent working class in the 1830s, were repressed, either by legislation (combination laws) or violence (use of the armed forces in 1834–6). The coalition of bourgeois forces that ruled France in the early nineteenth century had, then, some difficulty in assuring its hegemony (i.e. securing passive assent to its rule and thus making reliance on force unnecessary); a symptom of this is the chronic difficulty which it experienced in forming a party or parties to canalize its parliamentary strength. This meant that any concessions had to be wrung out of the political system by force; hence very often the régime had to collapse before concessions were obtained (e.g. the July Monarchy falls in 1848, after which universal male suffrage was conceded; the Second Empire collapses in 1870 as the price for the return to a fully parliamentary régime).

Such changes were often facilitated by three other factors. First, the high specific weight of Paris within French life. All major aspects of French life – culture, politics, administration, business – had their source in Paris, which dominated the passive and largely under-developed provinces. Crises occurred first in Paris, where it was possible for a revolutionary élite to mobilize the high number of under-privileged inside the capital and seize power. This could not last long, however, for soon the dead weight of peasant France, rallied by the overthrown *notables* would make itself felt and repression set in (June 1848, May 1871).

That this pattern could be repeated in the nineteenth century proves the importance of another factor, the slow rate of industrialization, to which reference has already been made. This meant that there was no sudden arrival on the political scene of a proletariat (i.e. a large manual working class, employed in big units of production and developing a strong class-consciousness and political organizations to correspond to it). On the contrary, rural exodus was slow, the growth of working-class consciousness and organizations tardy and fragmented. Hence the sense of political stagnation and *déjà-vu*, and the possibility for the ruling fractions to recover situations that seemed to be escaping from them.

A third important factor is the foreign invasions which France has experienced and which have often compounded domestic tensions to produce the reversal of a régime (cf. the collapse of the Second Empire in 1870 or the installation of the Vichy régime in 1940).

In short, these frequent changes of régime are best explained by the nature of the post-Revolutionary ruling class and the type of opposition, domestic and foreign, which it faced. Now, such uncertainty about the régime has had much to do with determining political stances, and it is far from being dispelled. If it is true that the republic has had general acceptance since 1870, and that since 1958 economic modernization, the emergence of a presidential executive and the increasing bipolarization of party politics have apparently forced most Frenchmen to accept the logic of the Fifth Republic, then it is equally true that this Republic has worked so far only because the politics of president and parliamentary majority have thus far coincided. If the right were to win the 1986 legislative elections, then real strains might be placed on the institutional consensus, for Mitterrand is in office till 1988.

The role of the church in French politics is also a long-standing issue. In Britain the relationship between religion and the state has been relatively easy for a century and a half, the established Protestant church coexisting comfortably with the state, as does the large Catholic minority. In Ireland of course — a country whose political culture is in many ways more similar to that of France than to that of Britain — the problem is posed more acutely. The French church was, before the Revolution, a privileged ally of the monarchy, occupying key positions in the state apparatus in return for moral and ideological support. The Revolution made an attempt to make the church more subordinate to the political authorities and in so doing began a battle which has never entirely finished. It centred on control of the education system, and it entailed an ideological quarrel which is part and parcel of the political culture. Because the church or its leaders at least tended to favour anti-republican régimes, republicans (and later on socialists and communists) built up an image of the church as a kind of anti-republic, a sort of lay version of Antichrist. Intellectual bases for this opposition were provided by the 'positivist' or 'scientiste' doctrines of early republicanism, which laid stress on human reason and implied that all phenomena could be explained scientifically, thus doing away with any need for the supernatural, or 'superstition' as they often called it. Such doctrines also pointed out that Catholic theories implied a natural and immutable hierarchy in the universe, which they contrasted unfavourably with their own theories of natural equality (whatever the shortcomings of these in practice, especially in the economic field). Catholics reacted accordingly, and to the republican stereotype of the Catholic as reactionary, servile and superstitious corresponded a Catholic myth of the republican as socially subversive, dictatorial and atheistic. Now although the Third Republic showed — particularly by the 1905 Act of Separation, which reduced the church from the rank of an ideological apparatus to something ressembling that of a sundry pressure-group — that republican democracy and Catholicism could coexist, the process of rapprochement was to take a long time. It would take the Resistance of 1941–4 and the emergence of a christian democrat political movement to confirm it. Even today, however, it would be simplistic to believe that the 'clerical question' is dead. There are still parts of France where politics are determined primarily by religious alignment or lack of it, and practising Catholics still vote in the majority on the right.

Nationalism occurs in all political cultures. Here the word is taken in a restrictive sense, i.e. a set of beliefs about one's nation and what it represents. In most political systems rulers will use some kind of nationalism to legitimize their rule; it may well be that a polity cannot remain in existence without the propagation of such sentiments. This propagation need not, however, take place directly or obviously — through formal instruction in schools, say. There are many more oblique means whereby nationalist values can be passed on to the citizenry, and the feeling of 'belonging' reinforced.

What is striking about French politics, though, is precisely the openness with which national sentiments are displayed compared with, say, the discrete way in which the British propagate their nationalism (though obviously this latter statement is becoming progressively less true). Today no major French political force dare take its distance publicly from nationalist sentiments (i.e. they all have to proclaim allegiance to the principle of 'France first'), though in private members of the political class can be heard to talk differently. It is true that what France incarnates for a Gaullist is not perhaps the same as what she represents for a communist; but both seem to employ nationalist rhetoric with equal ease.

The reasons for this go beyond the recent success of Gaullism and its revival of xenophobic sentiments, sloganized as *l'indépendance nationale*. Gaullism was simply building on a capital of nationalist feeling that existed since the Revolution. When the Revolutionaries began to construct a new kind of state, they came into conflict with other European powers attached to the *Ancien Régime*. The massive popular mobilization which resulted and which saved France from defeat succeeded probably because the participants knew that basic patriotic or national feeling (defence of one's soil) was inseparable from defence of a new kind of political system. Already, then, French nationalism had acquired this extra dimension of value.

From its republican and progressive origins, though, French nationalism was to undergo changes. The defeat by Prussia in 1870 led to a revival of the nationalist problematic, but this time on the right.[29] For theorists like Barrès and Maurras, the French decline was attributable to the republican form of government and the equalitarian theory on which it rested. A return to a régime of authority and hierarchy was needed; essential Frenchness lay in these qualities. Nationalism moved away from the left, but remained a burning problem, the more so as France was now acquiring an overseas empire second only to Britain and the schools were busy imbuing the rising generations with ultra-patriotic (and anti-German) values, in preparation for a war of revenge. Every political force had to define itself in terms of nationalism: for or against France? If for, then what sort of France? The problem was given a further twist with the emergence of socialist and then communist movements, in theory supra-national ('the worker has no country'). Even these were forced progressively, however, to present themselves in terms acceptable to an increasingly nationalist public opinion.

Since the Second World War, nationalism has bitten deeper if anything into French political culture. The humiliating defeat of 1940, Vichy, occupation and collaboration: the rise of the USSR and USA as super-powers, with the consequent decline of western European nations: the traumatic loss of the French empire after 1945 have all left their mark on at least one generation. All these events raised the question: what does France stand for? In short, given the peculiar historical experiences of the French over the last two centuries, it hardly seems surprising that the debate about nationalism should be so open and that no one can escape participation in it.

It was remarked earlier that Napoleon created much of the state machinery of modern France. It would be more accurate to say that he continued *Ancien Régime* traditions, notably those of Louis XIV, i.e. the use of a highly centralized administration, headed by a trained élite, capable of carrying the state almost irrespective of the nature or abilities of the government. Centralization means that important decisions are taken in Paris and as little initiative (and resources) as possible are allowed to lower tiers of administration elsewhere. In theory this is supposed to be more efficient because decisions are taken by the most enlightened; in practice, as those who have experienced it at first hand know, the lower one descends the administrative chain, the more frequent are the restrictive practices, blockages and inefficiency. It is certain, as Wright and others have shown,[30] that the potential power of the state is never as great as its real influence; none the less, the average Frenchman is conscious that the state casts a big shadow across his life and his relationship with it is in some ways odd.

Its presence appears in apparently anodine things, such as the use of identity cards, which must be produced on the demand of a policeman. This card is the most important of a series of official papers which French people carry with them in wallets specially made for the purpose. In this respect they are like most of their fellow-Europeans, for the majority of European states, east and west, have developed high degrees of administrative centralization. The author has heard French people say that they felt undressed without '*les papiers*'. This symbolizes in a way the close relationship of state and citizen; the state guarantees, literally, the citizen's identity. The state guarantee is, moreover, the only one that counts. In education, for instance, a teacher applying for a post in Britain would have to show references from someone in the professional hierarchy, but might well not be asked to show a degree certificate. In France, the opposite is true. The state is not interested in the opinion of private citizens as to the suitability of X or Y, only in its own proof of competence – in this case a certificate approved by the minister of education. (Usually the original must be produced; if not, a *copie conforme* is acceptable, provided it is stamped by some authorized state representative.) This is a small point, perhaps; but it does illustrate the difference between two systems, in one of which the state keeps its distance from the citizen, whereas in the other it intervenes more directly in his life.

This relationship with the state is ambiguous. On the one hand the state is seen as a benefactor: it dispenses credits, employs on a big scale and for a long time was seen as the classic means of social mobility by the lower classes. On the other it seems remote: often its local intermediaries are inscrutable or evasive: there seems to be something oppressive about this distant but powerful machine. So there is often a sort of reluctant tolerance of the state, without the individual ever giving it his full loyalty – a state of mind well evoked by the Radical philosopher Alain.

This mentality is often linked up with the fact, much stressed by such as Hoffmann[31] and Crozier,[32] that the French have always taken much less part in voluntary associations than the Anglo-Saxons, preferring to allow the state to occupy a maximum of terrain within civil society and making periodic insurrectional forays against it when it is felt to be deaf to sectional demands or plain oppressive. This is probably less true now than at any time. Wright has shown that the relationship between state and groups is much more fluid than the Hoffmann style of analysis suggests. Whatever the reality of the relationship between state and citizen, it still looms large in the consciousness of many Frenchmen.

The special historical development of French society after 1789: the nature of the régime: the problem of the church: the question of the nation: the relations of state and citizen — these would seem to be the constants of French political culture. All groups and forces will in their political activity have to refer, consciously or unconsciously, to these factors. How this process takes place will be seen below.

Chapter 3

The political framework

(1) The problem of constitution

The question of a constitution may seem at first glance to the apolitical student to be somewhat obscure, full of meaningless details which have little to do with any kind of reality. Yet the problem of the constitution has loomed large in French life for the best part of two hundred years. Ever since the Revolution of 1789, France has been searching for political stability and has sought it, via a written text, from several traditions in her history and political thought.

The British reader may ask at this point why a written constitution is necessary, but this is how the French define a constitution. (The dictionary definition being: charters, fundamental texts which determine a country's form of government.) This is the essential difference between the political traditions of Britain and France (and most other countries), in that the British constitution is not written. The average Briton knows that British society is, to a greater or lesser degree, governed by certain institutions (a monarch, a prime minister and his cabinet, a parliament, comprising a lower and an upper house). One who is more politically aware may also know that these have evolved over centuries, without there being any document which specifically confirms their existence as such. Since, too, there has been no revolution in Britain since the mid-seventeenth century, we may not unreasonably describe the British political tradition as being one of political stability. This tradition also has an effect on the political mentality of the British who, by and large, do not feel the need to call in question or to abolish British institutions, however much they may wish to see these altered.

Such is not the case in France which has had a large number of written constitutions since her first one in 1791. This has a number of important consequences: (a) unlike Britain, there is a different political tradition, one of instability and change brought about by revolution and (b) more important, the mentality that is engendered by such a situation. When a constitution has to be written, there is inevitably a need for great clarity of thought, and the choice which is finally arrived at implies a recognition of political values. Sophisticated as this approach may be, it also comprises within it an element of instability, since there can be no absolute conviction that the constitution will last. 'Les Français sont souvent comme le Poète: les pieds à peine sur terre et la tête dans les Etoiles. Spécialement dès qu'ils évoquent la Constitution, dont ils ont si souvent changé: ils rêvent toujours de la prochaine, tout en se référant à la défunte qu'ils ont fini par comprendre, tandis qu'ils vivent présentement avec un autre texte' (M. Jobert, 'Le partage du pouvoir exécutif', *Pouvoirs*, no. 4, 1978, p. 7).

Once a régime is established, it must face up to the supporters of its predecessor, it must inculcate into the nation at large a respect for the new institutions. It may be possible to assume general approval for the new régime, if there has been a referendum, for example, but this does not mean a pledge of undying support from a nation whose history has, since 1789, seen régimes come and go at an average rate of once every twelve years. Consequently, the political parties and groups all have to explain their situation *vis-à-vis* the institutions existing at the time, which cannot be taken for granted, as they tend to be in Britain.

In creating a constitution, both the *form* and the *nature* of government have to be considered. Form here is taken to mean the external appearance of power, as in (a) a monarchy (rule of one), whereby power is, to a greater or lesser degree entrusted to one individual, and handed on to a successor via the hereditary principle, or in (b) a republic, where again, as a rule, there is one individual – a president – holding a greater or lesser degree of power, but who has arrived at that pitch of eminence by process of election for a specific number of years. More important than the form, however, is the nature of government. The first distinction to be made here is also the most fundamental: a government is either free or it is not, which means that it permits or forbids the exercise of the basic human and civil rights. However, such a basic distinction can be modified in various ways. A government, whether republic or monarchy, may be described as authoritarian, if virtually all political power is in the hands of one individual, without there being any checks to limit its use (arbitrary power). On the other hand a government may be parliamentary, i.e. where most power is in the hands of the law-making body of elected representatives known as the legislature or parliament (comprised of one single assembly, or an upper and a lower house) and where the executive derives its authority to act from parliament. Inasmuch as this form of government derives its power from the election of national representatives, it may reasonably be assumed that it will ensure the preservation of the basic freedoms since it must, every so often, face an electorate at the polls. However, although a parliament is an elected body, this does not necessarily imply that the whole nation is involved in its election; there is therefore one further element which a constitution-maker may wish to take into account — democracy, which means that the nation as a whole has a substantial say in the election of its government. Normally we may expect to find in a parliamentary democracy a head of state, with purely formal and ceremonial duties, an executive comprising a prime minister and a ministerial team, taken from the majority opinion in the legislature, and deriving its authority from the legislature, to whom it is responsible. In opposition to this form of government, one might consider a 'presidential' system, with power stemming from the president himself. Furthermore, a government may be composed of varying and contradictory elements and merely tend more in one direction than another. Theoretically at least, an authoritarian government may be democratic as well, and some authorities would claim that a government may be both parliamentary and presidential.

Before the Revolution of 1789, there was no written constitution; France was governed by a hereditary monarchy in which, although there was provision for consultation by the king of the nation's representatives in assembly (the *Etats-Généraux*), the monarch himself was the fountain-head of all power — judicial, legislative and executive. This was particularly the case in the seventeenth and eighteenth centuries, when the monarchy is usually described as absolute. It was in 1789, even before the drafting of a new constitution, that different approaches to government were envisaged, specifically in the *Déclaration des droits de l'homme et du citoyen* (26 August 1789). This laid down a number of basic principles, which future governments would have to bear in mind. It declared that all men were equal before the law and that they had certain rights, such as freedom of thought, whether written or spoken, freedom of the person, the right to resist oppression, the right to own property. At the same time the political rights of the citizens were also defined, i.e. to be involved in the making of laws, directly or by representatives. The fundamental point was made that sovereignty (and hence authority) resided in the nation, consequently, any authority which did not explicitly emanate from the nation could not be exercised by any one individual or group. These statements were from this time on regarded as fundamental, at least in theory, for any constitution and the government which it established.

Between 1789 and 1799 there were a number of fairly short-lived governments, starting off with an ill-starred attempt at a modified monarchy, and thereafter a republic was established under varying forms. It is from 1799 that a clearer picture begins to emerge of French political tradition which, on the basis of her history since the revolutionary decade, and in the terms of the nature of government, has two essential aspects which are undoubtedly paradoxical, if not mutually exclusive, since they concern parliamentary government on the one hand, and authoritarian government on the other. The French parliamentary tradition derives initially in the nineteenth century from two attempts to establish a constitutional monarchy (on the British pattern, where the monarch's powers are very much reduced as compared with the eighteenth-century absolute monarchy). These two attempts, the Bourbon Restoration (1814-30), and the July Monarchy (1830-48) where the Orleans dynasty (younger Bourbon line) was brought to the throne, both failed, and were each brought to an end by a revolution, in 1830 and in 1848. The third attempt at parliamentary government was that of the Third Republic, which was born out of military disaster in 1870, gave itself a set of laws providing for parliamentary government in 1875, and fell in 1940, again as a result of foreign invasion. A further attempt at parliamentary government was made with the creation of the Fourth Republic, which, unlike its predecessor, lasted only twelve years (1946-58).

The second tradition may be described as authoritarian, where most of the power is in the hands of the executive, and where power of the legislature is weak or merely fictional. It could be said with justification that this tradition originates with the absolute monarchy of pre-Revolutionary days, but it is essentially to be seen in the régimes headed by the two Bonapartes. These were the consulate (1799-1804) and the empire (1804-14) of Napoleon Bonaparte: also (to a lesser extent), the Second Republic (1848-52), of which Napoleon's nephew, Louis Napoleon Bonaparte, was president; and the Second Empire (1852-70) in which he took the title of Napoleon III. In each case, the legislature was weak, and the powers of the executive were strengthened by the use of what was then known as a plebiscite (now called a referendum) – an appeal to the people on specific issues, like the establishment of a new régime (which often meant the ratification of a *coup d'état*), or some important change to be made to already existing institutions. The powers of the executive were also strengthened in the Second Republic by the election of the president of the republic by universal manhood suffrage. The use of the plebiscite conferred on these authoritarian régimes an aura of democracy. An appeal to the people, in itself democratic, could be and was used to bolster up régimes which, to a considerable extent, did not accord to the nation at large the basic freedoms as laid down in the *Déclaration des droits de l'homme et du citoyen*.[1]

As far as the form of government is concerned, the French tradition is more straightforward. We have seen that the attempts in the thirty years following Napoleon's reign to establish a constitutional monarchy were unsuccessful, partly because the members of the lower house of parliament (*chambre des députés*) were elected by a fraction of the population, but also because, in their different ways, the monarchs exercised more power than the constitution gave them, and than was consonant with the role of constitutional monarch; hence the use by some experts of the term 'Orleanist' to describe a constitutional head of state who exercised improperly wide powers. It is also a fact that the early attempts to form a republic failed, particularly in terms of durability. The First Republic came under the influence of varying political factions from 1792 onwards, only to end up as the authoritarian consulate of Napoleon Bonaparte. The Second Republic had an even shorter life, being killed off by its first president, Louis Napoleon, who felt that it did not give him adequate powers to govern effectively. The third attempt, the Third Republic, was much more successful in terms of length, and it can be said that this long-lasting, if rather unspectacular, régime consolidated the republican tradition in France. Yet it was republicanism of a parliamentary type (unlike the Second Republic, where the powers of the single deliberative body, the *assemblée nationale*, and of the president had been almost equally weighted); but added to it was universal manhood suffrage, in the election of its representatives.

The situation of the *président de la république* in the Third Republic was unusual, in that his powers were substantial, prior to the voting of the constitutional laws of 1875 which reduced them somewhat; although he still had the task of selecting the *président du conseil* (head of government). However, amongst the ceremonial and formal powers of the president (henceforth to be elected by the two houses of parliament) was one which should have given him some political influence. This was article 5 of the law of 25 February 1875, which gave the president, with the senate's (upper house's) agreement, the power to dissolve the *chambre des députés* (lower house) before the expiry of its mandate. Unfortunately, the second president of the republic, Marshal MacMahon, a royalist, chose to exercise this right against an increasingly republican *chambre des députés* on 16 May 1877 – circumstances which gave rise to such controversy that no president ever dared to use the powers of dissolution again. The significance of this is twofold: first, it gave rise, during the Third Republic, to great ministerial instability, given the number of political parties and the consequent need for coalition governments, since the right of dissolution had been intended as a weapon against the irresponsible overturning of cabinets. Every time a ministry was defeated and had to resign, there ought to have been a general election, when the deputies would have had to face their electorates; but since the right of dissolution was never used, this did not happen. Furthermore, the weakness of the president's powers meant that, in the main, those who sought the office tended not to be men of great personality or of authority. Any attempt to strengthen the office was stifled by parliament, and presidents who attempted to use wider powers were pressurized out of office by an outraged parliament.[2] As it was, the assumption tended to be that the president had no real powers; and at a moment of crisis, the president was left, rightly or wrongly, with an impression of total helplessness.

It would nevertheless be unfair to suggest that the Third Republic fell only because its institutions were at fault; however, the débâcle of 1940 did permit General de Gaulle to press for a very different type of constitution to be set up after the liberation. His concept of the ideal constitution for France was outlined in his speech at Bayeux, 16 June 1946, where he laid the blame for a number of France's problems squarely at the door of the political parties, whose disagreements had caused the national interest to suffer, giving rise inevitably to a lack of respect on the part of the French for their institutions. These therefore should be changed. His demands boiled down to two essential requirements: a strong executive (head of state) with wide powers, elected by a large electoral college (not merely the two houses of parliament), and the separation of executive, legislative and judicial powers. A further requirement stemmed from the separation of powers, namely that the powers of the executive should not, as had been the case in the Third Republic, proceed from the legislature (*président du conseil*, supported by a majority of the *chambre des députés; président de la république*, elected by the two houses of parliament).

These views were not heeded, and the Fourth Republic was established with a constitution very like that of the Third, providing for a head of state elected by the two houses of parliament, with powers which made of him merely a figurehead, the real power still remaining in the hands of the legislature. It was not until 1958, when the Fourth Republic virtually ground to a halt over the Algerian crisis, that de Gaulle had an opportunity to put his constitutional ideas into effect, and the constitution of the Fifth Republic was adopted by a large majority at the referendum of 28 September 1958 (17,668,790 in favour; 4,624,511 against; 4,016,614 abstentions).

Since that time, the Fifth Republic has given proof of its stability. Of all the régimes which have governed France since the Revolution of 1789, only the Third Republic lasted longer. It could be alleged that this stability stems in part from the continuity provided by the Fifth Republic's first three presidents: de Gaulle, Pompidou and, to a lesser degree, Giscard d'Estaing, shared broadly the same political standpoint. At all event, the right and centre in coalition held power in France for the best part of twenty-three years. No *alternance* was to occur until the election of F. Mitterrand in May 1981, and the subsequent election in June of an *assemblée nationale*, where the socialists gained an overall majority. Yet if the transfer of power from right to left has taken place so smoothly, after so long a dominance by the former, it must be admitted that the institutions of the Fifth Republic have proved their efficacy.

The constitution of the Fifth Republic provides for a lower house (*assemblée nationale*), an upper house (*sénat*), a prime minister and a president of the republic with very wide powers. First of all, his role is defined: 'le Président de la République veille au respect de la Constitution. Il assure, par son arbitrage, le fonctionnement régulier des pouvoirs publics ainsi que la continuité de l'Etat. Il est le garant de l'indépendance nationale, de l'intégrité du territoire, du respect des accords de Communauté et des traités' (article 5). This definition is important, because any incumbent of the presidency has a reasonably clear idea as to the extent of his role, and it is in order that he may carry out this task, that powers are allotted to him which presidents of the Third and Fourth Republics did not possess. He has, for example, the power to put to a referendum a proposed piece of legislation, thereby by-passing parliament – the normal law-making body (article 11). He also has the right to dissolve the *assemblée nationale* (article 12) and finally, the right to take special powers in moments of crisis (article 16). These powers represent a very substantial advance on those enjoyed by earlier presidents. Other, more ceremonial powers, remain much the same as for earlier presidents, such as the promulgation (official publication) of laws, and, if deemed necessary, the right to ask parliament to reconsider legislation which it has just passed (article 10), the appointment to civil and military posts in the state, the signing of ordinances and decrees (article 13), the accrediting of ambassadors (article 14) and the prerogative of mercy (article 17). Clearly the president of the Fifth Republic is no longer merely a constitutional head of state – that part of the executive dealing only with ceremonial, what Walter Bagehot would call 'the dignified parts of government', but a head of state who is politically active as well – a key figure in the 'efficient parts' of government.

As the president of the republic's powers have increased, so the role of parliament has been reduced, having suffered under the Fifth Republic what has been described as a 'constitutional assault'.[3] Very precise measures were introduced into the constitution to ensure that the political parties (and, hence, parliament) should no longer hold supreme political power. It is stated in the constitution, for example (article 34), that parliament votes the law, which is then defined in detail. This has a limiting effect, since anything outside the definition given is also outside parliament's competence, particularly when it is made clear (article 37) that matters not comprised within the definition of 'law' have a 'caractère règlementaire', which means that a minister may deal with them, without the need for parliamentary scrutiny. Furthermore, the existence of the *conseil constitutionnel* with powers to decide whether or not (a) a specific subject comes within the definition of 'law', (b) legislation passed by parliament is constitutional, and (c) the election of deputies has been conducted in a proper manner, limits the powers of parliament to conduct its own affairs.

Although in formal terms the government is still responsible to parliament, that responsibility has clearly been attenuated by the provisions of the constitution — representing an unequivocal endeavour by de Gaulle and his advisers in 1958 to reduce the extent of ministerial instability which had bedevilled the coalition ministries of the Third and Fourth Republics. A new prime minister, appointed by the president, seeks a vote of confidence from the *assemblée nationale*, on his political programme. As for censure motions, it is explicitly stated that a censure motion must be signed by at least one-tenth of the members of the *assemblée*, and the vote takes place forty-eight hours later. The only votes counted are those which support the motion (i.e. abstentions are counted as being favourable to the government), and there has to be a majority, not merely of those voting, but of all members of the *assemblée nationale*. Those who signed the motion may not sign another in that same parliamentary session. The prime minister may also ask for a vote of confidence on a specific text, which is considered as adopted unless a censure motion is proposed within the following twenty-four hours and a vote taken thereon as already indicated. It is clear enough that considerable obstacles are put in the way of any *assemblée nationale* wishing to bring down a government: the very precise nature of the procedure to follow, the required lapses of time, the requirement that ten per cent of deputies sign the motion, that they may not sign another in that session, all this means that the opposition, by definition more likely to oppose government policies, and also by definition in a minority, would have to be careful not to fritter away its numbers in vain attempts. The success of this in terms of governmental stability is that only one censure motion has ever been passed in the twenty-year life of the Fifth Republic — on 5 October 1962, when G. Pompidou's government was brought down over de Gaulle's decision to put to referendum the proposed election of the president of the republic by universal suffrage.[4]

In the Fifth Republic's constitution, we have seen that a very decided (and successful) attempt was made to cut down the powers of the parties. It may be asserted that, in support of this, an attempt was also made to deal with what was viewed as the excessive number of parties at source in the electoral legislation. During the Fourth Republic a form of proportional representation obtained. This system, thought to be too favourable to the existence of numerous parties, was altered in 1958 to one in which voters, instead of voting for several candidates, could vote only for one. If a successful candidate has an absolute majority (i.e. more than the total votes gained by his rivals), he is elected *député*. If, however, the majority is only relative, then there is a further vote in which those candidates who have gained votes totalling a minimum of 12.5 per cent of the number of registered voters, may stand again for election. In this election, a relative majority is sufficient to be elected *député*. It is at this point that parties in alliance may agree on a policy of *désistement*, whereby one unsuccessful candidate may stand down in favour of another and encourage his supporters to cast their votes in the latter's favour. One further innovation is the requirement that each candidate supply himself with a *suppléant*, to take over the *député's* seat in parliament, in the event of death, or resignation, thereby preventing by-elections. However, the principal reason for this innovation was the constitutions's insistence on the incompatibility of the office of minister and that of *député*. Any *député* acceding to ministerial office must give up his seat in parliament to his *suppléant*. Such a constitutional requirement is the logical consequence of the separation of legislative and executive powers, and, while it may shed a vivid light on the nature of the Fifth Republic's government, it causes no little inconvenience to the professional politician who, when giving up office, must either wait until the next general elections, or prevail upon his *suppléant* to resign in order that a by-election may be held, which virtually nullifies the principle of incompatibility.[5]

While the electoral system as put into effect under de Gaulle was clearly designed to control the power of parliament, later changes have put that design into some doubt. The first, under Giscard, was the law of 7 July 1977 which provided for elections of the French representatives to the European parliament to take place on the basis of proportional representation. It has been suggested by J. Hayward that had Giscard chosen to bring in proportional representation also for the legislative elections, his chances of reconstituting the centre alliance would have been greater, and his own position strengthened thereby. However, he chose not to do so, and it was not until the Mitterrand presidency that further proportional representation was introduced for municipal elections in towns with a population of 3,500 inhabitants or more. This tendency to return to proportional representation makes it more likely that in due course this electoral system will also be reintroduced for the legislative elections. There has been a good deal of discussion about such a possibility, which is not now likely to be brought in before 1986 (i.e. before the end of the present parliament). Yet such a change could have very significant consequences for the party system which at present obtains in France.

The provisions of the constitution, together with the electoral law, make parliament a much less powerful body than in the past. As a consequence, the nature of the régime is a matter for a great deal of discussion, as to whether it is essentially parliamentary or presidential. The views of the opposition (the left) have been consistent in condemning what they see as the anti-parliamentary nature of the régime (see, for a typical example, pp. 150–2 of the *Programme commun*, Paris, Editions Sociales, 1972). The principal architect of the constitution, Michel Debré, denies this categorically: 'Si les gaullistes . . . condamnent le régime représentatif, ils ne sont pas hostiles au régime parlementaire . . . les constituants de 1958 ont voulu rénover, en France, le régime parlementaire.'[6] It has however been suggested that the election of the president by universal suffrage, approved by referendum in 1962, marked a profound change in the nature of the régime. Nevertheless the change, in his view, does not mean that the prime minister, whose duties are defined in article 21, is stripped of power, but rather that a dyarchy (rule of two) is created – an opinion roundly denied by de Gaulle in his press conference of 31 January 1964 where, in describing the respective duties of president and prime minister, he implied that while the former indicated the outlines of policy, it was the latter's task to put this into effect. However, if we look at the way in which the president appoints and dismisses the prime minister, it may be possible to establish the relative powers of each, and hence the nature of the régime. In a purely parliamentary régime, the choice of prime minister is, as a rule, a very straightforward one: either he is the elected leader of the majority party (in a two-party system), or else he is the accepted leader of a coalition (in a multi-party system, either by presidential choice, thereafter ratified by parliament, or simply by an agreement between the parties concerned).

The prime minister in the Fifth Republic is only very rarely the party leader (as in the case of J. Chirac, who became leader of the Gaullist party while prime minister, but resigned the post with the explicit approval of the president). He is, as a rule, one of the party's leaders – possible exceptions here being Pompidou and Raymond Barre, the latter chosen more for his economic expertise than for his influence in any party. Since the Gaullists were the majority party (with or without allies) for over twenty years, it should theoretically have been possible (barring death or other incapacity) for the same individual to have held the post of prime minister for the whole of that time. This would be technically feasible in a parliamentary situation if one party remained in the majority throughout, and should, on the face of it, be equally possible in the Fifth Republic. Article 8 of the constitution concerning the appointment of the prime minister is couched as follows: 'Le président de la République nomme le Premier ministre. Il met fin à ses fonctions sur la présentation par celui-ci de la démission du gouvernement. Sur la proposition du Premier ministre, il nomme les autres membres du gouvernement et met fin à leurs fonctions.' A strict reading of this text implies that the president of the republic merely receives the prime minister's resignation, but does not provoke it. The only reference to the cause of a resignation is to be found in article 50, which indicates that if a censure motion is passed, or if there is formal disapprobation by the *assemblée nation-*

ale of government policy, then the prime minister and his government must resign. The theoretical inference, in strict terms, is clear: only the *assemblée nationale* can bring down a government. Furthermore, during the elaboration of the constitution in 1958, on 8 August, de Gaulle categorically denied that the president of the republic could dismiss the prime minister (see *Avis et débats du Comité consultatif constitutionnel*, Paris, Documentation française, 1960, p. 118). It is also a fact that proposals tending to permit the dismissal of the prime minister were not accepted. By 1964, however, de Gaulle, in his press conference, made it perfectly clear that the president could not only choose the prime minister, but change him when necessary (press conference, 31 January 1964), and a similar line was taken by President Pompidou during his term of office.

The practice of dismissing prime ministers has tended to follow the 1964 rather than the 1958 pattern. The exchange of letters between president and premier makes it clear that if one sticks rigidly to the texts, the following points emerge: that the resignation of M. Debré was the result of a 'gentleman's agreement' arrived at beforehand between president and prime minister; that General de Gaulle dismissed Pompidou but wished it to appear as if he had not done so; that Chaban-Delmas was dismissed by the president; and, finally, that Chirac felt that he had insufficient powers to carry out his task and therefore asked to be released from office.[7] In none of these cases was parliament in any way involved. It is noticeable, on the contrary, that in the case of Chaban-Delmas, the prime minister had been at pains to obtain a vote of confidence from the *assemblée nationale*; noticeable also that a successor was appointed during the summer recess, and that parliament had no opportunity to discuss the change until the beginning of the next parliamentary session.

It must be evident from these instances therefore, that although the prime minister may be said to have a formal and limited responsibility to parliament in the Fifth Republic, the bulk of his responsibility is towards the president who appoints and dismisses him. Clearly common sense would indicate the difficulty, in practical terms, of two men working closely together if one is uncongenial to the other; but it is not a problem which must be reckoned with in parliamentary government, where the head of state must put up with whatever the majority sends him. It is indeed an indication of how far the régime has travelled since 1958.

The government, as a consequence of the incompatibility principle, must depend much more on the support of the president than on that of parliament. Those who become ministers may have been *députés* but, in certain fields, are just as likely to be 'technocrats', for example in foreign affairs, where career diplomats have frequently been appointed (MM. Couve de Murville, Sauvagnargues, de Guiringaud) and in education, where academics with a career in administration have been appointed (R. Haby, A. Saunier-Seïté). This can be looked upon as a new departure, a step into the technocratic age, or as one more link with tradition (either pre-Revolutionary or Bonapartist), where experts were very often chosen to act as ministers and to aid the sovereign.

One further point must be mentioned, since it is furiously debated prior to every general (legislative) election. What happens if the president of the republic and the parliamentary majority are of different political persuasions; in other words, which expression of public opinion is to be taken as predominant? De Gaulle's answer to the problem was straightforward — the threat (or promise) of his resignation if he did not receive adequate support. Pompidou's response was rather more drastic in his press conference of 21 September 1972 (see *Le Monde*, 23 September 1972) where he made it clear that in the event of an electoral victory of the unified left, he would not call upon its leaders to form a government, and that if the government which he chose (presumably a minority one) were overturned, he would dissolve the *assemblée nationale*. V. Giscard d'Estaing's answer to the problem has been decidedly more subtle, namely to indicate that he would fulfil his term of office and put into effect the programme of the majority, a position which has been described as a *coup d'état*, in comparison with the attitude of his predecessors.[8]

The position of F. Mitterrand in relation to the rôle of the presidency is a curious one. His general attitude while in opposition was invariably critical of the Fifth Republic's institutions, to such an extent that one commentator has described as 'une sorte d'aversion viscérale envers le style et les moeurs gaullistes' (P. Valadier, 'François Mitterrand — des idées politiques pour prendre le pouvoir' in *Projet*, no. 170, December 1982, p. 1176). Since coming to power, however, he is on record as having stated that he would exercise to the full the powers accorded to him by the Constitution (see *Le Monde*, 2 July 1981). Thus it is that in the matter of relations between presidency and parliament, he has adopted a more Gaullian stance than his immediate predecessor. This is most clearly evidenced in the dissolution of the *assemblée nationale* by Mitterrand as soon as he assumed office (22 May 1981), in the (fulfilled) hope of obtaining a majority sympathetic to his political programme, which, given the scope of the reforms already initiated and of those still in preparation, he undoubtedly needed.

The use of article 12 by Mitterrand in this instance makes it as clear as ever that in the event of a disagreement between president and parliament, the former still has the whip hand, since he can dissolve the *assemblée nationale* if he so chooses. While it may be true, therefore, to say that the constitution of the Fifth Republic may be read as a parliamentary one, it could equally be suggested that this has scarcely been the case in reality as yet. From 1958 up to the time of writing, parliament and president have been fundamentally of the same political persuasion, and there has as yet been no opportunity to find out how the machinery of the constitution would function if the president and the majority in the *assemblée nationale* and in the *sénat* were to be politically opposed. On the other hand, another interpretation would indicate that the reliance of successive presidents on a sympathetic parliamentary majority makes clear where a substantial degree of power still lies.

As well as ambiguity in practice, there is clearly a good deal of ambiguity in the very text of the constitution itself, which makes a conclusion on its nature difficult to arrive at. The case of article 8 has already been mentioned. Ministerial responsibility (to parliament), always the hallmark of a parliamentary government, is only mentioned in relation to its very limited application of articles 49 and 50. The president of the republic, however, is said, by virtue of article 68, not to be responsible for actions committed by him during his term of office − except in the case of high treason. The political irresponsibility of the head of state is again the characteristic of a parliamentary government, but, as we know, in the Fifth Republic the president has wide powers bestowed upon him, and, in eight cases (articles 8, 11, 12, 16, 18, 54, 56 and 61) acts without the need of ministerial counter-signature. What is the reason for this ambiguity, which is to be found in the constitution's text rather than in its practice? The answer seems to have been one of political expediency in 1958, since, although at that time the constitutional ideas of de Gaulle were paramount, and those of Debré exceedingly influential, there were other parliamentarians who played a part in the discussions.[9] It can therefore be assumed that, although many of them wished to see the establishment of a more stable government, they might have considered de Gaulle's ideal régime as going too far in the anti-parliamentary direction, and that consequently a certain amount of 'masking' of de Gaulle's ultimate intentions was necessary.

> Certains d'entre nous dans les premières années de la Ve République, se sont parfois étonnés, devant le général de Gaulle, de ce qu'il ait accepté une Constitution plus traditionnellement parlementaire que ce qu'auraient normalement comporté ses prises de position antérieures et sa volonté bien actuelle d'affirmer l'autorité du Président . . . les explications données tournaient toujours autour de deux pôles: les milieux politiques y auraient vu du bonapartisme et le pays n'aurait pas compris. (B. Tricot *et al.*, *De Gaulle et le service de l'état*, p. 148)

Apart therefore from analyses of stronger presidential and weaker parliamentary powers, the controversial use of article 11 in 1962, the subsequent election of the president by universal suffrage, de Gaulle's admission allows us to put aside the 'Orleanist' interpretation, even for the period of 1958–62. It can be said that a substantially wider suffrage (*notables* plus parliament = 80–100,000 electors) represents a step towards universal suffrage; but, more crucially, as Léon Blum foresaw, the logic of the 'Bayeux system' meant inevitably a recourse to universal suffrage to elect a *président de la république*, to whom such wide powers would be given (see *Le Populaire*, 21 June 1946) – much wider powers than those enjoyed by even an 'Orleanist' constitutional monarch. The comparison which springs inevitably to mind is that between the president of the Fifth Republic and Napoleon III, as he would have been, had the Liberal Empire of 1870 not been swept away by the Franco-Prussian war. Provision was made specifically for responsible ministers, but the emperor still retained the right to appeal to the people via a plebiscite. Thus we may consider the Fifth Republic an undoubted descendent of the authoritarian/plebiscitarian tradition rather than of parliamentary government.

One further possibility has been suggested:

> Les constituants (of 1958) ont voulu que la Constitution puisse faire l'objet de plusieurs 'lectures' différentes. En fonction de la personnalité du Président de la République et de celle du Premier Ministre, de la composition politique de l'Assemblée nationale et même du Sénat, de la concordance entre la majorité parlementaire et la majorité présidentielle, la Constitution établit un régime qui peut être soit plutôt présidentiel, soit plutôt parlementaire. (J. -L. Debré, *La Constitution de la Ve République*, p. 327)

The very fact that the constitution of the Fifth Republic apparently lends itself to so many interpretations, is in itself a factor of arbitrariness and hence a link with the authoritarian tradition, since the president may decide as he sees fit how he will interpret the constitution's description of his powers. Far from being a factor of stability, such a situation could, in the long run, prove to be a danger at the moment when one interpretation supersedes another, possibly giving rise, not merely to theoretical controversy, but to political and civil strife in a country which easily accepts the legitimacy of revolution and the rise and fall of governments.

(2) Aspects of central government

The foregoing conclusion, arrived at almost exclusively on theoretical grounds, may be considered, for that reason alone, suspect. Since an interpretation of the theory suggests that the Fifth Republic is essentially presidential rather than parliamentary, more concrete proof ought to be adduced as well. This section will therefore attempt to focus on areas of the governmental machine which indicate this tendency.

It is perhaps worth noting in this context the fact that the deputy is no longer regarded by the general public as the all-powerful figure that he had been in the Third and Fourth Republics. (P. Birnbaum, *Les Sommets de l'état*, p. 79)

Like the simple deputy, parliament also has been stripped of power. The constitutional restrictions on her role have already been noted, but there are other practical restrictions which have been imposed by government regulations. For example, parliamentary sessions, two per year, now have a maximum life of ninety days each, which in fact means that there is invariably insufficient time to cope with legislation; this leads to undue haste and poorly drafted texts. The government decides on the day's business in both houses, the *ordre du jour*, with the opposition having no say in the matter; and it may also force on the *assemblée nationale* a single vote on the text which it has proposed, together with such amendments which it has suggested itself, or of which it approves. This reduces the power of both houses of parliament materially to affect government proposals during their legislative passage. Parliament's power of amendment is also restricted by article 40 of the constitution which disallows any amendment tending to reduce public resources (i.e. taxation) or implying the creation or increase of public expenditure. The idea behind this provision was clearly to deny deputies the possibility of demagogic gestures designed to appeal to their constituents, as well as to embarrass the government. While a measure of this kind could possibly be viewed as an aid to efficiency in the dispatch of government business, its interpretation may give rise to restrictions of the most ludicrous kind.[10]

Proposed legislation must be debated not only in parliament as a whole, but by one of six permanent committees: *commission des finances; commission des affaires étrangères; commission de la défense nationale; commission des lois* (dealing with legal and administrative questions); *commission des affaires culturelles, familiales et sociales; commission de la production et des échanges*. This system is unsatisfactory, since the committees are too large, some of them having well over one hundred members. Also, parliament is required to debate, not the draft legislation as amended by the appropriate committee, but the government's original version, which makes a mockery of the committee's labours. In the case of the budget also, parliament's rights are restricted: if the budget has not been passed in seventy days, the government can enact it by ordinance. Again, the amount of legislation to be dealt with in the short parliamentary sessions, makes proper parliamentary supervision impossible.

Yet with the maintenance, albeit in reduced form, of the government's responsibility to parliament, there must still be at least a measure of lip-service paid to that concept. Consequently, the government must keep parliament informed of its activities, either by statements to parliament, or by the method of parliamentary questions, whether oral or written. The use of questions requiring written answers is extensive, but the possibilities of parliamentary power in question time have not been exploited. As V. Wright has indicated (p. 138), deputies seem resigned to the fact that government pays little heed to their queries, and they themselves do not react firmly enough when the government acts in a way which improperly reduces parliamentary control over government. This, together with the legitimate methods used by government to restrict parliament's powers, is quite sufficient to engender in the deputies 'désaffection et désengagement à l'égard du rôle national' (see J.-C. Masclet, *Un député pourquoi faire?* Paris, PUF, 1982, pp. 181–6).

Many of these problems arose, however, as a result of the long pre-dominance in parliament of the Gaullists and their allies. Slightly more heed had to be paid to parliament during the presidency of Giscard d'Estaing. Some of his reforms suffered as a result of this, notably the imposition of a capital gains tax. Furthermore, the power of parliament to set up *ad hoc* commissions of enquiry (*commissions d'enquête* or *commissions de contrôle*) has performed a necessary service in bringing various types of malpractice into the open. Since the advent of Mitter-rand, the situation has reverted more to what it was under the first two presidencies. If anything, the tendency has been towards an increase of presidentialism.

In this respect, there is little if any fundamental change, and it is clear that the executive continues to enjoy wide powers which have resulted in a corresponding reduction in those of parliament. Even within the domain of law, as defined by article 34 of the constitution, the voting of *lois cadres* (laws indicating tendencies and principles) is often couched in the most general of terms. These can only be put into effect by the use of ministerial decrees which provide in detail instructions as to how the law is to be implemented, and consequently leave to the government, in the person of the appropriate minister, substantial interpretative powers as well as the faculty to choose when (or if) the law should be brought into effect. The complexity of the budget has given rise to an analogous process of *debudgetization*, which has taken certain areas of public spending out of the budget and consequently away from parlia-mentary surveillance, such as it is.

The government, thus, is powerful in relation to the body to which, in theory, it is responsible, and which has only once succeeded in overturning it, according to the terms of article 49. What must now be considered is the extent to which anything resembling cabinet government exists, i.e. to what extent there is any ministerial soli-darity or cabinet responsibility, which is assumed to exist in any British government (leaks and political memoirs apart).

The first point to consider is how ministers are chosen. In theory, the president of the Republic appoints the prime minister, who then chooses his ministerial team. In practice, the prime minister may well have imposed upon him by the president individuals whom he personally would not have selected. A notable example here is that of Mme Françoise

Giroud, who, having made no secret of her support for Mitterrand in the presidential elections of 1974, was asked personally by Giscard to take on the post of *secrétaire d'état à la condition féminine* in J. Chirac's government. The counterpart of this direct presidential involvement in ministerial appointments has been seen under Mitterrand with the removal of J.-P. Cot as *ministre délégué auprès du ministre des relations extérieures, chargé de la coopération et du développement* on 9 December 1982 by the simple expedient of the Elysée spokesman's declaration that the post was vacant, without apparent reference to the prime minister. Equally, cabinet reshuffles may well take place on presidential instructions. Under Mitterrand's presidency, the need has also been felt to ensure that all political currents within the PS (not to mention the PCF) should receive some representation in the government (very much as in the days of Giscard, when various centrist groups would be represented).

In political terms therefore, there is no principle of unity which obtains. With the principle of incompatibility between the position of deputy and that of minister, the prime minister is no longer obliged to choose or appoint deputies or senators, and there has always been in the Fifth Republic a percentage of ministers without parliamentary experience at the time of their appointment, although they may attempt to have themselves elected thereafter.[11]

Consequently, the solidarity of the government as a whole is not great. While the prime minister is usually at the very least *primus inter pares*, there have been cases where specific ministers have been known to be influential, over and above their ministerial rôle, as in the case of M. Poniatowski, when he was interior minister in the Chirac cabinet. An analogous situation could be said to exist in the Mauroy government, in two forms: (a) with the existence of so-called 'super-ministries' such as that of the economy, finance and the budget, at present occupied by J. Delors, and (b) by the presence in the cabinet of a minister enjoying the confidence of the president in the presentation of legislation, however controversial. A case in point here is that of A. Savary, education minister (see chapter 6 for his proposals for private and higher education). Under the first three presidencies, the importance of the cabinet meeting seems to have been slight. There was apparently little discussion — a prerequisite for decision-making. It was possible for ministers to intervene outside the area of their own competence, but few did so. F. Giroud's own description of cabinet meetings makes them sound unutterably boring.[12] She also indicates that when ministers had proposals to make, these had to be submitted to the prime minister, to the president, and to any relevant minister, in advance. Where texts were to be considered, or read out, these too were invariably handed out in advance. This seems to have changed for the better since 1981, with freer discussion and more participation by all ministers. Yet all ministers do not automatically attend cabinet meetings; since 1977 the *secrétaires d'état* are briefed by the *garde des Sceaux* on the proceedings.

However, there are other meetings, which may be clearly regarded as organs of decision-making. Apart from the regular meetings between president and prime minister, the former has similar sessions with the other senior ministers, of external relations, finance, and interior. There are also three further types of meeting: (1) *interdepartmental committees*, attended by senior civil servants from the ministries and chaired by one of the prime minister's own officials; (2) *interministerial committees*, with the prime minister in the chair, composed of ministers and possibly some senior officials, plus representatives from the president's own staff; (3) *interministerial council* or *conseil restreint*, chaired by the president of the republic, where the principal decisions are taken. These states are progressively used, if agreement has not otherwise been reached at an earlier stage. Such a system also means that it is possible for a prime minister to leave out a colleague whose presence is not thought desirable at certain meetings.

United, the ministers would seem to enjoy little influence on general lines of policy; within their own ministries, and at the head of their own civil service, at the centre and in the provinces they are relatively powerful figures. The minister is a member of the government, and as such he must make the needs of his ministry known to the president, as well as parliament. He is also at the head of his ministry, aided by his own personal collaborators (*cabinet*).

Powerful though he may seem, the decentralization legislation of 1982-3 (see below, chapter 3, part 3) is in process of stripping the minister of part of his power. The *services extérieurs* – ministerial field services – will pass in due course to the control of the *commissaire de la République* (the *préfet*'s new title, taken from the revolutionary tradition of 1848, but a title which is never used). Equally, the change in the rôle of the *préfet*, whose executive powers in turn pass to the elected presidents of the *conseil général* and *conseil régional*, are intended in theory to reduce centralization, and in so doing, to cut down on the power of the ministers in the provinces.

There are other areas too where the power of all ministers is limited, by their financial means, and their wishes are often blocked by the finance ministry, known until April 1978 as the *ministère de l'économie et des finances*. The problem relates specifically to the budget, over which many conflicts have arisen between the finance ministry and the spending ministries, for example education and agriculture. The preparation of the budget is a lengthy process, carried out initially by the directorates of forecasting and the budget (*directions de prévision et du budget*). In the budget directorate, work on the budget begins over a year earlier in November, the calculations being based on the previous year's budget, and on the one actually in operation. The forecasting directorate begins its preparation about the same time, and the first phase of its operations lasts about three months, during which it considers all possibilities, relating to the international situation as well as the state of the national economy. Both directorates present their findings to the minister in March, which gives him the material necessary to begin the first discussions on the contents of the finance bill. Once the government's priorities have been established, there follows possibly the most difficult period, between April and July, when discussions are held between the finance minister and the various spending ministries over running costs. It is at this stage that disputes may well have to go to the arbitration of the prime minister, if officials cannot solve them. The outstanding problems then go before the prime minister, the finance minister, and the relevant spending minister, and the prime minister's decision is final, although an appeal may be made by either side to the president of the republic. In the vast majority of conflicts, it is the finance minister's case which prevails.

While the finance ministry has been accused of inordinate conservatism, which has caused many proposals of reform to be stillborn, its position has perhaps been less assured during the Fifth Republic than under the Fourth. The reason is not hard to find; although de Gaulle may not have been interested primarily in economic and financial matters, they were always of interest to Pompidou; the same can equally well be said of Giscard as a former finance minister, and of Barre, who was chosen as prime minister by the president specifically for his economic expertise. Yet J. Hayward[13] suggests that the finance minister had regained a considerable part of his former powers because of the emphasis between 1963 and 1966 on the need for a balanced budget. It is true that every ministry has within it an official appointed by the finance minister, whose task is to exercise a preventive control over the ministry's expenditure. This is beneficial as far as 'good housekeeping' is concerned, but has caused the finance ministry to be considered as inordinately rigid and excessively conservative.

This was the position when, in April 1978 after the legislative elections, with the formation of Barre's ministry, the finance ministry was split in two, one part becoming the *ministère du budget*, under M. Papon, and the other, the *ministère de l'économie*, under R. Monory.

The size of the ministry seems to have been one of the reasons behind the change, since the number of principal directorates within the ministry, twelve in number, increased the possibility of blocking proposals either before their realization, or once work was in progress. The other reason for dividing the finance ministry may have been also to render it more vulnerable to pressure from the prime minister, Raymond Barre, whereas, as a single ministry, it was able to wield more influence. The present rearrangement conserves something of the division: J. Delors is now minister of the economy, finance and the budget, but there is a *secrétaire d'état*, at present H. Emmanuelli, who has specific responsibility for the budget. This latter post is an important one, since it comprises within it four powerful directorates: *direction du budget, direction générale des douanes et droits indirect, direction des impôts*, and *direction de la compatabilité publique* (public accounting). Up to now, this arrangement has not necessarily resulted in a unified ministry, and the ministry did not speak with a single voice on economic matters, where Delors and L. Fabius (Emmanuelli's predecessor) were by no means always in full agreement in their public pronouncements.

Two other bodies whose existence tend to shed doubt on the parliamentary nature of the Fifth Republic are respectively the *conseil d'état* and the *conseil constitutionnel*.

The former of these is a Napoleonic creation of 1799 – a renewed version of the pre-revolutionary *conseil du roi*. It had not only administrative and judicial functions in this early period, but also a legislative one, since it was consulted on the drafting of proposed legislation, and was responsible for the drafting of all the organic laws, as well as of the *code civil*.

The present functions of the *conseil d'état* are essentially of two kinds, consultative and judicial. The consultative functions are undertaken by the administrative sections – finance, interior, public works, and a section dealing with social questions. There is also a general assembly comprising all members, who meet at least once a week to consider and take a decision on the texts of draft bills, regulations, ordinances, as well as matters on which a separate section feels that further consideration is desirable. The consultative aspect of the *conseil d'état* is completed by the existence of a *commission permanente* which may pronounce on draft legislation in exceptional circumstances.

While the *conseil d'état* could be viewed as a body allied to the government whose powers impinged on those of parliament, the relations between it and the government were by no means cordial. De Gaulle was highly displeased with its ruling on his decision to use the referendum in 1962 to bring about a change in the election of the president of the republic, which he describes in his memoirs as 'abusive', since it permitted itself to pronounce a political judgment on his actions, instead of merely considering the appropriateness of the text itself. (It is also worth noting that it took the same line on de Gaulle's referendum in 1969.) The *conseil d'état* too may be seen as the protector of civil rights. Again, it incurred de Gaulle's wrath, when its judicial section pronounced the annulment of the military court which had been established in 1962 to try rapidly members of the OAS. One of these, M. Canal, was condemned to death by the court, and sought the ruling of the *conseil d'état*. The ordinance of 1 June 1962, setting up the military court, stated that there was to be no appeal against its ruling; it was for this reason that the decision of the *conseil d'état* was arrived at. In spite of de Gaulle's anger, there seems no reason to doubt that this was a totally unpolitical ruling on a matter of civil rights, and many of the judicial rulings of the *conseil d'état* deal with matters of this kind.

The creation of the *conseil constitutionnel* is a complete innovation, its essential task being to rule on the conformity of legislation to the constitution. It is composed normally of nine people – three appointed by the president of the republic and three each by the presidents of the two houses of parliament. Former presidents of the republic are members *ex officio*.

An appeal to the *conseil constitutionnel* for its decision (*saisine*) is provided for in the constitution, where it may be obligatory or voluntary, according to circumstances. Cases where an appeal is obligatory include regulations of parliament (by presidents of the two houses), organic laws (by the prime minister), the use of article 16 by the president of the republic, irregularity in legislative elections, where the matter may be taken up either by the justice minister or by the *bureau* of either house of parliament. Voluntary appeals to the *conseil constitutionnel* are concerned with ordinary legislation, and may be made by the president of the republic, the prime minister or the presidents of the national assembly and the senate. In 1974 this right was extended to groups of sixty deputies and senators, who now have also the right to query the constitutional propriety of legislation.

Initially, the decisions of the *conseil constitutionnel* were thought to be excessively timid, and orientated in favour of the government. Unlike the *conseil d'état*, it declared in 1962 that it did not have the competence to pronounce on de Gaulle's decision to put the election of the president of the republic to a referendum. Yet subsequently, its decisions were by no means pleasing to the government – notably on the question of modifying the arrangements for deputies and their *suppléants*, which failed since the *conseil* invariably maintained the principle of incompatibility existing between the position of minister and that of deputy.

Under Giscard's presidency, however, there were still criticisms made of its pro-government stance, notably in the matter of irregularity in elections. While the *conseil constitutionnel* has always declined to pronounce on the intervention of the president of the republic on the grounds that the head of state is responsible only to the *haute cour de justice*, it does have competence to decide on electoral irregularities committed by candidates or their supporters, and consequently it could be alleged that there is inequality as between government and opposition. Such was the view of Mitterrand himself (see *Le Monde* 20–1 August 1978), who wrote that he would prefer to see a non-political supreme court in charge of these matters. His criticism of the political tendency of the *conseil* was undoubtedly a fair one, the root cause being the lack of *alternance* between 1958 and 1981. Since nomination of members had for so long rested with the right, the political complexion of the *conseil* must inevitably seem suspect to the left, whether the question related to political questions of a controversial nature, such as the law on nationalization, which it considered twice, and which was modified in consequence, or to the propriety or otherwise, of an election. Yet even this situation is to be viewed as less invidious than that of the Fourth Republic, where parliament verified the legislative elections itself.

In the light of this cursory examination, is it possible to assess the tendency of the Fifth Republic? There is clearly no doubt as to the power of the state, particularly at the centre; whether the state will continue to wield power in the provinces remains to be seen. Furthermore, the state has at its service (and has had for two centuries and more) groups of highly trained officials, technocrats, capable of passing from one aspect of government to another, whether it be *conseil d'état*, or the central administration of a ministry. Equally, a large number of politicians have the same type of training, whether it be as members of the *inspectorat des finances*, *cour des comptes*, or other *grand corps*. We may therefore be justified in speaking of a political class which, by virtue of the *grandes écoles* and the *concours*, may be largely regarded as self-perpetuating.

If this is so, how may the Fifth Republic be regarded as presidential? It has been suggested, and rightly, that the president of the republic is not able to achieve all his policies, and that the state apparatus is by no means unified. Precisely the same comment could be made, for example, about the supposedly absolute monarchy of the *Ancien régime*, or the Second Empire, whether in its authoritarian or in its liberal phase. Another point which is regarded as significant, is that while the prime minister's staff is a relatively large one (at present over fifty persons), the president's is relatively small (forty-two, both civilian and military). Yet it should be remembered that initially the prime minister's task was to carry out in detail the policy outlined by the president. Even this emphasis has changed, however, and presidential involvement with specific policies and decisions is much more in evidence – inevitable when it is remembered that the present president and his two immediate predecessors have all had considerable ministerial experience. However it is possible to suggest that in the case of Mitterrand, the presidentialism of the régime has been further strengthened whether in relation to a weaker and more subordinate prime minister, or in terms of greater presidential control over the majority party (it is perhaps not without significance that L. Jospin, the PS secretary, is a regular attender of presidential breakfasts). It is clear that the stated wishes of the president take precedence over other legislative matters, which gives to him an initiative in this field hitherto the prerogative of the prime minister and the members of parliament. (See H. Portelli, 'Les Socialistes et l'exercice du pouvoir', in *Projet*, no 168, September–October 1982, pp. 922–31.) This being the case, there can be little doubt that political responsibility rests essentially with the president.

It is true that among the reforms which are at present either being debated or already in process of realization, there are a good many which could well be thought liberal in their inspiration. Yet it is perhaps worth noting that no attempt has been made to reform the constitution of the Fifth Republic (unless Mitterrand's stated preference for a single presidential mandate of seven years can be counted as a statement of intent). Possibly the scope and the controversial nature of much of the legislation render presidential authority even more necessary in the eyes of the government, in order that the changes be effected as soon as possible. Yet while it can be alleged that Mitterrand is not only continuing, but even increasing the presidentialism of his predecessors, the criticisms levelled against the Fifth Republic, under their auspices, will continue to be made during the Mitterrand presidency.

As well as political and administrative institutions at the centre and a network of personnel spreading over the whole of the country, the French state has a further string to its bow, in the shape of the use it can make of the mass media. This matter could well be regarded as a kind of appendix to the constitution, since, just as much as the latter, it confers power on the state – a power which régimes in the previous century did not enjoy – namely to communicate information and views immediately to the mass of the population. Such a technological advance may also subject the state to the temptation of abuse, of propaganda, hitherto impossible on such a vast scale. The use (or abuse) of these powers may provide yet another indication as to the essential nature of the Fifth Republic.

Censorship of the means of communication has a long history in France, dating back to the *Ancien Régime*. During the nineteenth century it existed to a greater or lesser degree, depending on the strength or tolerance of successive régimes. Yet the mass media have for long been subject to some control by the state. Before the Second World War, while a state monopoly existed in theory, private radio stations were allowed a measure of freedom to operate on a temporary basis. During the war all radio stations, whether privately run or state controlled, or, as in the occupied zone, taken over by the occupying power, suffered from their financial dependence on the authorities; in order to survive, they gave proof of their total docility by the constant broadcasting of propaganda. Such an experience was unfortunate for future developments, since it clearly indicated to postwar governments the political possibilities inherent in broadcasting, which they were consequently reluctant to let out of state control.

In 1945 the *Radiodiffusion-télévision française* (RTF) was established by decree which provided for a state monopoly responsible to the prime minister and the ministry of information. The RTF was headed by a *directeur général* appointed by the cabinet, and in practice was answerable to the information minister. Clearly, such a framework, together with financial dependence, and a lack of coherence in the administrative organization, meant that the RTF was very vulnerable to political pressure. Various attempts to reform the system were made during the Fourth Republic, but to no avail. However, the political pressures did not begin to make themselves felt until the Algerian war, when broadcasters came under strong pressure, if they advocated a political standpoint on the issue, which was hostile to the government. The broadcasting of news suffered, inasmuch as items relating to the Algerian war which were deemed embarrassing to the government, tended to be omitted.

It was evident that reform was necessary if broadcasting was in any way to revert to its role of honestly informing the public. The problem arose as to what mechanisms might ensure broadcasting integrity. One method might have been to authorize commercial broadcasting, which might have ensured genuine freedom of information, but was subject to other pressures which would not necessarily be calculated to maintain either a high standard of entertainment or the ideal of public service. This possibility was therefore not considered when a reform was introduced by ordinance in the early days of the Fifth Republic (4 February 1959).

Reform might indeed be regarded as too forceful a description, since the changes introduced were moderate. The RTF was henceforth to be a state establishment of an industrial and commercial nature, enjoying financial autonomy, since it would have its own budget. Yet the control of the state was still strong, as the RTF still came under the authority of the minister of information. It was, as before, to be headed by a *directeur général*, appointed by the *conseil des ministres*. While he was assumed to have charge of the organization and its personnel, he could not appoint his deputy, nor the directors of the various services, who were, like himself, appointed by the government. Political influence was equally evident in the two bodies set up to assist the *directeur général*. The *conseil supérieur* was made up of representatives of various ministries and the presidents of the specialized programme committees; the *comité de surveillance*, wherein were to be found parliamentarians and officials, only met at the request of the minister.

The involvement of the state became more evident in the early 1960s, when the numbers of people owning television sets began to rise (60,000 in 1954; one million in 1959; three millions in 1963), with the possibility which this factor bestowed on the government of exercising political persuasion over a substantial part of the population. De Gaulle himself was on the whole a notable television performer, and used his skill to the detriment of his political opponents and to the enhancing of his own relationship with the electorate. Television also provided him with yet another means of by-passing parliament, since important matters of policy could be announced directly to the nation, or to that portion of it that could afford television.

The problem which state control over the media provoked was that, with the Gaullists in power, the media were geared almost exclusively to the presentation of the Gaullist viewpoint, to the detriment of any equity or objectivity. While more autonomy for the RTF might have helped to correct the balance, there were financial and administrative difficulties. A further attempt was therefore made to reform the system by the law of 27 June 1964. Its main innovations were the transformation of the RTF into an *office*, no longer under the authority of the information ministry, but merely under its aegis (*tutelle*) and that of the finance ministry, and the setting up of a *conseil d'administration*, with half its members representing the state and half representing listeners, viewers, the press, and people working in the ORTF; they were to serve normally for a three-year period. They would elect a president and vice president from amongst their number. The tasks of the council were to define general policy, discuss the budget and see that it was put into effect, ensure the maintenance of quality and moral content in programmes, objectivity and accuracy of news and, in general, freedom of expression for the main tendencies of opinion and thought. As before, the men at the top, the *directeur général* and his deputies, were nominated by the government.

In terms of freedom of political expression, the reform changed nothing. The views of the government were still presented to the virtual exclusion of others, and journalists continued to lose their jobs because of their political views. Yet the political dangers to the ruling party itself do not seem to have been apparent until the presidential election of 1965. De Gaulle's poor performances at the first ballot clearly came as a shock to him. All candidates were allowed two hours' time on television in the fortnight before the elections, and some of his opponents, notably J. Lecanuet, proved more adroit than had been expected. De Gaulle, forced to descend from his Olympian approach of the first ballot, used all of his television time in the second, and adopting a different technique, he went on to win an adequate victory (55 per cent of the vote at the second ballot). Television, as well as being a new factor in electioneering, also proved a significant one in that, with a modicum of equity in television time for all candidates, it aroused political interest and helped to maintain a high standard in the electoral campaign.

Yet it was not until well after the events of May 1968 that further changes were made. After the strike of ORTF journalists, many were sacked or put in much less prominent positions. J. Ardagh suggests that attempts to stifle opinion had by this time become much more subtle, in that anything which could offend the susceptibilities of any important group, political or religious, was avoided; which gave rise to self-censorship. However, some positive changes were brought in, notably the abolition of the information ministry, as the consequence of a promise by Pompidou in his presidential campaign of 1969. That some further changes were still necessary, was clear from the so-called clandestine advertising scandal that broke in 1971.

The problem was this: commercial radio and television in France was not acceptable to the government, but the persistent financial difficulties suffered by the ORTF brought a measure of advertising, under state control, into the media. There had been since 1960 what was known as *publicité compensée*, that is, advertising for a type of goods, but not for a specific brand; this was paid for by commercial companies. In October 1968 advertising of specific brands of goods was permitted, to the tune of two minutes per day and by 1972 this had increased to nineteen minutes. However, in 1971 it was revealed that there were very close links between ORTF and an advertising agency and that these were being put to improper use. The names of specific brands of goods were brought before the public in tele-vision programmes, allegedly for pecuniary gain on the part of private individuals. The solution for this type of malpractice was felt to lie in decentralization, but such a solution would not have given the state the same hold over broadcasting. A further ominous note was the resurrection of the minister of information under a slightly different name – *secrétaire d'état de la fonction publique et des services de l'information* – in the person of P. Malaud, who was given the job of producing a draft bill on ORTF reform which, in due course, became the law of 3 July 1972. Its main innovation was in the creation of a *président-directeur-général*, still appointed by the government for three years; he not only headed the ORTF but also presided over the *conseil d'administration*, concocted as before. While the ORTF was still under the aegis of the prime minister or his delegate, one change seemed to be of very slightly liberal tendency, namely the right of reply, where an individual felt that his or her honour, reputation or interests had suffered as a result of the content of any broadcast. At the same time, however, another provision gave to the PDG powers to decide who, in the case of strikes, was to be regarded as essential for the continuation of the public service, and who was not – i.e. who could strike and who could not; this was inevitably viewed as as attempt to curtail the right to withdraw one's labour.

All in all, this did little to bring about the fundamental changes, for which successive reports (by Diligent in 1968 and Paye in 1970) had pressed, notably in the area of decentralization. Nor was the appointment of A. Conte, a UDR deputy, particularly reassuring. Yet less than two years later, Conte was to leave his post, making his reasons completely clear. In October 1973, Malaud had demanded the removal of two broadcasters for their political views, stating that unless this was done and unless France-Culture (which, he said, was a hotbed of communists and *cégétistes*) was reorganized, there would be no increase in the ORTF budget. In due course, Conte was sacked in what P. Viansson-Ponté described as 'une forte odeur d'autoritarisme' (*Le Monde*, 24 October 1973) and Malaud moved to another post, although not disavowed by the government.

Up to this point, it can be stated that the authoritarian tendency, inherited partly from Vichy and partly from the desire of the left-wing resistance to have no truck with commercial values and to rely on the democratic state for fairness and freedom of expression, had scarcely been modified over nearly forty years. With the arrival of V. Giscard d'Estaing as president of the republic, the format changes. Pompidou had had no doubts on the official role of the ORTF and its broadcasters. 'Qu'on le veuille ou non, le journaliste de la télévision n'est pas tout à fait un journaliste comme un autre. Il a des responsabilités particulières . . . Qu'on le veuille ou non, la télévision est considérée comme la voix de la France, et par les Français et par l'étranger' (*Le Monde*, 23 September 1972).

While the views of V. Giscard d'Estaing were less clear cut, it was likely that he would not share those of Pompidou. (His brother, O. Giscard d'Estaing, was a prominent supporter of commercial radio.) By August 1974, a law had been promulgated which disbanded the ORTF altogether, and reorganized television and radio in seven bodies: three television companies, one radio company, a company to produce films and plays, another to maintain equipment, and an audio-visual institute. It should be made clear that the state is the only shareholder, so that such competition as exists is simply between one state organization and another.

Opinions vary as to the success of the reorganization; for some, the experience of working in a smaller group of people after the impersonal ORTF system is beneficial; for others, it has brought about a lowering of cultural and artistic standards (see D. Korlin, 'Quelle nostalgie de l'O.R.T.F.?' in *Le Monde*, 24–25 April, 1983).

In one sensitive area, some benefit seems to have been reaped — freedom of political expression. Political parties and trade unions now have not only the right to broadcast on FR 3's *Tribune libre*, but also the main political groupings have a right to four party political broadcasts per year on the other two channels.

Yet initially, it did not seem as if much would change with the left, with a number of resignations from radio and television under government pressure, and their replacement with people more sympathetic to the views of the new majority. Then on 29 July 1982 a law was passed dealing with radio and television, and laying down the principle of freedom of the media. To ensure their independence a *haute autorité de la communication audio-visuelle* was established, to which they would be responsible. Its duties include the regulation of party political broadcasts, and programmes dealing with electoral campaigns, and the right of reply to government communications. Other responsibilities cover the protection of children, the maintenance of equality for women and men, the defence of the French language, but also support for regional languages and culture. More specifically it appoints at national and regional level the presidents of the radio and television companies. Whether these new arrangements will give the media greater freedom from state intervention remains to be seen.

In another area too, equally sensitive, the *haute autorité* has an important part to play. If the exclusive involvement of the state in media broadcasts seems oppressive, it must be remembered that it is viewed by some as the one bulwark, already weakened by the 1974 law, against commercialization.[14]

There was, in the last five years of Giscard's presidency, an upsurge in the number of private radio stations, which proved very embarrassing to deal with. Tough legislation was introduced in 1978, but when the left came to power, a decision was taken to authorize some of these, even before the establishing of the *haute autorité*, whose task this has become. There are now officially twenty-two authorized radio stations in Paris, and by the end of 1983, there were approximately one thousand throughout France. Commercialization, however, is still banned, and it is thus difficult to see how these private stations will survive.

The state's relations with the press are in many ways equally ambiguous if, perhaps, less tortuous. Freedom of the press has formally been recognized by the state since 1881, and the problem has been since how the state may best nurture that freedom.

The main danger in the post-war period was felt to come, not from the state, but from commercial interests. The ordinances of 1944 banned any papers which had appeared during the occupation, which effectively left the field clear for the clandestine publications of the resistance, since only the resistance groups were permitted to publish. A stricter definition of the *entreprise de presse* differentiated it from other types of publication in that its productions appearing at least once a month were essentially informative, yet not solely scientific, artistic, technical or professional. The *directeur de publication* had to be either the owner or the principal shareholder, or the editor of the company. It was hoped, in this way, to prevent the setting up of large press empires, yet in the main it must be admitted that the spirit of the ordinances has not been maintained, since the press groups still exist, the newest and largest being that of R. Hersant, which now owns not only the Parisian dailies *France-Soir*, *Le Figaro* and *l'Aurore*, but fourteen regional daily papers as well.

Yet if the anti-monopoly aspects of the 1944 ordinances have not been successful, the provision of state assistance which they initiated has undoubtedly helped to keep many papers alive – the principle behind these provisions being to maintain competition among news-papers and periodicals, and at the same time to guarantee a measure of equality to all these organs. State aid is essentially of two kinds: direct assistance in the shape of subsidies for the purchase of printing material, for export aid, or direct payments to the railways for trans-porting of newspapers, and to the PTT for the cost of telephones; indirect help, in the shape of reduced rate for postal charges, telegrams, etc., reduction in VAT, exemption, whole or in part, from other forms of taxation such as the *patente* (see below). In 1976 and 1977 this system was increased to take in not only daily papers, but weekly publications also, which have to have a national distribution and also be of such a nature as to enlighten their readers on national and inter-national news, and as such, be in the public interest.

Over all, the aid received by the press from the state in France is higher than in any other western country, totalling in 1983 over 5,200 million francs in direct and indirect aid. This gains for the country, in theory, a press which covers a wide range of political opinions and con-sequently a genuine freedom of opinion. However, without considering here the problems of censorship as applied to books or films, it is clear enough that the state has that power if it chooses to exercise it, and state-aided as it is, the press is ill-equipped to stand against the state if this should ever become necessary.

The present situation of the national press in France is not good. Over the past ten years, the circulation of national daily newspapers has gone down by some three million copies. Even a prestigious newspaper like *Le Monde* is in financial difficulties, having lost 14 per cent of its readership in the past two years. The weakness of the press is clearly a weakness for the democratic principle in France, should the state choose for any reason to exercise its powers against the press. 'Newspapers which accept help from the state, in money or in kind, are inhibited from keeping a cool watch on the state's performance which is among their main obligations.'[15]

A case in point is the legislation at present before parliament. It will provide for more selective, and thus it is hoped, more effective aid to news-papers. However the main aim of the draft bill is a far more controversial one – namely to limit the number of newspapers which may be held by one individual or group, in order to preserve what is called *la transparence financière et le pluralisme*, and essentially to reactivate the ordinances of 1944. The essential provisions are as follows: no one individual or group may own *either* a national daily paper plus a regional one, *or* more than three national dailies having in total over 15 per cent of the national daily readership, *or* an undetermined number of regional dailies, with the same percentage total of readership. It is also proposed to establish a commission to ensure adherence to these provisions. Since these proposals seek only to put into effect what should have been adhered to since 1944, it could be said that the measure is a healthy one – assuming it to be practicable. The problem is that there is virtually only one press empire which stands to suffer is this legislation is enacted, that of R. Hersant. Hersant makes no secret of his right-wing views, and hence of his opposition to the present government. It is therefore rather unfortunate that these proposed measures appear so obviously to attack one man, which allows scope for suspicions that the government is simply seeking a means to attack a powerful political opponent, who has a stranglehold on a very important part of the media.

If Hersant has to choose between his national or his regional papers, then the government will have achieved its aim. What it might also achieve is the disappearance of yet more national papers – not perhaps the long-term objective which is intended.

(3) Central government and local government

(i) Structures

The relationship of local and central government inevitably brings one to the terrain of myth. The problem is often posed from two contrasting viewpoints – Jacobins and decentralizers. The Jacobin archetype, suspicious of the reactionary provinces and seeing Paris as the sole source of leadership, technique and consequently of material and cultural benefits for the people, confronts his decentralizing opponent, for whom Paris is arrogant and remote, if not to say tyrannical, taking its decisions without knowledge of local realities and desires. For the Jacobin, Parisian leadership is the *sine qua non* of national unity: any weakening of it is the prelude to national fragmentation; for his adversary, Parisian tyranny will in the end, unless power is developed, produce so much discontent on the periphery that the nation may well break up anyway.

Jacobins justify their case with an ideology of the 'general interest' and a series of impersonal rules which are supposed to cover adequately any conceivable problem. Decentralizers delight in pointing out the innumerable delays, inefficiencies and examples of bureaucratic obstruction that the system seems to secrete. So the opposing cultures argue.

Behind this clash of stereotypes lies a more complex reality. It is true that the Jacobin and Napoleonic founders of the modern system of local government wanted to restrict local autonomy as far as they could, and by a barrage of legal and constitutional means at that. But it is also true that local politicians have long since adapted fairly comfortably to this Procrustean bed and are able to have a fair degree of power and influence within the system. What follows is an outline of the different layers of sub-central government prior to the 1982 changes, in terms of structures, responsibilities and resources, plus an attempt to grasp their real relationship to Paris. The lowest level is the *commune* (36,433 in 1983), dating from 1789 and based on the parishes of the *Ancien Régime*. Above it is the *département*, created in 1790; there are ninety-six in metropolitan France. Each of these is sub-divided into *arrondissements* which in turn split into *cantons*: but neither of these levels now has either elected authorities nor provides services. Above the departments stand the twenty-two regions, each of them grouping a number of departments.

All communes elect a municipal council (often referred to as 'la municipalité'); these are elected six-yearly, the system varying according to the size of the commune. Councils number anything from 9 to 163 (Paris): they are obliged by law to carry out certain services (gas and water supply, roads, etc.) and can expand into other fields unless specifically forbidden. The dominant figure is the mayor, elected by his colleagues after taking office and who cannot then be dismissed by them. He is the representative of the state as well as head of his commune. In his first capacity he thus performs duties such as marriages and electoral registration; but in his second, he represents his commune in dealings with other bodies (especially the prefect), assures its security and cleanliness, appoints its staff, draws up its budget and executes its decisions.

Each department has a *conseil général*, whose members are elected on a territorial basis (one per *canton*). The size varies from 17 to 163 (Paris again, for it is both commune and department). The council serves for six years, half of its members being elected at three-year intervals. Although it had an elected president (usually a figure of national standing), its executive was an appointee of the interior minister, the prefect. He it was who prepared agenda and budget, and implemented decisions. Like the commune, the department is obliged to provide some services (roads, school buildings, some social security services) and may expand into other activities, legal and financial possibilities permitting. An important part of its work was to give financial support to communes within it.

The region was not a full tier of local government, so it had no elective authorities. Its role was one of economic development, which it fulfilled in association with its constituent communes and departments, mainly by proposals and participation in state projects with its rather limited resources. It had three elements — an economic and social council, composed, like its national equivalent, of delegates from local interest groups, whose role was largely consultative; a regional council, of deputies and senators for the region plus nominees from communes and departments, which voted a budget and debated the allocation of central grants, and the executive, a regional prefect who drew up the budget and agenda, and who also doubled as prefect of the main department within the region.

The Defferre Act of March 1982 and its successors of January and July 1983 were an attempt to *decentralize* power (i.e. place it in the hands of local élites), as opposed to *deconcentrating* it (removing the effective locus of decision from Paris but placing it with the prefect or other local administrators). In the commune thus the mayor is now only subject to *a-posteriori* tutelage; his decisions are immediately implemented and it is up to the prefect to challenge them if he thinks fit, either in the administrative courts or, in the case of alleged financial impropriety, in one of the new regional courts of account that the act sets up. The mayor also receives new powers, especially in housing and town planning (it is now he who grants building permission). He has more latitude for intervention in the fields of employment and economic enterprise generally, being able to support firms with public money (within limits) and even take over certain kinds of enterprise. Although *la tutelle* was often exaggerated in its importance and in any case had been weakened legislatively by previous governments, the above changes are more than symbolic. They certainly place more responsibility on mayors, as Wright observes, thus making it harder for them to blame Paris or 'le pouvoir' for their inadequacies.

At departmental level the prefect loses his executive power to the president of the assembly, which also gains new powers, particularly in transport, housing and social services. Again tutelage is exercised *a-posteriori*. The prefect retains overall control of field services, which continue to be available for use by the department and its communes. In time some of these services will be transferred to departmental control so as to enable the department to discharge its new responsibilities. This process of transferring powers and services will go on in a fairly piecemeal way through 1985. In order to better co-ordinate their new tasks and their new assets, some departments have taken on the virtual equivalent of the chief executive of an English borough, i.e. a senior administrator of high calibre and experience. Many of these are, unsurprisingly, ex-prefects, often Giscard supporters fallen on hard times after May 1981. Their job is to support and advise the departmental leader in his dealings with their ex-colleagues in *la préfectorale*.

The region is now a full tier of local government, which will now elect its council by universal suffrage (Corsica and the overseas regions have already done so and France will probably follow after 1984). As with the department, the prefect loses his executive role to the president, and his tutelary power also. The advisory Economic and Social Council has had its composition changed to give more weight to working-class interests. The region's powers will be increased especially in economic development, housing and vocational training, and it will presumably have to create some services to this end. In some ways the idea of the region as a level of decision-making involves questions beyond the scope of local government *stricto sensu*, and we shall return to this in conclusion.

(ii) Dependence or autonomy?

Local authority finance comes from three main sources – local taxes, central government grants and borrowing.[16] These resources may be supplemented by the bigger or more fortunate communes with revenue from their own assets, either industrial or commercial. In 1981 the great mass of communes (with a population below 10,000) derived their income as follows (if the big towns were included, there would be more grants and less borrowing). For their *recurrent* expenditure (staff overheads, maintaining equipment and paying off debts) they found 12.6 per cent out of their own assets, 34.3 per cent from government in the shape of the *dotation globale de fonctionnement* or DGF (see below), and 46.2 per cent from local taxes. The other part of their income, which goes on *capital* expenditure (mainly new investment on infrastructure, some 77 per cent of which is done in France by the communes) was made up out of previous surpluses (28.1 per cent), grants from government and from the departments (27 per cent) and miscellaneous sources (9.7 per cent). The remaining 35.2 per cent was borrowed.[17] Communes and departments may raise local taxes, two-thirds of which go to the former, one-third to the latter. Three of these are based on property values and the fourth, the old *patente* (now re-baptized as *taxe professionnelle*) on business activity; many regard the latter as arbitrary and rather unjust in the way it was levied.

It does however bring in over half of the total local tax receipts, so it cannot simply be scrapped as some of the business community would like. Local taxes have risen sharply in the last decade, outstripping both national tax rates and the growth of GDP, as communes strive to meet expanding demands for services from a growing population. As elsewhere in Europe governments are glad enough to let local authorities assume the heavier responsibility, but less keen when it comes to handing over additional resources.[18]

All told, government transferred to the local authorities in 1982 some hundred billion francs, half of it through the DGF. This replaces income lost to local authorities through the disappearance of obsolete taxes, and its financing is guaranteed because the government puts into it a fixed proportion of receipts from VAT. It has an inbuilt corrective mechanism (*prérequation*), whereby poorer communes receive proportionally more than better-off ones. Thus within the unavoidable limits of size, natural resources, etc. some effort at ironing out discrepancies is made.

Finally communes need to borrow (35 billion francs in 1982). Two-thirds of this is done through special public banks, mainly the *Caisse des*

Dépôts, which are usually able to offer interest rates below commercial ones. This is partly due to government's ability to persuade the public to subscribe heavily to local authority saving schemes (e.g. Livret A): certainly the response seems better than in the UK.

The overall financial position of local authorities is, then, one of increasing need for resources. Often the choice seems to be between increasing taxes (within parameters set at the centre), with all the difficult political choices involved, or trying to extract more from government, which may involve numerous political compromises. It is a familiar dilemma in Europe today.

This scheme hides much of the real centre-periphery relationship in France. Does the legal and financial muscle exerted by the centre mean that local autonomy is inexistent? An examination of the forces involved suggests that the answer should be a nuanced one.

The prefect is often set up as the embodiment of Parisian tyranny. His formal powers are great: he is the state's representative in his department (hence the elaborate uniform he wears on official occasions). He is appointed by the head of local government in France, the interior minister, and as such exercised supervision, *la tutelle*, over all local authorities. He could dissolve councils (though he never needed to, in fact); he could veto a budget; he has the last word on law and order (so can prohibit demonstrations, etc.); he is the 'eyes and ears' of the government, expected to pick up and pass on the views of politically important (or dangerous) people to his superior in Paris. He was helped in his task by field services (*services extérieurs*) of ministries in his department, which will have office staff and a direct labour force also. The most important are from the ministries of finance, infrastructure, labour and agriculture; the prefect was supposed to be overall co-ordinator of these services in his department (except for those of justice, labour and education, which have their own heads). Prefects will also participate, along with their own expert staff and heads of the field services, in the regional administrative conference, where important decisions about regional planning are effectively taken.

In practice there were limits to this power even before 1982: some of the prefect's formal powers (e.g. *a priori* control of budgets) had been cut back; he has probably never had a great deal of control over the field services, which may well deal with Paris or local notables behind his back. The prefects' career structure is another source of weakness: they are moved frequently, whether as a reward or as a punishment. Above all, the prefect has never managed to shake the hold of local notables in his department, some of whom will be parliamentarians or ministers; they are thus powerful figures whom a prefect will annoy at his peril. Such figures often obtain various favours for their departments (building grants, the location of job-creating public or private enterprise, etc.) over the prefect's head, which gives them at least as strong a local clientèle as the latter. J. Chirac was reputed, for instance, during his premiership to have a full-time staff in Matignon, channelling resources busily into the Corrèze, where Chirac is deputy and general councillor. In fact the prefect has long been a 'Janus', facing two ways. On one hand, he must try to implement the will of Paris; on the other, he finds himself increasingly the advocate of the local grievances and demands to which he must listen every day. Recent studies have dwelt on the similarity of the prefect and the mayor, both in the sandwich-position between grass-roots pressure and Parisian imperatives, and hence very much objective allies, despite the potential for conflict that their relationship contains. Small wonder that the prefect's is a difficult task; yet the profession still attracts men (there were no women prefects before 1981) of the highest intellectual and political skills, remaining one of the most prestigious 'grands corps' of the French administration.

The other main pressure for centralization is alleged to be the atomized structure and the financial dependence of local authorities. The financial structure has already been described, and whatever the ability of notables to channel resources into their departments, dependence on central aid remains a powerful check on local autonomy — and not just in France, one might add. As regards the existing levels of local government, there are again some unpalatable facts for the defender of local autonomy to digest, starting with size. Ninety per cent of all communes have fewer than 2,000 inhabitants; 50 per cent fewer than 300. Some 996 have fewer than 50 people, even. But at the other end of the scale, some 73 per cent of the total population live in a mere 12 per cent of the total communes. Now all communes are supposed to be equal: i.e. Paris has the same legal status as a hamlet in the Lozère with 120 people. In practice there is a huge disparity between big communes like Lille or Marseille, with considerable revenue of their own, and small rural villages which raise precious little revenue. Many big towns are famous for their urban planning, their business enterprise or their cultural activities; many rural communes are too poor to put tarmac around the telepone box, assuming that there is one. Autonomy, then, is proportional to resources. A big town can afford its own specialists and finance much of its development plans; its small 'equivalent' might have one part-time official (probably the primary school teacher) who does municipal business one evening a week. Clearly, such communes are at the mercy of the prefect for resources and technical expertise. Of late, attempts have been made to palliate such fragmentation by encouraging communes to merge, more by offers of financial inducement than by legal pressure. But local pride and fear of losing office have meant resistance. In the seven years following the 1971 act on mergers, only 2,179 of these had occurred. One way forward which sacrifices comparatively little civic pride, is via the various forms of inter-communal co-operation: a *syndicat à vocation unique*, when they combine for one particular purpose, such as bussing school-children; *syndicats à vocation multiple*, for any number of common services. In big city suburbs there are *districts*, which group local communes for several services and where the communes pool much of their finances. Nine big towns have gone even further with the *communauté urbaine*, which takes over compulsory services from its member communes and has its own council of nominees from the latter.

It seems then that French communes fall into two categories – the small and fairly dependent ones which have, however, great civic pride and interest on the part of their citizens, and a minority of big and powerful ones. Government has generally moved only slowly to change this imbalance. At the end of Giscard's septennate the government was considering projects, such as reductions in VAT, better time off and pay for mayors, an improved career structure for local officials, increased technical aid, a guaranteed minimum income for communes and changes in the reviled professional tax.

The Defferre reforms clearly aim to give more responsibility and freedom of action to local élites. Yet there are gaps in the framework which might prove hard to fill. Firstly, there is still some uncertainty as to *la répartition des compétences* (which level carries out which functions and with which resources). The eventual shape of this will result from a lengthy struggle between the interested parties – prefects, local officials, ministries and parliamentarians. Secondly, there is the problem of career structure. Most mayors and their *adjoints* are short of time and expertise. For the reform to work properly, there will need to be a full definition of their status, covering such issues as remuneration, time off and legal and technical training. Similarly a revised pay and career structure is needed for local government officers if this branch of the public service is to recruit good people to fill the new posts. At present it is the poor relation, compared to a career in a Parisian ministry: certainly few *énarques* would be happy to make a career in provincial prefectures.

The most serious gap remains the financial one. Although the law pledges government not to transfer responsibilities without commensurate finance, there is as yet little sign of a reform of local finances, and the situation of local authorities here is still one of relative dependence.

(iii) Elections

Local elections have become more party-political of late and are becoming even more so; yet it is unwise to underestimate the electoral pull of a popular *conseiller général* in the countryside or a dynamic town mayor who might choose to hide his political feelings behind an ideology of 'service to the commune' or technical expertise. The electorate does tend though to use such elections as a test of the government, often voting against it in mid-term as a 'warning'.[19] Such has been the fate of the present government which faced cantonal elections (for the

departmental assemblies) in March 1982 and municipal ones a year later.
In the former category, out of 2.014 seats to be filled, including 166 new
ones, the RPR gained 146 and the UDF 69: their right-wing allies gained
a further 51. The PS lost 5, the PCF 44 and their Radical and other left
allies some 50. This meant in terms of the control of the new departmental executives that the right now controlled 60 and the left 36.
Ironically the new powers were going to be first used by those who had
spent much of their time opposing them.

A similar trend emerged from the municipal polls of 1983 where the
right waged a very hard campaign, stressing national issues rather than
local ones and harping much upon law and order and immigration.
Some of its candidates in big towns went beyond limits which civilized
people would find acceptable. The usual index of performance in these
contests is the vote in the 227 towns of over 30,000, as smaller and
especially rural communes tend to have many candidates difficult to
classify politically.

The government had prepared these elections by changing the voting
system, combining proportionality and majority weighting in a clever
attempt to reconcile representativity and efficacity in terms of government. In communes of 3,500 and over, each party presents a list (one
name for each seat on the council). Electors vote for lists *en bloc*. If a
list gets over 50 per cent at the first ballot it wins half the seats plus a
percentage of the remainder in line with its own percentage of the vote.
Otherwise there is a second ballot. For this, any list that won over 10
per cent may stand again but the usual procedure is to bargain with
whichever of the two leading lists is closest to you and thereby obtain
good places on it. The second round is thus usually a two-horse race in
which of course one list is bound to obtain over 50 per cent, with seats
distributed as above. This weighting is very fine in fact, meaning that a
slim majority in votes gives a big lead in terms of seats. Thus in the second
ballot at Châlon-sur-Saône, the RPR list took 12,105 votes (50.21 per
cent) against the outgoing PS 12,003 (49.78 per cent). This is a narrow
lead, but on the new council there are 34 RPR and 11 Socialists. But at
least there is now an opposition in the town halls compared with the
previous winner-takes-all system where 50.01 per cent of the votes
meant 100 per cent of the seats. Judging by the grudging way in which
the winning lists welcomed the opposition into the *mairies*, however,
cheerfully denying them office space, briefing papers and facilities in
general, it seemed that traditional triumphalist attitudes would not
change overnight.[20]

An added refinement was introduced for Paris, Lyon and Marseille.
The latter is a socialist stronghold; the other two are never likely to be.
In the hope of gaining some foothold here, however, the socialists
created, rather furtively it must be said, a new tier of administration,
the *conseil d'arrondissement*. Elected simultaneously with the full town

council, these bodies were to have limited resources and some say in housing and use of amenities; in short they were the means to creating a socialist clientèle in the right-wing fortresses. The tactic blew up in their faces as the right made a clean sweep in Paris and Lyon and came very close to unseating Defferre in Marseille.

Elsewhere in the towns of 30,000+ the left lost a net total of 30 (in 1977 it had gained over 40), and remained in control of 127 of the big 227 (66 PS, 59 PCF, 2 MRG). These figures needed adjustment in the light of several re-run elections in the autumn, called because the *conseil d'Etat* disqualified a number of victorious PCF mayors for electoral fraud. Nearly all these elections were lost.

(iv) Regions

The very idea of the region as a level of decision-making involves problems of a different nature from those of commune or department. In many cases it brings in a political or cultural dimension, where the identity of those in the region is perceived as being opposed to or at least not synonymous with the national identity, as incarnated by the capital and its officials. It is wise to remember Hayward's remark that 'France is a unitary state superimposed on a multinational society'.[21] Historically France spread out from the Paris region, absorbing such peripheral peoples as Alsacians, Basques and Bretons: but this assimilation has never been entirely successful. There are in fact many possible causes of alienation on the periphery and these causes are often complex and interlocking.[22] It is certainly true that regionalist feeling is not exclusively inspired by economic decline, whereby the regions are exploited by an acquisitive centre which impoverishes them while enriching itself (cf. Hechter's thesis of 'internal colonialism'). In some cases there may be some truth in this accusation; in others it may be that those on the periphery *believe* it to be the case, even though statistically the argument can be disproved. In the areas of militant nationalist or even separatist feeling, the main factor is cultural, i.e. Paris is seen as trying to destroy a local culture (often symbolized by its language) by normalizing the region so as to make it like the rest of France. It would seem that when cultural resentment and a perception of economic decay coincide then militant regionalist arguments gain their best audience.

Of equal complexity and variation also are the possible responses which the centre can make to a discontented periphery. In recent years peripheral demands have grown in volume, and they range from demands for increased financial and administrative power for the twenty-two regions to fully-fledged nationalist demands in the case of some regions with a strong historical sense of differentiation (notably Brittany and Corsica): though such demands are still very much a minority phenomenon.

The state has in fact chosen different responses to regionalist demands, the main one being to develop the twenty-two regional structures, from their initial formulation as economic planning units in the 1950s to the 1982 law which put them on a par with existing units of local government. The logic of this approach (which Hayward usefully describes as functional *regionalization*, in contrast to the *regionalism* of peripheral groups) was to concede resources where necessary, but as little as possible in the way of powers.[23] Thus the regionalization of the 1960s meant using the regional prefect as the pivot of the economic development effort. By channelling funds he would, it was hoped, enlist the co-operation of local notables in modernizing their areas, thereby making them forget any illusions about the usefulness of such notions as 'regional power'. Another key policy instrument was DATAR (*Délegation à l'aménagement du territoire et à l'action régionale*), basically a high-powered team of economic planners with funds at their disposal and access to the prime minister's office, whose task was to speed up the process of job-creating investment in the provinces by by-passing much of the traditional administrative procedure. The strategy was not wholly successful: local élites did not co-operate fully, fearing a diminution of their influence and DATAR for its part was able to get some firms to move out of Paris, but mainly into the west or the Paris basin. Thus the struggling departments in the south-west or the Massif Central missed out. The notables helped defeat de Gaulle in 1969, and when Pompidou's regional law was passed in 1972 it recognized their influence. Thus the regional councils were not elected by universal suffrage, were not fully-fledged units of local government, had minute tax-raising powers and were obliged to use the regional prefect as their executive. Grants still tended to be doled out piecemeal by prefects to rural mayors (*le saupoudrage*). Town mayors tended to try and bypass this system either via DATAR or via their contacts in Paris. Above all, no alterations were made to existing regional boundaries, either on cultural grounds (to please regionalists) or economic ones (many planners wanted eight or even five regions). Giscard's governments did not alter these arrangements significantly, as even their special plans for different regions (south-west or Massif Central) were centralized exercises, done with an eye to electoral advantage. Thus when Mitterrand arrived in 1981 it could be said that there was some scope for a new initiative in the regional field.

The post-1982 regions suffer in fact from a number of weaknesses. Although now a full level of local government with its own executive (the president of the council and his bureau), not subject to tutelage and able to raise its own taxes and create its own services, although its council will be elected by universal suffrage, the region is far from being the state-within-a-state which M. Debré claimed to detect when, in the National Assembly debate, he accused the socialists of trying to turn France into a federal state. No concessions have been made to cultural regionalists, as the twenty-two regions remain mere agglomerates of existing departments, deliberately cutting across traditional provincial boundaries. Many of them show grave economic imbalances. The structure of tax-raising is still not clear, nor is that of staffing. More seriously, as Sadran shows, some powers have gone to the departments which could usefully have been given to the regions.[24] The departmental assembly with its overrepresentation of rural areas is traditionally, as Hayward observes, a locus of immobilism and precisely where the notables gather in strength. Many socialist parliamentarians who have won local office are in fact becoming a new generation of notables in their own right, and they can be expected to try and keep the departments strong. Hayward is doubtless correct when he says that the only way to put teeth into the regions is to attack the *cumul des mandats* and bring forward a new sort of local élite without Parisian connections.[25] But it is a moot point whether this will be done.

Against those who believe that regional power is best able to deal with local economic or cultural problems, there is still a persuasive Jacobin literature. Wright argues shrewdly that regional authorities might be taken over by obscurantist élites bent not on growth but on thrusting the values of obsolete cultures down the throats of local inhabitants, who may well desire to escape just such a fate.[26] Not all Scotsmen like the sound of bagpipes, as he remarks: and it may be that the protection of liberties, generation of growth and redistribution of its fruits are best guided from the enlightened centre. Against this, regionalists would doubtless claim that in several centuries Paris has still not succeeded in performing adequately these very tasks. Clearly this is an argument which will go on long after the laws of the Mitterrand presidency have begun to take effect.

Mention must be made briefly of two regions with autonomist tendencies. If Breton autonomism seems stagnant with the failure of the UDB (*Union démocratique bretonne*) and its right-wing rivals to break into electoral politics in a significant way, then Corsican autonomism has undergone an upswing during the last decade. It has been fuelled by rising unemployment and high land prices, leading to increased emigration by young people, plus resentment at the fact that the better-off seemed increasingly to be from the mainland. As the local notables, or the *clans* as they are often called (they belong usually to old-established families with wide ramifications), proved unable to assuage discontent by their traditional methods of clientelism (they secured benefits from Paris in return for votes for them), particularist and nationalist ideas gained more hearing. By 1981 at least two strands were competing for nationalist support: the moderate UPC (*Union du peuple corse*) led by E. Siméoni, which aimed at a sort of home rule (with defence and diplomacy left to France), and the partisans of armed struggle in the FLNC (*Front de libération nationale corse*). Giscard's reply was the time-honoured one of the hand-out: thus a second department (i.e. an appreciable number of jobs) was created, grants and transport subsidies stepped up. In 1982 the socialists went for a bold and imaginitive solution, trying to conciliate local feeling on the island with the need to keep control of national unity. Thus a Corsican Act was passed whereby the island gets its regional assembly early but one with slightly increased powers (notably to create agriculture and transport boards and to provide extra schools): suitable acknowledgment was made of 'la personnalité corse' but it was clear that the island was still part of France. In the August elections the autonomists did well in a very fragmented poll, with 7 seats out of 61. But so did the *clans*, working through the traditional parties. Under its president P. Alfonsi, a pragmatic notable willing to govern with the help of the autonomists and the left, the assembly began its difficult task.[27] But as violence increased through 1983, some of it is due to the operations of rival squads of secret police-men working unbeknown to one another, the prospects of rule by consensus seemed to recede. In September 1983 the government dissolved the nationalist groups CCN, generally regarded as a front for the FLNC.

Sub-central government in France is clearly in the throes of a poten-tially far-reaching reform. Clearly there are gaps to be filled in the law, notably the crucial one of finances. There is a clear will to develop more initiative and to reduce the feeling of dependency on Paris. But it is too soon to say what the results will be. We may guess that those most able to use the new powers, i.e. urban mayors and presidents of strong departments, will probably make full use of them. But such people will not be in a majority, and for the mass of rural mayors little will change.

Above all it seems hard to imagine that the secular relationship between technocrat and notable, prefect and mayor will alter overnight. The new arrangements still call for much co-operation between the representative of Paris at the head of his services and the notable, articulating his local interests. Their sometimes frictional but unavoid-able collaboration will last for some time yet. We may agree with Wright that they are 'condemned to live together in a chaos of surreptitious bargaining, illicit agreements, hidden collusion, unspoken complicity, simulated tension and often genuine conflict'. *Plus ça change, plus c'est la même chose . . .*

Chapter 4

Political forces

(1) The French party system

Parties are nowadays deemed essential to the workings of a democratic political system. Their functions are complex; but their prime one is to organize and give coherent expression to the political demands of various groups. The latter may be a single class or fraction, or a wider grouping. Although the origins of most parties are clearly traceable to different class fractions, the nature of a party may well change over time; in particular, it may well come to attract support from other class fractions than those on which it was first based, thus qualifying for the title of a 'catch-all' party. Such a process is usually a long and oblique one, and in general it is safe to say that the way in which parties mirror (or deform) class interests is a complex one. At any rate, parties aim to capture political power or a share thereof, so as to translate their demands as far as possible into public policy. Much of their activity will consist, then, in mobilizing supporters; and such mobilization need not be restricted to electoral competitions, though the latter obviously occupy a privileged place in the activity of most parties. A final function of parties is to produce élites who will be able to govern. In other words parties are essential to the upkeep of what is often called the political class.

In democratic systems, parties always function alongside each other. The way in which they relate to each other, the party system, is thus crucial for understanding the politics of any country. In the UK or the USA, politics are dominated by two large, stable and apparently unshakeable parties, with no really crucial differences between them; commentators contrast this stability, which they see as reflecting or maintaining a widespread consensus about the nature and objectives of Anglo-Saxon society, with France, where the party system seemed for a long time to offer a model of acute instability.

Under the Third and Fourth Republics, governments were coalitions whose member parties were divided on a number of bases: class differences were important, but so were ideological ones and plain sectional interests. It has been suggested that this division gave an artificial and exaggerated image of French society, i.e. that underneath

151

the rhetoric of party professionals there was a high degree of consensus as to the nature of the society that suited France most. But the consensus never made its way into party politics. Parties remained numerous and divided. Even the rise of a relatively well-structured socialist party, and later on a communist one, did not really affect the fragmentation of the party system. Neither of the above was able to enlarge its audience beyond a certain point; and when their initial militant ardour had cooled, they too were admitted from opposition into the coalition system. The older parties of the right never developed much of an organization, but they never needed to, managing even after the advent of universal suffrage to maintain hegemony within French civil society and stop the left from gaining too much support.

By 1958, then, France had a party system of coalitions between parties which could agree provided that little positive action were taken, but not if urgent action were needed, and which could in fact quarrel bitterly about seemingly trivial issues. This contributed of course to the debacle of 1958.

Since then there has been something of a mutation. New parties have appeared; old ones have been forced to tighten up their organization: and all have been forced into durable alliances, with the result that France seems to be moving towards a two-block party system ('bi-polarization'). The Fifth Republic enjoys widespread legitimacy, but its system of government displaces power away from parliament (the natural terrain for parties) towards the head of the executive, the president. This means that their ability to influence policy is lessened. At the very least, a party wishing to influence government must have presidential endorsement in elections, i.e. it must already accept a number of common policies or objectives. The president, on the other hand, needs a sympathetic majority (of one or more parties) in the lower house; for if his legislation were consistently refused by a hostile lower house, his constitutional position could become untenable. Hence the majority in the national assembly must be disciplined; and so also must any opposition hoping to supplant it. Thus there are considerable pressures towards tighter party organization and alliances arising from the presidential function itself.

The president himself, though claiming to rule only in the national interest and to be 'president of all the French', could never win his election in the first place without the help of party machinery. The very existence of the second ballot, which is limited to two candidates, forces parties to line up in two conflicting blocks. So far as legislative elections are concerned, one should note the system of *scrutin d'arrondissement* (single-member constituencies), with two ballots again. Seats are rarely won at the first ballot (over 50 per cent of the votes cast being needed), whereas a relative majority suffices at the second. Parties have thus a clear interest in making alliances for the second ballot with those nearest them, and not getting in each other's way. What usually happens is that the principle of 'republican discipline' (as the left calls it) obtains, and the best-placed candidate on left or right benefits from the withdrawal (*désistement*) of the candidate closest to him; the result is usually a straight right–left duel (this was the case in 96 per cent of the seats in March 1978). In some cases withdrawal is automatic, because in order to reach the second ballot candidates require the votes of 12.5 per cent of the registered electorate, i.e. probably over 15 per cent of the poll. Now, the parties which benefit least from such a system are ones with a strong identity, especially the communists; this is so because 'at the first ballot the voter chooses, but at the second he eliminates'. This also means that there is no connection between the percentage of votes obtained in the first ballot (the truest index of a party's audience) and the percentage of seats which it will win in the end.

Here is an example of the system:

Eure 3 (Louviers), March 1978 (main candidates only)
First ballot: Montagne (UDF) 20,431   Loncle (MRG) 14,775
               Desbordes (RPR) 6,164   Binay (PCF) 11,820

Between ballots Desbordes withdraws in favour of Montagne, and Binay in favour of Loncle, with the following result:

    Montagne   31,061
    Loncle   30,939

Montagne thus wins by 122 votes, illustrating perfectly the importance of a good alliance.

It is also suggested that many other factors which made for party fragmentation in the past are disappearing. Thus economic modernization, the drift from the land, the beginnings of a relative affluence and the decline of religious observance, plus an increasing consensus on the merits of the Fifth Republic are all adduced to explain the trend towards a two-block system. One could suggest limits to how far these processes have gone. As regards the consensus on the régime, it would seem better founded if the régime had passed the acid test, i.e. what happens when presidential and parliamentary majorities no longer coincide? It might also be true that modernization, far from solidifying voters into blocks, actually increases the centre mass of 'floating voters' without strong allegiance to left or right. In fact the main pressure towards bipolarization is almost certainly institutional; electoral systems always have a greater effect on political behaviour than is immediately apparent.

Today, then, two blocks of parties confront each other in France.

They are referred to here as left and right — terms which might appear more ideological or polemical than the 'opposition' and 'majority' currently preferred by government and media. For years now it has been fashionable to say that the terms are meaningless: that left governments have behaved like conservatives and that many of the right's policies have been progressive. Whatever the truth of such assertions, the great majority of French people seem to identify with the terms; for many they bear a strong emotional, if not irrational charge. They are part of the political culture, in fact. Historically of course the left has stood for change and the right for resistance to change, hence the tags of 'movement' and 'order' which some analysts use. Clearly the content of the terms has varied from the Revolution, when they were first coined (in the Revolutionary assemblies the most radical elements sat in the high benches on the speaker's left). Thus to be in favour of the republic and universal suffrage in 1815 was to be well on the left; whereas to demand no more today would place one equally firmly on the right. None the less the movement/order polarity exists in France as elsewhere, and today it is not difficult to identify its content. The parties of the right are those which accept the broad social and economic structures of French capitalism. The left in contrast is composed of those who aspire to structural change in the direction of socialism. It follows from this that the room for manoeuvre of any centre force is slight; it can only define itself negatively, occupying such terrain as left and right leave to it. Of late this has become so slight as to be non-existent; bi-polarization has forced the centrists to choose sides and most of them are now firmly aligned with the right.

A final curious point concerns vocabulary. Unlike politicians of the left, who revel in the title, those of the right never like to be described as such. They have always preferred a label such as *modéré, indé-pendant* or even *centre-gauche*; only the very muscular right likes to call itself *la droite*. Such a curious practice is puzzling only to those who, as Rémond remarks, have not yet plumbed the depths of French political vocabulary; but it does show the odd mystique which political concepts can sometimes take on.

Before examining the parties in detail, it is necessary to make some remarks, necessarily brief, about political behaviour. At its most basic level (voting) or at more sophisticated levels (being active in parties, holding office, etc.), political behaviour is usually analysed in terms of a series of classic variables, all of which involve high degrees of speculation. For the motives of individuals or groups are seldom as transparent as might be suggested by empirical surveys, even when these are subjected to strict statistical tests. In many cases those concerned may be ignorant as to their 'real' motives or perhaps reluctant to admit these. Subject to such obvious limitations we can say that French people are influenced in their behaviour by the classic variables which obtain elsewhere – class, age, sex, religion, type of socialization (how they are exposed to cultural norms and values) and so on – and that, at the risk of excessive brevity perhaps, three traits could be particularly underlined.

Firstly religion continues to be very important, showing its persistence at the expense of class, and this despite the increasing urbanization of French society, which as elsewhere seems to have resulted in a decline in religious observance. The divide between religious (even in a vague sense) and *laïcs* remains one of the lynch-pins of the left/right polarity. Even the greater readiness of some Catholics to vote left or even to be active in the left parties has only begun to weaken this very deep cultural divide, and it is unwise to underestimate its importance.

A second crucial trend is the growing political awareness of women, who now outnumber male voters. The key factor in this seems to have been work experience, with women learning the importance of politics as a consequence of their experience in the workplace. The emergence of an articulate feminist movement testifies to this much more subterranean process of the politicization of women. The long-term consequences of this trend for established political forces are far from clear.

A final factor is the rise of the salaried middle classes, whose role now seems pivotal, with small variations in the behaviour of this category apparently crucial in deciding electoral outcomes. Relative newcomers on the social stage and lacking the deeply rooted culture and traditions of older social groups, they seem more volatile and are increasingly seen by political forces as a key target to capture.

These trends and the influence of the wider political culture into which they fit will be seen as we now analyse the workings of the main political forces in France.

(2) Parties of the right

The parliamentary majority supporting presidents de Gaulle, Pompidou and Giscard d'Estaing has increased steadily in terms of parties, even if the latter represent a declining share of public opinion. But despite being forced into close collaboration by the presidential system, these parties have all striven to keep a separate identity; we shall examine them in turn (see Table 4.1).

Gaullism – le Rassemblement pour la république (RPR)

Development   Gaullism has been the dominant party or 'movement' (as the faithful prefer to call it) of the Fifth Republic. It has had numerous changes of name. If one leaves aside the Gaullism of the Resistance, based largely on personal allegiance to the General as a

Table 4.1   Majority parties since 1958

President	Years of office	Constituent parties of majority
De Gaulle	1958–62	UNR + varying numbers of MRP, SFIO and Independents (only PCF in outright opposition)
	1962–9	UDR + RI
Pompidou	1969–74	UDR + RI + Duhamel Centrists
Giscard d'Estaing	1914–81	UDR (RPR) + RI (PR) + remainder of Centrists (Lecanuet and Servan-Schreiber)
Mitterrand	1981–	PS + MRG + PCF

symbol of the will to fight the German invader, then it can be said to have entered its organizational phase with the RPF (*Rassemblement du peuple français*) in 1947. Despite a massive initial surge of membership and popularity, the movement had broken up long before 1958, over the question of support for Fourth Republic governments. But de Gaulle's return to power in 1958 necessitated speedy rebuilding of the Gaullist machinery. The UNR (*Union pour la nouvelle république*) developed into the UNR-UDT (*Union démocratique du travail*) in 1962, to be succeeded by the UDV^{e}R *(Union des démocrates pour la cinquième république)* in 1967 and the UDR (*Union pour la défense de la république*) in 1968. This changed to the *Union des démocrates pour la république* in 1971, and in December 1976 the movement was refurbished as the RPR.

Beneath the changing nomenclature, the party grew steadily in organization and influence, particularly after 1962 under Pompidou's guidance, as it became steadily apparent that de Gaulle's charisma alone was not enough to obtain automatic compliance from the electorate. During these years it supported presidential policy unflinchingly, often being rewarded with favours to be distributed among the constituencies on a fairly clientelistic basis − a technique which led sarcastic critics to compare the UDR with the other great historical masters of clientelism, the Radicals. Gaullism was the biggest party in parliament, its ministers were most numerous in government: Gaullists were given key posts in ministries and other parts of the state apparatus (media, education, public enterprise, etc.). Small wonder that by the late 1960s opponents denounced the Gaullist 'colonizing' of the state and coined the derisive slogan of 'l'Etat-UDR'.

The 1973 elections showd a relative decline in Gaullist strength, and when the UDR lost the presidency in 1974 its rapid demise was predicted. Energetic action by Chirac, making full use of the resources of his two-year premiership, revitalized the movement. The RPR that he launched in 1976 was already a well-oiled movement, and it was able to win over 22 per cent of the first ballot vote in the 1978 election, running neck and neck with the socialists for the title of France's biggest party.

Ideology   Gaullists like to see their movement as part of a tradition that resurfaces 'when France is in danger'. Less indulgent analysts usually place it within what Rémond calls the Bonapartist right, as opposed to the 'Orleanist' right (see below). The Bonapartist right is essentially nationalist, populist and, within varying degrees, authoritarian. Gaullist nationalism emerges in its foreign policy of independence, whereby France is to play as autonomous a role in world affairs as is commensurate with her strength as a medium-sized power, resisting in particular the hegemony of the USA. In domestic policy, it emerges in the doctrine of national unity at all costs; for Gaullists the ties of nationhood override, or should override, class or sectional interests. Hence *inter alia* their ready acceptance of the Jacobin state and their hostility to anything resembling decentralization. In the Bonapartist tradition, national unity also involves clear and firm leadership; hence Gaullist dislike of parties and of parliamentarianism in general and their preference for personal leadership based on a popular mandate (presidential election, referendum, etc.), which they claim will provide rational and impartial government in the 'national interest'. Such views are often accompanied by strictures on the primacy of law and order, and hostility to any attitudes that could at all be described as permissive, the whole often being expressed in a commonsense and fairly anti-intellectual language.

For the fairly authoritarian Gaullist conception of the state is also a populist one, i.e. it postulates an indistinct mass of *peuple* rather than a society divided into classes or fractions and believes that it can satisfy them all. This explains why in economics, the Gaullist-Bonapartist tradition keeps its distance from liberal economic theory, talking of a 'voluntaristic' economic policy which uses planning mechanisms and gives the (neutral) state an important arbitral role. Another facet of this economic populism is the various attempts at workers' participation, or *l'association capital/travail*, whereby the Gaullist state has tried, unsuccessfully, to persuade employers and workers to sink their differences in the name of national unity. It is this aspect of the doctrine that also accounts for the persistence over the years of left-wing Gaullists, whose influence on the movement has not, on the whole, been great.

This populism has its limits, however. Gaullism is vocal about the sanctity of property and particularly virulent in its denunciation of marxism, especially the communist party.

Given this ideological basis, then, one can see why Gaullism regards the Fourth Republic as a kind of Antichrist. For them its impotent multi-party system was the result of putting sectional priorities before the national interest; its foreign policy consisted merely of cowardly endorsements of American *Diktats*; and even its social and economic achievements, when these are actually recognized, are attributed to the good work of de Gaulle's provisional government before 1946! One cannot underestimate the importance within Gaullist discourse of the ideal antibody, the Fourth Republic, mere mention of which is enough to legitimize Gaullist rule.

None of the above should be taken at face value, of course, especially the claim to be above the interests of any one class or fraction. Historically *régimes d'exception*, to use Poulantzas's phrase, whether of the gentler Gaullist type or the tougher Napoleonic variety, occur when there has been a loss of hegemony, i.e. when dominant social forces and their political representatives lose political control over society, at least temporarily. Now, so long as there are no social forces to challenge them radically (forces which demand a qualitatively different society, that is), political equilibrium can only be restored by some kind of compromise until the old forces recover or renew themselves sufficiently to reassert control. Perhaps Gaullism was such a compromise. Its assumption of power came only two and a half years after decimation at the polls in January 1956; but in the meantime the impotence of the older right, centre and even its allies on the non-communist left had been confirmed, notably by the Algerian fiasco. It was this crisis which let in Gaullism; the political class, not to mention large sectors of the population, wanted a solution. So too did certain advanced sectors of French capitalism, for whom re-orientation of the French economy was paramount. If the established parties of the régime could no longer guarantee the necessary political stability for this, then perhaps Gaullism could (whatever reservations one might have about some non-economic aspects of Gaullist policy). The Gaullist élites, with their ideals of public service and the national interest, were in fact quite favourably predisposed to economic modernization, and thus ready to perform the task required to speed up the modernization of French capitalism. This task consisted in using the power of the state to pressure industry, and to a lesser extent agriculture, into expansion, mainly by concentrating production into bigger units and opening the economy out towards European competition. Such a course involved a certain amount of pressure from the state, and this the parties of the classical right, especially Pinay's CNIP, had been unwilling to exert, even though it was necessary if French expansion were to continue. Now, this does not imply that Gaullism is simply the tool of 'monopoly capitalism' as the communists have alleged; such an analysis does not explain away Gaullist economic and political nationalism, for instance. But one can suggest that there was a convenient symbiosis between the political needs of Gaullism and those of progressive fractions of French capital, which should perhaps make one look with some scepticism on claims to be above class or other interest.

Although it sought, by packing the state apparatus with its own people and by bringing government and administration closer together (*technocratie*) to give the state some autonomy from capital, this autonomy was in the end only a relative one. Gaullism could in the long run only impose its expansionist policies within certain limits; sooner or later it would have to make concessions to fractions hurt by these policies but who still pulled considerable electoral weight. Pompidou's presidency already showed considerable clemency to smaller and medium-sized capital. One might wonder what the future of Gaullism could be, once it had closed the colonial question, brought political stability and expanded the economy as far as possible. Could it retain an identity once these primary tasks had been fulfilled or would it, like earlier Bonapartist régimes which had had similar cleaning-up operations to perform, simply melt away and allow the return of more conventional capitalist forces? Perhaps an examination of the movement's structures might shed light on this.

Structures   The RPR has the vertical structure typical of mass parties. Its basic unit is the constituency union, though smaller groups may meet at the level of the commune or even of the workplace. The constituency union elects two-thirds of the delegates to the federation, the departmental level of the movement; the other third consists of party officials, office holders and ex-officio members. The federation can send policy proposals and suggest candidates for office to the secretary-general in Paris, but the federation secretary can be elected only with the latter's approval. Federations send delegates to the national conference (*assises nationales*) in proportion to their membership and the number of their office-holders. There is another tier of activity between federal and national level, the regional councils, but these do not seem to be very active.

At national level four bodies are important. The two-yearly *assises* are open to all members (40,000 attended the inaugural one in 1976), though only delegates from federations, parliamentarians and members of the Economic and Social Council have voting rights (there were 14,000 of these in 1976). These elect the president of the movement some 170 members of the *comité central* which is supposed to run the movement in line with policy approved at the *assises*; the other members of this body are, since March 1978, all deputies and also members of the *conseil politique*. This body advises the president and consists of the secretary-general (a presidential appointee, currently Bernard Pons), ex-prime ministers, the chairmen of RPR senate and national assembly groups, and other central committee nominees and co-opted members.

If the central committee, is the RPR parliament, then its executive is the *commission exécutive*. This veritable shadow cabinet, which is an oligarchy of presidential nominees, has a dozen national secretaries, who specialize in different areas of policy; it includes the best-known Gaullist leaders, as well as rising stars such as Alain Juppé and Jacques Toubon.

Today the RPR claims over 800,000 members. We do not have a complete sociological analysis of members, but the 230,000 members aged under twenty-five which the movement claims have been broken down as follows: workers 19 per cent, lower white-collars 16 per cent, students 22 per cent, cadres moyens 13 per cent, professions 8 per cent, artisans and *commerçants* 10 per cent, farmers 4 per cent. If this shows a preponderance of intellectual categories (which would doubtless be corrected if the 'adult' membership were taken into account), it also suggests that the popular base of the RPR is far from negligible. Attempts to enlarge this base have led to the setting up of workplace branches (852 with over 25,000 members claimed in 1983) and efforts to get closer to 'moderate' trade unions like FO and CGC (see below). But as C. Ysmal shows, the main effort has been made towards small employers and cadres — precisely the categories tempted by Mitterrand in 1981 and who may have lost out since.[1] In local government, long neglected by Gaullism, strenuous efforts have been made to organize RPR supporters, making full use of the facilities of Paris town hall. In 1983 the RPR gained from both Giscardians and the left; it now controls 151 out of 862 towns above 9,000. Its mayors are organized under the leadership of M. Giraud, the dynamic president of the Ile-de-France region, who recently succeeded A. Poher as president of the influential lobby, *l'Association des maires de France*.

Finance is a crucial ingredient of any political party, both for running expenses and for campaigning. A would-be deputy probably needs 50,000 to 100,000 NF to conduct a decent campaign; the three main presidential candidates in 1974 spent over five million. One might be tempted to think that the *patronat* finances parties of the right, but this verdict needs some refinement. While it has often had money for certain candidates in the past, and while it still employs a full-time political staff under M. de Mourgues, whose main task is to give logistic and financial support to chosen candidates, there is no automatic collusion between the employers' organizations as a whole and any one party of the right. Money tends to come from individuals or sectors within the *patronat* and to be doled out rather reluctantly, and very much on the basis of local situations. It is also widely known that there is a *'caisse noire'* of unspecified proportions in the prime minister's office, which is disbursed at election time.

How, then, do Gaullist finances fit into this picture? As with all parties they are hard to assess. There are probably individuals and groups of employers who donate. Crisol and Lhomeau suggest that the figure of twenty million NF advanced by the RPR is too low to pay staff and other overheads and that Chirac, 'le grand argentier', still has access to considerable but unspecified funds.[2]

The party press is slight for such an important movement. Local efforts apart, there is only really the broadsheet *La Lettre de la nation*, edited by Pierre Charpy, which is rather hard to get hold of. On a more intellectual level there are revues such as *Etudes gaulliennes* or *L'Appel*, which are not official RPR publications but are run by militant Gaullists, usually of the more ideological kind.

Compared with the average of the French population, the Gaullist electorate (see Table 4.2) seems very masculine and middle-aged. Sociologically, there is a high percentage of farmers, retired people, petty-bourgeois and top bourgeois. The working class is under-represented, however. It is also worth pointing out the low number of RPR voters who are either irreligious or belong to a union.

If this suggests that much RPR support is conservative, the hypothesis

Table 4.2   Electorate of major parties (percentages) in the 1970s

	PCF	PS/ MRG	CDS/ Radical	PR	RPR	French electorate
CSP						
Agriculteur, salarié agricole	4	8	13	10	12	9
Artisan, petit commerçant	3	5	9	8	7	6.6
Cadres supérieurs, professions libérales, industriel, gros commerçant	4	8	17	14	13	9
Cadres moyens, employés	19	24	18	17	19	20
Ouvrier	46	31	11	16	20	28.5
Inactif	24	23	32	35	29	26.9
Sex						
Male	52	51	57	46	50	48
Female	48	49	43	54	50	52
Age						
18–24	17	13	9	9	13	15
25–34	24	26	8	17	18	20
35–49	26	26	29	26	25	25
50–64	20	21	28	20	21	20
65 +	13	14	26	28	23	20

Source: September 1977 poll by Louis-Harris-France, *Le Matin*, 6 February 1978.

is confirmed when we look at areas of geographical strength – Alsace and Lorraine, with strong Catholic and nationalist traditions, Brittany and the south of the Massif Central. These are all old conservative areas. But Gaullism has also done well in more industrialized areas such as the Paris region and the north. It has never been very strong in the south, with its long anti-clerical and republican traditions.

All the evidence today suggests that the core of RPR support is increasingly conservative. In 1967–8, the structure of the Gaullist vote was very near to that of the electorate at large (see Table 4.3). Since then it is clear that it has lost much working-class support in particular, and the major task for the RPR is to try and win it back.

Recent polls suggest that the RPR electorate is very close to that of the rival UDF. Thus in a test of voting intentions carried out in June 1983, the two parties ran neck and neck among upper and middle management, lower-white-collars and manual workers, i.e. the whole of the wage-earning strata.[3] The RPR had a fair lead (38 per cent to 27 per cent) among industrialists, artisans and *commerçants* and also among the professions, whereas UDF led among the aged and retired. These figures suggest that beneath the different ideologies and traditions of the right voters perceive a common conservative core.

Politically Giscard's defeat proved just the catalyst that the RPR needed. As the organizational fragility of Giscard's support emerged, leadership of the opposition swung back to the better-structured and

Table 4.3   The right's electorate in the 1960s (percentages)*

	France as a whole (1968 census)	Gaullists + RI 1967	1968
Age			
21–34	29	29	55
35–49	29	26	
50–64	22	26	45
65 +	20	19	
CSP			
Cadres supérieurs, professions	6	5	6
Commerçants	9	11	14
Cadres moyens, employés	17	16	18
Ouvriers	32	28	25
Agriculteurs	12	16	18
Inactifs	24	24	19

* Includes the votes for RI candidates standing in alliance with Gaullists.
Source: J. Charlot (ed.), *Quand la Gauche peut gagner*, Moreau, 1973, p. 52.

tougher-sounding Chiraquians. The RPR has seized its chance. Organization has been tightened; a team of ex-prefects has been hired to run the central office and the older generation of Gaullist 'barons' has now been virtually replaced by younger men, often *énarques* such as Juppé and Toubon, or M. Noir and P. Séguin. Decision-making in the party does remain a largely personal affair, Chirac working closely with a team of preferred advisers, notably C. Labbé (leader of the RPR deputies), C. Pasqua (electoral expert and organizer of mass rallies) and the under-rated Pons. A less aggressive tone is used towards the Giscardians (gone are the days when Chirac could accuse the ex-president of being 'le parti de l'étranger' as he did in 1979) and fences have been mended with historic Gaullists like Chaban-Delmas, hurt by the abrasive thrusting tactics of Chirac. Even left Gaullists such as the UJP youth movement have now drawn closer. This smoother style is allied to the clever use which Chirac makes of his position as mayor of Paris, visiting and receiving heads of state and government, and suggesting that he is a world statesman (and of course a future president).

Programmatically the RPR has been affected both by the effects of socialist government in France and by foreign imports in the shape of Thatcherism and Reaganomics: it now advocates extensive denationalization, tax cuts, privatization of health, educational and welfare services to varying degrees and reduction of government spending to below 40 per cent of GDP. But this type of theory is now shared more or less by all the parties of the right. So too is the other theme which has figured of late, viz. law and order, often linked, and not very subtly, to immigration; here there is clearly a moving towards the themes of the extreme right, whatever disclaimers the moderates might make. Much of the RPR economic theory stems from *Club 89*, a think tank close to the party run by Juppé.

Giscardism – le Parti Républicain (PR)

Development The ancestry of the PR goes back to the *notables* of the early nineteenth century. Representing the post-Revolutionary bourgeoisie, these politicians were staunch defenders of economic and political liberalism, wanting to restrict the state's role to one of maintaining law and order. Originally supporters of a constitutional monarchy based on restricted suffrage, these 'Orleanist' liberals were able to adapt themselves to universal suffrage and parliamentary democracy, merging imperceptibly after 1870 with new political currents based on the middle and lower bourgeoisie. Such were the origins of the moderates or independents of Third and Fourth Republics. If by ideology and temperament such groups were loose and ill organized, consisting of deputies clustered around one outstanding leader and potential prime minister (Ferry, Poincaré, Flandin, etc.), their members often held key posts in government. After 1945 the Cold War and the break-up of tripartism gave them the chance to refurbish a reputation tarnished by the fact that many of them had collaborated more or less willingly with the Nazi occupier. They thus became a key element of coalitions, especially after 1951 under the leadership of A. Pinay. During the Fourth Republic Roger Duchet made energetic but only partially successful attempts to federate these chronic individualists into something resembling a modern conservative party – the *Centre national des indépendants et des paysans* (CNIP).

Most independents were glad to see de Gaulle back in power in 1958. But while liking his financial orthodoxy, they found his presidentialism opposed to their parliamentary mores; and his moves towards Algerian independence clashed with their colonialist views. There thus ensued a split in their ranks in autumn 1962 (over the referendum on the system of presidential election), most of them going into the *cartel des non* and suffering electoral disaster for it. Some thirty-five of them followed de Gaulle, however, and they were led by the young deputy for Puy-de-Dôme, first elected in 1956 and widely recognized as a Pinay protégé – Valéry Giscard d'Estaing. In 1966 they set up a party of their own, the *Fédération nationale des républicains indépendants* usually known as the RI.

Until 1974 the RI played a useful secondary role in French politics. Always within the majority, they used the Gaullist umbrella to prosper, roughly doubling their parliamentary strength. They held some key posts (Giscard at the finance ministry, Marcellin at the interior), and were fully associated with Gaullist policy during its dominant period. Yet they were never Gaullists by temperament, ideology or origins. Their position was summarized in Giscard's famous 'Oui, mais . . .'; they agreed broadly with Gaullist policy but reserved the right to express differing views – notably on European affairs and on questions of economic and political freedoms. Needless to say their dissent did not go far, except for the referendum of 1969 where their hostile vote (Giscard was temporarily excluded from government by the General at the time) effectively sealed de Gaulle's fate. Many Gaullists still cannot forgive Giscard for this; but it meant his return to power under the aegis of Pompidou. The RI were clearly awaiting the end of the latter's mandate so as to install their leader in the Elysée in 1976, but their wish was granted earlier than foreseen when Pompidou died in 1974.

Since then the RI have struggled to develop a party machine to match that of Gaullism, so as to support the actions of their leader. Despite the much publicized metamorphosis of their movement into the PR in May 1977, it does not seem that they have been too successful. But by the 1978 elections they had managed to unite the non-Gaullist parties of the right into a loose electoral organization, the UDF (*Union pour la démocratie française*), very much under PR hegemony. In the new parliament the UDF deputies formed a group; but it was too early to say if this meant the beginnings of a new non-Gaullist mass party of the right.

UDF's problems loomed large after May 1981 when its inspiration and to some extent its *raison d'être* lost office. As UDF recovered from the traumatic loss of half its deputies, its fissiparous tendencies became apparent. The Radicals talk increasingly of reuniting with the MRG (see below); CDS stresses its christian-democrat identity more, and the direct members of UDF who do not belong to one of the constituent parties seem rather lost. Symptomatic of these difficulties is the organizational wrangling which led to the sacking of UDF secretary-general M. Pinton (admittedly not the most adroit of politicians, for all his enthusiasm). Lecanuet and a team of four vice-presidents took over his functions on a basis that seemed temporary. But the ultimate future of UDF depends of course on wider factors than mere internal ones.

Ideology   Today's PR is characterized above all by its style, which could be described as one of moderation. Its spiritual leader, Giscard d'Estaing, is urbane, aloof and coolly intellectual — the very opposite of Chirac, who cultivates an image of hardworking and uncomplicated directness. The style of the parties matches that of their leaders. The RPR goes for what it thinks is a plain man's language, full of appeals to 'common sense'; it is never afraid of polemic and at times positively welcomes noisy public dispute. PR discourse is a more subtle affair, resting on carefully calculated appeals to different categories and not so much on muscular denunciations of 'collectivist' opponents (though these are not to be ruled out in extremis). These differences in style conceal a number of characteristic ideological themes.

First among these is an appeal to individualism against what is seen to be the all-encroaching power of the state — 'donner à l'épanouissement individuel priorité sur l'organisation de l'Etat.[4] This theme, a constant of liberal thought since the early nineteenth century, contrasts with the more Jacobin view of the Gaullist right, which tends to sublimate individuals into the framework of the nation. In the economic field this involves a greater commitment to free enterprise, with no talk of the voluntaristic planning dear to Gaullism; indeed the PR recommends hiving off sectors of nationalized industry to private capital. The PR has something to offer small businessmen and farmers, promising support to those wishing to set up on their own; but it also admits the necessity of rationalizing further both agriculture and industry, speaking of 'une politique industrielle sélective', so as to increase exports. In other words it attempts, somewhat uneasily, to reconcile the claims of big and smaller capital.

Individualism also characterizes the PR view of social relations, where the accent is put on participation and decentralization of responsibilities. This contrasts with the RPR, which the Giscardians like to present (usually more by implication than by direct statement) as being further to the right than themselves. The PR sees society not as a homogeneous block, and not in terms of class cleavages either; rather it is a loose agregate of groups, with the middle groups between the very privileged and the very deprived becoming steadily more numerous. These middle groups can, the PR hopes, be won over. To structure this society, and to ensure greater participation by individuals in decision-making, the PR counts, like its ancestor Tocqueville, on the *corps intermédiaires* — voluntary or public bodies situated between citizen and central government. The PR proposes to give greater powers to voluntary organizations, but there are limits to how far decentralization and participation will be taken: on the level of sub-central government, for instance, the PR, although it claims that it will abolish the tutelary powers of prefects, refuses the creation of regional authorities with proper powers. In the field of industrial relations, while it promises *cadres* a significant say in decision-making inside the firm, it offers workers merely an increased (but quite unspecified) say in the organization of conditions on the shop floor.

Finally, on the level of foreign policy, the liberal tradition has always been less nationalistic than its Bonapartist rival. Thus, Giscardism has always been more favourable to European political integration than Gaullism. The PR programme wants increased co-operation between the developed capitalist democracies — 'une communauté de peuples libres' — in an unspecified way; but the tone of this proposition is in stark contrast to the Gaullist stressing of French priorities. The PR is also characterized by a definite lack of the anti-American feeling which was and is an important emotional constituent of Gaullism.

Structures   Despite the presence of its moral leader in the Elysée and the sophistication and ubiquitousness of its publicity, it should not be thought that the PR was a particularly well-structured organization. When Giscard came to power in 1974, he was in roughly the same position as de Gaulle in 1958 — he had supreme power, but in order to use it fully, he needed an adequate party machine. The old RI fell a long way short of requirements and it is not certain how well today's PR fits the bill.

At local level the significant unit is probably the departmental federation, with its centrally appointed secretary; constituency associations would seem to be fairly weak. At national level the network of committees that ran the old RI has been reduced to two — a *bureau politique* and a *secrétariat national*. These are appointed by the secretary-general, himself elected by the three-yearly party congress The secretariat contains eighteen persons who are responsible for different areas of policy and are in effect PR spokesmen on these topics. The *bureau politique* is a more powerful body, 'le véritable exécutif du PR', and it determines the main outlines of policy. Chaired by the secretary-general, assisted by his two national delegates, it contains twenty-four people, all of them notables. The PR programme has much to say about listening to grass-roots initiatives, but with the long intervals between congresses, the wide powers of appointment accruing to the secretary-general, the PR would seem to be a centralized machine, especially if, as Ysmal claims, party leaders have a monopoly of the congress platform anyway.[5] A generation of ambitious young deputies are currently on their way up the hierarchy and could expect office in any future government where Giscardians figured, notably F. Aubert, A. Madelin and F. Léotard (presently secretary-general).

Little is known about PR finances; the proportion of gifts from companies and individuals is probably high. Campana recounts the unsuccessful attempts of V. Chapot, a senior PR organizer and very close to Giscard d'Estaing, to raise some finance from industry after 1974 by the device (which most political parties in France use) of floating a company which is largely fictitious but whose services can be paid for generously (and legally).[6] The PR probably relied heavily on government for loan of ministerial staff and also for financial support when in office. Clearly since 1981 its resources will have been somewhat strained.

In terms of press the PR is badly served, not managing to produce a regular journal. The cynical would no doubt point out that the radio and television in France did a more than adequate job in propagating Giscardian ideals. There are also a number of weeklies, notably *Le Point*, which, though having no organic connection with the PR, present Giscardian views in an intelligent and readable way.

As regards membership, the PR claimed 90,000 in March 1978 – an improbable figure. Some of these will also be members of the youth movement *Autrement* (previously *Génération sociale et libérale*), which claims 15,000 members and which Wright describes aptly as a movement for well-bred youths. More important are the clubs *Perspectives et réalités* who claim 20,000 members; under Fourcade's chairmanship these clubs are 'think-tanks' which contribute policy ideas and more importantly, attract and groom suitable candidates for local and national office from among the educated and better-off sectors of the population.

The PR is proud of the youth of its membership (one-quarter under twenty-five, 69 per cent under forty-five) but rather more cautious about its sociological composition; it uses an analytical breakdown that does not correspond to the normal system of CSPs. Thus some 11 per cent of members are listed as *fonctionnaires*, which could cover anything from a train-driver to a *chef de cabinet ministériel*. One or two features do stand out, however; there are relatively high proportions of lower petty-bourgeois (18 per cent of *employés*) and of retired or non-working people (over 16 per cent). Workers represent a mere 8 per cent of the total, suggesting that the militant audience of Giscardism at least has not penetrated far below the petty-bourgeoisie.

The PR electorate is of interest as it is very close to that of the Gaullists. If one compares the answers given by both sets of voters to various questions (limitation of the right to go on strike, role of the family within society, opposition to structural changes within society), one sees that the difference between the two is minimal.[7] One can say that the PR and the RPR are fighting for the loyalties of the conservative Frenchman (certainly the PR does well in areas of conservative tradition – Normandy and Brittany, the east, the Alps). It may well be that in the first ballot local considerations and personalities decide which party does best; but in the crucial second ballot there is almost an automatic transfer of support both ways. Conservative voters seem able to recognize that agreement on essentials runs deeper than argument about lesser details.

Giscardian allies

These are the CDS (*Centre des démocrates sociaux*), plus some minor groups. CDS is by far the most significant.

Development   CDS has a long history, inseparable from that of the church. The reader is familiar with the long antagonism of church and republic since the Revolution; but with the consolidation of republican democracy, the church decided to come to terms with the inevitable and encourage Catholics to participate in republican politics, so as to conserve as much influence as possible. The result is christian democracy. Never having much of an audience or organization before 1939, it owed its dramatic start in 1945 to the upheaval of the occupation years and the part played by Catholics in the Resistance. These were the people who launched the MRP (*Mouvement républicain populaire*) at the liberation. It was to become a key party of the Fourth Republic, attracting on occasions up to 28 per cent of the vote and sitting in most governments, sharing power first with the left, then with the right.

This thankless position in the centre of French politics reflected the fundamental contradictions of the MRP, torn between a reformist leadership often close to the socialists on some points (notably social policy and European union) and a conservative electorate. The latter voted for it only because (a) it was Catholic and (b) older conservative parties were discredited by their record during the occupation, and Gaullism was not yet available as an alternative. The revival of both these forces after 1947 took support from MRP, which moved steadily to the right in an attempt to regain this. The MRP was really in a cleft stick; if it supported traditional Catholic demands, such as state aid to church schools, it fell out with the left. But if it turned against conservative vested interests (e.g. that of the home distillers' lobby, responsible for much of the alcoholism in France) it stood to lose votes in vital seats. By 1958 its stock had shrunk steadily, and being identified with the Fourth Republic it shared the opprobrium generally incurred by the régime. Although the MRP supported the arrival of Gaullism and shared in government till 1962, it broke with the General over Europe and the presidential election question; the November election dealt it a death blow, much of its support going over to Gaullism.

After momentary thought about reviving the old alliance with the socialists, the rump of the movement decided to go it alone. It ran a candidate, J. Lecanuet, in the presidential election of 1965 and he scored over 15 per cent on the first ballot. Convinced that there was still a solid bedrock of christian-democrat support in France, he launched a movement, the *Centre démocrate*, in December 1965 to canalize this (the old MRP was wound up in 1967). This 'opposition centrism' fought elections (as the *Centre pour le progrès et la démocratie moderne*) and formed a parliamentary group; but their opposition lacked conviction, to say the least. Some of them joined the majority of G. Pompidou in 1969, under the leadership of J. Duhamel, leaving Lecanuet still in opposition. He joined with another rump-party, the Radicals of Jean-Jacques Servan-Schreiber, in 1971 under the umbrella of *Les Réformateurs*. This coalition scraped together enough deputies to form a parliamentary group (a minimum of thirty is required) in the 1973 elections, but only thanks to Gaullist with-drawals at the second ballot. Giscard's campaign in 1974 was the signal for Lecanuet to abandon his opposition, and he supported the eventual victor right from the first ballot. The reward was a generous share of ministerial portfolios for himself and his friends. It now remained only to unite the two halves of the old CD, as both were now in the majority. This duly took place at Rennes in May 1976, the new formation taking the title of CDS. We can thus summarize its rather untidy evolution in diagrammatic form:

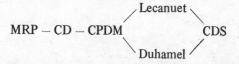

Ideology The CDS has retained much of the character of the main-stream MRP (the members of that organization who took its progressive aspects seriously having long since departed to various parts of the non-communist left). It makes as much as possible of its centrist title, implying that it occupies a happy medium between a 'collectivist' left and a hard, inflexible right (read Gaullism), which is incapable of change. It implies that it is the left wing of the right, as it were, and thus that it is best able to pull Giscardism towards a policy of reforms and even one day (for politics is sometimes made of dreams) serve as a link between Giscardism and the socialists. Lecanuet often casts himself in the unlikely role of siren, attempting to lure the socialists away from their communist partners. CDS discourse is suitably moralizing, and it borrows a lot from a humanistic type of vocabulary developed by the MRP: words like 'justice' and 'responsibility' figure prominently. Yet this is usually mixed with a fairly elementary anti-communism which is certainly cruder than that of the PR. The CDS is clearly reformist, i.e. it does not seek to change the structures of French capitalism but believes that these can be improved by legislative measures, such as income redistribution through the tax system or participation for workers in the workplace (in which they might perhaps go further than the PR). A characteristic theme is the CDS view of the family as the matrix of society and their wish to shape social policy around the family. This and the humanistic discourse are the surest signs of the CDS catholic origins, though the movement denies strenuously that its christian appeal is limited to anv one denomination. Politically, CDS favours greater decentralization. Above all, CDS is committed to European political unity. This has long been its major trademark (and the main source of Lecanuet's opposition to the régime before 1974). CDS leaders can be heard to remark in private that the idea of an independent foreign policy is a myth, although naturally their public pronouncements are more nuanced. A proof of the Euro-peanism of the CDS is its membership of the *Parti populaire européen*, an international grouping of christian democrat parties.

Structures   Apart from traditional Catholic areas (Brittany, Alsace, Auvergne), organizations at constituency level are weak. Departmental federations send delegates to a two-yearly national congress, which elects a president and secretary-general; but in the interim, power resides with the top committees. These are, first, the *conseil politique* composed of departmental delegates and parliamentarians, and theoretically responsible for overall policy guidelines. It also elects thirty members to a *comité directeur*, who sit with various co-optees of the president and secretary-general. Within this latter committee lies the real locus of power, the *bureau politique*, which meets monthly and is composed of president, secretary-general and assistants, treasurer and six others.

Power is thus concentrated in a few hands, mainly those of parlia-mentary notables; this is an adequate structure for a party whose task is not to put on massive displays of militant activity but to rally the *bien-pensants* of provincial, and mainly petty-bourgeois, France. The personality of its godfather, J. Lecanuet, senator and mayor of Rouen, looms large over CDS, though his hegemony is now under threat from a generation of rising stars such as P. Méhaignerie (agriculture minister) and J. Barrot (commerce minister) up to 1981. Méhaignerie's election as CDS president by two-thirds of the vote against B. Stasi (regarded as the leader of the party's 'left') shows the continuation of Lecanuetist orthodoxy and probably the limits to any possible opening towards the left.

If relatively weak in terms of deputies, CDS has a strong base in local government with its 4,000 mayors and 355 departmental councillors, 13 of whom chair their *conseil général*. The CDS also boasts a youth wing, the JDS (*Jeunes démocrates sociaux*), which probably contains most of the real activists; some of them confess disappointment at CDS support for the austere policies of recent governments. There is also a women's movement which claims 4,000 members and which, while by no means militantly feminist, is still very critical of the inadequate life-chances which are offered women in French society.

Membership of CDS as a whole is estimated at 35,000, no sociological analysis of membership being made.

Lack of militants on the ground is compensated by an excellent publicity machine, the best of the right parties. In addition to numerous broadsheets produced by local groups and federations there is a very competent weekly *Démocratie moderne*, which sells 25,000 copies. *Commune moderne* is a specialized review for local councillors: and there is the more theoretical periodical *France Forum*. The ably produced election manifesto *Une Autre Solution* sold 22,000 copies.

The remainder of the Giscardian alliance is made up of random elements, starting with the Radical party, whose history will be recounted at greater length in the following section. It has shrunk sadly from the days when it was the pivot of the republic; today it lives on only through its local councillors and its handful of senators and deputies (most of whose seats are secured by some very subtle electoral alliances); there is also the financial backing of Jean-Jacques Servan-Schreiber (JJSS). Little remains of the old Radical spirit except rhetoric and nostalgia. Lately the party has benefited from the general revival of the right's fortunes. It claims 10,000 members and has 29 mayors in towns of over 9,000. Its future progress depends on electoral reform: if some kind of proportional system is introduced, it might escape from the logic of bipolarization and figure anew as the centre-left pivot in a looser multi-party system. For this reason rapprochement with the MRG (who split off in 1971) is vital; the question is whether to do it now or to wait until MRG deserts the left, as many believe will happen. The battle for the party presidency in 1983 was fought on just this question, and A. Rossinot, defending the second tactic, beat O. Stirn, an unconditional *unitaire*. But electoral change does not depend on the Radicals, and without it their future looks bleak.

Of slightly more significance is the CNIP, that relic of the Fourth

Republic which confounded many who had believed it to be dead by doing quite well in the 1978 elections. The CNIP is really the last stand of the notables of earlier republics, very much the representatives of an earlier phase of capitalism, when the small and medium-sized businesses still weighed heavily in the economy. They are too individualistic to join either Chirac or Giscard d'Estaing. In their numerous brochures and their monthly journal, the independents propound a rugged liberalism. They have never really accepted the welfare state, any kind of government intervention in the economy, women's rights, or moral liberalism; church and family are still very important to them, and most of them regard Giscard as a crypto-socialist. Their anti-communism is the most uncompromising of all. Presided over, curiously, by an *énarque* (P. Malaud), CNIP was alleged by 1983 to be a convenient link between the respectable parliamentary right and the extreme right which prefers battles in the street to duels at the hustings (see below).

(3) Parties of the left

These are essentially the socialists and communists, which are assumed to be on the left because they seek to transform the structures of capitalist society, instead of reforming or managing it. Since 1972 these parties have been combined in a left union, along with the left Radicals (a small left-over from previous republics, which will be discussed briefly). Stimulated by the common programme of government (CPG), which committed its signatories to a precise legislative programme if elected, the union progressed well in terms of popular support until September 1977, when the renegotiation of the CPG broke down, resulting in a drastic deterioration of relations between the partners and the loss of the 1978 elections by the left. But the left union, though at a low ebb, is not dead; the two main partners still claim to be committed to it, and it is hard to see how in the foreseeable future either could find a realistic alternative alliance. For this reason, we shall insist somewhat in this section not just on an analysis of the separate components of the left, but also on their inter-relationship in all its conflictual dynamism.

Socialism – the Parti socialiste (PS)

Development   In 1905 a number of marxist and near-marxist fractions united to form the SFIO (*Section française de l'internationale ouvrière*). The new party was an unstable mixture; its revolutionary marxist rhetoric belied a leadership much more inclined to reformism and the conquest of power through parliament. This contradiction was plastered over, brilliantly, in the theoretical writings and the political action of Jean Jaurès, the effective party leader until he was murdered in 1914. By this time the party's one million votes showed that it had a solid working-class base and was also making inroads into the lower petty-bourgeoisie and peasantry.

A revolutionary party in theory, aiming to establish social owner-ship of the means of production, the SFIO excluded collaboration with bourgeois governments – at least to the point of joining one. But this temptation grew stronger between the wars under the leader-ship of Léon Blum, especially as the party was challenged for the working-class vote by a new and intransigent movement, communism. Pressure came to a head in 1934-6, with the worsening international situation. The threat posed by fascism persuaded communists (with the blessing of the Soviet Union), socialists and radicals in several European countries to join together in Popular Front alliances, the object of which was not to promote socialism but to shore up the wavering capitalist democracies for what seemed an inevitable war against fascism. In France the Popular Front alliance scored a clear win in the 1936 elections, Blum forming a government with communist support, but not participation. Though short-lived, the government implemented a number of changes (forty-hour working week, paid holidays, representative status for trade unions) which have retained a nostalgic, almost mythic odour for people on the left; they are seen as an example of what the left can do when united, and in an odd way 1936 marks a peak of left unity that has never been achieved again.

If its first spell as dominant partner in government had been reluctant, the SFIO was to find itself a frequent member of Fourth Republic coalitions, sharing power first with communists and MRP, later with MRP and Radicals of various hues in the 'third force' type of government – this despite having committed itself in 1946 to a rigorous marxist doctrine under its new secretary-general Guy Mollet. The SFIO record up to 1958 was not brilliant; if it could point with pride to its share in setting up the welfare state institutions of the liberation period and the beginnings of economic recovery, then it had also presided over wage freezes and brutal strike-breaking, as part of the policies demanded by French capitalism for its post-war consolidation. Most of all, in colonial policy, the Mollet government of 1956-7 was responsible for the decisive escalation of the Algerian war. It undertook the disastrous Suez expedition, allowed the forces of repression a free hand in Algeria and made a steady erosion of civil liberties at home. In other words it contributed decisively to that weakening of government authority that in the end killed the Fourth Republic. By 1958 the electoral and militant support of SFIO had sunk as low as the prestige of a régime of which it was now a pillar. It gracelessly admitted defeat and helped de Gaulle to power.

The 1960s were spent exploring various alliances to try and revive the machine. In an early phase it was hoped to revive the old centre-left or third force alliance (MRP to SFIO), an idea particularly associated with G. Defferre, who hoped it could be the platform for a presidential campaign of his own. Lack of enthusiasm by Lecanuet (and also by the communists, who were shut out of this deal) ensured that the idea was stillborn. The mid-1960s saw then a dwarf version of the centre-left alliance called the FGDS (*Fédération de la gauche démocrate et socialiste*). This embraced the SFIO, the Radicals and a group of near-Radical remnants from the Fourth Republic clustering under the leadership of F. Mitterrand known as the CIR (*Convention des institutions républicaines*). This alliance did reasonably well in the 1967 elections, with Mitterrand emerging as a leader of national dimensions, but failed to withstand the electoral disaster of 1968. Since then the logic of bi-polarization has told, and the socialists have been pushed back towards the communists. The rapprochement of the two had been getting under way as early as 1962, in fact, when the communists withdrew a number of second ballot candidates in favour of the SFIO. In 1965 the communists took the dramatic initiative of not running their own presidential candidate and supporting Mitterrand as the united left candidate. In 1967 they again stood down in the second ballot for FGDS candidates and in February 1968 signed a joint declaration with the FGDS in which both partners listed policy points on which they agreed and disagreed. There seemed to be the possibility of a common programme of government emerging as the basis of a united left campaign. But the electoral defeat of 1968 and the Soviet invasion of Czechoslovakia, condemned by the communists with no great enthusiasm, again drove a wedge between communist and non-communist left.

The division was not to be durable, though. During 1969-71 the SFIO rebuilt itself, becoming the PS and formally absorbing Mitterrand's CIR and some smaller groups. The unification congress of 1971 at Epinay-sur-Seine elected Mitterrand as first secretary. As well as changing its name, the PS changed its leaders and its ideas: its 1972 programme *Changer la vie* leaned markedly in the direction of the political philosophy of *autogestion* (see below). Visibly taking on new life, the PS felt strong enough to talk to the communists again; in July 1972 a common programme was actually signed. Fighting the 1973 elections with the CPG behind it, the PS did almost as well as the communists. After Mitterrand's narrow failure in 1974, the party drew in new blood in the shape of several thousand members of the PSU at the *assises du socialisme* of October 1974.

From then to the defeat of 1978 came a steady flood of new members and election wins. But the 1977 quarrel with the PCF and the failure to win in March 1978 posed some questions about the inevitability of PS progress. 1978-81 were very sticky years for the party, marked by factional strife, pivoting on the Rocard/Mitterrand rivalry for the presidential nomination. This personality clash did have ideological and political foundations (see below), and the unhappy display of internecine strife at the Metz congress of 1979 led to some talk of splits. The campaign efforts and the 'divine surprise' of Mitterrand's win, followed by enjoyment of the spoils of office and the difficulties of governing, have healed wounds remarkably. The party is by no means solidly united (it is the nature of democratic socialist parties not to be so), but it is once more a major force.

Ideology   If so much space has been devoted to the history of French socialism, then this is no accident. First, the political and social analyses made by the PS are properly historical, as befits a socialist organization. Second, its own view of itself and its relations with other forces is heavily coloured by memories of its past. The PS sees itself as continuing and extending the old republican tradition, with its attachment to democracy and civil liberties. But it is also a socialist party, believing that capitalism is based on exploitation of the majority and that full democracy and freedom can only be achieved under socialism, when private control of the means of production and exchange is ended. Today the conditions for such a transformation exist: recent monopolistic trends in French and international capitalism have increased exploitation and redrawn the map of society, pushing downwards strata of petty-bourgeois who were previously in a fairly comfortable position. These can be won over, along with the working classes and that part of the petty-bourgeoisie which is employed by the state (and which was for a long time the main activist base of the SFIO), in a 'class front'. This front would seem to involve less of the middle bourgeoisie than the communists' 'anti-monopolist alliance'.

Aware of the poor governmental record of the SFIO, the new PS refuses the label of social democracy (managing capitalism without trying to change its structures, but at the same time trying to redistribute a few social advantages). But it is equally critical of the Soviet type of one-party socialism, with its evident lack of democracy. It has thus developed a third model, *le socialisme autogestionnaire*. Its keynotes are decentralization and responsibility. So far as possible, in any area of activity, power will be brought nearer to the grass roots — whether in the workplace, the school or university, or the local community. The key area of activity, the economy, will be brought progressively under workers' control, starting with the public sector, and extending, it is hoped, into the domain of private capital; intermediary structures between state and private sector, such as self-managing co-operatives, will be encouraged. The risks of economic fragmentation will be avoided by a revitalized and more democratic form of planning, with inputs coming in from the self-managing firms rather than from central ministries.

The PS believes that the transition to *autogestion* can be sponsored by a government based on the left alliance to which it remains fundamentally committed and that it can be done without revolution. It also believes that such a project has more chances of success on a European scale than on a French one, hence its attachment, warts and all, to the EEC and its wish to implement common European socialist policies agreed across national frontiers.

PS programmes are criticized for their utopian character. It is true that *autogestion* is a vague and open-ended ideology, but it does have a clearly libertarian tinge which distinguishes its protagonists from the PCF and helps the PS to appeal to the numerous new middle classes. Moreover, the PS can be very pragmatic or even opportunistic if need be; thus it has changed from supporting unilateral nuclear disarmament to enthusiastic endorsement of French deterrence in response to what seems to be enduring public support for this. Its economic strategy (cf. chapter 1) was again designed pragmatically, appealing to notions of efficiency and greater material benefits. In other areas, the party can be overtly traditionalist if not archaic, cf. its attachment to the doctrine of *laïcité*, which helps tie in to the party categories for whom this concept is central (e.g. teachers in state schools). It is this mixture of idealism and pragmatism in policy choices that helps explain the party's rise, as it gets through to such different publics.

Structures   Basic units (*sections*) exist at workplace or residential level; their delegates attend the departmental federation, which in turn elects to regional and national bodies. The most important of these, constitutionally speaking, is the two-yearly national congress, where delegates are sent by federations in proportion to membership.

Federations also elect delegates to the national convention, which meets twice yearly and which is supposed to check that the sovereign decisions of congress are being upheld by the party executive, the *comité directeur*. This is elected by congress and supervises in the interim the party's office-holders, members and press outlets.

Places on the CD are allotted proportional to votes cast by members for general policy motions presented to congress. Each of these bears a list of signatures in order and is effectively sponsored by one of the fractions or *courants* (see below). Thus congress is the moment when the *rapports de force* between fractions are measured, and it is of course fraction leaders who take the seats on the CD. Thus at the Bourg-en-Bresse congress of 1983 motion I (Mitterrandists + Mauroyites + Rocardians) got 77 per cent of the votes, Motion II (CERES) 18 per cent, and Motion III ('dissident' Rocardians led by Alain Richard) 5 per cent. Seats on the 135 member CD were thus alloted as follows: I — 102 seats,

II – 23, III – 6.

The CD delegates responsibility for day-to-day-running of the party to a smaller nucleus the *bureau exécutif* (BE) whose twenty-seven members meet at least weekly. Again it is elected proportionately. But the real locus of power and initiative inside the party lies inside the BE, in a body called the secretariat (currently fifteen full and fifteen part-members). This is a sort of inner cabinet, with each secretary in charge of one policy area; the first secretary (L. Jospin) is thus a sort of party prime minister. Usually the secretariat is the exclusive preserve of the majority fraction, unless it does a deal (*la synthèse*, in party jargon) with the sponsors of rival motions, in which case the latter are offered secretarial posts in return for signing a revised, unitary motion (whose content can sometimes be quite contradictory!). When there is no *synthèse*, then the BE and CD are like a parliament to the secretariat's government, i.e. it has to get its initiatives past their scrutiny or opposition. But this it can usually do as it has a majority. From 1979 to 1981 the party was governed by a Mitterrand-CERES axis against Mauroy and Rocard.

The fractions (*les tendances*, as they are pejoratively called) have now become central to the party's functioning in a way that few can have imagined in 1971; indeed rule 4 of the party statutes specifically forbids their existence! Yet exist they do with their own internal structures, resources, premises, and publications; they have all the trappings of parties within a party. Usually formed out of groups that pre-existed the rebirth of the party in 1971, they have maintained and consolidated their identities, ensuring that the party is a place where ideas circulate and debate is vigorous, albeit at the risk of that sectarian infighting which, if taken too far, can destroy a party electorally. Such was the experience of the British Labour party in 1983, whose fractions are ironically much less organized. Apart from the 1979 to 1981 period, the fractional leaderships have usually known when not to prolong their disagreements, and the Bourg congress was a perfect illustration. Here the CERES motion criticized the government for its austerity policies and its foreign policy (seen as too anti-Soviet), but in the end CERES accepted a *synthèse* with the pro-government motion of Jospin when the latter made them some concessions.

Fractions are sometimes hard to identify, amid a welter of sub-groups, some of which in turn split from time to time into further sub-groups. Also some of them remain underground, as it were (i.e. they keep their organization intact, but refuse to present motions and hence to 'stand up and be counted'). Thus the Rocardians have signed Mitterrandist motions ever since 1981 (on humiliating terms, as a rule). But most analysts discern four abiding fractions:

(a) the Mauroyites: mainly ex-SFIO members, based on municipal bastions in areas like the mining and textile zone of Nord-Pas-de-

Calais and parts of the *Midi rouge*. Despite marxist language, fairly pragmatic reformists, near to North European social-democracy, and pro-Europe.

(b)   the Rocardians: strongly influenced by 'new left' ideology. Mistrustful of the state and traditional parties as means of social and economic change, relying more on voluntary and co-operative institutions in civil society. Anti-communist and lukewarm on *laïcité*; probably more Catholics here than elsewhere in PS. Derided by rivals, especially CERES, as liberal wolves in socialist sheeps' clothing. Probably the fraction least at-home in the party.

(c)   CERES: marxist left fraction. Sees party as necessarily revolutionary, and determined to make it so. Socialism to result from a fusion of vigorous government action and mass pressure in street and workplace, canalized by party. Most attached to union with PCF, which it sees as transforming both parties. Deliberately nationalist, anti-American and anti-German. Long considered *autogestionnaire* and open to Catholics, but the struggle with Rocard brought it back to its *dirigiste* and *laïciste* roots. Exceptionally obstinate and able leader in J.-P. Chevènement.

(d)   the Mitterrandists: the least cohesive group. Includes Mitterrand loyalists (Joxe, Mermaz, Laignel, etc.) often from a Radical culture with a veneer of marxist economics. Also classic marxists like the sect which follows the ex-PCF notable J. Poperen. Plus a majority of new members from the 1970s without previous experience, including many careerists. Generally the most sectarian *laïcs* (which has facilitated rapprochement with CERES on occasions); claim attachment to left unity, but mainly on electoral grounds. Divided on foreign affairs between Atlanticists and the more independent-minded. Mitterrand's skill and presidential personality was the real cement of this fraction in opposition: since his elevation to the presidency, fear of Rocard and the power of government patronage have been adequate substitutes.

It is hard to judge the exact weight of each fraction, as lately only CERES has had the courage to put up its own motion. But the percentages at Metz were as follows; Mitterrand 40 per cent, Mauroy 14 per cent, Rocard 20 per cent, CERES 14 per cent. These seem to have served as a rough guide to Mitterrand when he composed his governments, for the different posts were distributed with remarkable subtlety between fractions, a procedure known as *dosage*.[8]

The fractions exist thus with all their differences under the banner of the *autogestionnaire* philosophy which they all in theory share. They are not just launching pads for the presidential ambitions of various leaders, though that is one of their roles,[9] but genuine ideological communities which group the faithful under their particular version of the true creed. As such they give the party a suppleness shared by few of its colleagues in the Socialist International.

PS electoral support has undergone a similar evolution to that of successful democratic socialist parties elsewhere. Beginning as a narrow-based workers' and small farmers' party, it has spread to the point where it takes votes across the whole social spectrum (see Table 4.4) functioning as a 'catch-all'. Its membership can best be understood as a series of concentric rings: the nearer you are to the leadership bodies of the party, the higher up the sociological scale you will be.[10] Thus if there are still manual workers and lower white-collars among the 213,000 members claimed in 1983, federal and national élites will come increasingly from the new middle class, especially its intellectual components and among these, especially public sector teachers and lecturers; right at the top, graduates of the *grandes écoles* abound. The weight of these public sector intellectuals is reinforced by the absence of a feature common to North European social democracy, viz. organic links between the party and the labour movement, especially its trade unions. This gap, which makes it very hard for working-class people to rise up through the PS, is such that in the view of some theorists (H. Portelli, A. Bergounioux) the PS and its Latin neighbours should not really be called 'social democratic'. The one organic though unofficial link that the PS has with a union is with the teachers' union FEN (see below), whose input in terms of membership, finance, and last but not least, ideology should not be underestimated.

In regional terms, the party still does best in old republican regions, mainly south of the Loire (especially Burgundy, the Rhône valley, the south-west and Languedoc) and in the old mining and textile areas of the Nord and Pas-de-Calais; it has grown of late in the conservative east and west, even in 1981 to the point where there are seats to show for it.

Finance comes from classic sources. Local and national office-holders pay in a part of their emolument, and members' dues are supposed to amount to 1 per cent of disposable income. In fact they are usually banded in broad categories according to income; thus in 1983 a lecturer, say, would pay around £15 per *month* (as compared with £6 per *year* to the British Labour Party). The party's town planning advisory service *Urba conseil* is a useful source of income, and clearly office has meant that the party gets staffing and doubtless financial help from government. In the past, reformist employers, often friends of Mitterrand, helped out.

The PS has some interesting press outlets. *Le Poing et la rose* is a compact monthly for members, and the weekly *Unité,* under the astute editorship of C. Estier, publishes party documents as well as news and analysis. There is also the *Nouvelle Revue socialiste*, ten times yearly, which aims at a more cultivated public. But the most interesting papers are those with the least formal connection with the PS. Apart from provincial dailies such as *Le Provençal* (owned by

Table 4.4 Electorate of major parties, June 1981, first ballot

N.B. The columns total 100% *horizontally*, i.e. the figure in any box is the percentage of that category which voted for a particular party

	PCF	PSU + far left	PS + MRG + allies	UDF	RPR	other right	Ecologists
Total Electorate	16	1	39	19	21	3	1
Men	17	2	39	20	20	1	1
Women	15	1	38	18	22	4	2
Aged 18–24	18	2	44	14	17	3	3
25–34	17	2	46	16	15	1	3
35–49	17	2	37	18	23	2	1
50–64	18	1	42	19	16	3	1
65+	10	1	27	27	30	5	1
Agriculteur: salarié agricole	6	2	32	28	32	–	–
Artisan: commerçant	10	–	35	19	31	5	–
Cad. sup; profn. libérale: industriel; gros commerçant	7	2	38	19	28	3	3
Cad. moyen: employé	16	2	45	18,	14	3	2
Ouvrier	24	1	44	15	14	1	1
retraité; inactif	16	1	29	23	26	5	–

Source: Nouvel Observateur, 4 July 1981

Defferre) which support the party, there is the Parisian daily *Le Matin* which achieves the difficult synthesis between readability for a mass audience and reasonably sophisticated political analysis. There is a stream of lively theoretical reflection from reviews like the CERES *L'Enjeu*, or the Rocardians' *Interventions*.

Communism – the Parti communiste français (PCF)

Development   Like most of its sister-parties in Europe, the PCF began as a split from an existing socialist movement, in the aftermath of the First World War and the Bolshevik revolution. Thus the SFIO congress at Tours in December 1920 saw admirers of the Russian revolution leave 'la vieille maison' to form a new party, the PCF. Accepting the rigorous twenty-one conditions for membership laid down by Lenin, the PCF was admitted to the Third International (Comintern), and for a long time carried the sub-title SFIC (*Section française de l'internationale communiste*). If its founders were enthusiastic about Leninism, however, they had still much to learn about the theory and application of that doctrine. It would take over a decade to 'bolshevize' the new party and make it something like the disciplined instrument demanded by Leninism. During this period the PCF remained a marginal force in French politics.

Its future depended, then as now, on its relations with socialism. Until the mid-1930s it would attack the SFIO with the slogan of 'classe contre classe', stressing the necessity of a revolutionary break with capitalism and denouncing the reactionary nature of the SFIO for implying that this could be achieved without a vanguard party (like the PCF). In this it was faithful to the policy laid down by the Comintern, the co-ordinating body for all communist parties under firm control of the Soviet Union. When the Comintern made its famous tactical 'turn' of 1934, however, and recommended the adoption of Popular Front tactics, things changed rapidly for the PCF. Its new tone of social consensus for class-struggle, patriotic nationalism for working-class internationalism and defence of parliamentary democracy instead of denunciation of 'bourgeois freedoms' gave it huge gains in membership, parliamentary seats and trade-union support – a base which it has never lost since, in fact.

A good resistance record (especially after the Nazi invasion of Russia in 1941) helped the party's reputation, and it shared power from 1944 to 1947 with SFIO and MRP. During this time it made every effort to preserve political and social stability in France and to boost production, succeeding so well that de Gaulle acknowledged this in a letter to the widow of Thorez (PCF leader) on his death in 1964. This was the party's peak period for electoral and militant strength. But the Cold War brought its eviction from government and the return to a ghetto from which it has tried to escape ever since. Permanently shut out of government, despite holding a steady fifth of the popular vote, the PCF could at first only retreat into a doctrinaire shell, with the occasional flexing of its industrial muscle as sole response to its isolation. But by the early 1960s the start of de-Stalinization in Russia, the end of the Cold War and the logic of bi-polarization were all leading to a situation where alliance with the non-communist left might seem more feasible. The slow genesis of the 1972 alliance has already been described. But it was always a conflictual one, and from 1974, when it was clear that the PS was the major beneficiary, the conflict worsened to the point where the PCF was ready to weaken the alliance and in effect lose the 1978 elections. But in so doing it held back socialist growth and kept intact most of its own positions in terms of votes and seats.

This on-off relationship with socialism, characterized by mutual need but equally strong hatred, has hardly changed at bottom over six decades. It raises the question: what sort of party is the PCF?

Ideology   Marxism sees historical development as working through class-struggle: a new type of society only comes into being when a ruling class is supplanted, probably violently, by a rising one. Under capitalism the rising revolutionary class is that of the workers: only it could destroy capitalism and establish a social order not based on exploitation. Lenin added to this proposition a significant rider, namely that, left to itself, the working class would probably develop no more than a reformist consciousness. For it to become revolutionary (i.e. to see its situation clearly and to realize the task awaiting it), it needed guidance from an external factor, the party. Formed of those who had acquired a Marxist understanding of history (and thus an organization which placed a premium on quality rather than quantity) the party would organize the class for the seizure of power, the dismantling of the bourgeois state apparatus and the building of socialism.

The party must thus be disciplined. In Leninist language it would practise 'democratic centralism' — democratic because the party hierarchy is freely elected and preliminary policy options freely discussed, but centralized because, once policy has been decided, it must be implemented by the base without question. The existence of organized tendencies inside communist parties has been forbidden since 1921. How democratic centralism operates in the PCF will be seen shortly; but such was the Leninist concept which marked it from its outset — hierarchized, disciplined and dedicated to revolutionary class-struggle under the aegis of the Soviet Union.

Over the years a number of factors have eased the PCF away from its purist origins. The evident shortcomings of Soviet socialism: the fact that conditions under French capitalism have never been catastrophic enough to drive huge sectors of the population into the PCF's arms: the division of Europe into two spheres of influence, with France firmly in the capitalist one – all these have led the party to reconsider its role and to move, along with the Italian and Spanish parties notably, towards what is rather sloppily called 'eurocommunism'. For the PCF at least this means that there is no universal model of socialism, certainly not the Soviet one; France must invent its own. Moreover, such a socialism is now considered attainable by non-violent means: electoral victory of the PCF and its allies will usher in a period of 'advanced democracy' where economic and social reform will create conditions for a later stage, socialism, whose characteristics are not specified. The basis of this analysis is the theory of state monopoly capitalism (SMC); it is held that the high degree of interpenetration between the state apparatus and vast industrial and commercial concerns has raised productive capacity to a high level, but only at the cost of increasing hardship and deprivation for many sectors of the population – all, in fact, except the very top layer of bourgeois, 'une poignée de milliardaires insolents', as G. Marchais is wont to put it. This means that an electoral alliance of all the deprived is feasible, 'l'union du peuple de France', under PCF hegemony, of course. The PCF is so committed to the idea of a French socialism that it has made its own the Gaullist notion of independence in foreign affairs, even to the point of accepting the French nuclear deterrent which it opposed for years.

This theoretical revision explains a number of points conceded by the PCF of late. It now admits the possibility of political pluralism during the phase of socialist construction or even of power returning to the right after a period of socialist-communist government; previously it had held to the theory of proletarian dictatorship (which meant in practice irreversible one-party rule), but this was struck off the statutes at the twenty-second congress in 1976. The PCF proclaims its attachment to civil liberties and the necessity to extend these; previously it tended to regard them as 'formal' (i.e. not worth very much). On numerous occasions it has criticized the Soviet Union, timidly at first (cf. the mild reproaches over Czechoslovakia in 1968) but with growing firmness (cf. its obtaining the release of the dissident Plyutsch or its approval of an underground film condemning labour camps in 1976). But this has by no means cleared up the party's problems of identity, either for itself or for others. Perhaps this will become clearer if we examine PCF structures.

Structures   The PCF hierarchy is as follows:

Paris   Congress (elects Central Committee, which elects
                 bureau politique (BP) and secretaries)

Department	Federation conference (elects federal committee, which elects *bureau* and secretaries)
Workplace or locality	Section conference (elects committee, which elects *bureau* and secretary)
Workplace or residential	cell (has own bureau and secretary)

The national congress is the sovereign body of the PCF; its authority is delegated to the two-monthly central committee, which leaves day-to-day affairs to the *bureau politique*. In 1983 the CC had 145 members including 24 substitutes; the BP had twenty-two members, seven of whom enjoyed the rank of secretary. G. Marchais is secretary-general.

The organigram shows a pyramidal structure which appears un-exceptional in that the lowest level elects delegates to the next level, and so on upwards. Thus the national leadership, vested in the BP, should be an emanation, albeit indirect, of the grass-roots, and thus amenable to its ideas and proposals. If anything, the reverse is true; it seems that the leadership (and some would even claim the secretary-general) is able to decide changes in policy or tactics (cf. the volte-face over the nuclear deterrent in May 1977) and have them executed by an obedient membership. Revolts do occur in the lower echelons (e.g. after the Soviet crushing of the Budapest insurrection of 1956, or after the electoral disaster of 1978): and in the past, purges were used to restore order. Probably two features explain the relative ease with which the BP runs its machine. One is the party's vertical system of communication: there are no sideways links between cells, which effectively prevents grass-roots discontent from gaining momentum. The second is the hold exerted by *les permanents* (full-time party employees, hence unlikely to cross the leadership) who occupy key positions in the apparatus, notably at the level of federal secretary. Although they are elected, their candidacy has to be approved by the candidates' commission of the CC; in other words they have to have BP approval. Hence this system of filtering ensures that only loyalists win office; and they are expected to 'bien tenir' sections and cells below them. Thus compared with the PS or the parties of the right — although we have seen that one can exaggerate the extent to which the grass-roots influence policy here also — the PCF seems to have perfected a watertight system whereby a small professional élite decides and imposes policy.

Several other features characterize the PCF as a party 'pas comme les autres'. Its strength in the workplace is well known — 9,922 cells in late 1977, with a very strong presence in the public sector. Linked to this is its symbiotic relationship with the CGT (see below). In 1978 eight out of sixteen of the CGT leadership were communists, as were eighty-eight out of ninety-six federal secretaries. It is customary also to remark on the party's influence over other associations in civil society, professional and voluntary alike. The main secondary and higher teachers' unions, the SNES and SNESup, are led by PCF militants; so too is the small farmers' union MODEF. The party's influence spreads across bodies such as the *Mouvement de la paix, l'Union des femmes de France* and even ex-soldiers' associations. In all these bodies, communists attain hegemony not because they are 'submarines' or infiltrators, but by hard graft and dedication — qualities for which there are no substitutes in politics.

The party is also important in the publishing world. Its *Editions sociales* produce an impressive range of marxist work at fair prices. There is the party daily *L'Humanité* (claiming sales of 240,000) and three dailies based on provincial towns. The weekly *La Terre*, aimed at farmers and passionately opposed to enlargement of the EEC, is very readable. The main theoretical review is *Cahiers du communisme*, which often has important party texts. PCF economic theory is treated in *Economie et politique*, now more popularized, and the more difficult *Issues*. The weekly *Révolution*, a fusion of two previous publications run by vaguely dissident elements, has lost the dynamism of both its predecessors. In this connection one should mention the immense effort that the PCF puts into education; as well as running many levels of schools for its activists it has a permanent research institute, the Institut de recherches marxistes.

A good deal is known about party finances. In 1981, 84 million NF were collected in dues and from office-holders (who turn over their salary to the party and are paid back the wages of an OP); a further thirteen millions came from collections, donations and fêtes. This would not suffice to pay the wages of the several hundred full-time officials which the party uses in Paris and the provinces. The PCF has thus developed a commercial sector of some importance, involving up to 300 firms and solidly competing with capitalist enterprise. Its activities include property, printing and agriculture, especially the Interagra export company directed by the 'red millionaire' J.-B. Doumeng. Commentators show some smugness in criticizing the PCF for possessing this veritable capitalist empire; but as, unlike its rivals, it receives no help from government or private capital, it must finance itself somehow. It can hardly be expected today to rely on handouts of 'Moscow gold', for which it was stigmatized in the 1930s. Writers like Montaldo still insist that the party is funded by the USSR but their case is not proven.

In February 1982 the PCF claimed 710,000 members in 27,700 cells; these are believed to turn over at a high rate (maybe 15 per cent p.a.), leaving a relatively stable core at the centre of, say, 50,000 activists who are really the heart of the party. Nugent gives the following figures for 1979 to describe their sociology:[11] farmers 3.4 per cent, artisans/*com-merçants* 4.1, lower white-collar 28, intellectuals 13 and manual workers 51. Although the weight of the latter categories may be exaggerated, there is no doubting the strong popular base of the PCF. And it is true that with rare exceptions it is working-class people who rise to the top of the party, in a way unthinkable in other parties: a typical career begins with union work in the CGT, followed by responsibilities at cell or section level, then, after following courses at a party school, perhaps office as a federal full-timer and so on to eminence in late middle age as a member of the central committee. Nowadays the party is more feminine (35.7 per cent women) and seems readier than others to give responsibilities and winnable candidacies to women. It is also young, half the members being under forty.

The PCF vote held steady at 20.6 per cent in 1978. Its bastions are where one would expect them to be, among the working class – Paris suburbs and those of other big towns, Nord and Pas-de-Calais, Lorraine steel area, Bouches du Rhône. But the party has grown in audience in the poorer departments of the south-west, Limousin and Languedoc-Roussillon, thanks to its diligent espousal of the small farmer's cause. Its weakest areas are, unsurprisingly, Alsace and Brittany.

The 1981 elections were a disaster, as many supporters seemed to sanction the PCF's retreat to more sectarian positions. The presidential poll brought 15.3 per cent and the parliamentary one 16.2 per cent. A quarter of the vote had gone. More seriously, only 24 per cent of the working class now voted PCF, compared with 44 per cent PS; and other popular categories showed a similar loss of support. These trends continued through the municipal polls of 1983, as seen in the loss of several 'red belt' suburban towns, very much the bastions of the party and long considered impregnable. This suggested that 1981 was more than a passing accident.

The left Radicals – Mouvement des radicaux de gauche (MRG)

The MRG is heir to a proud tradition. Radicalism was a major force of earlier Republics, notably the Third, where it was in the vanguard of the struggle for parliamentary democracy and the secular state. Perhaps the peak of its achievement was in 1905, when both could be said to have been achieved. Radicalism was based on the petty-bourgeoisie and parts of the peasantry of the provinces: its typical *notable* was the small-town professional man, usually well-entrenched as mayor or deputy and operating on a fairly clientelistic basis, distributing favours obtained from Paris in return for electoral support. The slow rate of change in pre-war France meant that such categories remained important long after the movement had achieved its political aims.

Hence it could only become conservative, winning elections on the strength of its progressive rhetoric and then governing in a timorous way, often in alliance with the right. This led to the joke that a Radical was someone whose heart was on the left but whose wallet was on the right.

The revival of 'third force' politics after 1947 enabled the Radicals to continue this performance under the Fourth Republic, the only exception being the energetic premiership of P. Mendès-France in 1954–5. This capable and far-sighted leader cut several Gordian knots in foreign policy before his appetite for reforms aroused the hostility of the more cautious Radicals and split the party into two. The decline continued through the Fifth Republic and the movement split yet again in 1971, some following JJSS into alliance with Lecanuet (and later Giscard d'Estaing), others joining the left alliance and signing the CPG. These, under R. Fabre, set up a separate party, the MRG.

MRG discourse continues the republican, 'humanist' tradition. For free enterprise (but against its logical outcome, big capitalism), for private property (so long as it does not become 'gigantisme industriel'), against bureaucracy and for civil liberties, the MRG emerges as what it has always been — the champion of the small man. It likes to suggest that it is the salutary leaven in a dough consisting of doctrinaire communism and socialist adventurism — so much so that one wonders why it ever signed the CPG. The answer is that MRG deputies need communist votes on the second ballot.

The 1981 presidential elections vindicated MRG's decision to field a candidate, M. Crépeau, both in terms of votes won and rewards afterwards, in the shape of ministerial office for Crépeau and others. But survival remained a problem, as in late 1981 two MRG deputies switched to the PS. The election of J.-M. Baylet (whose family owns the famous old radical newspaper *la Dépêche*) as party president in 1983 hinted that the search for unity with the other Radicals might be about to begin seriously, as MRG doubts about the left's chances in 1986 grew.

(4) Fringe parties

On the left

The most notable of these is the *Parti socialiste unifié* (PSU). It began life in 1960 as a refuge for those disgusted with the established left, its early militants including leftish catholics, communists driven out by the rigidity of the PCF, socialists repelled by Molletism and Mendesists alienated from the stagnant Radical party. Always prone to faction-fighting, its role was to gather and to stimulate debate.

Its electoral weight was slight (a handful of deputies, Rocard's defeat of Couve de Murville in a by-election in 1969 and his 3.7 per cent of the first-ballot vote in the presidential election of that year); but electoralism was never a PSU priority. It aimed to create a new socialist movement, neither social-democratic nor Leninist. In particular it helped to develop and vulgarize the theory of *autogestion*: Though critical of the CPG, the PSU supported Mitterrand's 1974 campaign — a sign perhaps that some members felt the PS to be moving towards their policies. Confirmation of this came in October 1974 when Rocard took 3,000 militants with him into the PS after the *assises du socialisme* meetings. But the *pur et dur* minority remained active: in 1974 C. Piaget was the inspiration of the work-in at the Lip watch-factory.

The PSU presidential campaign in 1981 was disappointing, but it has given critical support to the government since. History was made in 1982 when Huguette Bouchardeau accepted the post of environment minister, becoming the first PSU member to enter a government. Typically the party was badly split on the issue, fearing that it would be exploited as a fig-leaf to cover Mitterrandist austerity. Increasingly, as well as providing critical ideas for the left in general, the party's future would seem to lie in its ever-closer involvement with movements in French civil society, outside the ambit of formal party politics. Hence its leading role in the French equivalent of CND, CODENE (*Comité pour le désarmement nucléaire en Europe.*)

France also boasts a plethora of organizations of the classic extra-parliamentary left, viz. Trotskyists and Maoists. Of the latter, the best known is probably the PCMLF (*Parti communiste marxiste-léniniste de France*), which publishes the paper *L'Humanité rouge*. French Trotskyism is marked by the mutual suspicion and internecine sentiments which characterize Trotskyist movements elsewhere. Of particular note are the *Ligue communiste révolutionnaire*, of which A. Krivine is the best-known spokesman. *Lutte ouvrière* is probably associated for most people with Arlette Laguiller, bank clerk and presidential candidate in 1981, where she took one vote in forty on the first ballot.

Small but committed, the far left organizations put most of their energy into campaigning — for conscripts, for women's rights, for tenants, for immigrants, against nuclear power stations. Often they discover themes which are 'recuperated' by the official left for electoral purposes. They also provide many young people with their first experience of active politics and introduce them to a marxist analysis of society — both of which acquisitions may well be put to use later on within the parties of the official left, when revolutionary ardour has cooled somewhat. As such, the far-left organizations may well play within the political system a role somewhat different from that which they intended.

On the right

Like most of her neighbours, France has not been spared from fascism. In the 1930s, a number of semi-fascist 'leagues' flourished, and under Vichy genuinely pro-Nazi elements eventually came to the fore. After 1960 there was a revival of fascism with the OAS, which did not flinch from terrorism in its resolve to keep Algeria French at all costs. The economic recession of the seventies, with its unemployment and tendencies towards economic nationalism, has given fascists in France and elsewhere a new target, the black immigrant worker. In France today there are still people who preach the traditional themes of fascism – the 'strong state', seen as the only barrier to marxist collectivism, total commitment to nationalism, and racialism. The main groups are the PFN (*Parti des forces nouvelles*) run by people close to the newspaper *Minute*, and the *Front national* of J.-M. Le Pen, ex-Poujadist deputy and OAS supporter.

Although it was widely believed that the far right represents less than 1 per cent of electoral opinion, it has undergone an upswing of late. In the by-elections of late 1983 the FN, exploiting themes of insecurity and unemployment, which it blames with brutal simplicity on immigrants, had several scores of above 10 per cent, some in working-class suburbs. At Dreux it was offered places on the victorious list led by an RPR sympathizer, and Le Pen's fame grew to the extent of being interviewed on BBC television. Part of this revival is due to the fact that the official right has started using these themes; and indeed it seems that the far right has striven hard to infiltrate the moderate parties, especially CNIP.[12] It is too early to say whether this collusion will establish the FN as a serious political force or whether (as happened in the UK in the 1970s) its new-found support will drift back to the conservative parties as they adopt some of its themes and vocabulary. Indeed there is already tension in these latter parties as they argue about the nature and extent of possible alliances with the hard right.

Associated with this latter but not synonymous is the new right, a group of intellectuals concerned not with party organization but with the ideological renewal of the right.[13] To this end they have updated in a new language some very old themes, appealing to biology to demonstrate the truth of what they see as inevitable natural inequality, and stressing the superiority of Western Christian civilization over what they call the totalitarianism of the Soviet system. This highly Parisian mode is well publicized in the media (especially *Figaro-Magazine*): it would be hard to say how influential it has been in the ideological development of the established right-wing parties or in their convergence with the extreme right.

Ecologists

This new force cannot yet be classified in traditional terms. They made a spectacular impact in the 1977 elections (270,000 votes: more than 10 per cent in Paris and other big towns). The burden of their protest is familiar — the waste and probable exhaustion of natural resources by industrialized societies, the social ills which result from pollution and other nuisances, the dangers of nuclear power. But it is not clear how ecologism fits into existing political structures. Is it just a self-interested pressure-group, of the type that does not want a motorway in front of its own garden, but has no objection to one in front of someone else? Or can it become a new political movement, traversing existing parties and creating a new politics on the basis of its particular problematic (the use/misuse of nature)? Alternatively, will the movement be 'recuperated' by existing parties, all of whom are rapidly straining to develop an ecological dimension?[14] Ecologists themselves are a heterogeneous collection, as shown by the existence of candidates from two movements (a radical one and a more 'apolitical' one) in 1978, and voting behaviour in the second ballot (some ecologists voting on the right, some on the left).

Despite Lalonde's success in 1981, the ecologists remain bedevilled by personal rivalries and conflicting ideological and strategic options. The 1983 municipal elections showed a loss of half the vote from 1977, due to division among ecologists (some of whom were on right-wing lists and some on the left) and in some cases clever absorption of certain demands by established parties. The 1984 European elections were a chance to present a united list and hence to work towards a unified movement (in 1979 the ecology list almost broke the 5 per cent threshold necessary to elect representatives).

It is hard to place the *Mouvement des démocrates*, led by M. Jobert, once Pompidou's foreign minister. They are basically left Gaullists, alienated by what they see as Chirac's betrayal of traditions. This small formation contests elections and it supported Mitterrand in 1981. Jobert was rewarded by appointment as minister of foreign trade but resigned after two years in protest at apparent lack of government will to protect French industry. Typically this enigmatic figure had no real alternatives to suggest. Politically he has always claimed to be neither on the right nor the left but 'ailleurs'. In 1983 it looked as if 'ailleurs' really meant 'nulle part'.

(5) The parties today

On the right it is clear that the Chiraquian RPR has staged a remarkable comeback. After 1974 it was predicted that Giscardism with its control of presidential patronage would weaken or even absorb its rival. This was to underestimate both the strength of ideological traditions and of party apparatuses; thanks to the 'premeditated treason' of May 1981 the RPR has turned the tables. Its organizational superiority and the growing sophistication of Chirac make it the leader of the right; and Chirac must start favourite in the 1988 race for the presidency.

The UDF suffers from organizational fragility and from the fissiparity inevitable when different political traditions are hastily ground into an electoral machine. Its future depends on its ability to overcome these handicaps and present a unified and plausible liberal alternative to the populism of Chirac. 1988 is the crucial date but there are three stages on the way. First are the direct elections to the European Assembly in 1984. If UDF joined a united list, it would have to take the terms offered by Chirac, which might be seen as a sign of weakness. If it ran separately and finished behind the RPR, that too would imply weakness. The choice will again have to be made at the 1986 parliamentary elections, where the UDF must decide if there are to be one or two right-wing candidates at the first ballot. But whatever it does then, the UDF must stand up and be counted in 1988; for the presidential competition is where real power is allocated, and no serious party dare shun it. But there are problems here. Giscard now seems stuck with the tag of loser and would probably be seen as a liability. The logical alternative, R. Barre, for all his intelligence, suffers from severe handicaps. One is his over-weening arrogance, which frightens even his close supporters, and the other is that he was after all jointly responsible for the policies – and failures – of the last septennate.

For these reasons there is growing talk, including in the moderate left press, of a bid by Simone Veil, popular former president of the European Assembly and ex-health minister under Giscard. This liberal and humane figure might be better placed than others to pull votes from the floating centre ground. UDF thus faces some hard choices. Yet it will survive, even if its constituent parties do not knit any closer together.

It may well be that programatically the right-wing parties are today closer than ever: to a greater or lesser extent they are all in favour of denationalization, tax cuts, reduction of public spending and privatiz-ation of welfare services. In foreign policy they are all born-again Cold Warriors, yet apprehensive about the reliability of the USA and aware of the need for greater European self-reliance in defence. Their divergences are comparatively minor (e.g. length of the presidential term of office). Sociologically and indeed on most political or ideological questions, their electorates are very close. But none of this means that France will end up with a single conservative party, for two factors pull strongly against this unitary pressure. One is the weight of tradition and history; movements with a long past and a record of achievements do not easily lose identity, especially as their activists sustain themselves with a myth-ology which pivots on their own distinctness and exclusivity. The other factor is more material; parties are apparatuses aiming at state power. They contain leaders and supporters able and willing to fill posts in the state so as to implement their policy goals. Supply of such places is limited and demand great; and the mechanism which allots them is at bottom the party. So the parties will continue their separate ways. UDF will have to convince voters that it is sufficiently like RPR to be trusted with the running of a conservative France, but sufficiently different as to justify voting for it. RPR will be trying to do exactly the same. Differences will be stressed but always within the fundamental parameters of conservatism. This process will last a long time yet.

The break-up of September 1977 did raise acutely the question of the conflictual relationship of the PCF and PS.

The PCF's desire to break was prompted by simple considerations. It was not simply that the PS was prone to reformism and hence potentially disloyal to the CPG (this was as true in 1972 as it was in 1977); behind PCF allegations of a socialist 'virage à droite' and readiness to strike a bargain with Giscardism, lay the unpleasant truth that the PS was benefiting more from union than the PCF. The PS was growing and appealing to the better-off workers and lower petty-bourgeois, but the PCF seemed incapable of extending its appeal beyond the 20 per cent of its hard-core support. It thus faced the prospect of entering government as a junior partner, with slight influence; it might find it difficult to get the CPG implemented, never mind extended (especially as economic growth, on which the CPG was predicated, had been less rapid since 1974). The PCF thus needed either to get extensive guarantees from the PS (which were not forthcoming in the re-negotiations) or failing that, to make sure that the left failed to win. For marxists, power is not worth having unless one is able to use it to make significant change.

What does the PCF stand for, then, and how does it see its role? Today it has moved further away from the Soviet Union than ever before; but it has still made no detailed analysis of the shortcomings of that system (perhaps because this would involve questioning the role of the Soviet communist party, hence of itself). There are several views of the party: a revolutionary Bolshevik party, still: a rallier of the exploited and discontented: a potential party of government: or even, as Kriegel claims, an 'alternative society' with its own life-style and values. Perhaps the PCF is all of these at once; what is sure is that it is still a Stalinist party, albeit, as Kriegel says, a degenerate one. By this is meant that it is still a blunt instrument, wielded according to the calculations of an entrenched leadership.

In fact the PCF has been in acute discomfort since 1981. It has ministers, but in a sense is half in and half out of government. The ministers do their job with impeccable cabinet solidarity, while the party press and the CGT snipe at the policy outcomes, especially in economic and foreign affairs. Periodically Jospin calls the PCF to order, and commentators pit their wits as to when it will leave government, either voluntarily or by eviction. Realistically the party can only hope that the Mitterrand experiment is enough of a failure to drive 'les deçus du socialisme' back into its arms. Readers will probably think that this is not much by way of a political project.

Yet this relationship with the PS probably remains the main determinant of party behaviour. In a sense these Siamese twins are competing for the same ground, even if in a good period the PS can stretch its support further to the right. No one knows if the recent electoral erosion of the PCF is definite; but it must start quickly to regain its working-class support as well as that of the middle strata, especially technical and intellectual, which some see as the groups which are hardest for it to attract.[15] Paradoxically it is one of the party's greatest strengths which makes the widening of its appeal most difficult.

This strength is its real working-class identity. It is not just that its activists and supporters are workers; the party has helped foster a proletarian culture or way of life which stresses the profound differences between workers and the rest. This implies a sort of angry pride in belonging to the class and 'le parti qu'elle s'est donné'. And this culture is maintained by the activity of the PCF through all its antennae and institutions. Many believe that the unattractive features of the party (its mechanical Stalinist structure, its dogmatism and its attachment to 'real socialism') are somehow part of this identity.[16] At any rate it seems hard for the party to abandon them in an attempt to please middle groups who might not be attracted anyway. Yet in the long run the PCF will have to change itself to some extent if it is to avoid ghettoization as the representative of a traditional and declining working class. It cannot go on forever purging people who ask awkward questions, such as J. Elleinstein or H. Fiszbin.

The real problems of the PS will begin when it loses office, and the inevitable recriminations set in as to whether there was too much or too little socialism. This is when the full potential for conflict which the party's fractional structure implies will be released. But the PS will probably prove resilient enough to show that it was no mere flash in the pan which could cobble together an alliance of the new middle classes and workers temporarily alienated from the PCF long enough to win an election, but nothing more. In terms of votes and seats it is bound to descend some way from the high point of 1981. By the end of the decade its ideological discourse will doubtless be as maximalist as ever and as strident. But by then people will be able to see it better for what it is, namely an inter-class, reforming party of a type which historically seems necessary to occupy the middle ground in the sociologically diverse industrial states of the developed world.

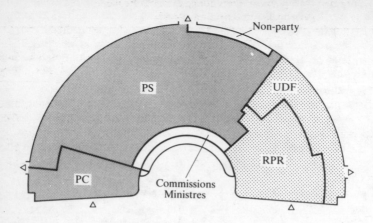

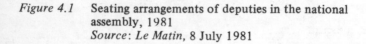

Figure 4.1   Seating arrangements of deputies in the national
assembly, 1981
Source: *Le Matin*, 8 July 1981

(6) Interest groups

Political parties compete for power in the hope of translating their
supporters' demands into public policy; besides them one finds, in
pluralistic societies, interest groups. The aim of these is more modest;
bringing together people with common objectives (economic, ideological, etc.) with a view to furthering such objectives by common
action. When they try to influence public policy in this direction
(i.e. by trying to influence decisions within the state apparatus) they
are termed pressure groups.

France has her share of these, but observers have always been
struck by the much looser relationship that they enjoy with the state
than in, say, the Anglo-Saxon countries. In the latter, some groups
appear so well integrated into the process of political decision-making
as to be almost parts of the state apparatus. Much has been written
on French groups, and the current debate has been so well summarized
by Wright that only a few remarks need be made here.[17] Basically,
there is no single model which covers adequately all the possible
relationships between the French state and groups. The latter are not
always natural enemies of the state, prone to violence so as to extract
concessions from a rigid bureaucracy. Nor are they passive clients,
'recuperated' by the government so as to implement its policies more

Table 4.5 Main political forces during the Fifth Republic, performance in general elections*

		Election date						
		Nov. 1958	Nov. 1962	March 1967	June 1968	March 1973	March 1978	June 1981
Communists								
	A	18.9	21.8	22.5	20	21.3	20.6	16.2
	B	10	41	73	34	73	86	44
Socialists								
	A	15.7	12.5	19[c]	16.5[c]	20.7[e]	24.7[e]	37.5[e]
	B	44	66	116	57	101	114	283
Radicals								
	A	11.5	7.8					
	B	40	39					
Christian democrats								
	A	10.8	16.8[a]	17.9[a]	10.3[d]	13.1[f]		
	B	57	55	41	33	64		
Independents								
	A	19.9					21.5[g]	19.2[g]
	B	192					137	62
Gaullists								
	A	17.6	37.7[b]	37.7[b]	44.7[b]	36.4[b]	22.6	20.8
	B	206	268	245	360	238	148	85

* The percentages in every case do not total 100, as the scores of minor formations are omitted; A = percentage of first-ballot votes; B = number of seats eventually won.
a   combined total of MRP and opposition independents.
b   combined total of Gaullists and Giscardian RI.
c   combined total of SFIO and Radicals allied as FGDS.
d   centrists' group, CPDM.
e   combined total of PS and MRG.
f   30 of these were centrists elected in alliance with the majority: the total also includes those Radicals allied with Lecanuet as *les Réformateurs.*
g   combined total of UDF (PR + all remaining centrists).

easily. Nor are they so strong as to dictate policy to certain ministers – although one could easily find examples of all these situations. There are in fact an infinite number of possible relationships between state and groups, and the extent to which groups can extract concessions depends on several variables: their organization, finance, capacity for publicity, access to decision-makers and so on. One point that most observers would concede is that the groups' targets have shifted some-what; today access to ministers or the Elysée is much more important than access to deputies — a far cry from the deputy-centred republics of old.

Another factor which is sometimes forgotten is that there are obvious limits to what any state can concede within the framework of a capitalist economy. The state's function in such situations is to ensure that accumulation of capital proceeds as smoothly as possible. Now, there is never one unambiguous way for this to occur; there are always strategic and tactical choices to be made (concessions to big capital or to small? or to skilled workers at the expense of unskilled?). Equally there are certain choices which must be ruled out, because they would be damaging to capitalism as a system. One of the interesting aspects of French groups is that some of the most powerful are militantly anti-capitalist.

Bearing this parameter in mind, the next pages will outline concisely the major economic pressure groups, while trying to suggest by what means and with what effect they influence policy.

Working-class unionism

Development   Modern unionism dates from the Second Empire with its modest surge of industrialization. Prior to that the labour movement had known the fate of its counterparts in other countries which experienced industrialization, viz. legal and physical repression. The law of 1864, passed by a régime looking for support among a growing working class, went halfway towards granting freedom of association and was completed by the law of 1884.

A working class that was still small, scattered and divided, both ideologically and in terms of the size of workplaces, might be expected to evolve differently from the UK, where industrialization and urbanization were much quicker. At any rate, in 1895 when the first major national grouping of unions was set up with the title of CGT (*Confédération générale du travail*), it had as its doctrine the theory of revolutionary syndicalism. Largely inspired by skilled workers with a high level of political consciousness, this ideology presumed a high degree of technical and political competence among workers: so much so that they were now able to run the economy and society for themselves, the bourgeois class becoming redundant. Not that the latter would hand over control peaceably, however; a short period of violence triggered by a general strike would be necessary to expropriate them. The *syndicat* (union branch) was seen as the basic political unit, both for the seizure of power and for political and economic decision-making afterwards. Political socialism (the SFIO) was despised as irrelevant or reactionary. Such were the tenets of revolutionary syndicalism, which failed to survive World War I as a living force, but which marked French unionism powerfully. Its most notable legacy is the famous *apolitisme*, enshrined in the CGT's Amiens charter of 1906, which insists on the total independence of the union movement from all political parties; in a different way, the ideology of *autogestion* also owes it something in the way of theoretical ancestry.

Between the wars the CGT was the arena of a struggle for control between socialists and communists, which ended in the victory of the latter; the decisive phase was probably the occupation where the outlawing of the unions by the Vichy régime put a premium on the qualities of resolution and leadership which the communists possessed. By December 1947 the 'moderates' (SFIO sympathizers) were ready to split off; they were helped financially by the American unions and, it was later discovered, the Central Intelligence Agency. The result was a new union CGT-FO (*Force ouvrière*). Since then CGT and FO have gone their separate and antagonistic ways.

The third major union began life in 1920 as the CFTC (*Confédération française des travailleurs chrétiens*). As its title shows, it was for catholic workers and was long characterized by extreme deference (at one point it had an advisory council of clergy). Inevitably its militancy increased as members learned that catholic employers are still employers. After 1945 the movement became more politically conscious, developing a theoretical reflection in which themes of class-struggle and socialism became prominent. This led in 1964 to a retitling of the union as the CFDT (*Confédération française démocratique du travail*); the minority for whom religious convictions remained paramount continuing as the *CFTC maintenue*. The CFDT was heavily involved in 1968, which helped its radicalization no end; it has been in the forefront of the *autogestionnaire* movement and has probably done the most to awake interest in this notion. Yet it has avoided becoming an appendage of the PS; with its radical socialism and its syndicalist mistrust of political parties it seems very much the *enfant terrible* of French unionism today.

It is clear, then, that the French labour movement is heavily politicized; and this is logical. For unions always have a political dimension, whatever their members may think to the contrary. This is so for many reasons. Often members are direct employees of the state; even when working for private capital, their everyday demands (wages, holidays, etc.) will have a direct effect on government economic policy. This explains the increasing state involvement in wage-bargaining at all levels. So even when people join unions for non-political reasons (job protection, better rewards, etc.), they are joining bodies that have a political role to play. Now French unions are well aware of this. It is true that they carry out the normal bargaining which members expect of them; but they have also thought deeply about the kind of society they wish to see (a socialist one) and the means to

attain it. Clearly at the heart of any such analysis will lie the relationship between unions and political party, to which we shall turn shortly.
But let us first examine union structures.

Structures   The following structures are those of the CGT and FO:
with slight variations, they are valid for all major unions.

The basic unit is the *syndicat*, organized as far as possible on the
basis of one big industry (thus the *fédération des métaux* would group
syndicats of workers ranging from general labourers to very skilled
steelworkers, who in Britain would probably be in specialized unions
of their own). The organization of the union is both vertical and
horizontal, or to put it another way, both geographical and professional. Professionally, the *syndicats* are part of a federation (a national
grouping of all *syndicats* in that particular industry) and the different
federations are then joined in a confederation. But geographically
they are linked at local, departmental or regional levels with *syndicats*
from other industries which share the views of the confederation as a
whole. These geographical levels are represented on the national
(confederal) bodies, as are the professional levels. The hierarchy thus
reads:

confédération

fédération   union départementale

union locale

syndicat

At national level the sovereign body is the national congress (two- or
three-yearly), which delegates power in between to other bodies.
First of these is the *comité confédéral national*, which is elected by
federations and departmental unions and which between its six-monthly
meetings passes on power effectively to the *commission exécutive*
and *bureau exécutif* (from within the latter's ranks). Thus the CCN
is roughly the union parliament, and the CE and *bureau* its executive.
The situation in the CFDT is similar, although the names of the top
bodies are different.

In general unionization in France is low, compared with similar
industrialized countries; it is rated at below 25 per cent of the workforce. Union membership is always difficult to assess in any country,
for numerous reasons, but the following estimates give some indication
of strength.

In late 1982 the CGT (secretary-general H. Krasucki) claimed two
million members. Its strengths lie in mining, the metal-working
industries, building, chemicals, printing, electricity and transport,
and it is weaker in the tertiary sector. The CFDT (secretary-general
E. Maire) claims 960,000, with special strengths in metal, oil, rubber,

textiles, banking and insurance. FO (secretary-general A. Bergeron) numbers around 1,100,000 and is strong in non-industrial sectors — banks and insurance, transport, commerce and the lower ranks of public employees in general. The CFTC has some 250,000 members, under the leadership of J. Bornard.

All these figures show a sharp drop over the last four or five years. As the crisis generates unemployment and demoralization, unions find it hard to hold existing members, let alone recruit. At the same time employers go on the offensive, increasing procedures such as fixed-term contracts and part-time working, which make it harder for unions to defend workers. Such practices are currently estimated to apply to a quarter of the workforce.[18] The loss in membership has hit especially at those areas predicated on traditional industries like engineering or textiles.

It may be that of late overpoliticization has weakened the more radical unions. The CGT is known to have suffered for pushing members to support Marchais's presidential campaign, and earlier in 1978 CDFT decided that even its always critical support of the Left Union was detracting from basic union tasks in the workplace. Hence its adoption of *recentrage* (forsaking electoral politics in favour of day-to-day union struggles in the workplace). But neither union seems able to halt its erosion.

In terms of resources, Reynaud believes French unions to be the weakest in Europe, along with Italian ones. Most *syndicats* fix dues at 1 per cent of members' salaries, varying parts of which are taken by the higher levels of the union. Unionists who are members of the Economic and Social Council usually turn in their salary, but this represents a small amount (700,000 NF out of a budget of 21 million for the CGT in 1975). There is little advertising revenue from union journals and although the government gives a certain amount in the form of training and research grants, the CGT and CFDT both believe that their more moderate rivals obtain a higher proportional share than is justified by their membership. Also, the grants could be bigger (they covered 19 per cent of the CGT's 1975 budget). This means *inter alia* that strike funds are low and that in prolonged disputes unions must rely on collections and other manifestations of solidarity.

Unions devote an important part of their resources to publicity. There are abundant publications, ranging from local broadsheets to work aimed at specific categories (e.g. papers for immigrants in their own languages). At national level, the most important are the CGT weekly *Vie ouvrière* (in a popular style which sells 200,000 copies) and the more theoretical *Peuple*. The CFDT issues the weekly *Syndicalisme* (55,000 copies) which has important confederal texts as well as practical advice for active unionists and discussion of current problems. There is also the more advanced *CFDT aujourd'hui*. FO publishes the essence of its views in *FO Hebdo*.

Unions deal with the state in various ways. It recognizes only the four major industrial unions, plus the specialized CGC and FEN (see below) as representative. This entitles them to the aid described above and to seats on the Economic and Social Council, its regional equivalents and some public companies. Unions also help to manage a number of bodies in the field of social affairs (vocational training funds, unemployment benefits) and also the *comités d'entreprise*. Since 1968 they have had the right to set up branches openly in large firms, with time allowed for meetings and other business; though there are still large firms where *bona fide* unions are kept out by violence and intimidation. To some extent, union influence can be measured in terms of their performance in the elections for the above bodies, where in the first ballot representative unions have a monopoly of candidacies in theory.

Union strengths are given in Table 4.6. They must be read with caution, as for each type of institution the electorates, conditions of participation and of course turn-out are different. But they do show that the major centres are widely representative, as well as indicating their strength relative to each other. Of late 'moderate' unions have gained at the expense of more radical ones.

A further interesting feature is the way in which the regional strengths of unions parallel those of the political left. CGT thus does best in the older industrialized regions of northern France and in those parts south of the Loire where there is a long socialist or communist tradition. CFDT strengths lie more in Normandy, Brittany and Alsace, areas which of course have markedly Catholic electorates.[19]

A more significant measure of strength perhaps is the way in which

Table 4.6   Union strength in elections to social institutions, 1945–83

	Social security Funds				Comités[1] d'entreprise	Prud'hommes[2]	
	1947	1955	1962	1983	1978–9	1979	1982
CGT	59.3	43	44.3	28.3	36.7	42.4	36.8
CFDT	26.4	20.9	21	23.5	20.5	23.1	23.5
CFTC				8.5	3	6.9	8.5
FO	–	16.2	14.7	17.8	10	17.4	17.8
CGC	–	–	4.7	9.6	6.3	5.2	9.6
CSL[3]	–	–	–	–	1.2	2.8	1.7

1 When vertical columns do not total 100, the remaining votes went to non-union lists.
2 The *conseils des prud-hommes* are arbitration tribunals, jointly run by employers and workforce.
3 Confédération des syndicats libres: so-called independent unions, largely kept alive by certain big employers.
Source: adapted from *Le Monde* 10 December 1982 and 22 October 1983.

negotiations are conducted. As regards private employers, these are hardly ever conducted nationally, the employers being strong enough to keep negotiations to the level of the branch, region or even the firm. Only in the public sector have unions managed to sign national agreements since the premiership of Chaban-Delmas, but this practice is by no means universally established. And only in two areas – part of the newspaper industry and the docks – is there a closed shop. There are clearly limits to what the unions can obtain from the state or from private capital.

Certainly – with the exception of teachers' and farmers' organizations (see below) – there is nothing like the corporatism alleged to flourish in the UK and northern Europe. By this is meant arrangements, largely informal, whereby unions take part in the elaboration of economic policy along with government and private capital. In return for being allowed an input into the policy process they are then expected to 'deliver' their members into acceptance of the final package, possibly even becoming involved in the administration of this. The arrival of the French left in office has not heralded any such development. If socialist attitudes and legislation are obviously sympathetic to organized labour, the government cannot count on uncritical support by any means, even if by the end of 1983 the unions had given it, by British standards, an easy ride.

Ideology   The unions' discourse reveals the double nature of their preoccupations – on the one hand, defence of everyday interests and, on the other, long-term political goals. We shall concentrate especially on the latter.

The CGT is predicated on revolutionary class struggle and aspires to socialism. What such socialism would be is uncertain; if the CGT has recently begun to talk seriously about *autogestion* instead of sneering at it as 'utopian', its own view of socialism would probably centre on what it calls 'gestion démocratique', i.e. a fairly centralized economy with some power of decision devolved to plant level, where the union would pay a key role. This obviously involves looking at the relationship between union and party (a socialist government would obviously be based on the left parties), and confronting the charge that the CGT is merely a conveyor-belt for the PCF. This charge is indignantly refuted by both, in the name of union independence; but it is well known that most of the departmental secretaries are communists and so are half the BE. Le Guen and Krasucki are on the *bureau politique* of the PCF. Ross has shown plausibly how the PCF has tried to use the CGT in an aggressive or consensual way over the years, according to its current policy needs; but there are limits to such a process.[20] Any active member of a union knows that members cannot be brought out on strike at the drop of a hat, or even cajoled back to work if they are in dispute; May 1968 was ample proof of that.

If the CGT still appears in some respects to hanker after eastern European practices, then the CFDT presents a frankly leftist image. Although it agrees about extending the public sector, the CFDT wants neither a bureaucratic state capitalism nor an improved private one. Its self-managing socialism aims at a decentralized economy, with authority in firms exercised by works councils, elected by the whole of the workforce, who would elect and supervise management boards. The latter would negotiate with the national plan, which the CFDT wishes to democratize *à la* PS by placing greater emphasis on inputs from local units. Even the CFDT's immediate demands, such as reduction of all differentials to a scale of one to six have a radical ring about them which distinguishes them from British or American demands. The CFDT stresses intensely the importance of union autonomy from political parties. This explains its refusal of an organic relationship with the PS, which it has long fuelled with militants and ideas, and its refusal to sign the CPG, although it obviously supported the left union.

FO by contrast has no project for a socialist society, although it occasionally talks about class-struggle. Its outlook is pragmatic and reformist; it sees its task as to extract as much as it can from management and state. It is reluctant to take industrial action and has staked much of its reputation on signing agreements in the public sector (where a good half of its members work); if this policy were to prove impracticable through government austerity, FO could have trouble with its members. FO pays the ritual lip-service to union autonomy from parties, and mixes it with some fairly stiff anti-communism, directed at the CGT; this is logical enough, given its origins. A final ideological flourish is provided by FO's keen support for European integration: Europe is seen as a framework that can solve problems too vast for individual states to cope with.

French labour unions are thus divided politically and ideologically, as well as by normal competition for members. One can appreciate union pluralism in that it offers workers a choice, keeps debate alive and the union apparatchiks on their toes; but undoubtedly it also means that the employers face a weaker challenge.

Employers' unionism – the Conseil national du patronat français (CNPF)

Employers' organizations in France are as old and as complex as workers'. The CNPF dates from 1946 in its present form, being really an umbrella organization which tries to co-ordinate the activity of employers from all fields (except agriculture, the professions, the *artisanat* and some of the public sector). Its organization is both horizontal and vertical; in other words, it groups geographical organizations embracing more than one

economic activity and also the local, departmental and regional organizations of any one individual activity. Individual firms do not join, membership being by geographical or professional bodies. It is estimated that
over 80 per cent of these do belong to the CNPF, whose national structures
are crowned by an executive council and president (Y. Gattaz), assisted
by a number of full-time staff.

This is not to suggest that the CNPF is particularly homogeneous.
It has numerous internal tensions, the most important being that
between large and smaller capital. The latter has its own organization,
the CGPME (*Confédération générale des petites et moyennes entreprises*), founded and led for many years by L. Gingembre, and which
has representation inside the CNPF. The smaller employer tends to see
himself as being a real boss, closer to the daily realities of the firm,
in contrast to the remote and 'technocratic' head of a large corporation.
Another split is between reformists and traditionalists, the latter
preferring repression of or confrontation with the unions, whereas
the reformists are prone to dialogue and consultation (within limits).
Many of them are to be found in the *Centre des jeunes dirigeants*. The
actions of the CNPF are in the main discrete; it provides services to
members (expertise in fields such as management techniques or export
markets, and also information on unions or political parties). It also has
a more public role in that it publicizes heavily the virtues of capitalist
enterprise, employing to this end some twenty staff whose task is to
insert the employers' viewpoint into as many newspapers and other
media as possible. This operation is conducted with increasing success,
if one recent analyst is to be believed.[21]

As regards direct influence on government, it would be naïve to
think in terms of the latter being teleguided by a clique of employers
with clear-cut interests. The reality is more complex than this
conspiratorial vision suggests. It is known that the *patronat* disliked
some Gaullist policies of the 1960s and that Giscard d'Estaing was
for a long while mistrusted by them. But there are limits to political
action set by the logic of the capitalist system, from which no right-
wing government dare depart, and also certain broad objectives which
will suit all fractions of capital. Within these parameters, the CNPF
functions as an effective lobby. The reader is familiar with its staff
of political experts under M. de Mourgues; one of its functions is to try
and influence legislation at the committee stage and to supply deputies
with employers' viewpoints.

Since 1981 CNPF's task has been harder. While avoiding total opposition to Mitterrand, it has campaigned hard against the Auroux Acts (it
dislikes their cost, insistence on annual negotiations and the fact that
they encourage unions at all) and against attempts to stiffen wealth
taxes, with some success.[22]

The most militant employers' opposition has come from a sub-group of the organization the SNPMI (*Syndicat national de la petite et moyenne industrie*), led by G. Deuil, a self-confessed admirer of the late Marshal Pétian. In the *prud'homal* elections of 1982 this Poujadist type of formation scored well, illustrating the fears of many small employers.

At the end of 1983 as the working-class unions flagged, and the government moved increasingly to conciliate employers, Gattaz set out CNPF demands with increasing clarity: wages to be held below the rate of inflation; prices to rise freely; costs and taxes to be cut; firms to be freer to lay workers off. The sophisticated rhetoric of CNPF can conceal some familiar realities.

The self-employed: the Comité d'information et de défense – Union nationale des artisans et des travailleurs indépendants (CIDUNATI)

The long slow decline of small commerce has already been referred to, as have the sometimes violent reactions of the disgruntled small businessman. Poujade canalized much of their discontent in the 1950s, but in the 1970s his mantle has fallen on to the shoulders of G. Nicoud and the CIDUNATI. The movement was a fusion in 1970 of groups dissatisfied with the work of their traditional professional associations (which are grouped in departmental chambers of commerce), with regard to government policy on tax and social security. The movement soon made a name for itself by a series of energetic demonstrations, including raids on government offices and seizure of records. Although Nicoud was imprisoned it was not long before the government was engaged in dialogue with CIDUNATI, showing that a delinquent group is still able to frighten Paris into giving something away.

CIDUNATI caters for the small, essentially family business; though members may own up to three or four shops, and there has been an influx of small industrialists also. It is above all for activists, who feel their business threatened and who want safety by all means, even legal ones, as the tag has it. 'Le commerçant ne se rue dans les brancards que quand il se sent le couteau à la gorge': thus did one regional organizer put it, in the down-to-earth idiom typical of the movement. CIDUNATI has a distinct ideology, which stresses the virtues of the small 'independent' man – his hard work, his professional knowledge and care for the customer (compared with the anonimity and shoddy quality of the big supermarket). It is rather impatient with normal legislative procedures, seeing deputies as weak-willed creatures, manipulated by faceless technocrats in the finance ministry. Its basic demands are three: to pay less tax and suffer less interference (read tax inspections: CIDUNATI newspapers often carry stories of honest shopkeepers hounded to suicide by odious tax-inspectors): to have a simpler and more comprehensive system of social security: and most of all, to stop 'unfair competition' from big capital in the shape of the large supermarket or hypermarket.

The movement's muscular actions have wrung a number of concessions, mainly in the pensions and insurance field, but also including
the Royer law of 1973 directed against big supermarkets. Royer is the
one commerce minister (the member of government who has the thankless task of appeasing small businessmen) who has at all pleased the
militants; but the movement is characterized by a perpetual mistrust
of all governments. It knows how to use its political weight, however,
and its votes are solicited by all parties.

CIDUNATI membership is hard to assess, as it deliberately publishes
no figures. But it could well be over 200,000. There is an impressive
new headquarters in the Isère, Nicoud's department (a gesture typical
of the provincial flavour of the movement), and two journals with a
style all their own. CIDUNATI claims to have few permanent staff,
relying on voluntary work at all levels. The national leadership seems
dominated by Nicoud, a waiter turned café-owner, and very much a
self-made man; by origins and temperament he is an ideal spokesman
for his followers.

In 1981 Nicoud supported Mitterrand; but probably only about a
third of the *artisans/commerçants* vote on the left.

Of late the movement has been quiet, having also suffered from
splits. It is hard to say when or if it (or a similar phenomenon) will rise
up again. Certainly *les petits* seem to have been frightened by the left's
win and some have spoken of a 'crisis of confidence' in this sector.[23] It
may well be as Gresle states,[24] that this 'petty-bourgeois populism' for
all its verbal violence has limited aims, i.e. getting more protection from
government. But so long as the small men feel that the latter is backsliding
in its duties towards them, a resurgence can never be ruled out.

Managerial unionism — the Confédération générale des cadres (CGC)

If the traditional petty-bourgeoisie has its own organizations like
CIDUNATI, then this is also true of the newer, wage-earning variety.
Since 1946 *cadres* have been organized in the CGC. There is some doubt
as to who is a *cadre* (one who has a position of managerial authority),
the CFDT claiming for instance that proper *cadres* are relatively few in
number; the CGC recruits its 320,000 members over a rather wide range
of white-collar jobs, however, from senior managers and engineers down
to foremen, and including such disparate categories as commercial travel-
lers and nurses. The problem, for real *cadres* or sundry white-collars, is
however the same one of identity. On one hand they are put off by the
mass industrial unions, whose style and image are very much that of the
skilled worker; indeed they are encouraged to think of themselves as being
different from these. On the other, although culturally they may feel
nearer to the employers, they themselves are decidedly not employers;
rather their function is to secure compliance with the latter's decisions

from workers. CGC unionism reflects the discomfort, in many ways, of this median position. Strictly apolitical, it has no vision of society other since 1974). The CGC was not militant. It saw the economy as an arena of 'concentration', i.e. reasonable bargaining between moderate partners, with satisfaction on both sides.

In the late 1970s many felt that CGC was at last being forced to change under the weight of the crisis. Its seemingly greater firmness towards employers and willingness to speak even to working-class unions suggested that it might be about to become what it had never been before, 'un véritable syndicat des classes moyennes salariées'.[25] This flicker of militancy, symbolized by the election of J. Menu as president, helped a crucial fraction of *cadres* to vote Mitterrand in 1981. But since then enthusiasm has cooled rapidly as *cadres* feel themselves to be victims of socialist financial policy. Menu and the combative P. Marchelli were among the first to attack Mitterrand systematically; there have been three major CGC demonstrations of late (previously unheard of) and the leadership is rumoured to be close to RPR.

Today with its 320,000 members and over 40 per cent of the vote in the *cadres*' college at professional elections, CGC is clearly the main managers' union. But like many white-collar unions it still hesitates between being a real trade union and providing an uneasy lobby for the aspirations of those who feel superior to the shop-floor but who know in their hearts that few of them will make it to the summits of the bourgeoisie.

The CGC is for *cadres* happy with their position between worker and employer. Some *cadres* have joined the special sections of the CGT or CFDT, however, which are called the UGITC and UCC respectively. This means that they have made a political choice, seeing their fate as a class-fraction to be linked to that of the working class. Such a choice clearly involves accepting that in a socialist society the role and privileges of *cadres* might well be changed; they would have to learn, as Maire put it, 'la richesse des relations égalitaires'. For the moment, though, the CGC undoubtedly commands the loyalty of the majority.

Farmers' unionism – the Fédération nationale des syndicats d'exploitants agricoles (FNSEA)

Farmers' unionism reflects many of the contradictions in French agriculture. Chronic peasant individualism and the slow rate of economic development ensured weak and fragmented farmers' organizations, until the depression of the 1930s forced some unity. The Vichy régime with its heavy rural and traditionalist bias attempted to organize and discipline farmers into its peasant corporation. This was not particularly successful, but the idea of a single national farmers' union was revived by the left-wing governments of the after-war period in the shape of the CGA (*Confédération générale de l'agriculture*). Within a few years the FNSEA, which was merely one of the constituent elements of the CGA, had become so strong as to supplant it; in other words, farmers did not want a leftish union imposed from Paris. This clearly tells us something about the character of the FNSEA. Under the Fourth Republic, it liaised closely with the CNIP group in parliament, and from 1951–6 the agriculture minister was always one of its nominees. Since 1958 its contacts with the régime have been at least as intimate; the agriculture minister has weekly meetings with the FNSEA, which is recognized as the only representative farmers' union.

Today the FNSEA claims 850,000 members (some would say 750,000).

Long under the leadership of M. Debatisse, it incorporates departmental chambers of agriculture, producer groups (for specialized products, e.g. beef, lamb, etc.) and related bodies like the CNJA (*Centre national des jeunes agriculteurs*), source of many ideas and capable leaders. It is dominated by the big farmers of northern France, its congress being effectively controlled by eighteen departments, because delegates are elected in proportion to dues paid, thus privileging the richer areas. This control explains perhaps the existence since 1959 of the MODEF, more or less under PCF hegemony and claiming some 200,000 members, especially among the small farmers of the south-west. There are also smaller movements of leftish and rightish complexion, but they cut little ice besides FNSEA; in the elections to departmental chambers of agriculture in 1976 it obtained 65.11 per cent of the seats, compared with 17.47 per cent for MODEF and 5.97 for the rightish FFA.

As Keeler shows, the FNSEA is a classic case of corporatism, indeed a largely state-created 'official union'.[26] In return for securing members' compliance with government policy it is rewarded in various ways. These include: inputs into policy formation, notably at the annual conference where prices are fixed; extensive subsidization, open and covert; privileged representation on the various boards which administer grants and land transfers; virtual capacity to replace prefectoral administration on certain matters and, last but not least, repression of rival unions by the state. By these means FNSEA has often taken 90 per cent of votes in elections to departmental chambers of agriculture and reconciled members to policies which it has largely helped to shape. Even if results have not always matched rhetoric (e.g. in terms of prices or incomes obtained) farmers clearly feel that a more traditional, market-oriented unionism might have defended them even less well.

In 1981 the new agriculture minister, Edith Cresson (whose appointment was a bold innovation in a milieu renowned for its sexist values), switched government strategy by recognizing the smaller, usually leftish unions. This was part of a PS analysis which sees farming as very much divided between the big (who control FNSEA) and the small and exploited (whom the party has courted diligently). FNSEA under its new leader F. Guillaume was furious and not even mollified by such gestures as the socialists' Gaullian defence of the wastemaking CAP or their steadfast refusal to admit Spain and Portugal (highly competitive in wine and vegetables) into the EEC. Sensing the problems of governing against such powerful vested interests, the new minister, M. Rocard, was at the end of 1983 taking steps to undo the representativity of the small unions. Corporatism is a difficult dragon to slay.

Teachers' unionism – the Fédération de l'éducation nationale (FEN)

Teachers have by far the highest rate of unionization of any profession in France. Their profession has always had close links with the republican state, which looked towards the teacher, especially in the primary school, to propagate democratic ideals and form the citizens of the future. Public sector teachers have thus long been part of a republican, secular tradition. The counterpart of their loyalty has been higher prestige, better rewards and better conditions than those enjoyed by their colleagues, at least in the UK. After a long struggle for existence (because the republic was not so keen to grant the right of unionization to its own employees as it was to other categories of workers), teachers' unions were incorporated into the CGT. When the latter split in 1947 the teachers avoided the brutal choice between communism and the SFIO by creating a separate organization, the FEN.

Today this 'state within the state' numbers 559,000 members, led by J. Pommatau. The FEN is in fact an umbrella organization for teachers of different levels. The bulk of its troops are, as always, primary school teachers (320,000) and some 99,000 secondary school teachers, organized in the SNI (*Syndicat national des instituteurs*) and SNES (*Syndicat national de l'enseignement secondaire*) respectively. Teachers in France are radical in their views; a poll in *Le Monde de l'éducation* in February 1978 showed that 59 per cent considered themselves to be on the left, and 21 on the centre-left. Thus within the FEN as a whole, factional struggles are between different shades of left. The movement has officialized tendencies, dominant among which is that of Henry, probably best described as moderate PS or social-democratic; it easily beats off the challenge of communists and extreme leftists. Within SNES, however, the PCF is held to be prominent.

Outside the FEN all the other main unions have their teacher branches, from CGT to CGC; and there are independent unions, especially in the private schools. But their membership is to be counted in tens of thousands, and they cut little ice besides FEN. It is accused of corporatism, i.e. of accepting a consensual role within the state apparatus, in return for rewards given to its members. The claim is only half true. The FEN is recognized as the one representative teachers' union, and the state in practice allows it considerable say in matters such as appointment, promotions and transfers of teachers (especially in the primary sector). It is also true that it has great veto power (cf. its perennial ability to stop governments from cutting school holidays, and its resistance to the Haby reform and its predecessors).

In 1981 A. Henry, FEN leader, became minister of leisure. This was a sure sign of the movement's strength and of the PS debt to it, both ideological and financial (the latter extending far beyond the gift to the party of its headquarters in rue Solférino). Today FEN is a financial empire as well as a teachers' union. Active in property, health care, pensions and insurance, retail co-ops and travel, it offers members services in these areas, from cradle to grave, at very keen prices. It employs thousands and has assets worth ten billion francs.[27] Such affluence has not weakened its republican and *laïcard* idealism; that flame is kept very much alive by the control of the SNI over the movement and its strong links with organizations such as freemasonry and the main secularist lobby CNAL (*Comité national d'action laïque*).

FEN is not without contradictions, notably between the SNI, which wants to bring secondary teaching into the orbit of its (underqualified) members and SNES, which naturally seeks to prevent this. It remains a strange mixture of successful semi-corporatism and left-republican ideology *à l'état pur*.

Chapter 5

External relations

(1) Values, purposes and organization

The external relations of a contemporary society such as France are greater in scale and complexity than at any time in history. Their importance for individuals varies according to class, occupation or sub-cultural grouping, but no one can be immune from their impact in an age when energy resources, food, clothing, equipment at work and in the home, cultural and recreational activities, are all more or less dependent on foreign imports and influences. The increase in scale of external relations can be analysed quantitatively by using statistics on, for example, mail and telecommunications, foreign travel or inter-marriage; qualitative change is harder to analyse but undoubtedly it has made life both more vulnerable and more fascinating.

A society's external affairs relate either directly or indirectly to its political, economic and social systems. Politically there is a basic need for security in peace or success in war. Economically there is a need to ensure supplies of essential food, energy and raw materials; depending on the size and character of the economy there might be further needs, such as foreign financial investment or vital military supplies. Within a capitalist society there are influential groups seeking particular benefits from external relations; for example banks and insurance companies profit from external financial exchanges and large companies profit from facilities abroad for creating new branches or market outlets. Finally, the values of a social system, its images of itself and of its place in the world, will influence attitudes to foreigners and preferences for relations with other societies having perhaps a similar language, a similar politico-economic structure, or an historical tradition of friendship.[1]

History has a great influence on France's image of herself and her role in world affairs. It is less than five hundred years since the emergence of the modern nation-state international system. For about half that period, while Europe was predominant in world affairs, France had the largest population, the largest standing army and the greatest cultural influence in Europe, French being the international language. After a period of relative decline in the nineteenth century,

210

French primacy was revived briefly by victory in the First World War. Experience from the age of Louis XIV to very recent times, therefore, has convinced French people of their political importance in the world.

There have been differing interpretations, however, as to which were the most important international influences emanating from French society. The Revolution of 1789 was the origin of modern French nationalism, with the attempt by Jacobin patriotism to extend France to the 'natural frontier' of the Rhine and to extend principles of republicanism to other societies. Subsequently Bonapartism undertook to export the revolution in a bastardized form. The French, moreover, made significant contributions to the ideology of nineteenth-century liberalism, for instance by introducing universal manhood suffrage in 1848 before other European societies. From another standpoint the French experience in the commune of 1871 was an important stage in the international development of socialism. A different experience, derived from Monarchist and Bonapartist traditions, had laid emphasis on the values of hierarchy rather than equality, the general will of the nation rather than the interests of individuals and groups within it, centralization rather than particularism, the state as actor rather than arbitrator. Such diverse elements in the French tradition have influenced not only Europe but the world at large through the impact of the former French empire.

French nationalism has been particularly self-conscious owing to recurrent struggles for identity in the face of defeat, partition and occupation by enemies during the past two hundred years. Defeat in war or weakness in the face of an external threat has invariably led to a change of régime. Conversely, each new régime has proudly proclaimed its ability to restore national honour, to recreate a sense of security and to defend national interests effectively.

Thus, the Third Republic after 1875 believed that it would regenerate France and her empire with strength derived from liberal principles and possibly persuade Germany to renegotiate the peace treaty of 1871 or, if not, get revenge in battle whenever an opportunity presented itself. By the 1890s many Frenchmen were protesting that the régime had failed to uphold the national interest, but were soon to be proved wrong by the victorious outcome of the First World War. The Fourth Republic emerged from the disasters of the Second World War with a surge of ambition: to reorganize western Europe in such a way that there would be neither the urge nor the opportunity for Germany to attack France again. Whatever its moderate success in Europe, however, failure to deal effectively with problems in the empire led to the Fourth Republic's replacement by a new régime claiming ability not only to reorganize the French community on a new footing, but also to re-establish French national independence in the face of foreign pressures. Before long, however, the Fifth Republic too was being subjected to bitter accusations that it was failing to uphold vital French national interests in its foreign relations.

Thus the French experience of insecurity, together with political instability, has resulted in patriotic feeling becoming inseparable from the support or rejection of a particular political system. The state is seen as having a specific role to play in world affairs and is always on trial; to put it another way, it is never a neutral but always an ally or an enemy in the eyes of different sections of French society, depending on the way it represents French national interests. Some may judge it according to its pursuit of certain economic or military interests; others may demand that it should uphold a certain ideological tendency; and then there are the simple patriots, lacking political commitment or opportunity for personal profit, who will derive satisfaction nevertheless from the exercise of any kind of French influence in the world. It is important to recognize, therefore, that assessments of the success, or otherwise, of French foreign policy will always vary according to the optics of diverse politico-economic interest groups in French society.

In the perennial pursuit of security from enemy attack, French policy assumptions underwent an agonizing reappraisal following the disastrous experience of defeat and occupation in the Second World War. Traditionally, ever since 1870 when Germany had become the dominant land power in Europe, France had depended on allies to restore the balance. This policy had worked well in the First World War when Russia, Britain, and ultimately the United States, helped France to achieve victory and to recover lost territory. The same policy was pursued in the period leading to the Second World War, but in 1940 France had to face the German onslaught with Belgium and Holland trying to preserve neutrality, Britain giving token assistance, and the United States and Soviet Union remaining studiously neutral. Since the bitter disappointment of 1940, therefore, French policy has consistently tended to seek independent means to achieve national security – a policy of 'France first'. Nevertheless the harsh realities of the post-war world, a devastated society requiring Marshall Aid for reconstruction and the division of Europe into hostile Soviet and American armed camps, requiring a choice as to which bloc France should join, combined to make France more than ever subject to external constraints and dependent on allied support.

This ambivalent collective attitude towards allies was held and articulated most strongly by de Gaulle, who had struggled in exile to recreate French national identity and unity between 1940 and 1944. He found it easier to win the support of various resistance organizations in France than that of the United States, who refused to recognize his provisional government until a very late stage in the liberation of

France in the autumn of 1944. As for the British, in spite of his doubts about their interest in a French recovery, his dependence on outside support led de Gaulle to propose to Churchill on 13 November 1944:[2]

> que l'Angleterre et la France s'accordent et agissent ensemble dans les réglements de demain, elles pèseront assez lourd pour que rien ne se fasse qu'elles n'aient elles-mêmes accepté ou décidé . . . L'équilibre de l'Europe, la paix garantie sur le Rhin, l'indépendance des Etats de la Vistule, du Danube, des Balkans, le maintien à nos côtés, sous forme d'association, des peuples que nous avons ouverts à la civilisation dans toutes les parties du monde, une organisation des nations qui soit autre chose que le champ des querelles de l'Amérique et de la Russe, enfin la primauté reconnue dans la politique à une certaine conception de l'homme en dépit de la mécanisation progressive des sociétés, voilà bien . . . ce que sont nos grands intérêts dans l'univers qui s'annonce. Ces intérêts, mettons-nous d'accord pour les soutenir de concert. Si vous le voulez, j'y suis prêt. Nos deux pays nous suivront.

The proposal was abortive, for Churchill and his successors preferred to pursue a special relationship with the United States, but it articulated poignantly the frustrated ambition of de Gaulle and that of other post-war French leaders who were later to see Britain remain aloof from the European Coal and Steel Community and the treaty of Rome.

Despite the success of socio-economic reconstruction in France by the mid-1950s, the sense of a relative decline in political power in world affairs became increasingly painful. The impact of the Cold War not only forced France to become a satellite of the United States by joining NATO in 1949, but also to accept the rearmament of West Germany within NATO by 1955. Equally unexpected crises in the French empire led to defeat in Indo-China by 1954, subsequent withdrawal from Morocco and Tunisia by 1956, and even the loss by 1962 of Algeria, which had always been regarded as an integral part of France. These reductions in power were made even more intolerable by the reluctance of French allies to treat these crises as part of the Cold War, and by their refusal accordingly to provide sufficient allied help to ensure a French victory. Perhaps the most bitter blow was at Suez in 1956 when American opposition to European colonial ambitions in the Middle East thwarted an Anglo-French military expedition. French decline seemed to be the will of allies and enemies alike.

French leaders had a marked awareness that their interests did not coincide to any great extent with those of the super powers, the United States and the Soviet Union. When the latter reached a state of deadlock in the 1962 Cuba crisis, followed by a period of *détente*, there was a corresponding sense in France that the time was ripe to pursue long-repressed national ambitions. Hence the articulation in the 1960s of a philosophy of national independence.[3]

What were the forces in French politics and society behind the pursuit of an independent foreign policy? Some analysts have tradition- ally attached excessive importance to the personal influence of de Gaulle (e.g. Newhouse), as if he were able to impose an eccentric policy on a reluctant society. There was, of course, his 'certaine idée de la France . . . (qui) n'est réellement elle-même qu'au premier rang',[4] a conception developed into a fully-fledged philosophy of indepen- dence by 1965 in one of de Gaulle's histrionic television broadcasts. After a preamble summarizing the problems involved in the French transition from being 'un peuple colosse' to 'un peuple affaibli', de Gaulle proclaimed a total contrast between acceptance of what he dis- paragingly called the 'sirènes de l'abandon' before 1958 and the pursuit of independence since his return to power. A policy of independence, he postulated, must fulfil certain rigorous conditions – political, military and economic – and in his view France was managing to fulfil these requirements.

In international politics, he said, while maintaining friendship with the United States, the emphasis in French policy had been to reassert European interests by seeking real solidarity among the six members of the EEC, while also reviving historical links with eastern European states, in so far as they freed themselves of their 'écrasantes contraintes'. The ultimate ambition was: 'rétablir d'un bout à l'autre de notre continent un équilibre fondé sur l'entente et la coopération de tous les peuples qui y vivent comme nous'. This vision contrasted, by im- plication, with an alternative Atlantic community, or an integrated community confined to western Europe. As for the world at large, de Gaulle's view was opposed to hegemony, intervention or repression by one state in relation to another, and favoured instead the indepen- dence of each nation, free from restrictions and able to receive outside help without being forced into obedience in its policies. On these grounds French policy condemned the American war in Vietnam, while supporting the development of South American and African states, and forging friendly links with China. This, de Gaulle claimed, was a distinctively French policy, formulated in Paris.

Military security, he argued, required that in the nuclear age France should have adequate weapons to deter a possible aggressor so that, while not disrupting alliances, France could ensure that her allies did not hold her fate in their hands. Such a military force, he claimed, France was creating by her own efforts. This project necessitated considerable re-equipment but would cost no more than contributing to the NATO integrated military force which, in any case, would not afford such a secure protection if France remained merely a subaltern member. Thus, de Gaulle contended, France was reaching the point where no power in the world could inflict death and destruction on her without suffering a similar fate in return, and that was the best possible guarantee of security.

In the economic sphere, according to de Gaulle, independence implied maintaining activities essentially under French administration and direction. France must keep up with competitors in the key sectors essential to an advanced economy. If it were advantageous to share inventions and projects with another country, France must combine with one that was unlikely to have the power to dominate her. That was why, in his view, financial stability was important in order to avoid the need for foreign assistance. French stability was upheld by, for instance, changing into gold the surplus dollars imported as a result of the deficit on the American balance of payments. He proceeded to list economic successes that met the above conditions. In recent years research investment in France had increased sixfold; a common industrial and agricultural market was operating jointly with Germany, Italy, Belgium, Holland and Luxembourg; France and Italy had joined up to build a tunnel under Mont Blanc; the Moselle canal was being constructed with the Germans and Luxemburgers; France had joined with Britain to build the first supersonic transport aircraft in the world and there was the possibility of further Franco-British co-operation in civil and military aviation; France had recently concluded an agreement to set up her colour television system in the Soviet Union. To sum up he used a homespun image: however big a glass others might offer, France preferred to drink from her own, while amicably clinking glasses with those around her.

De Gaulle argued that, although the Americans had been disconcerted by French self-assertion, a time would come when they would appreciate the valuable friendship of a France able to stand on her own feet. Now that she had re-emerged as a nation with full sovereignty, the world game begun at Yalta, which seemed to be confined indefinitely to two players, had obviously been transformed. In that world divided between two hegemonies the principles of liberty, equality and fraternity counted for nothing. It was therefore in the interests of peace that a new equilibrium, a new order, should prevail. Who was better able, concluded de Gaulle, to maintain such a new order than France so long as she was true to herself?[5]

De Gaulle's philosophy of international relations clearly favoured a diffuse system of nation states rather than a polarized system of integrated alliances or blocs, according to Holsti's definition of different types of international systems. The rejection of the post-war hegemonies of the two super-powers reminds us, not merely that de Gaulle was born in 1890 and was perhaps fond of the 'good old days', but also that the three fundamental rules for conducting relations between states, namely political sovereignty, territorial integrity and legal equality, originated in the sixteenth century. The rules have been broken with great frequency but remain the conventional practice even today thereby lending substance to de Gaulle's contention that the nation-state is more important than integrated alliances or international ideological forces.[6]

One of the best known French analysts of international relations tended to support the Gaullist view regarding the importance of the nation-state and the primacy of political over economic relations between states. Raymond Aron was rather sceptical towards arguments that EEC economic integration, for example, would prevent a recurrence of Franco-German political rivalry. He further suggested that pursuit of higher status and independence by middle-sized powers like France would tend to have multiple effects in detracting from status and willingness to assume world responsibilities on the part of a super-power, perhaps driving it to adopt policies of isolationism.[7] The American setback in Vietnam and the failure to maintain a stable currency in the 1970s, lent weight to an interpretation that the US hegemony was in decline. But an alternative interpretation was that such setbacks were merely minor adjustments leading to the exercise of power by more effective methods, and that super-power hegemony was likely to prevail indefinitely.[8] Sharing this view, Waltz argues that the activities of a middle-sized power like France serve merely to illustrate a chronic inability to change the stable bipolar balance of power. Indeed, the fact 'that American policy need not be made for the sake of France helps to explain her partial defection', for example, from NATO in 1966; and attempts to challenge American power by states like France are thus seen as utopian and doomed to failure.[9] But analysts such as Wallerstein believe that there is a process of power redistribution in the world that offers prospects of promotion, implying that the adoption of an ambitious policy by France and other middle-sized states is both inevitable and practicable.[10] De Gaulle's articulation of French ambitions struck a chord in harmony with public opinion over many years; over half those people consulted in opinion polls consistently expressed the view that France should be neutrally independent of Soviet-American rivalry.

Why were many non-Gaullist voters and their political spokesmen attracted by the ideology of independence? To the left of the Gaullists there was a revival of centrist groups by the mid-1960s, who were much more enthusiastic than de Gaulle about European integration in the EEC. One of their principal motivations was that a large accessible market in Europe would stimulate growth and maximize business opportunities and general prosperity. This belief involved a particular brand of anti-Americanism that envied the high living standards in the US and resented the profits US companies tapped from branches that had penetrated the European economy. Hence the urge to pursue independence but at a European level, because it was felt that a national economy would be too weak to resist American influence and competition. Centrists like Lecanuet, and independent-republicans like Giscard d'Estaing, went along with de Gaulle's anti-Americanism, but rejected his view that an independent France was worth more than an independent EEC. Their philosophy of dynamic economic modernization was articulated in a best-selling book, *Le Défi américain*, brought out in 1967 by Servan-Schreiber, a publicist who became leader of the Radical party. Describing American investment as a bird of prey feasting on the European economy, he went on to argue that to regain control would require a new awareness among Europeans that must transcend mere economic nationalism in order to strengthen the economic and political sinews of the EEC.

To the left of centre in French politics, some socialists held to a philosophy that social reform would be most easily achieved as a by-product of rapid economic growth which in turn would be most attainable through European integration. They tended to share the resentment of centre-party politicians towards American influence, as well as sharing their enthusiasm for the EEC as a vehicle for politico-economic progress. Typical of this group were André Philip and Claude Brudain. More left-inclined socialists accepted the EEC while insisting on the need to direct it in the interests of the working class.

Paradoxically the politicians further left had views that had more in common with Gaullism than with those of the centrists. Naturally there was hostility towards the US as the capitalist Mecca. Then there was suspicion that the EEC was serving big business interests and operating beyond the control of French politicians in the national assembly, a view which sympathized with de Gaulle's resistance to further integration in the EEC. Moreover some socialists, and particularly communists, regarded the EEC as an economic reinforcement of western Europe within NATO and therefore as an organization perpetuating the division of Europe into hostile blocs. This too was a view that chimed in with de Gaulle's pursuit of a diffuse international system and an end to polarization so that European links could be forged beyond the confines of the EEC.[11]

Some fundamental requirements of the French economy worked in favour of de Gaulle's independence policy. First and foremost was the need to secure markets for surplus agricultural produce; this was achieved through the EEC common agricultural policy which became firmly established in 1966 as a system protected against competition from the US and other world producers. It made it expedient for de Gaulle to keep France within the shelter of the EEC. Another vital need was a guaranteed supply of oil to fuel rapid industrial growth in France. At first Algeria met the need, but firstly the expense of extraction then nationalisation without compensation in 1971 led France to look to alternative sources in the Middle East. Good relations with oil-supplying Arab states were created and maintained in the teeth of American and some European support for Israel.

Finally, there was an obvious cultural motive for the pursuit of an independent foreign policy that would consequently win the support of most French people. The relative importance of the French language and culture had declined considerably during the previous century and by the 1960s only about 12 per cent of the world's population used French for everyday or business purposes, compared with over 50 per cent who used English. Even if the French community had by then shrunk to only seven member-states, there was a compelling reason for the French government to maintain numerous links as closely as possible with the French-speaking world by means of the operations of the franc zone and a foreign aid programme that had especially large educational and cultural elements quite apart from profitable military and economic components. The counterpart to this policy was a sustained effort to restrict the penetration of the French-speaking world by the English language.[12] His enthusiasm for *francophonie* and the *rayonnement* of French culture generated for de Gaulle a considerable groundswell of political support.

Conjunctural conditions for the independent foreign policy of de Gaulle to flower fully occurred after 1962 when the end of the Algerian war left him free to concentrate attention on foreign affairs having created a firm political power base including acceptance in France of a presidential policy sector. Moreover, the outcome of the Cuba crisis of 1962 freed de Gaulle of Cold War constraints by revealing that the Soviet Union at least did not intend to push super-power rivalry to the point of nuclear war. In an atmosphere of *détente*, France had scope for divergence from the USA. De Gaulle proceeded with a series of independent initiatives to create links with West Germany, China and the Soviet Union on the assumption that those powers would enjoy as much as he did the freedom and flexibility of a diffuse nation-state system.

De Gaulle discovered, however, that the insecurity of West Germany in relation to eastern Europe first of all made her unwilling to diverge economically or militarily from the US, and furthermore it made her anxious to explore the possibilities of *détente*, not through France as an intermediary but directly through her own *Ostpolitik*. He also discovered that China's interest in containing the power of the Soviet Union made her anxious that not just France but the whole of the EEC should support her policy against Moscow, and ultimately China looked to the United States to use leverage on her behalf against the Soviet Union. Like West Germany, China was looking for a reliably structured system of international relations rather than an unpredictable diffuse arrangement with France. But the most severe blow to de Gaulle's policy came from the Soviet Union, who attached such vital importance to her integrated alliances with eastern European states that she organized military intervention in Czechoslovakia in August 1968 to ensure that a totally loyal régime should replace one subject to doubt. For a time there was fear that Warsaw Pact military operations might escalate into confrontation with NATO and de Gaulle was impelled to co-operate to a very considerable extent with NATO for the purposes of French security, combining operations, for instance, of the French navy with the American fleet in the Mediterranean to monitor the movements of Soviet ships. There were residual trade links with Russia and other communist states but otherwise French bridge-building policies directed towards eastern Europe were in jeopardy when de Gaulle fell from power in 1969.

If the Czechoslovakian crisis had revealed significant French military dependence on the United States, events in France in 1968 destroyed the financial stability essential to his policy of economic independence. Inflation, and speculative attacks on the franc in world money markets, forced de Gaulle to borrow massive credits from the United States and other powers in his desperate attempt to maintain the value of French currency. A combination of international crises and domestic political problems therefore recreated serious constraints on de Gaulle's foreign policy during his last year in power.[13]

His successors at the Elysée, Pompidou, Giscard d'Estaing and Mitterrand, had to endure a long period of even greater financial instability exacerbated by the quadrupling of oil prices following an Arab-Israeli war in 1973, and by the doubling of prices in 1979 during a second oil crisis associated with a revolution in Iran. Combined with more profoundly structural economic problems, the two oil crises drove the world into a major economic recession. At the same time there were political upheavals: American withdrawal from Vietnam was followed by a long war in Kampuchea; Portuguese withdrawal from Mozambique and Angola led to widespread armed conflict in southern Africa, and Spanish withdrawal led to conflict in the western Sahara; super-power moves towards *détente* gave way to mutual suspicion and a spiralling arms race that led to widespread speculation about the likelihood of a third world war. Political instability and economic upheavals in all parts of the world, in a climate of mounting violence, intensified external constraints on French foreign policy to the point of becoming a *force majeure*.

As a middle-sized state in a world crisis French interests and activities were subject to three principal interpretations. The classical liberal view emphasised the need for France to react flexibly to unpredictable forces and events in order to keep upright while awaiting a new world equilibrium. The reformist liberal view emphasized French links and comparisons with other states, *'le plus faible des forts et le plus fort des faibles'* as the 1981 Bloch-Lainé commission's economic report put it, needing actively to seek unrestricted co-operation with all parts of an interdependent world to derive mutual benefits of peace and prosperity. The marxist view emphasized the need for France to adopt a competitive but circumspect role befitting an intermediate position in a world structurally divided between dominant, semi-dependent and dependent states.[14] With a liberal perspective, Pompidou accepted realities such as US predominance but looked to European co-operation for greater influence than was available to France alone:

> Il n'est pas question, bien entendu, de faire ce qu'on appelle la guerre au dollar, car une crise du dollar serait une catastrophe pour tous les pays d'économie libérale. Ce qu'il faut, c'est d'une part, que le gouvernement américain prenne toutes les mesures nécessaires pour . . . rendre le dollar réellement stable et c'est, d'autre part, que les nations européennes, à commencer par la France, essayent ensemble de créer . . . une certaine union monétaire qui fasse que les pays européens puissent, en quelque sorte, équilibrer par leur masse économique le dollar . . . Le problème de la coopération, c'est précisément de se rencontrer, de discuter, de s'informer, de se rapprocher, pour aboutir un jour à . . . une confédération européenne, . . . le jour où on aurait une union politique européenne, à coup sûr l'Europe pèserait d'un grand poids dans le monde . . . Il faut donc beaucoup de patience, mais il faut aussi la foi. Patience et foi, c'est ma devise, si vous voulez.[15]

Pompidou insisted that a Europe conscious of its own destiny would not set out to oppose other powers, especially the US. But, while welcoming moves towards *détente* between the super-powers, he saw dangers in a rapprochement that might end in condominium, neutralising or effacing a Europe that must therefore defend its identity.[16] If Gaullism required the effective pursuit of major national interests then Pompidou could argue that they were best pursued through European co-operation. His liberal policy of opening up the French economy did allow American investment to double between 1968 and 1971, but that was outstripped by EEC investment which quadrupled during the same period. Giscard d'Estaing adopted a more reformist liberal policy, taking initiatives to promote co-operation in Europe and among the world's major capitalist powers, but also calling for a new international economic order to help the 'third world'. He insisted that worldwide problems required worldwide solutions. France, with a global presence and wishing to be a friend of all nations, had adopted '*une politique mondialiste et de conciliation*'. Giscard's foreign minister, J. François-Poncet, later admitted that the international environment had deteriorated considerably but insisted that with courageous and imaginative measures France could master her difficulties so long as she remained open to the world and affirmed her international presence as a great power.[17]

By the early 1980s the internationalization of France's economy in pursuit of dynamic growth had created serious problems. Unable to compete directly with the US or Japan, France directed 51 per cent of her trade towards EEC partners and 25 per cent towards the 'third world', areas where her bargaining position remained significant; but as world trade contracted in 1982 France had a trade deficit with all EEC states except Greece and only kept a surplus with developing states by dint of export credits to them costing 20 billion francs. Moreover, foreign penetration of the French market had risen from 12 per cent in 1966 to 19 per cent in 1973, 23 per cent in 1978 and 26 per cent by 1983. Mitterrand gave priority to economic revival, renaming the Quai d'Orsay the ministry for external relations as a sign that it would augment internal policy by improving world conditions. Some of his socialist colleagues recommended a marxist policy of competitive protectionism; but he opted eventually for a reformist liberal approach by March 1983, calling for American and European co-operation with the 'third world' and keeping the economy relatively open while introducing austerity measures in France to enforce adjustment to world trading conditions. This policy enabled France to borrow 25 billion dollars in 1982 but, while over half that sum was used to credit 'third world' trading partners, France was becoming one of the world's leading debtors.[18] Mitterrand's awareness of the French position as a middle-sized power with limited freedom of action led him to emphasize co-operation with allies rather than independence. He maintained Giscard's rearmament policy begun in 1976, but dispensed with his search for an East-West convergence of interests in favour of a balance of power approach that involved encouragement to US rearmament and installation of Cruise and Pershing II missiles in western Europe to counter perceived Soviet advantages. Although Mitterrand could take a strong line on military security, for example when stating on 14 July 1983 that French national independence and territorial integrity was decided not in Moscow, nor in Washington, nor at Geneva, but in Paris by himself, his foreign minister, C. Cheysson, spoke later in more cautious terms of a diplomatic '*marge de manoeuvre*'.[19] And however laudable the efforts to make heard the voice of justice and reason, at least one analyst wondered whether Mitterrand was reaching the point beyond which 'verbal diplomacy is no longer sufficient to compensate for the loss of prestige due to the weakening of the economy'.[20] Whatever the persistence of *traditions gaulliennes*, it was necessary for France in the 1980s to relate her objectives very clearly to her resources.

A remarkably wide range of political opinion accepted the government's decisive choice in March 1983 of a strategy combining austere deflation at home and co-operative Atlanticism abroad. Although socialists resented the dollar's being used as the oil currency and supported by high interest rates, so that it had risen 25 per cent against the franc in little more than a year, they were nevertheless able to give virtually

unanimous support to the government's policy at the annual PS conference in October 1983. The CERES group on the left merely argued that
deflation should be defined as *'une logique de l'effort'* necessary for an
effective independence policy. The PS leaders received some criticism at
their meeting with communist partners in government on 1 December
1983 to *vérifier* their original agreement of 23 June 1981 though there
was no question of a rupture; the communists looked for a contribution
to East-West *détente*, for example by allowing French weapons to be
taken into consideration to facilitate a disarmament agreement, and
they hoped for an early withdrawal of French troops from the Lebanon
in case they served US interests at the expense of Syria instead of merely
keeping the peace. Among the opposition parties there was considerable
satisfaction with government policy abroad. The Radicals supported a
strong defence policy though calling for efforts with European partners
to build *'le pilier européen'* of the western alliance; this call was echoed
by the CDS who proposed the creation of a European security council.
The PR of Giscard d'Estaing looked for better consultation between
Europeans and Americans and new structures for effective partnership
to discourage pacifism in Europe and isolationism in the US. The Gaullist
RPR accepted the policy of Atlantic co-operation to cope with what it
saw as the risk of domination by international communism, and even
attacked the government for not approving American intervention in
Grenada in October; on the European level the RPR sought *'une
réflexion approfondie pour élaborer une politique de défense étroite-
ment coordonnée et modernisée'*, and when Chirac visited West Germany
to propose on 17 October an improved association between the two
countries in communal security questions, even on the nuclear level, it
became clear that Gaullist foreign policy was in a state of profound
mutation. Opposition criticism of the PS government was specific rather
than general, urging greater efforts on armed forces to make possible a
more energetic intervention in Chad and elsewhere, but at the same
time recognizing budgetary problems and especially the risk of costly
embroilment in disputes overseas.[21]

By the 1980s, France was permanently represented by ambassadors
or consuls in 160 different states in the world. The responsibilities for
the policies they had to implement were defined by the Fifth Republic
constitution as follows: article 5 makes the president the protector of
the nation's independence, its territorial integrity, its treaties and
community agreements; articles 13 and 14 state that ambassadors and
envoys are appointed in the council of ministers and are then accredited
to foreign powers by the president; article 15 makes the president
head of the armed forces and chairman of the higher councils and
committees of national defence; article 16 gives the president full
powers in a state of emergency arising, for example, from a threat to
the independence of the nation or to the integrity of its territory;

article 20 states that the government decides and directs national policy and is served by the administration and the armed forces; article 21 makes the prime minister responsible for national defence with power to appoint to a number of civil and military posts; article 35 gives parliament the power to authorize declarations of war; articles 52 and 53 give the president power to negotiate and ratify treaties except for peace treaties involving international organizations, financial obligations, or modification of territorial possessions, which have to be approved by act of parliament; article 86 allows for states to be members of the community while being totally independent. Although articles 5, 15 and 52 give the president extensive powers, there is no mention of a *domaine réservé* and his powers are clearly subordinate to those of the prime minister under articles 20 and 21 while parliament has important powers of decision under articles 35 and 53. The hybrid nature of the constitution could not be better illustrated than in the field of foreign and defence policy.

Nevertheless the experience of the Algerian war, the personality of de Gaulle, and a docile national assembly combined to establish a convention by which the president determined the direction of foreign policy as part of his *domaine réservé*, while the prime minister made it possible to carry out the policy within the context of general government programmes and priorities (in particular the prime minister would have to ensure a majority vote in the national assembly regarding treaty laws or questions of confidence or censure). It was then the responsibility of the foreign minister to carry out the policy in dealings with representatives of foreign powers, a recognizably standard role on the same lines as in other countries.

It is worth looking a little more closely, however, at the role of the prime minister and his office and at their influence on French foreign policy. Although the convention is for the president to have the last word on policy, served by a small group of personal advisers at the Elysée palace, the important process of co-ordinating different issues and policies usually takes place in the prime minister's office at the Hôtel Matignon. The principal official in the prime minister's office, the *secrétaire général du gouvernement*, prepares the agenda for weekly meetings of the council of ministers, takes minutes and keeps a record of decisions taken at those meetings. The rest of the staff in the prime minister's office, particularly the *chef de cabinet*, play a large part in co-ordinating negotiations between ministries which precede and follow each meeting of the council of ministers. This process of negotiation is often conducted between relevant ministers in the presence of the prime minister. The latter's close relationship with his colleagues contrasts with that of the president who has weekly meetings with the ministers for foreign affairs and finance separately and never sees the two ministers together except in the presence of the prime minister. Negotiations also take place among officials from various ministries, but again the initiative for convening and presiding over these meetings comes from the Hôtel Matignon. This system gives considerable potential influence to the prime minister in various spheres of policy including foreign affairs. A final point about the traditional system of government established under de Gaulle is that neither prime ministers nor foreign ministers appointed after 1958 could be deputies, and consequently they were unlikely to have an independent power base apart from presidential favour.

During the presidency of Pompidou, the organization of government underwent significant modifications which affected foreign as well as domestic policies. For most of the period 1969 to 1974, the prime minister, Chaban-Delmas, was a leading Gaullist party politician who was therefore a potential rival to Pompidou quite apart from coolness in their personal relations. The result was that the prime minister was virtually cut out of policy-making in various fields including foreign affairs (on one occasion he simply wanted to attend an England-France rugby match at Twickenham but was prevented from going in case he became involved in talks on British entry into the EEC, an issue which Pompidou was determined to handle personally). Normally during this period the president worked with his foreign minister in a tandem relationship, and the Elysée staff took over the work of co-ordinating foreign with domestic policies, thus reducing the importance of the prime minister's office. The secretary-general at the Elysée under Pompidou was Michel Jobert, who, for example, personally arranged a series of Franco-British negotiations regarding the EEC. After the defeat of foreign minister Maurice Schumann in the March 1973 elections, Jobert was appointed foreign minister by Pompidou, whose illness, leading to death in the spring of 1974, incapacitated him to such an extent that in practice Jobert assumed personal control of French foreign policy and had significant influence, for instance, on a resurgence of anti-Americanism in France at that time.

Under Giscard d'Estaing, after 1974, power to direct policy still lay with the president but Giscard's interest and sense of purpose in foreign affairs was more superficial and intermittent than those of his predecessors. His book *Démocratie française* gave very little attention to world affairs and had a bias reflecting his earlier career as finance minister. He replaced Jobert at the Quai d'Orsay with a career diplomat and personal follower, Jean Sauvagnargues, who was not very able and appeared even less so as a result of Giscard's tendency to improvise during press interviews and policy statements without consulting his foreign minister whose ignorance led to a series of gaffes. (It was not always Giscard's fault – on one occasion the muddle-headed Sauvagnargues greeted the great pianist Artur Robinstein as 'monsieur Toscanini' and was evidently in the same league as President Ford of the United States, who once greeted the then Egyptian leader, Anwar Sadat, as 'President of Israel'.) Evidence of incompetence mounted and in August 1976 Sauvagnargues was replaced by the able and more reliable Louis de Guiringaud, a diplomat respected for his work in the 'third world' and as French representative at the United Nations. Although conscientious and loyal to the president, Guiringaud had a dour, colourless personality subject to depressions that were eventually to undermine his career. Meanwhile Giscard had leant heavily on the services of his Elysée staff, particularly his secretary-general and confidant, Jean François-Poncet, who came from a family famous in both business and diplomacy. François-Poncet replaced Guiringaud at the Quai d'Orsay in November 1978, thus emulating his predecessor, Jobert, and proving to be the most effective of Giscard's foreign ministers. Nevertheless, his appointment reaffirmed the importance of the Elysée and the personal grip of the president on the making of foreign policy. The prime minister from 1976 to 1981, Raymond Barre, was also finance minister and during the economic crisis had little time to involve himself in foreign affairs, apart from prime ministerial responsibility for defence.[22]

Mitterrand made it clear when elected president in 1981 that he would retain the conventional *domaine réservé* in order to decide personally on matters of foreign and defence policy. His authority was reinforced by the way in which the PS majority in the National Assembly was elected in June on the platform of his 110 propositions in the presidential election rather than on the agreed 1980 party programme. He had less experience of foreign affairs than his predecessors, and his concern for domestic issues was clear when he renamed the Quai d'Orsay the Ministry for External Relations to reflect that priority. What experience he did have related to the 'third world'. His interest in Africa brought him into close contact during the Fourth Republic with rising politicians like Houphouët-Boigny of the Ivory Coast, and as interior minister in 1954 he had responsibility for Algeria at the beginning of the civil war. He also had an interest in Latin America, particularly the writings of Che Guevara. Mitterrand's own writings showed a deep attachment to the French language and culture which he was eager to strengthen at home and abroad. While in opposition his most notable foreign policy action had been to vote against leaving NATO in 1966, and as president he soon made clear his commitment to the Atlantic alliance.

Mitterrand made up for any lack of experience on his part by appointing a team of ministers that was arguably the strongest since the beginning of the Fifth Republic, and he allowed them exceptional freedom of action while reserving the right to redefine or take control of policy whenever he saw fit.[23] As minister for external relations he appointed Claude Cheysson, a trained diplomat who learned the political ropes as *chef de cabinet* to Mendès-France in 1954 and later experienced multilateral diplomacy in the EEC and the 'third world' as the commissioner in Brussels who masterminded the Lomé I and II association agreements with African, Caribbean and Pacific states in the 1970s. Serving under him at the Quai d'Orsay from 1981 was a *ministre délégué* for European affairs, initially Chandernagor then from 19 December 1983 Roland Dumas, who had won the Périgueux seat for the PS and could understand south-western French problems in the EEC; there was another *ministre délégué* for co-operation and development (francophone states overseas), initially Cot then from 8 December 1982 Christian Nucci, mayor of Beaurepaire, born in Algeria and educated in Morocco before moving to France, who was therefore ideally suited to his ministerial responsibilities. Other ministers particularly concerned with external relations were at Defence, where Hernu was the PS oracle, and at Finance, where Delors brought considerable banking experience as well as political experience as adviser to Chaban-Delmas when he was prime minister. Mitterrand's prime minister, Mauroy, was energetic in organizing government business and relations with parliament and the party; he took seriously his responsibility for defence and often paid visits abroad.

The perennial question as to whether the president is in total command of foreign and defence policies can be answered affirmatively in principle but with reservations in practice. Mitterrand's Elysée staff, which includes foreign affairs advisers such as Guy Penne for Africa, Hubert Vedrine for liaison with the Quai d'Orsay, Régis Debray for the 'third world' in general, Jean Saulnier for liaison with the armed forces, and François de Grossouvre for the secret services, is slightly larger than Giscard's staff but with about forty advisers in all, however energetic, it is quite incapable of acting as a parallel government. The staff have varied backgrounds and overlapping responsibilities (*chevauchements de compétences*) so that Mitterrand has available the widest possible range of information and opinion. The views of his leading ministers are sought at least once a week; and his staff make frequent direct contacts with ministries such as external relations. The Quai d'Orsay has reorganized itself in recent years to provide structured advice from a *centre d'analyse et de prévision*, created in 1973 and now headed by Gergorin, and from directorates for world regions, created between 1976 and 1978; the department employs four times as many personnel (6,600 including one-third in France) and handles fourteen times as many telegrams (1,400,000 a year) compared with the late 1940s. But this has not resulted in increasing influence.[24]

Everything depends on what is considered to be high policy, under presidential control, or low policy, under the control of ministers and officials. In high policy-making much depends on who has the presidential ear and eye. Mitterrand allowed his ministers exceptional freedom subject to his authority, and he kept very open ears and eyes, so that

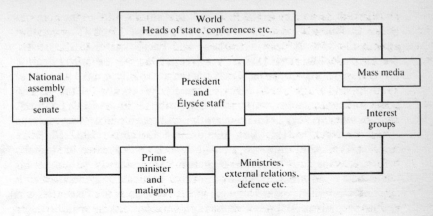

Figure 5.1 Influences on external relations

observers had difficulty in identifying his imprimatur and the specific influences that lay behind it.[25]

(2) Defence policy: purpose and structure

A peaceful world does not depend on a sudden change towards benevolence in human nature. It depends rather on methodical procedures to control and reduce tensions before they lead to explosions. In a world where the privilege of some relates directly to the deprivation of others, there must be scope for anger, hostility and violence to show the limits of tolerance. Failure to indicate such limits merely conveys indifference. Anger, hostility and violence are costly, however, and sometimes increase with expression; they therefore need to be controlled and directed at particular causes of tension in order to bring relief without harmful side-effects. To achieve successful management of tense situations, anger, hostility and violence must be accepted as inevitable and expressed so that the other party will make amends; this may require an explanation of the interest or attitude that gives rise to anger. To cultivate co-operation, sympathy and responsibility in others, feelings and requirements should be made clear without insulting or alienating them. If crisis management fails, owing to the determination of the other party to refuse co-operation, an escalation of violence may have to be considered while balancing likely risks and costs against the importance of the need to remove the particular causes of stress and hostility.

Such is a typical contemporary psychologist's approach (actually that of H. Ginott, University of New York) to friction and violence in civil society and international relations. It is perfectly in tune with the 200-year-old dictum of Clausewitz that war is nothing more than the continuation of politics by other means. The French experience of major wars and invasions over the past two centuries had led them to attach vital importance to their security and to the need for armed forces to back up their policies. In the recent history of France the army has been at the centre of passionate debates dividing public opinion almost as much as the schools. It is not possible in France to discuss military questions with sole regard to their technical specificity. Any definition of defence policy automatically relates to a system of political values.

At the beginning of the nineteenth century the revolutionary experience had created a view according to which the soldier was the defender of liberty, and it was among republicans of the left that militarism was most pronounced. Half a century later, however, having witnessed the crushing of the 1848 revolution and the *coup d'état* to establish the empire of Napoleon III, public opinion regarded the soldier as serving order rather than liberty. After the defeat of 1870 there was more consensus on the need for a strong army, and by a new system of universal conscription the politicians of the Third Republic sought to reconcile military strength with political reliability: it was to be a nation-in-arms that would be primarily citizens rather than soldiers, abjuring authoritarianism at home and irresponsible adventurism abroad, but generating an irresistible patriotic dedication to defend the soil of France against an invader, thus following in the tradition of the triumphant *levée en masse* of 1793.

The Dreyfus Affair split French opinion once again over an issue that appeared to demonstrate the incompatibility of justice and military discipline. Consequently one group of Frenchmen regarded the army as incarnating the values of patriotism, social order and respect for hierarchical authority; others saw it as a force for reaction, hostile to the progress and liberty of civil society. These stereotypes of militarism and anti-militarism influenced controversies over military organization. When the socialist leader, Jaurès, argued in 1905 in his book *L'Armée nouvelle* that conscription could be reduced to six months and still provide an army perfectly capable of defending French territory, he was more concerned with making the army politically reliable than with its technical efficiency. In practice a system of three years' service was used at the time of the First World War and proved its value by providing vast reserves of trained manpower. Victory in 1918 ensured the retention of the nation-in-arms philosophy so that proposals for change such as those in de Gaulle's book in 1934, *Vers l'Armée de métier*, were rejected owing to their élitist, apparently anti-republican tendencies, irrespective of the military case for highly trained units using technically advanced equipment that might have been more effective in battle.

In spite of the French defeat in 1940, the same system of conscription prevailed after the Second World War, partly owing to the influence of resistance leaders and partly because conscription had the advantage of being cheaper during a period of perennial budgetary difficulties. By the 1970s a changing French role in world affairs revived controversy as to whether the existing system of conscription for twelve months, possibly even reduced to six or eight months, was more appropriate to French needs than a professional volunteer force. But the debate was still as much concerned with the political significance of military organization and its purposes as with its technical efficiency. Raoul Girardet summed up this persistent French tradition (in *Défense nationale*, April 1977, pp. 21-7) with the proposition that the nature and composition of an army are always closely correlated with the social and political structure of a nation.

One of Mitterrand's presidential election campaign commitments in 1981 was to cut conscription from one year to six months, in keeping with the precepts of Jaurès. But defence minister Hernu hesitated and then kept it at twelve months, while introducing in 1983 the option for some conscripts (up to 15 per cent) to volunteer for specialized training for sixteen to thirty-six months. Opposition criticism of unfairness and weakness over the number of conscripts exempted was rejected with statistics indicating that over 105,000 exemptions in 1974 had declined to 88,000 in 1982, and only 0.5 per cent of conscripts were conscientious objectors. Thus 76 per cent of Frenchmen did their service compared with 57 per cent of Italians, 54 per cent of West Germans and only 10 per cent of Chinese. '*Dieu merci!*' exclaimed one deputy. Much more concern was voiced over a decision to reduce numbers in the forces by 35,000, mostly from the army whose chief of staff resigned in protest over inadequate personnel and equipment. Hernu was thus economizing and reducing the unemployment figures while maintaining the nation-in-arms system as was to be expected of a stalwart of the *Club des Jacobins.*[26]

As we have seen, successive French governments since the Second World War were concerned to create an adequate instrument of defence, operating in relation to allied forces but not dependent on allies for vital security. De Gaulle defined an independent policy in April 1965 as one by which France herself should have the capability of deterring a possible aggressor; and in the nuclear age this meant having a nuclear force capable of retaliating against any state in the world that might attack France. How far has France achieved that aim?

Table 5.1 shows the resources and military power of France compared with those of several other states, revealing the nature of her status as a middle-sized power and the gap between her and the super-powers. After 1962 the French armed forces were organized in three sections: the *force nucléaire stratégique*, the *forces de manoeuvre*, and the *défense opérationelle du territoire*. The nuclear force, commonly known as '*la force de frappe*', consisted in 1983 of five nuclear-powered submarines each carrying sixteen ballistic missiles (these vessels had M-20 missiles with a range of 1,800 miles and warheads about ten times as powerful as the bomb dropped on Hiroshima in 1945). A sixth nuclear submarine, *L'Inflexible*, equipped with new M-4 missiles each with six warheads, would enter service in 1985; and the other five submarines would also be refitted with M-4 missiles. Construction of a seventh submarine, the first of a new generation, would begin in 1988 so that it could enter service in the early 1990s. In addition there were two squadrons each with nine S-3 surface to surface missiles based on the Plateau d'Albion in Haute-Provence. To complete the strategic nuclear force there were thirty-four Mirage IVA bombers carrying bombs about five times as powerful as the one dropped on Hiroshima. Then there were the tactical nuclear forces including two Mirage III E squadrons, three Jaguar squadrons, and a fleet of Super-Etendard planes based on aircraft carriers, quite apart from the *Pluton* surface-to-surface missiles (see below). Research and development relating to the neutron bomb (*l'arme à rayonnement renforcé*) had not reached the point of decision on production.

Among the operational forces, the army was partly restructured from 1979.[27] There were by 1983 eight armoured divisions, each comprising 8,000 men divided into two tank regiments, two mechanized infantry regiments and two artillery regiments; there were also some four infantry divisions, each comprising 6,500 men — divided into three motorized infantry regiments, one armoured-car regiment and one artillery regiment (a fifth infantry division was also scheduled). In addition there were several specialized Alpine, marine and parachute divisions; and five regiments equipped with thirty *Pluton* surface-to-surface missiles for 'tactical' use, each carrying one 20-kiloton warhead equivalent to the power of the Hiroshima bomb. A number of other regiments were equipped with Hawk and Roland surface-to-air missiles.

The deployment of the army in 1983 was as follows: 48,500 in West Germany, plus another 2,700 in West Berlin; 3,520 at Djibouti, 2,911 in Lebanon in Multi-National United Nations Interim Forces; 1,170 in Senegal; 3,000 in Chad; 450 in Gabon; 900 in the Ivory Coast; another 16,500 men from all services were deployed overseas in Antilles-Guyana, South Indian Ocean, New Caledonia and Polynesia. The remainder of the army was based in France.

The navy was growing steadily in 1983 and it was expected that by the early 1990s France would be able to match Britain as a world naval power. To the existing eighteen submarines five more would be added soon; to the twenty destroyers five more would be added; and to the twenty-five escort ships three more would be added.

Table 5.1 Defence force comparisons, selected states 1982

	France	United Kingdom	German Fed. Repub.	USA	USSR
Population	54,270,000	55,965,000	61,600,000	234,516,000	271,800,000
GDP 1982, estimated in $	537.4 billion	473.4 billion	659.2 billion	3,011.6 billion	501.0 billion roubles
Defence expenditure 1983	$17.93 billion (Fr. 132.22 billion)	$25.17 billion (£15.987 billion)	$18.934 billion	$240.5 billion	17.05 billion roubles
Military service	12 months	voluntary	15 months	voluntary	24 months
Personnel:					
Total armed forces	492,850 (inc. 253,200 conscripts)	320,623	495,000 (inc. 236,000 conscripts)	2,136,400	3,500,000
army	311,200 (inc. 195,000 conscr.)	159,069	335,500 (inc. 185,000 conscr.)	780,800	1,800,000 (inc. 1,400,000 conscr.)
navy	68,000 (inc. 17,500 conscr.)	71,727	36,400 (inc. 11,000 conscr.)	569,000 (plus 195,000 marines)	460,000 (inc. 350,000 conscr.)
air force	100,400 (inc. 38,500 conscr.)	89,827	105,900 (inc. 40,000 conscr.)	592,000	360,000 (inc. 220,000 conscr. approx.)
Paramilitary	85,000 gendarmes		20,000 border guards	152,000	450,000
Combat aircraft	522	620	501	3,700	5,950
Major surface combat vessels	46	64	20	213	315
Submarines	18	27	24	95	276

Source: Compiled from *The Military Balance 1983–1984*, London, International Institute of Strategic Studies, 1983

Apart from normal deployment of vessels in the Atlantic and Mediterranean, one-sixth of the French navy was deployed in the Indian Ocean (the largest allied fleet there, according to Admiral Lannuzel, commander-in-chief of French naval forces).

The air force possessed 522 combat aircrafts in 1983. It was divided into a tactical air force comprising seventeen fighter-bomber squadrons equipped with 135 Mirages and 120 Jaguars, and a number of reconnaissance and conversion squadrons; an air defence command with 164 Mirage fighter-interceptors, twelve missile squadrons and four communication squadrons, then an air transport command and a training command.

Figure 5.2 shows the decision-making structure for French defence policy. The president exercised overall command of the armed forces, assisted particularly by the *Conseil supérieur de la défense nationale*, the *Comité de défense* and the *Comité de défense restreint* which formulated directives for the president's approval. But there was the unwieldy constitutional arrangement by which the prime minister was responsible for national defence and was served by a number of bodies, notably the *Secrétariat général de défense nationale*, which were quite separate from the president and his military advisers. The only institutional liaison, as clearly revealed in the figure, was in the council of ministers when the president and prime minister met. Otherwise, co-ordination among relevant ministers was achieved in the *Conseil de la défense nationale* which met approximately once every two months under the chairmanship of the prime minister; it was essentially a forum in which other ministers had the opportunity to react to the proposals of the minister of defence. Under de Gaulle's presidency defence policy was separated from other aspects of government, particularly from economic policies. But after de Gaulle, budgetary problems had considerable effects on defence policy by upsetting programmes for military spending during the 1970s. For example, the fourth military programme from 1977 to 1982 had set out to raise defence spending to 20 per cent of the budget by increasing conventional equipment even faster than the nuclear sector; but in practice a combination of economies, inflation and technical hold-ups hit the conventional sector hardest and thus defence remained at about 17 per cent of the budget and its rise from 3.6 to 3.9 per cent of GNP enabled the nuclear programme to keep its privileged position.[28] Table 5.2 indicates projected spending under the fifth military programme, intending to emphasize equipment rather than other sectors and keeping nuclear spending at about 30 per cent of the total for equipment. But the inflation allowance was only 6.2 per cent for 1984 and 5 per cent after that. If sacrifices had to be made the conventional sector was most vulnerable and the plan for a Rapid Action Force of 47,000 might also be affected.[29]

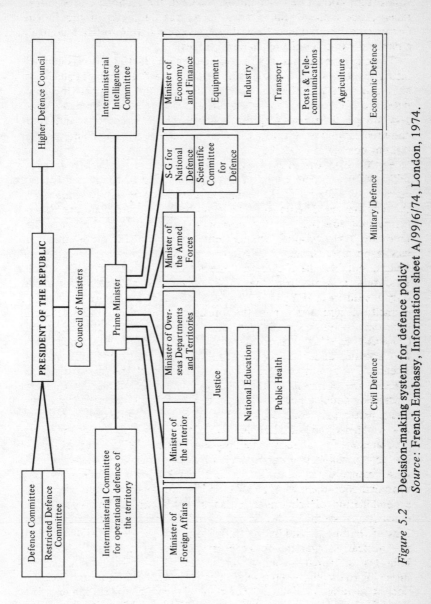

Figure 5.2 Decision-making system for defence policy
Source: French Embassy, Information sheet A/99/6/74, London, 1974.

Table 5.2   Defence expenditures, 1984 to 1988 (millions of current francs)

	1984	1985	1986–8	Total
Section Commune	34,492	36,648	125,632	196,772
Section Air	30,350	32,354	117,846	180,550
Section Terre	37,887	40,309	143,224	221,420
Section Marine	26,097	28,205	102,353	156,655
Section Gendarmere	13,274	13,984	47,345	74,603
Total	142,100	151,500	536,400	830,000
Titre III	75,500	78,500	261,000	415,000
Titres V et VI	66,600	73,000	275,400	415,000
– Equipements nucléaires	21,742	23,810	85,913	131,465
– Equipements classiques	44,858	49,190	189,487	283,535

Source: *Assemblée nationale, Rapport*, 18 May 1983, no. 1485, p. 168

The problem of increasing armaments expenditure without creating budget deficits and domestic inflation could be overcome to a considerable extent by the export of war materials to other countries. By 1978 France had become the third biggest arms exporter after the United States and the Soviet Union. Table 5.3 indicates the rapid increase in French arms exports, particularly after 1972 when arms sales tripled within five years. It was estimated that one-third of armaments industry production was directed towards the export trade, and arms sales in 1975 represented 3 per cent of total external trade. This needs to be seen in the context of global arms sales: between 1965 and 1974, for instance, the United States sold 49 per cent, the Soviet Union 29 per cent, France 4 per cent, and Britain 3 per cent. Nevertheless, French arms exports were the result of an official policy to maintain independence in defence and foreign policies; arms sales were intended to serve the political purpose of guaranteeing an autonomous defence structure and extending French influence in Europe and the world. The continuing success of the policy in an expanding world armaments market could be seen from calculations of sales in billions of dollars: 1.388 in 1974, 1.934 in 1975, 2.436 in 1976, 2.994 in 1977, 3.819 in 1978, 4.807 in 1979 and 5.775 in 1980. In 1981 orders from abroad for French arms were about 40 billion francs, and in 1982 orders rose to about 53 billion francs. But in the first half of 1983 orders dropped 27 per cent back to the 1981 level, though this decline was reversed by a Saudi Arabian order at the end of 1983 worth 35 billion francs.

In the 1960s French arms sales were directed as much to developed

Table 5.3 Exports of war materials from France (millions of francs)

Year	Air	Land	Sea	Electronics	Total
1965	1,912	600	50	250	2,812
1966	2,540	320	129	250	3,239
1967	1,686	360	187	380	2,613
1968	2,823	615	143	495	4,076
1969	1,990	400	41	140	2,571[a]
1970	5,242	605	1,055	386	7,288
1971	5,219	1,500	79	324	7,122
1972	3,688	300	80	650	4,734[b]
1973	5,470	2,421.2	234.3	1,310.7	9,436[c]
1974	9,987	5,701	2,224	1,831	19,743
1975	9,210				20,000

Sources: [a] *Le Monde*, 28 February 1970; [b] *Le Monde*, 23 December 1973; [c] *Les Informations*, 9 December 1974.

as to developing states; but during the 1970s there was an increasing bias towards the latter, amounting to 90 per cent by 1980. The Middle East and North Africa took 79 per cent of all French arms sales in 1980, Europe and North America 7.5 per cent and Latin America 7 per cent. The world recession made the market volatile and in the first half of 1983 the Middle East and North Africa only took 62.5 per cent while Latin America and the Caribbean took 25.6 per cent of French arms sales. The most important components of sales were aircraft, helicopters and tactical missiles, making up 59 per cent in 1979. Relevant sections of French industry became export-dependent; in 1970 arms production for foreign markets was only 14.8 per cent, but it rose to 38.1 per cent by 1977 and was still at that level in 1983.[30]

Success in arms markets not only offset costs incurred by energy imports but also reduced the cost of arms production, research and development and made it possible for France to maintain the military independence underpinning the philosophy founded by de Gaulle. That philosophy was one of dissuasion, or deterrence, by which any attack on France and her allies would incur massive retaliation from the *force de frappe*. This was carried to its apogee by 1967 when the then chief of the general staff, General Ailleret, proclaimed a defence strategy of *tous azimuts*, a multi-directional system that would be valid against attack from any part of the world. De Gaulle endorsed the strategy in 1968, but politico-economic problems related to the events of May that year made it unlikely that France would have the resources to create a credible multi-directional nuclear force. Moreover, the invasion of Czechoslovakia by Warsaw Pact forces in August 1968 renewed the polarization of the Soviet bloc as a possible threat to western security just at a time when Franco-American relations began to improve. Both before and after de Gaulle's fall from power in 1969, French strategy reverted to a specifically anti-Soviet posture in liaison with NATO. By 1974 General Maurin was chief of the general staff and was speaking in terms of engagement in battle in the framework of the alliance and in consultation with NATO leaders, rather than independent French action.

During the 1960s French strategy was to use the *force de frappe* for three variable purposes: first, to threaten an attacker with unacceptable levels of damage; second, to act as a 'trigger' to ensure use of American nuclear forces in a situation where there was doubt about their commitment in a crisis; third, to obstruct American plans for a 'flexible response' to aggression in Europe by which conventional forces would be used initially in the hope of preventing escalation to the level of nuclear warfare without sacrificing vital interests (the French fear was that the Soviet Union might be tempted to attack in the hope that some areas of western Europe would not be regarded as of vital interest to Washington). Many American and European analysts criticized the French *force de frappe* for involving dangerous proliferation of nuclear weapons and for being prone to obsolescence owing to the apparent inability of middle-sized powers to keep up with super-power technology. Nevertheless, some French analysts believed the *force de frappe* would have sufficient credibility to act as a deterrent to an aggressor, if only on psychological rather than military grounds, regarding deterrence as a matter of risk rather than certainty.[31] The political debate involved opposition from the left on the grounds that a French nuclear force increased proliferation and the risk of war and that it wasted resources needed in other fields, opposition from the centre on the grounds that the French force should be integrated in a European or Atlantic force, and support from Gaullists and their allies on the grounds that it increased French political prestige and military security, while also having spin-off value in raising the general level of French technology. Variations of opinion in France in the 1960s settled into a consensus in favour of maintaining the *force de frappe* in the 1970s; to reverse policy by scrapping it would involve waste of many years of national investment. Moreover it had two attractive political advantages: first, it ensured a French superiority over the growing power of West Germany, and second, it apparently offered some possibility of independence from the United States.

In the 1978 general election campaign, not only had the left ceased to dismiss the *force de frappe* as 'la bombinette', but the communists were even advocating renewal of the *tous azimuts* strategy in order to make it possible to adopt a neutral stance between the Soviet Union and the United States. There was considerable communist criticism of Giscard d'Estaing for not maintaining de Gaulle's policy of independence by means of an appropriate nuclear strategy. This view was expressed more forcefully, of course, by Gaullist diehards.[32]

French government interest in developing conventional forces was in response to criticism that a strategy of massive retaliation reduced freedom of choice, and therefore independence, in a war crisis involving French allies. Was there not a similarity between the *force de frappe* and the Maginot line of 1940 in that they both left France without alternative means to influence hostilities beyond her frontier and involving other kinds of weapons (cf. the view of J. Huntziger, right-wing PS)? Just as France might upset American flexible response strategy by 'triggering' a nuclear response, so might West Germany upset French strategy by engaging in military operations that left France the choice between massive retaliation (and suicide) or doing nothing. Moreover, developments in Africa revealed a possible need for conventional armed forces to operate outside France. Whereas de Gaulle had adopted the position that a Soviet attack on West Berlin, for example, would automatically meet with massive retaliation from France, by 1975 Giscard d'Estaing was asserting French freedom to assess a crisis with a view to ensuring 'à tout coup la sécurité de nos frontières'. It was pointed out to him that, although compatible with the Atlantic Alliance of 1949, this attitude diverged from the Brussels Treaty of 1948 which required automatic assistance to be given to allies; moreover, it would hardly reassure West Germany of French reliability in a crisis (see the article by A. Grosser in *Le Monde*, 17 November 1975).

The deployment of *Pluton* tactical nuclear weapons from 1974, nevertheless, made it possible, even necessary, for France to develop a strategy of flexible response to aggression. The 1976 military programme indicated the change of strategy; and both General Méry, chief of the general staff from 1975, and Giscard d'Estaing explained that the use of tactical nuclear weapons served the vital purpose of showing the adversary that he had reached the threshold beyond which he would incur the threat of strategic nuclear weapons (see article by P.-M. de la Gorce in *Le Figaro*, 3 March 1978). By the late 1970s the research into a neutron bomb added a new dimension to French thinking about tactical counterforce weaponry. In 1981 Mitterrand took the view that such weapons might dilute the deterrent value of the strategic nuclear force. No decision to produce a neutron bomb was taken but tests were continued. By the time Hernu presented his 1984–8 military programme he had undertaken to replace the Pluton with longer-range Hadès missiles by the early 1990s; although he insisted that no decision to deploy a modernized tactical nuclear weapon had been taken yet, it was clear that neutron bomb development might provide an ideal arm for Hadès. Such weapons, together with the creation of a Rapid Action Force for use either alongside allies in Europe or independently overseas, raised obvious questions regarding security relations with allies, and particularly with West Germany where there was much soul-searching during the Euro-missile crisis between 1979 and 1984. Both Mitterrand and his principal rival Chirac, the Gaullist mayor of Paris, went to Germany to discuss improved co-operation in security matters; this was no doubt a reflection of the anxious speculation in France at that time regarding a possible German withdrawal into neutralism if their allies failed to satisfy their security needs.[33]

After the onset of the cold war, and even more after the Algerian war, a major French preoccupation had been security against communist subversion within French frontiers. To achieve this a number of overt and covert activities were regularly pursued. First of all there was the domestic intelligence organization controlled by the ministry of the interior, called the *Directoire de surveillance du territoire*, essentially the French equivalent of the American FBI. Second there was an external intelligence service under the ministry of justice, the *Service de documentation extérieure et de contre-espionnage* (SCECE), which was very much the equivalent of the American CIA in that, although officially restricted to an external role, there was criticism in 1978 that 80 per cent of its work had been within France in recent years, including spying related to tax returns — the worst possible offence according to conventional French values — and carrying out 'witch-hunts' against some radio technicians whose membership of the CGT was equated with 'communist penetration' of the intelligence service. Half a dozen men in the SDECE were replaced by the ministry of defence but there was residual public resentment that the organization had overstepped its bounds and was extravagant with its large budget.[34]

There are two more overt organizations active in internal French security. First there is the *gendarmerie nationale*, serving the ministry of defence. It had been given an organization in relation to the division of France into seven defence zones, seven military regions and twenty-one territorial sub-regions, each involving co-ordination of civil and military authorities. There were in 1983 85,000 men serving in the paramilitary force of the *gendarmerie*, including 8,700 conscripts. The force was equipped with 38 light tanks, 124 armoured cars and 38 helicopters (see *The Military Balance, 1983–4*, p. 34). In April 1977 the director of the *gendarmerie*, J. Cochard, announced the formation of seven new *pelotons d'intervention rapide*, one in each military region, each *peloton* consisting of eighteen men with highly sophisticated equipment and a high degree of mobility; the ultimate aim was to provide such a *peloton* for each of the 400 companies of the *gendarmerie* (see *Armées d'aujourd'hui*, July 1977).

The second internal security force was the *Compagnies républicaines de sécurité* (CRS), serving the ministry of the interior via the *direction générale de la police nationale*. As distinct from the *gendarmerie*, the CRS had the normal right of the police to form a trade union but not to strike. The CRS in 1977 had 15,800 men divided into ten groups and sixty companies. Their organization by the Minister of Interior reflected that just as their numbers were lower than the *gendarmerie* they were also less widely dispersed; moreover their equipment was limited to individual weapons and two light machine-guns for each company. In emergencies, however, such as during the Algerian war, they can be specially equipped with heavier equipment and armaments. The CRS was essentially a flexible force capable of rapid intervention, by order of the minister of the interior, to prevent civil disorder effectively without a provocative show of force such as involvement of the *gendarmerie* would entail; though the CRS trade union had unsuccessfully sought guarantees that in civil disorders where firearms were used the *gendarmerie* would be called in rather than the CRS. The roles of the two forces were therefore not as distinct as their organizations would suggest. In addition to dealing with civil disorders such as occurred in February 1934 and in May 1968, the internal security forces would also be expected to organize resistance in France to an invasion such as that of 1940; this is the wider significance of the division of France into seven zones of defence, so that internal and external security forces are organized to support the various aims of French foreign policy.[35]

After coming to power in 1981 Mitterrand tried to improve the relationship between the authorities and various dissident groups such as Breton and Corsican autonomist movements. He abolished the state security court and encouraged his interior minister to bring in legislation to create more effective regional assemblies, beginning with Corsica. But by 1983 it had become clear that the Corsican FLNC separatists had refused to be reconciled with the new institutions. On 29 April, for example, there were fifteen FLNC bomb attacks in major French cities and on 23 May there were forty-three more attacks in Corsica itself. On 13 June Mitterrand visited the island in a vain attempt to restore calm. Just at that time Orsoni, an FLNC leader, disappeared and later in the summer a government official was murdered in reprisal, and rumours began to circulate about a counter-terrorist initiative in Corsica by a Captain Barril who had links with the Elysée. On 5 October the *Groupe d'intervention de la gendarmerie nationale* (GIGN) was asked to hold an enquiry into Barril's activities, and it was significant that at the end of October the anti-terrorist cell at the Elysée was reorganized. This problem, like that of reorganizing the SDECE to reduce its collusion with the American CIA and the Israeli Mossad, illustrated the difficulty of combining firm political control with efficiency in the security services.[36]

(3) Main directions of foreign policy

France has a long tradition of vital interest in relations with both
super-powers, the United States and the Soviet Union, and has a
tradition of bridging or balancing their influence rather than becoming
merely a satellite of one or the other. In the First World War, for
example, France began with an alliance with Russia which saved her
from defeat on a number of occasions between 1914 and 1916, then
she finished up in close association with the United States which
assured victory in 1918. Neither power joined France at the beginning
of the Second World War, but both played their different parts in the
eventual liberation of France in 1944; thus, although physically more
directly attached to the American government and its armies in western
Europe, de Gaulle hastened to Moscow to sign a treaty of non-ag-
gression with the Soviet Union in December 1944 on behalf of the
provisional French government, believing that Franco-Russian solidarity
was in harmony with the natural order in view of the German threat
and the Anglo-Saxon attempts at hegemony (see C. de Gaulle,
Mémoires de guerre, vol. 3, p. 54). But the 1945 Yalta conference,
which mapped out spheres of influence in east and west, and the
ensuing deterioration of the Cold War, detached France from the
Soviet Union and entrenched her firmly in the western sphere
dominated by the United States. When a period of relative *détente*
eventually began after 1962, de Gaulle had returned to power in
France and resumed his earlier policy of seeking freedom of manoeuvre
between the super-powers, thus creating an ideology of independence
to which his successors have also formally subscribed. What effects
did this policy have on relations between France and each of the
super-powers after 1962?

In pursuit of political independence from the United States, whose
role according to de Gaulle should be to provide a security umbrella
for Europe but otherwise to leave her alone, French policy was to
propose (in the 17 September 1958 memorandum[37]) equal power-
sharing in NATO or otherwise a progressive French withdrawal of her
forces from that integrated structure under American command.
This policy, culminating in February 1966, was characteristic of de
Gaulle's essentially negative achievements during those years; other
examples were preventing the American 'Trojan horse', Britain, from
entering the EEC in 1963 and 1967, and refusing to sign the 1963
treaty sponsored by the United States, Britain and the Soviet Union
banning nuclear tests on land or sea. American governments during
that period were constantly frustrated by de Gaulle's blocking tactics
regarding initiatives not only in Europe but, for example, in the Congo
or Laos.[38]

De Gaulle's concept of political independence, judging by his speech on 27 April 1965, seemed to focus on developing friendly relations with West Germany, eastern Europe, the Soviet Union, China and states in Africa and South America. But his intention to handle the German problem in a purely European context was rebuffed by the Germans themselves who were the third most important trading partner of the United States, and who preferred to trust American security guarantees in NATO rather than a less credible protection from France. The Franco-Soviet consultation agreement in 1966 did not enable France to do anything to forestall the Warsaw Pact invasion of Czechoslovakia in 1968 which destroyed French assumptions that a free dialogue was possible with eastern Europe; and by the end of de Gaulle's rule, France was co-operating with NATO once more against a possible Russian threat. Technical problems required French reliance from September 1968 on NATO naval surveillance and radar networks. In fact this was related to dependence on the United States in advanced technology; in spite of de Gaulle's efforts to minimize American penetration of French industry he was not very successful as shown by the 1963 takeover by General Electric of Machines Bull, the leading French computer firm, and the subsequent evasion of de Gaulle's obstructive policy by General Motors who built one of the largest European car factories in Belgium and were then able to penetrate the French market from across the frontier. West Germany was warned off joining in de Gaulle's obstructionist policy, and France alone could do very little.[39]

The fact that de Gaulle's stand for independence merely amounted in practice to a *'politique déclamatoire'* indicates the limitations on the freedom of even middle-sized powers to initiate change in the world politico-economic system, beyond frustrating initiatives taken by others. This is not to argue, however, that the aim declared in 1965, to work for the freedom of all nations from outside intervention, restriction and domination, was not worth while, but merely that France alone did not have the necessary power to fulfil de Gaulle's ambition.

It is often stated that, whereas under de Gaulle foreign policy had priority over domestic policy, under his successors the opposite priority applied. Although in general this was true, foreign policy continued to have great importance for French governments after 1969 for two reasons: first, that Gaullist politicians, with communist support, kept a close watch on any divergences from independence in world affairs, particularly *vis-à-vis* the United States, and second, that the pursuit of economic growth in France had internationalized the economy to such an extent by the 1970s that foreign economic policy inevitably proved to be a major preoccupation.

Problems for France arising from the events of May and the Czechoslovakia crisis in August 1968 brought about an improvement in Franco-American relations. During the 'gold war', France had refused to sign a Group of Ten financial proposal to increase international liquidity by means of special drawing rights, but eight months later, in November 1968, France borrowed two thousand million dollars from the Group of Ten. On 5 December defence minister Messmer made it clear to the national assembly that there was no question of French neutralism and that France was in the Atlantic alliance to stay. General Ailleret was killed in an air crash and his successor, General Fourquet, accepted in March 1969 the American nuclear doctrine of 'graduated response' directed specifically at the Soviet Union to the east.

Certainly there was the encouragement for France of a more flexible policy in Washington: American forces ceased to bomb north Vietnam at the end of March 1968 and on 5 May Paris was chosen as the centre for Vietnam peace talks (hardly the most peaceful place to talk at that time). The newly-elected president Nixon visited France in February 1969; in April de Gaulle attended General Eisenhower's funeral in Washington and had a further round of cordial conversations with Nixon. When de Gaulle's successor, Pompidou, devalued the franc in the summer of 1969, American policy co-operated in helping to stabilize the French currency at its new level, while the French reciprocated by ending their doctrinaire resistance to US sales and investment in France.

There was a general expectation in Europe that after the Vietnam war, which ended in 1973, American foreign policy was likely to be more cautious and less domineering. The devaluation of the dollar in 1971 and its further weakening after 1973, accompanied by persistent American balance of payments deficits, all made it clear that successive American administrations were in deep trouble, quite apart from the Watergate affair in 1973–4 which led to the resignation of president Nixon. There was considerable speculation about possible American decline from power and withdrawal into isolationism. It therefore became much more acceptable to French public opinion to see Pompidou and his successor, Giscard d'Estaing, discussing co-operation with the American government in efforts to control the effects of a major world economic crisis after 1973.

The immense scale of American power, nevertheless, meant that it took only the nervous muscular reflexes of weak government to maintain the essentials of world political control. Moreover, the social pluralism and diffuse economic dynamism characteristic of American capitalism enabled it to recover from excessive dependence on short-term state contracts connected with the Vietnam war and to expand other profitable business interests. Although recession and unemployment hit some sectors of American industry, such as steel, there was remarkable buoyancy in other sectors such as plastics, electronics and even consumer durables; furthermore, profits were maintained through manipulation of overseas assets in American multi-national companies.

The American government preserved its grip on the world currency system by means of policy co-ordination between foreign ministries and central banks between 1973 and 1976. A set of guidelines for indefinitely floating currencies were agreed. France changed her policy in December 1974 to agree that currencies would not necessarily be linked to gold and that there would be no official international gold price; for its part the American government agreed that gold should be realistically valued according to market price and made available to governments with balance of payments deficits. By January 1976 a new international monetary regime had emerged to replace the 1944 Bretton Woods system: first, floating rates were legalized according to a set of conditions over which the United States had a veto; second, special drawing rights were made the principal international reserve assets in order to reduce the role of gold; third, the International Monetary Fund had powers of firm surveillance over exchange rate policies and was to lay down certain guidelines; fourth, a trust fund was established for poor countries to liberalize credit facilities (the caucus of underdeveloped countries made acceptance of the whole system conditional on that point).[40] This system involved a degree of Franco-American co-operation inconceivable in the time of de Gaulle. The importance of the dollar remained such that its subsequent devaluations were as much an American lever to manipulate world trade as a sign of instability or weakness.

Faced with an unprecedented threat to oil supplies in 1973, the United States reacted by forming an International Energy Agency as a pressure group against oil producers. France alone among EEC members declined to join the Agency, preferring a wider arrangement with producers as well as consumers of oil to ensure French supplies. There was a brief period of friction between Jobert, acting for the sick Pompidou, and Kissinger in 1974; but by 15 December Giscard d'Estaing had restored tentative agreement with the United States on the desirability of some joint action by oil consumer states. American muscle, including a threat to use military action against Arab states to prevent any embargo on vital oil supplies, restored the flow of oil at more stable prices.

By 1976 there was increasing speculation about 'eurocommunism', a tendency among western European communist parties to seek power by accepting fuller integration into local political systems by means of liberal democratic methods. Some observers anticipated the possibility of communist parties coming to power in Italy, France and Portugal. The American government reacted firmly in April 1976 with the Sonnenfeldt doctrine to reaffirm that the United States accepted Soviet predominance throughout eastern Europe, and at the same time a

Kissinger doctrine declaring United States opposition to any communist participation in western European governments. In spite of protests about US imperialist interference, it was clear that the polarization of power in Europe between the two super-powers would continue indefinitely. Moreover, France joined with other EEC members to reinforce this situation. At Puerto Rico on 27–28 June 1976, France, Britain and West Germany reached agreement with the United States that international financial assistance to countries such as Italy should be conditional on there being no communists in the government.[41] This represented a threat to the left in France in view of its alliance involving the communist party in the common programme of government adopted in 1972. The danger of American interference receded, however, when the French left split over various issues in the summer of 1977 and subsequently lost the 1978 elections.

Mitterrand's victory in the 1981 presidential election was a surprise to most observers, and the character of his government was provisional until after the legislative elections in June. Moreover, his platform had been 110 personal propositions rather than the common programme. The sweeping PS victory enabled him to choose to bring four communists into the government and thereby to present the United States with a *fait accompli* that directly challenged the Kissinger doctrine. When this was accompanied by adoption of a reformist liberal, or Keynesian, economic policy which contradicted US liberal, or monetarist, policy, this appeared to confirm American worst fears; Mitterrand was warned that Franco-American relations could not have the same tone or content so long as communists were in the government. It may therefore have been for self-protection that Mitterrand reassured Washington that France would remain a firm supporter of the Atlantic alliance and of its December 1979 decision to instal cruise and Pershing II missiles in western Europe (though not in France) unless the Soviet Union agreed to scrap her new SS20 missiles. While refusing to meet Soviet leaders unless they removed troops sent into Afghanistan in 1979, Mitterrand met president Reagan three times during his first year in office and left a deep impression of his opposition to communism. If there was an element of tactical diplomacy in this, there was no doubt of Mitterrand's firm conviction of the need for an East-West balance of power requiring an American commitment to counter what he saw as a Soviet advantage that threatened the security of France and her allies. Thus France became the staunchest (non-integrated) member of the Atlantic alliance in the 1980s, allowing the NATO council to meet in Paris in June 1983 for the first time since the rupture of 1966.

It is true that Mitterrand's economic policy involved nationalizing some French companies under American control; for example CGCT and LCT were bought from ITT in October 1982, and in 1983 CII was bought from Honeywell. This, following Giscard d'Estaing's decision in

January 1981 to sever the link between Framatome and Westinghouse, recovered a considerable degree of independence for French advanced technology. Such actions, when added to Mitterrand's determination to trade freely with the Soviet Union and his election campaign call for a reform of the western alliance, could be interpreted as potentially dissident as regards US leadership.[42] Mitterrand even opposed US intervention in Central America and the Caribbean, and sold arms to the Marxist government of Nicaragua. However, in 1983 French troops joined Americans in a Lebanon intervention by a multi-national force, while others intervened in Chad in liaison with American action to prevent a Libyan expansion there. Giscard d'Estaing's promotion of an EEC peace initiative in the Middle East from June 1980 was abandoned by Mitterrand who supported the American Camp David approach to piecemeal Arab-Israeli agreements. Only Giscard's 1978 proposal for a European Disarmament Conference was brought to fruition in Stockholm in 1984; and even then it was made clear that nothing substantial was likely until after the November 1984 US presidential elections. Thus were French hopes for a general arms control agreement including the super-powers kept alive; but French economic troubles and dependence on foreign loans reduced their influence, and it did not augur well for American commitment to the conference as a door to *détente* that the official in charge of their delegation was a Mr Goodby. Thus the French role was that of a semi-dependent power within the United States's orbit rather than the independent middle-sized power that had been the ambition of de Gaulle.

As one would expect, French relations with the Soviet Union were the converse of those with the United States. Relations had appeared to be good in the 1960s when de Gaulle left NATO and obstructed the expansion or integration of the EEC. During the last year of de Gaulle's rule, however, French policy retreated from *rapprochement* with the Soviet Union owing partly to the Czechoslovakian crisis, but also because a Russo-German dialogue was in progress as part of Brandt's *Ostpolitik* and de Gaulle was finding financial relations with West Germany particularly difficult after May 1968 when the franc came under pressure. It was the Russian turn to show anxiety in 1969 when the newly elected Pompidou showed enthusiasm for integration and expansion of the EEC and for improvement in Franco-American relations. Nevertheless Pompidou maintained friendly relations with Moscow, particularly in the form of trade agreements. As the Soviet Union began to develop a policy of *détente* with the United States in the 1970s it began to treat the earlier *rapprochement* with France as a model for relations with other western states. To develop this approach Brezhnev paid a state visit to France in October 1971. Paradoxically, this was just at a time when France was obdurately opposing proposals for mutual and balanced force reductions in Europe on the grounds that it tended towards a Russo-American condominium at the expense of the Europeans. But the Russians pressed ahead, emphasizing the importance of the Grand Commission founded with de Gaulle in 1966 to foster trade and scientific co-operation. They had since formed similar commissions with other powers including the United States. In October 1970 they had persuaded Pompidou to create a political counterpart to the Grand Commission, a protocol providing for regular consultations on international issues every six months and at other times when international tension might develop. In October 1971 Brezhnev proposed that they codify the principles of their co-operation. Clearly the aim was to make up for the break in relations in 1968 and to maintain apparent French determination not to re-enter NATO nor to allow the EEC to become closed to the east.

But this muted form of *rapprochement* came to an end in 1973 when French policy perceived fully the risks involved in a Soviet-American condominium. It is possible that strident anti-Soviet criticism came at the same time as attacks on American oil policy as a result of Pompidou's illness and Jobert's impetuous handling of French policy during 1973–4. Whatever the reason, Jobert warned the Helsinki conference on European security in June 1973 against a 'moral disarmament deadening the spirit of resistance, deceiving vigilance, and leading to servitude'. This was followed up by the French declaring that they intended to keep up their own military development, and appealing to the United States to maintain their existing conventional and nuclear forces in Europe. At this stage French anxiety regarding a super-power condominium was as much directed at the United States as at the Soviet Union; thus, on his visit to China in October 1973 Pompidou resisted the temptation of his hosts to fulminate against the Soviet Union. Back in Paris, however, Jobert continued to castigate both Washington and Moscow for ignoring European interests in the Middle East crisis of that autumn.

When Giscard d'Estaing was elected French president in 1974 anxiety increased in the Soviet Union that he was likely to commit France to integration in the EEC and to be influenced by colleagues like Lecanuet towards Atlanticism. But Giscard visited Brezhnev in December 1974, and returned convinced that, on the basis of a Soviet wish to avoid war, it was possible to pursue ambitious solutions to international problems with a *mondialiste* perspective. Regular Franco-Russian meetings were arranged, and trade contracts were sought with eastern Europe. French successes in East-West trade, however, were being more than matched by West Germany. The Soviet will to assert world power ambitions clashed with French interests in Africa and the Indian Ocean. Nevertheless, Giscard's trust in the limited nature of Soviet aims led him to attach little importance to their military intervention in Afghanistan in 1979, arguing that the assets of *détente* in the form of trade and cultural exchanges between East and West should not be jeopardized in order to support anti-Soviet Afghans whom he called 'rebels' rather than resisters. When he saw Brezhnev to exchange views in Warsaw in May 1980 he was derided as *'le facteur de Varsovie'* by Mitterrand, who sought to exploit the absence of nationalism from Giscard's reformist liberal discourse. When Mitterrand came to power he ostracized the USSR and relations reached a nadir when he expelled forty-seven Soviet diplomats in April 1983. But some views were shared, for example on the Middle East, and the Franco-Soviet dialogue was revived when Mitterrand received a visit from foreign minister Gromyko on 9 September 1983.[43]

The idea of European union has a long history related to early ideals of Christian unity and to efforts to prevent recurrent outbreaks of war which, by the eighteenth century, were already seen to involve greater losses than gains. France was involved in the problems of Europe as the leading power over a long period and was naturally the source of some of the concepts of unification. The prevalence of Monarchism, however, prevented the European idea from making institutional progress until at least the mid-nineteenth century, by which time the emergence of democratic and liberal thought encouraged a more systematic approach. Hence Victor Hugo's call for a United States of Europe in 1848. But this approach was short-lived as the consolidation of nation-states and politico-economic nationalism diverted interest in France and elsewhere, from the European idea.

It took the suffering of two World Wars and the discrediting of nationalism to bring the European idea back to the surface. The first time it was taken up seriously by a statesman in power was by Edouard Herriot in 1924, and his thoughts were developed tentatively by Aristide Briand into a plan for European union in 1929. But the onset of the depression of the 1930s, fascism and war killed the plan at birth. By 1945 not only was nationalism discredited, but also the machinery of the nation-state had been smashed. International principles involved in communism, socialism and Catholicism, among others, had more scope in the immediate post-war period than ever before; from another point of view, the development of capitalism as a system, and the scale of economic reconstruction problems facing Europe, encouraged serious thought on methods of international co-operation. American influence encouraged federal concepts, but ruled out communism as the cold war set in. Christian democracy and socialism were therefore the two principal movements that proceeded to promote the European idea.

Why did France play a leading part in promoting European unity? First, the two most important political parties under the Fourth Republic were the socialists and the christian democrats. Second, French national interests were to create a security system that would remove both the urge and the opportunity for future German aggression against France, and furthermore to achieve economic reconstruction in harmony with France's natural trading partners in western Europe. So far as timing was concerned, external American pressure in favour of German reconstruction and the organized sharing of Marshall Aid made the creation of some kind of western European institutions a matter of urgency.

Initially the British were involved, having strong interest in European security and stability. The Dunkirk defence treaty of 1947, followed by the 1948 Brussels treaty for mutual assistance against aggression, involved the British not only in military matters but also in discussion of socio-economic and political methods of co-operation. But French policy became attached to the concept of supra-national institutions designed to prevent the danger of Germany recovering the independence and power to threaten France once again. The federal ideas of J. Monnet and R. Schuman proceeded to lead the French government to propose the European Coal and Steel Community, and ultimately to join the European Economic Community, while leaving out the British who gave priority to relations with the Commonwealth and the United States for both economic and cultural reasons. The new West German state was willing to enter into federal agreements in Europe partly because it was shakily built on a divided society, and therefore needed outside political support during its early years, but even more because firm backing from western Europe was considered essential to avoid becoming submerged in the Soviet bloc to the east.

There were countervailing attempts to adopt confederal methods of co-operation between independent states in the 1950s. One example was Western European Union, which included the British, with a view to improving defence and other systems; but lack of political interest on the British side allowed such institutions to remain empty shells. When de Gaulle returned to power in France he did in fact favour confederal rather than federal methods, as shown by his Fouchet Plan launched in 1960; but at the same time he was anxious to avoid weakening the EEC in the face of what he regarded as 'Anglo-Saxon' hegemony, moreover he found it possible to work in harmony with West Germany under Adenauer. The result was a veto on British entry into the EEC during a period when de Gaulle otherwise obstructed further progress towards federalism and created so much ill-feeling that his own confederal ideas made no progress either.

Quite apart from differences of view in France and Europe regarding the form of European unity, there were different conceptions of the purpose and role of Europe in the world at large. Socialists in France were of widely differing tendencies, but generally regarded western Europe as a possible 'third force' developing a distinctive socio-economic system and pursuing independent political interests from those of the United States and the Soviet Union. The christian democrats and many of the Radicals, on the other hand, saw western Europe rather as a second western force, co-operating fully with the United States and sharing Atlanticist economic and political principles while also creating a bulwark against Soviet power and communism. These currents of thought and political tendencies converged, however, in the belief that a united Europe should maintain and develop close links with the under-developed world, thereby sustaining the influence of the French empire: 'Eurafrica' was one of the evocative catchwords of the 1950s. There was a further point of convergence in French opinion, which was appreciation of the importance of the EEC in providing an outlet for French agricultural surpluses and as a dynamic force for economic and social change.

By the end of de Gaulle's rule, in 1969, there were two problems that were preventing the EEC from progressing as smoothly as originally expected. First, there was a deadlock between de Gaulle and the other five member-states which had centred on the issue of British entry. Second, the fact that there was a deadlock at all was an indication of the growth of West German power and independence since the signing of the treaty of Rome. French policy under Pompidou from 1969 undertook to find a solution to both problems at once: the British would be brought in to provide a possible counterweight to West Germany, but on terms that would prevent her from disrupting the EEC organization in any way harmful to French agricultural interests. Thus Pompidou proposed a three-stage programme to achieve a *relance européenne* at the EEC summit conference at the Hague in December 1969: *achèvement* (involving completion and consolidation of the common agricultural policy, CAP), *approfondissement* (involving plans for complete economic and monetary union by 1980) and *élargissement* (involving the entry of Britain and several associated applicant states). This formula was intended to secure the interests of France and the EEC as a whole before British entry. In the event, British acceptance of the CAP and agreement to run down the independent role of sterling as a reserve currency, together with a favourable French referendum in April 1972, cleared the way for enlargement of the EEC in 1973. Nevertheless, this was made possible essentially by an informal understanding reached by Pompidou and the then British prime minister, Edward Heath, at a meeting in Paris in May 1971, and much of this personal understanding proved ephemeral when both men ceased to hold office in 1974.

Unexpected difficulties were encountered by France and the EEC as a result of the world financial and economic crisis which began with the Middle East war of October 1973. During the crisis, France, who was heavily dependent on imported oil for her energy needs, made full use of her special status as a state friendly to the Arabs and consequently received privileged oil supplies; in contrast, Holland was denied supplies of oil for a time and received no support from France. A common energy policy in the EEC proved impossible to achieve and all members except France accepted US leadership in the oil consumers' International Energy Agency. Moreover, world financial confusion disrupted progress towards monetary unity in the EEC. A 'snake in the tunnel' system had been created in September 1972 allowing member currencies to move 2.4 per cent above or below a normal parity. This was complicated when the dollar was floated freely during 1973 and France had to leave the system in January 1974, returning the following year, but leaving again in 1976. Moreover, Britain, Italy and Ireland had even earlier left the 'snake'. Considerable friction arose during this period, particularly as the German mark was clearly the strongest currency and attracted the envy of neighbouring states, including France. Thus, when Pompidou died in 1974, his policy was in shreds: although technically completed on a permanent basis, the CAP had been severely weakened by financial instability; monetary union had been thwarted; and British reactions to the economic crisis had tended towards solidarity with the US rather than with the EEC.

Giscard d'Estaing undertook from 1974 to stabilize and develop the French economy within the context of greater European co-operation. Disappointed with British policy, with its disruptive demand for re-negotiation of its terms of EEC membership in 1974, Giscard preferred to base his hopes on close relations with the West German chancellor, Helmut Schmidt, paradoxically using English as their common language and ignoring jibes from nationalists like Jobert that *'ils se tutoient en anglais'*. Thus Franco-German relations became closer than at any time since the early 1960s, proving once again that their harmony was the necessary and perhaps even the sufficient condition for progress in the EEC. Institutional progress on confederal lines was made by creating a European Council to enable heads of government to meet three times a year to promote political co-operation. Moreover, it was agreed that the European parliament should be directly elected by universal suffrage in 1979. It had already acquired significant powers to add to the EEC budget in April 1970 and these were confirmed in July 1975. Assertion of budgetary powers and the right to be consulted on legislation became more pronounced once the parliament increased its status through direct elections, though even after 1979 it forbore to use its supreme power under the treaty of Rome to dismiss the Commission in its entirety and remained a subordinate institution.

Giscard also pursued energetically the drive for monetary union. Although the 'snake' system was destroyed by the 1974 oil crisis, dissatisfaction with floating currencies, which would have sabotaged the CAP but for the invention of more stable 'green' currencies for calculation of common prices and monetary compensatory amounts (MCAs) to relate prices to changes in real currencies, led Giscard and Schmidt to launch a European monetary system (EMS) in 1979 whose members were sufficiently committed yet adaptable to withstand pressures arising from the second oil crisis in 1979 and the ensuing world recession. Most EEC members felt that the EMS and CAP were beneficial assets derived from a budget no larger than 20 per cent of the French budget. The oscillations of an oil-based currency prevented the British from joining the EMS and they objected to making large net payments into the EEC budget. While agreeing to give *ad hoc* rebates to the British, Giscard and other EEC leaders insisted on maintaining the 'own resources' system of automatic financing through customs levies and VAT payments created in 1969.

Mitterrand adopted an ambivalent attitude to the EEC in 1981, defending it against British attacks and criticising Giscard for his agreement to rebates each year, yet attributing to it responsibility for increasing disparities between wealthy and poor regions. To protect the latter he was more adamant than Giscard that Spanish and Portuguese entry into the EEC would require a long transitional period and a Mediterranean policy to safeguard farmers' interests. Even his 1981 plan for European economic revival caused anxiety in West Germany where his Keynesian approach was seen as damagingly inflationary and protectionist. After his retreat into a deflationary policy of *rigueur* from March 1983, however, his relations with the new chancellor, Kohl, became harmonious and he had valuable West German support for his efforts as EEC president in 1984 to resolve serious problems regarding new members, an increase in the budget and restructuring the CAP. He announced an impressive *projet politique* at the Hague on 8 February 1984, proposing a European space satellite programme as part of a wide-ranging plan for greater economic, political and military co-operation in the EEC. But such proposals depended on the outcome of disputes which threatened either to destroy the EEC or to make it divisively hierarchical according to varying levels of economic development and political commitment among its members.

French relations with the 'third world' were transformed by the traumatic experience of rapid decolonization between 1954 and the end of the Algerian war in 1962. De Gaulle established an ambitious policy of co-operation with independent francophone states and encouraged non-alignment among other states in accordance with his philosophy of independence for all nations. Thus France maintained extensive cultural, economic and military connections with ex-colonies, so that up to thirty states in the world continued to use French as their official language. Although over half French trade was geared to the EEC compared with a quarter to the 'third world', the importance of oil and gas imports from Arab states and valuable supplies of minerals from Africa ensured that France would maintain an energetic 'third world' policy. Moreover, the poverty and political fragility of many ex-colonies ensured that they would remain extremely dependent on French support.

French aid to the 'third world' was in three forms: public technical and cultural aid, private business and banking aid, and international aid through EEC agreements. French aid policy was traditionally more ambitious than that of other developed states. In 1963, for example, French public aid was nearly one billion dollars, 1.33 per cent of GNP, double the British figure. But, in spite of the 1963 Jeanneney report's advocacy of 1.5 per cent GNP, France followed other states by gradually reducing her aid programmes and shifting the emphasis from public to private aid which involved more interest payments and strings. In 1971 the International Development Assistance Committee asked its seventeen most developed member states to commit 0.7 per cent of the GNP to developing countries but the average aid actually given in 1977 was 0.3 per cent of GNP. The national figures were: US$4.1 billions, West Germany $1.31 billions (0.26 per cent GNP), Britain $907 millions (0.38 per cent GNP), France $2.394 millions (0.63 per cent GNP). Nevertheless, at least two-thirds of French aid still went to the franc zone countries, and the aid figures included grants to overseas *départements* like Réunion which were otherwise supposed to be integral parts of France. Furthermore, much of French aid was cultural with the understandable intention of maintaining the world-wide influence of French civilization; for example, the forty thousand teaching and technical assistants sent by France to 'third world' countries amounted to about half those sent out by all the developed nations. Then, like most other aid donors, France tended to attach strings to aid so that, even if it were not repayable with interest, it often required the use of French equipment and personnel. Thus it was hardly surprising that the debts of ninety-four developing countries increased from $71.7 billions in 1970 to $216.6 billions in 1976.[44]

Responsibilities for aid distribution by the French government were divided. The ministry of finance dealt with trading agreements and subsidies, though money was often sent out by other ministries directly concerned. After 1966 the ministry for foreign affairs organized co-operation with all parts of the under-developed world. There was a *secrétaire d'état* dealing with economic aid to the sixteen African francophone states. Then there was a *directeur des affaires techniques et culturelles* to organize educational and technical assistance to all countries receiving aid from France. Altogether the Quai d'Orsay normally spent up to half its budget on co-operation programmes.[45] Within the French government as a whole there were also the activities of the *ministre d'état* for overseas French *départements* and territories, and then of course the activities of the ministry of defence. In terms of trade there was a tremendous decline in the importance of the franc zone to France over a twenty-five-year period: in 1954 about 30 per cent of French trade was with the franc zone countries; by 1964 it was down to 17 per cent; and by 1975 it was down to less than 5 per cent. It was significant, however, that it provided France with an increasingly favourable balance; for example exports in 1975 were worth over three billion francs more than imports from the franc zone and nearly seven billion more in 1979.

The EEC, from its birth in 1957, organized a number of aid and development programmes with the 'third world'. This was important to France in helping to support the French empire and subsequently the independent states in the franc zone. In 1975 the EEC signed the Lomé convention with forty-six states in various parts of the 'third world'. But the agreement did not improve significantly on the existing EEC generalized system of preferences, in terms of tariffs. For example, it did not allow for goods to have tariff-free entry unless at least half their value was created in the signatory country concerned (thus blocking the development of finishing processes in 'third world' industry); there was, moreover, a safety clause enabling EEC members to block access to 'third world' products if they seriously disturbed a sector of their economies. Financial provision to help stabilize 'third world' countries' export earnings in the face of world market fluctuations was no more than £50 million approximately in any one year for a particular country's commodity (in fact the total aid provision under the convention was only £1,500 million approximately over a five-year period). The Lomé convention was signed by forty-six countries, and Lomé II in 1979 by fifty-eight needing trade assistance in a period of declining levels of aid; and it did encourage a few incipient 'third world' industries in spite of its general emphasis on trade in agricultural products and raw materials. The free trade provision in the convention were characteristic of the relationship between an advanced and a dependent economy, allowing penetration by the former without much risk of competition from the latter.[46]

Apart from cultural and economic relations with the French-speaking countries in Africa, France had equally extensive military connections. Ten years after their independence in 1960 many African ex-colonies were beginning to reduce their dependence on French military assistance, and president Pompidou had not concerned himself about that tendency. But after 1974 Giscard d'Estaing re-established close relations with ex-colonies. The third summit of French-speaking African states in May 1976 in Paris was attended by nineteen members compared with only eleven at the summit in 1973. At the fourth summit in Dakar in April 1976, president Senghor of Senegal welcomed renewed French interest in Africa, saying that if Europe did not appreciate the security risk in Africa other continents would take control. This reference to Chinese and Soviet intervention in Africa was echoed by a number of African leaders seeking military aid which they very often used for the internal security of their personal power base. Whatever the reason, France renewed military pacts with Congo-Brazzaville, Gabon, Ivory Coast, Cameroun and Senegal; and new technical military co-operation agreements were made with Benin, Chad and Togo. A force of 5,000 French troops was permanently stationed in the new republic of Djibouti, a situation which facilitated links with the large French naval force in the Indian Ocean and with another military base in Réunion. The most notable French military interventions in Africa were in the western Sahara in 1977, to support the Mauritanian government against Polisario guerrillas, and in Chad in 1976, to support the government against Libyan-backed rebels; Giscard d'Estaing was given the title *'gendarme* of Africa' in April 1978 when he used U.S. transport aircraft for French para-troops to intervene to preserve the government of president Mobutu in Zaire. The most significant point is that France was the only one of the ex-colonial powers to maintain permanent military bases in Africa.[47]

The reason for the importance of Africa to French security was explained by the French chief-of-staff, General Méry, in a statement of policy on 3 April 1978:[48]

il existe entre ce continent et la France un ensemble de liens établis par la géographie et l'histoire, que la complémentarité de leurs économies fondées sur les matières premières pour l'un et sur leur transformation pour l'autre, vient encore renforcer. Or, il règne actuellement en Afrique un climat d'instabilité qui ne peut, en conséquence, nous laisser indifférents et cela pour deux raisons principales que je rattacherai aux deux notions de sécurité et de responsabilité.

La sécurité de la France ne dépend pas, bien sûr, uniquement de la sécurité de l'Afrique, mais elle est, me semble-t-il, très fortement liée à celle-ci. Elle l'est, en premier lieu, parce que le territoire français est proche de l'Afrique en Méditerranée, proche aussi dans le canal de Mozambique avec Mayotte, et à la Réunion. Elle l'est ensuite, parce que 260,000 ressortissants français vivent et travaillent en Afrique, pour l'essentiel en Afrique du Nord et en Afrique Occidentale. Elle l'est enfin et peut-être surtout, parce que les routes maritimes qui entourent l'Afrique servent à acheminer la plus grande partie du pétrole et des matières premières dont nous avons besoin et sont donc vitales pour notre pays. Ces routes passent au plus près du continent africain en plusieurs endroits et sont alors à portée des moyens aériens et navals des pays riverains: à cet égard les zones de Dakar, du Cap, de Tunis revêtent une importance toute particulière, car elles constituent autant de passages obligés et 'singuliers', plus faciles à contrôler que les longs couloirs du Mozambique ou de la Mer Rouge.

He went on to speak of military aid agreements with a number of African states made by their own request and which involved a responsibility France was willing to fulfil in order to contribute to the development and stability of Africa.

Soon after he became president in 1974, Giscard d'Estaing spoke of the need for a new international economic order and subsequently initiated a north-south dialogue (*la conférence sur la coopération économique internationale*) in Paris from December 1975 until June 1977. The emphasis of his approach was on the need for new mechanisms in world markets to ensure a better balance in world trade. His ideal was to remove political and economic obstacles to the evolution of a natural economic order in the world. Nevertheless, Giscard d'Estaing admitted to the existence of structural imbalance in the world economy, and suggested in 1976 a 'Marshall Plan' for Africa. American policy under president Carter was sympathetic to this view, but its commitment of 0.27 per cent of GNP to aid in 1978 was cut to 0.18 per cent by 1980 under president Reagan.

Mitterrand made a clearer commitment to aid than Giscard, planning to raise it from 0.57 per cent GNP in 1980 (which included DOM-TOM payments) to 0.7 per cent GNP by 1985 (excluding DOM-TOM payments). This *tiers-mondiste* policy still involved a bias towards private aid with strings attached so that, as Léopold Senghor of Senegal once put it, out of every four francs given in aid five went back to France. In the Middle East Mitterrand sought to resolve the Israeli and Palestinian disputes, but in 1983 was drawn into an American-led multi-national force in the Lebanon. Like Giscard before him, he preferred a less prominent role within a United Nations force but the UN authority was in question. Similarly, Mitterrand sought a solution to the Chad civil war through the Organization of African Unity, but its authority too was in question and 3,000 French troops were sent in August 1983 to defend the Habre government against Libyan-backed rebels, who had previously been in power and defended by French troops against Habre! Thus France was helping tribes, factions, sects or families in various insecure states to preserve artificial frontiers established under colonial rule.[49] Mitterrand's greatest success was in bringing to fruition in 1983 the renewed co-operation with Algeria begun by Giscard in 1980. This was the cornerstone of Mitterrand's policy of association with the non-aligned states intended to reduce the world division into two hostile blocs.

France recovered a degree of self-determination after the Second World War that varied considerably between the two extremes of dependence and independence. The gradations between those extremes must be taken into account to give French external relations meaningful analysis. While distinguishing negative forms of independence from more positive forms, it is also important to vary the focus from relations with super-powers, in which French freedom is restricted, to relations with European partners, in which France plays an influential role, to relations with the 'third world' in which France sometimes determines the very survival of rulers and governments. In the 1980s serious political and economic challenges were met by France with a determination to enjoy the freedom and relationships essential to her unique identity.

Chapter 6

The education system

Introduction

It might perhaps be thought that education is a topic which has little to do with politics, yet it is one which, in recent years, has become the object of an increased political interest in France (as also in Britain). One reason for this is plain enough in economic terms: in a technological society, such as France, it is no longer sufficient for a worker to sell his unskilled labour; if he wishes to command an adequate salary, he requires a technical qualification, which only education can provide. It has been calculated that in October 1981, out of 23,262,701 men and women forming the working population, 5,516,657 had no qualification whatsoever and 5,003,137 had only the *certificat d'éducation professionnelle* (*Collections de l'INSEE, Démographie et Emploi, Enquête sur l'emploi d'octobre 1981*, INSEE, June 1982).

At the level of government and the higher administrative echelons also, it is higher education which provides the requisite personnel. In every respect, therefore, as W. D. Halls says, 'education in modern society is about power',[1] and the distribution of power is the natural pre-occupation of political parties.

This is not to say that there was no realization in the past as to the political usefulness of education. Napoleon, for example, laid down as one basis of education 'la fidélité à l'Empereur, à la monarchie impériale, dépositaire du bonheur des peuples, et à la dynastie Napoléonienne, conservatrice de l'unité de la France et de toutes les idées libérales proclamées par les constitutions' (Decree of 17 March 1808, Titre V, art. 38). This endeavour to gain political support via education may be viewed as indoctrination. Subsequent régimes do not appear to have regarded education in quite such a 'party political' light, even though education was considered a means whereby the social order might be maintained without violence, by including in the curriculum teaching on morality and on the values accepted by society. However, the need to adapt education to republican principles seems to have dominated the legislation of the 1880s.

Yet other opinions on the purpose of education, some going back to antiquity, are today not without significance; i.e. the need to bring up good citizens in general, to teach discipline, devotion to duty, to provide character training, and also to train individuals of superlative ability to serve and lead the state. Such views have exercised a considerable influence on the education systems of Europe, and should not wholly be disregarded. To these should perhaps be added, particularly from the sixteenth century onwards, the more aristocratic concept of the man of culture — a concept regarded by many as outdated, narrow, and over-literary, but still able to wield some power over the content of the curriculum.

The question of what should be regarded as culture is of particular importance. At a time of greater illiteracy when the teacher was the sole purveyor of information, he was viewed with greater respect, and the information which he had to convey was accepted accordingly. Today, in a period of mass communication, the teacher is only one of many providers of information, and his is often considered less relevant or interesting than the others', and undoubtedly less up-to-date. Whereas, in 1954, only 1 per cent of French households possessed a television set, in 1976 the figure had gone up 85.8 per cent. By 1981 93.1 per cent of French households had a television (9.7 per cent of that total owning two or more), and 95.7 per cent of the population possessed a radio. The printed word, still the most habitual medium for the teacher fared less well, a total of 80 per cent of households possessing books, and of those, 22.5 possessing more than 200 in 1981.[2] Pop music, jazz, science fiction, sport, all these have a claim to be regarded as part of any national culture, but are not necessarily so regarded in scholastic terms.

In the last few years, too, education has had to face the challenge of the computer age. It is therefore not surprising that the education system, influenced by age-old theories, adjusting with difficulty to the needs of mass society, finds itself criticized for its conservatism and narrowness in relation to what it teaches. Since it is now viewed also as a means to social advancement it is criticized for its inadequacies, or, more accurately, for its success. On the one hand, it is alleged to block the access of the working classes to higher education, in order that the necessary work force for the capitalist economy should still be available;[3] on the other, it is held to transmit the dominant culture from one generation to another, which in turn ensures not only the dominance of the upper classes (from whom the dominant culture proceeds), but also the preservation of the established order.[4]

In view of the criticisms made of the system, the uncertainties surrounding it, and the hopes (often disappointed) which it arouses, education undoubtedly warrants the political interest with which it is now regarded. What follows does not claim to be exhaustive, but is an attempt to provide a survey of the essential aspects of the subject. While French education has undergone major reforms over the last two decades, some elements in its make-up seem hard to shift, or even to reform. In this context, not only education at school and university will be considered, but also some of the more intractable problems left to present-day educators by centuries of history, notably that of centralized administration, and of Catholic education in France.

(1) The centralized administration?

The organization of French education owes its present framework to Napoleon, although centralizing tendencies may be seen at the end of the preceding century. If the French Revolution was unable to put its reforms into effect, some of the ideas propounded at that time were to be particularly influential. For example, Condorcet's proposals for reform in 1792 stated that education should be national (provided by the state). Its essential purpose was to give to each citizen the possibility of developing his talents to their utmost, in order to render effective the political equality recognized by the law. The vicissitudes of the Revolution made it impossible to implement these views on a large scale, if at all, and it was consequently left to Napoleon to interpret them as he saw fit.

Napoleon devised a system which followed one part of the Revolution's principles, whilst wholly neglecting the other. A state education system was established, but the need to supply education for all was disregarded. Between 1806 and 1808 the *université* was established which comprised the whole of French education at all levels. The monopoly was absolute in theory but in practice left primary education and women's education to the church; secondary and higher education was Napoleon's main concern, but here too, it was possible for private secondary schools to exist, if authorization were obtained.

The state 'monopoly', such as it was, may be said to have consisted of two elements: the conferment by the *université* alone of all qualifications, at that time the *baccalauréat* at the end of secondary education, the *licence* (either in letters, law or science), the first university degree and the *doctorat*, the post-graduate degree, together with the obligation for all teachers to obtain the appropriate qualification; the surveillance exercised, not by the state itself, but by the *université*, in the person of its own officials. Such a surveillance, extending over primary schools, secondary schools (whether *lycées* with a six-year course of study or *collèges* with a less extensive programme) and the *facultés* for higher education, required an administrative network to cover the whole country, which was divided up into twenty-seven[5] *académies*, each headed by a *recteur*, appointed for five years. This official was aided by one or more *inspecteurs d'académie* and a *conseil académique*, and his task was to supervise all levels of education within his *académie*. He was directly responsible to the head of the *université*, the *grand-maître*, by whom he was appointed. The *grand-maître*, appointed by the emperor, was himself assisted by a *conseil de l'université*, the members of which were appointed for life, and a number of *inspecteurs généraux*, whose task was, simply, to inspect all levels of teaching. He had at his disposal a wide range of patronage, since he appointed to administrative and teaching posts, and all matters pertaining to the *université* were within his province.

The purpose of this administrative system was to ensure, as far as possible, a high degree of uniformity both in pedagogical and political terms. Napoleon was very conscious, after the disuniting effects of the Revolution, of the need to weld the country together, and education seemed to him to provide the means to that end. This meant inevitably that the education system was used for political propaganda. Among the bases for teaching required in the university were 'la fidélité à l'Empereur, à la monarchie impériale, dépositaire du bonheur des peuples, et à la dynastie Napoléonienne . . .' (Decree of 17 March 1808, Titre V, art. 38). Education, for Napoleon, was essentially a political aid, one which would provide him with the educated personnel to assist him in the running of his empire, and, at a more general level, to provide the state with 'des citoyens attachés à leur religion, à leur prince, à leur patrie et à leur famille' (ibid.).

Overall, the administrative system established by Napoleon was retained in the nineteenth century and for a good half of the twentieth. At some periods, the *conseil de l'université* enjoyed more power (July Monarchy), at others the minister of education (the subsequent title of the *grand-maître*) and the administration (Second Empire). In spite of criticisms levelled at the *université*'s centralized administration (less strong than criticisms of the prefectoral system), commentators seem to have assumed that its authoritarian origins were not incompatible with the more liberal forms of government, and that the latter's ethos would prevail. 'Ce grand établissement eut ses vices, ses lacunes, témoignage de ce qu'il y avait de vicieux et d'incomplet dans le régime impérial . . . Enfin les maximes d'autorité et de centralisation absolue, qui caractérisaient tout le gouvernement impérial, tenaient là aussi une place exagérée et nécessairement transitoire' (Guizot, speech of 1 February 1836, *Archives parlementaires*, vol. 100, Paris, Imprimerie et librairie administratives et des chemins de fer/P. Dupont, 1899, p. 85). Such optimism seems to have been a little misplaced, since the administrative system has remained, while parliamentary régimes have come and gone. In this context, it is perhaps worth noting the attempts made in the 1880s and 1890s to bring to higher education an element of decentralization and independence. This initiative began with two decrees of 25 July 1885 which re-affirmed the *personnalité morale* of the faculties, i.e. their right to accept gifts and bequests made to them, and also to receive subsidies from towns, departments, *communes*, etc. – all gifts and subsidies to be noted under a specific heading at the ministry of education, and to be used as the faculties thought desirable. In December of the same year, a decree provided for the composition and powers of the representative bodies of the faculties: the *conseil général des facultés*, presided over by the *recteur* and comprising the deans of the faculties, and two academics elected from each faculty: the *conseil de faculté*, composed of professors, dealing in general with finance: and an *assemblée de faculté*, comprising all teaching members of the faculty and concerned essentially with pedagogical matters. In 1890 the faculties were given the responsibility of organizing their own budget, within limitations.[6] In April 1893 *personnalité civile* was bestowed on groups of faculties within the same *académie*, and the crown of the edifice was put in place with the law of 10 July 1896, which gave the groups of faculties the name of *universités* – but this change of title appears to have altered little in fact.[7] In the face of a centralized administrative system, covering all aspects of higher education not explicitly mentioned in the reforms, the latter had little chance of succeeding, given that their terms of reference were so limited. At all events, they seem to have remained enough of a dead letter for C. Fouchet, then education minister, to have stated in 1966 at the *colloque de Caen* on higher education that the texts of 1885 and 1890 provided adequate autonomy if the faculties were capable of profiting therefrom. Yet Georges Vedel, an academic of great experience, is of the opinion that at the level of higher education, centralization was very much less than is commonly supposed. 'La décentralisation et l'autonomie . . . ont existé sous le régime de ce qu'on appelle, chez ceux qui ne l'ont pas connue, l'Université "napoléonienne". Le ministre était à l'Université ce que la reine d'Angleterre est à l'Etat britannique: il signait tout et ne choisissait rien. Tout s'y décidait entre universitaires dans les conseils nationaux et locaux'[8]

It is possible that for academics higher education was less centralized than it appeared to be. Yet May 1968 is there to give a totally different picture of the administrative system up to that time. 'Virtually no powers of decision are in local hands; all administrative decisions, all budgetary allocations, all staff appointments, are the exclusive prerogative of a distant and faceless bureaucracy in Paris. A French university . . . works to norms ordained by the centre. All 23 universities in the country are state-run, on rigidly standardized lines, like a government department. The local administrative staff is impotent, the students resentful, their mutual relations hostile. Discussion is pointless seeing that decisions are taken elsewhere.'[9] Even if the students held totally erroneous views on the degree of centralization (and the consequent lack of participation) which obtained in French education, their views would still have to be taken seriously, as the *image* of itself which the system had conveyed. Yet the substance of such opinions received indirect backing from a sociological study which indicated that students prior to 1968 were by no means well integrated in society. There was little in the way of corporate life as between students of one faculty or of another, no encouragement from the universities.[10] Such problems could well arise from a situation where a centralized system made the student feel alienated and solitary.

As a result of May 1968, the *Loi d'Orientation* was pushed through Parliament in an endeavour to reform the education system, where it had given cause for complaint. In this context, the centralized administration of education was one element considered by E. Faure to be in need of reform. 'La conception napoléonienne de l'Université centralisée et arbitraire est périmée.'[11] Whatever the successes and failures of Faure's legislation, it must undoubtedly be looked on as a watershed – as a conscious effort to roll back the traditions of centuries. Such changes as there have been in terms of *déconcentration*, as well as moves towards decentralization, have been introduced since 1968 – and not only since 1981. The *Loi d'Orientation* and subsequent legislation will be looked at in more detail below (see Section 4), but at this stage, it should be sufficient to see how far the present post-Faure system (together with the changes that are being introduced by A. Savary) can be considered a decentralized one.

At the present time the *ministre de l'éducation nationale* (as he has again been called since 1981) is placed at the head of a large army of employees (1,121,868 persons in 1984 including 109,948 in private education) – teachers, administrators, and ancillary staff of all kinds. He is responsible for a budget of nearly 169,333 million francs, which is now the highest budget in the state, and which represents 18 per cent of the total. The minister's tasks are many: appointment of officials (*fonctionnaires*), which includes teachers, decisions regarding organis- ation and policy (this is of particular importance since legislation concern- ing education tends to be of the *loi cadre* variety, which indicates the general lines to be followed, and leaves the ministry to work out its practicalities and interpretations), the signing of official documents. He presents and defends his budget and his policies to parliament. He must also receive deputations from unions and other organizations, give inter- views, press conferences and the like. He has, to assist him in his decision- making, a body which he can consult, the *Conseil supérieur de l'éducation nationale* (CSEN). This comprises a maximum of twelve *ex-officio* members, representatives of the ministry; the unions and other interested bodies have at least thirteen representatives, and there are twenty-five elected members from the teaching profession and five from private education. While it is a consultative body, although the minister is free to reject its advice, it also acts where necessary as an appeal court in disciplinary matters.

The education minister chooses his own immediate advisers (his *cabinet*), which ceases to exist when he himself resigns. The ministry received its reorganization in the spring of 1982. There is no longer a central directorate by which all other directorates are controlled. As before, the *inspection générale* has direct access to the *cabinet*, as do the various *missions*. A number of directorates have been made common to all parts of the ministry. The emphasis on the unified nature of the ministry seems to allow for greater access to the *cabinet* (see Figure 6.1). The one exception to be made here concerns higher education. From 1974, when it became first an independent *secrétariat d'état*, and later a ministry in its own right, higher education was removed from the orbit of the education ministry – at least in theory. It could have been thought that this could have reduced the degree of centralization, but it simply put two heads at the top of the administrative pyramid, which did not necessarily make for efficiency in the event of disagreements over policy.[12] Higher education was re-attached to the education ministry in 1981 (whilst still separate geographically in the rue Dutot), with a general directorate overseeing the work of the four directorates and one *service*.

The education minister may also have a secretary of state, with or without clearly defined attributions, as the minister sees fit. In the case of the present *secrétaire d'état*, R.-G. Schwartzenberg, some specific duties have been allotted: buildings and equipment at school and university level, international affairs, cultural action, and environment as it relates to education. There is also a proviso that he may deal with any other matter entrusted to him (Decree no. 83–305, 14 April 1983).

As in the time of Napoleon, an administrative network covers the whole of France, which provides for the passing down of ministerial directives to all levels. There are now twenty-seven *académies* (including Corsica – a separate *académie* since 1975) each with a *recteur* as its head (see Figures 6.2 and 6.3). The *recteur*, appointed by the government, is the minister's representative in the *académie*; he passes on ministerial instructions to the relevant areas, and sees that they are carried out. He also acts as the minister's informant, as to what problems have arisen as a result of decisions implemented; his opinion may be sought by the minister, and he may make suggestions to the latter when appointments are to be made. It is his task to supervise all state schools, and private schools under contract in his *académie*, in terms of teaching, administration and finance. He is assisted in his task by *inspecteurs d'académie*, one for each *département* within the *académie*. At *académie* level, his role is similar to that of the *recteur*, in that he passes on orders from the *recteur* and the minister.

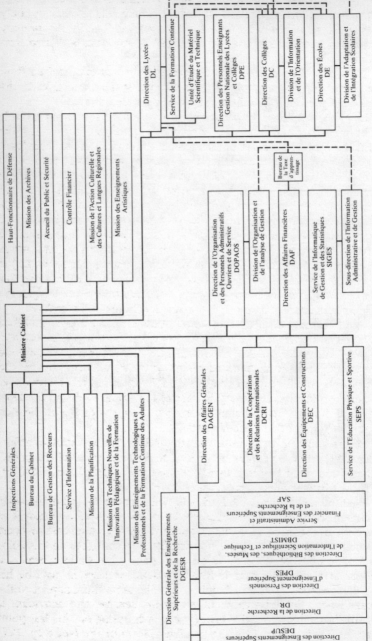

Figure 6.1   Organization of the education ministry, 1983
Source: Ministère de l'éducation nationale

He, too, provides information to his superiors as required. His role at primary level is particularly important, where it is his task not only to suggest appointments, but also to assess and mark the primary school teachers. In this task, he is assisted by *inspecteurs départementaux*.

Thus it is that an element of supervision which is organized from the centre covers the whole of the education system, and gives to the top of the pyramid (the minister) apparently wide powers.[13]

In 1976, a measure of *déconcentration* changed somewhat the role of both *recteur* and *inspecteur d'académie*. (*Déconcentration* may be defined as the transfer of decision-making from central to local level, whereas *decentralization* implies a transfer of powers and finances to elected local representatives.) The *recteur* was deputed by the central authority to decide on the posting of *instituteurs*, pupil-teachers and teachers in the *écoles normales* (teacher training institutions), the *carte scolaire* for secondary education. (The *carte scolaire* − school map − is essentially the educational geography of France, whereby the appropriate number of school places are provided each academic year, and where necessary, in terms of population and environment, extra schools.) It was further provided that the following powers should pass from *recteur* to *inspecteur d'académie*: appointment of *instituteurs*, and designation of teaching posts and supplementary teaching hours in the *collèges*.

On the other hand, the powers of the *recteur* have been modified since the *Loi d'Orientation* in respect of higher education. He has become *chancelier* of the university in his *académie*. The existence of an elected university president has reduced the scope of his activities, but he still has powers to alter the university budget if it does not meet with either his, or the ministry's approval (see Decrees of 14 June 1969 and 5 August 1970), although this will almost certainly change with the application of the *loi Savary* of 21 December 1983.

Before going on to describe the attempts to alter this state of affairs since 1981, it will perhaps be helpful to indicate some of the consequences produced by more than a century and a half of centralization, to show what the present government is up against.

First of all, the heads of schools, with whom the administration communicates, are themselves likely to be as much administrators as teachers, if not more so. Administration is considered an essential part of their duties which they are not permitted to shirk (see on this point *Le Monde* of 18 May 1978, on the suspension of V. Ambite, head of a *collège* at Cassis (Bouches-du-Rhône) caused at least in part by his unwillingness to act as an administrator. The same thing applies to the *lycées* where the triumvirate of *proviseur*, *censeur* and *intendant* is essentially an administrative one. (It is worth noting on this last point that the *Rapport Prost* on the possible reform of the *lycées* (p. 197) recommends the possibility of teachers' being able to take on the role

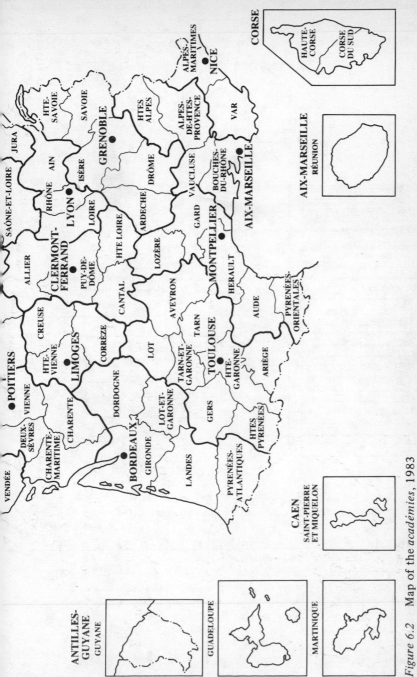

Figure 6.2 Map of the *académies*, 1983
Source: Ministere de l'éducation nationale

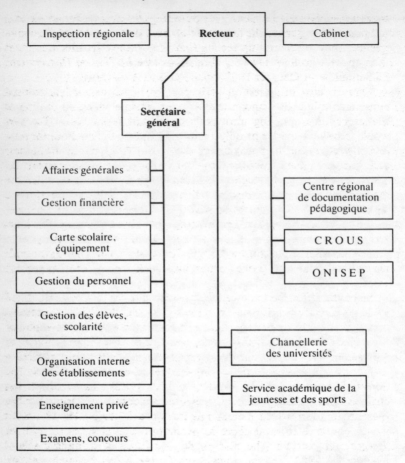

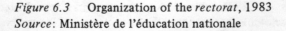

Figure 6.3   Organization of the *rectorat*, 1983
Source: Ministère de l'éducation nationale

of *proviseur* for a limited period of time, part of the training to include
a period of work experience as a *censeur*.

   This administrative predominance has a considerable effect on
teachers too. While they may hope to be sent to a specific area and to a
specific type of school, there is no guarantee that their aspirations will
be realized (see the example given by S. Citron, *L'Ecole bloquée*, p. 22
and M. Lemoine, 'LEP story' in *Autrement*, September 1981). A further
problem, which secondary school teachers (those with the CAPES qualification) have to face is the fact that the post to which they are appointed
may be very far from home – as much as 600 kilometres. This càn

cause not only added expense, for travelling and extra accommodation, but possible dangers to the family life of those that are married. In consequence, they often end up feeling that they receive harsher treatment than those who have fewer qualifications (see *Le Nouvel Observateur*, 25 September–1 October 1982, open letter to A. Savary).

There is also the question of inspection which has of late aroused considerable hostility among teachers, for reasons which an outline of the procedures applying until recently should make clear. Teachers would receive a mark not only from the head of their school (*la note administrative*) for their general attitude, punctuality, conscientiousness etc., but also a mark from the inspectorate for pedagogical competence, which seemed to many teachers to mean simply the extent to which the teacher followed the 'ministerial line'. (See N. Delanoë, *La Faute à Voltaire* p. 20.) The impression was often given that the inspector was trying to catch the teacher out by arriving without warning. The long-term consequences on a teacher's career could be considerable, determining whether promotion would be fast or slow, and an unfavourable inspection could also prove a stumbling-block for any teacher seeking work.

Since the left came to power, the government has to some extent had its hand forced on this issue, notably by the SGEN-CFDT. A national campaign first to refuse, and in due course to bring about the abolition of inspection in its existing form, was begun. The SGEN wished to replace old-style inspection with, on the one hand, assessment of teaching in groups (*équipes collectives*) and on the other, self-assessment. The minister's reaction (see *Le Monde*, 12 May 1982) was to admit that changes were necessary, that existing arrangements were unsuited to the present situation, whilst maintaining them provisionally. The two *notes* would continue to be decisive in promotion and changes of post for *agrégés* and *certifiés* (the most highly qualified of secondary school teachers) in 1982. Yet the possibility of a teacher's refusing inspection was recognized; those teachers who did refuse would be given a *note d'attente* of 12/20 unless their previous marks were lower, in which case these would be registered. Later in the year (28 October 1982) the need for change was re-emphasized, and the ministry promised that there would be a revision of inspection procedures at the end of the year. In the meantime teachers who wished for inspection were to request it. One other change to be introduced was a more open form of recruitment with candidatures to be sent for consideration to a commission composed of both teachers and *inspecteurs-généraux*.

Finally in January 1983 (see *Le Monde*, 21 January 1983), the proposed changes were consolidated. Whilst individual inspection and assessment was maintained, it was now to be preceded by visits of the inspectors to the school and specific class to gain an overall picture of the school's objectives. Teacher would in future have the right to reply to the inspector's report, and there was also the right of appeal in the event of a lower mark. Where teachers refused inspection, and no *note pédagogique* could be made, it would adversely affect the total mark, and possible promotion.

Other areas where administrative centralization have intervened not wholly successfully, are those of time-table and size of classes. The imposition of a fixed number of classes, without reference to the abilities of the children concerned led not only to rigidity, but also to unreasonably long hours for children.[14] Earlier attempts to liberalize this state of affairs at ministerial level proved to be both difficult, and ponderous. An example of this can be seen in a circular published in the *Bulletin officiel* on 1 September 1977. The then education minister, R. Haby, stated that in future the organization of school work would not be decided at national level, provided certain norms were respected, i.e. school work should, in term-time, occupy a minimum of five mornings per week, a minimum of two and maximum of four afternoons per week. This meant that a school head could, after obligatory consultations with other school heads and other interested persons, decide whether to leave Saturday or Wednesday free of classes. A further innovation was the reduction of each lesson from 55 to 50 minutes, the extra five minutes to be used by the teacher to become better acquainted with his or her pupils.

The question of time-table is very closely linked with administrative norms for class numbers, the so-called *grille Guichard*, in primary schools. Theoretically, primary school classes were not supposed to have more than twenty-five pupils, but in practical terms this was not so because of the global norms imposed. For example, if a primary school wanted to have four classes, it had to have at least ninety pupils; if not, one class would automatically be closed. A primary school population of 120 pupils was necessary in order to obtain a supplementary class. The *grille Guichard* has now been abolished, which should allow a greater degree of initiative. Yet this kind of problem is still found in other areas, for example, in the *lycées*, where the norm of forty pupils per class still obtains.

One further effect of the centralized system is an enduring respect for the hierarchy of seniority and qualification. It has been alleged that in the past, an *agrégé* would invariably gain a better *note* from the school head than a less qualified colleague *for that very reason* (see Delanoë, op. cit., pp. 19–20). Another indication is to be found in the difference in salary between teachers according to qualification (see Table 6.1), not surprising in itself, but coupled at present with the fact that the higher the qualification, the lower the number of hours required. The situation thus arises that the lowest paid have the heaviest time-tables.[15]

Up to this point, we have looked at specific questions exemplifying

Table 6.1 Teachers' salaries per month as at 1 July 1983

Grades	1er échelon	7ème échelon	Echelon terminal	Complément indicaire maximum lié à l'exercice d'une fonction, quel
Instituteur	5 116,03	6 074,03	7 736,96	que soit le grade de l'enseignant
Instituteur spécialisé	5 380,65	6 317,69	7 996,61	
P.E.G.C.	5 380,65	7 148,48	8 723,59	Directeur d'école (nouveau régime): 259,63
Professeur de C.E.T.	5 380,65	7 321,56	9 156,30	Directeur d'établissement specialisé: 588,50
Professeur certifié	5 909,88	8 382,33	11 198,70	
Professeur agrégé	6 715,76	10 800,60	14 020,00	Directeur adjoint chargé de section d'éducation spécialisée: 865,44
Professeur agrégé hors classe ou de chaire supérieure	11 198,70	–	16 476,35	Principal de collège: 1 730,87
Maître assistant de 2ème classe	7 009,05	–	11 198,70	Proviseur de L.E.P.: 2 163,59
Maître assistant de 1ère classe	10 592,90	–	14 020,00	Proviseur de lycée: 2 596,31
Professeur d'université de 2ème classe	11 198,70	–	16 476,35	
Professeur d'université de 1ère classe	14 020,00	–	19 956,91	
Professeur d'université de classe exceptionnelle	21 791,59	–	22 673,06	

Source: Ministère de l'éducation nationale.

Note: the only allocation added here is the residence allowance as in the second zone, where 2 per cent is added to the monthly salary. Zone 3 has 1 per cent, and Zone 1, 4 per cent. The three zones are composed at the present of the following académies:

Zone 1: Paris, Créteil, Versailles

Zone 2: Bordeaux, Caen, Clermont-Ferrand, Grenoble, Lille, Montpellier, Nancy-Metz, Nantes, Nice, Rennes

Zone 3: Aix-Marseille, Amiens, Besançon, Dijon, Limoges, Lyon, Orléans-Tours, Poitiers, Reims, Rouen, Strasbourg, Toulouse the problems posed by administrative centralization, together with solutions and proposals made by the present government. While there is certainly a liberalizing tendency in the action of the government, it could not be termed radical. Yet there is no doubt of the government's wish to reorganize education on a decentralized basis. One proof of this is the report by L. Soubré, produced at the government's request, on the decentralization (and democratization) of the education system. The *Rapport Soubré* proposes autonomy in several areas: (1) in that of teaching – within the limits imposed by the maintenance of national qualifications; (2) administrative and financial autonomy, with the removal of *a priori* financial control from the centre; (3) autonomy in terms of organization via three sets of *conseils*. These are: a tripartitie *conseil d'établissement* composed of representatives of 'school users' (parents, pupils, etc.), of the state, and of elected local authorities, to vote on the budget and school policy (*projet d'établissement*) amongst other things; *conseils d'enseignement*, where a collective pedagogical approach would be worked out, and the *conseils de classe*. *Lycée* and *collège* pupils would have responsibility, and would be encouraged to exercise it. The *chef d'établissement* would not necessarily be the president of the *conseil d'établissement*, and his role would be altered in relation to the greater degree of autonomy available to the other partners involved.

These suggestions must also be seen in the light of the government's wish to introduce administrative decentralization into local government. While the laws of 2 March 1982 and 7 January 1983 lay down respectively the principle of self-government and the transfer of power, it is the law of 22 July 1983 which enters into the details of how education will be decentralized (not later than January 1986).

Essentially, it is provided that primary schools will be the concern of the *communes*, *collèges* of the *départements*, and *lycées* and establishments providing specialized education of the regions, whether in relation to the *carte scolaire*, construction, maintenance, financing, or running of schools. The state will merely provide money for 'educational expenses': (machine-tools, audio-visual equipment, and the like).

As for finances, the region will receive an annual *dotation régionale d'équipement scolaire*, to be apportioned out in relation to the region's school-age population; the *département* will be treated in a like manner, receiving a *dotation globale d'équipement* from the interior ministry. Neither region nor *département* will have the power to create teaching posts. Yet the *maire* will have some power of decision over matters such as school buses, school hours and the use of school facilities outside school hours. There will also be created, in each *académie* and *département*, *conseils de l'éducation nationale*, whose tasks and composition have not yet been determined.

Under these circumstances, it is clear that the role of the *recteur* should change very considerably. From being the decision-maker, he is presumably intended to become an adviser and a negotiator between the different bodies which will then be in existence.

Since the education system in this area, as in others, is in a state of flux, given the changes in prospect, it is difficult to come to any firm conclusion. Yet, where attempts are made to decentralize, there is a temptation to create too many bodies, whether decision-making or consultative. This case is no exception. It could indeed be asked how teaching can be done, how decisions can be taken when so very many people must be consulted, and whether the disease of *réunionnite* (excess of meetings) may not drag the experiment to a halt.

Nor is it at all clear that all will equally approve of so much power being removed from the centre. The FEN, for example, has already declared its intention of opposing decentralization as far as it concerns private schools — admittedly a special issue (see *Le Monde*, 7 January 1984). The possibilities of disputes between differing groups involved in the *conseil d'établissement* is not unlikely[16] (see *L'Ecole libératrice*, 25 September 1982).

While there was certainly enough criticism of the old system to make it clear that there should be enough good will to enable the new one to succeed, there is no doubt that the infant decentralization faces dangers on either side. It could fail because of in-fighting between the various groups involved in *participation*; it could fail through the cumbersome nature of its institutions. If either of these turn out to be the case, there is still a wealth of experience of administrative centralization, and a centuries-old tradition, to drag it back in the opposite direction.[17]

Finally, it cannot be denied that the initiative of the minister limited though it may sometimes be by pressure groups, is still all-important in the determination of policy.

(2) Church and state: Catholic education in France

This question goes back beyond the Revolution of 1789, to the France of the *Ancien Régime*, when the Catholic church and the French state were closely intertwined. One of the former's recognized and traditional duties was education, of which it had virtually sole charge. During the Revolution, this task was taken away from the church, which suffered greatly from persecution and eventual suppression. The Revolution had laid down the principle that it was the state's duty to provide national education, which implied that in the future France would be a secular state, with a correspondingly secular education.

Although Napoleon distrusted intellectuals, and felt that education could be dangerous, he nevertheless had a clear idea of its value as an inculcator of political values, and of the consequent need of a body of suitably trained teachers. 'Il n'y aura pas d'Etat politique fixe, s'il n'y a pas un corps enseignant avec des principes fixes' (Napoleon, *Pensées politiques et sociales*[18] p. 213). The church was excluded from the monopoly which he established in secondary and higher education (except for institutions known as *petits seminaires* in which novices were prepared for the priesthood). This is not to say that the church had lost all influence; Napoleon was prepared to entrust to it those areas which he did not consider important – namely, primary education and the education of women. Yet the whole, paradoxically, formed part of the *université*, under state supervision. A thoroughly secular state however was not established, since the church was useful to Napoleon as a factor of social and political stability, even although it had been much disorganized and weakened by the Revolution. By the terms of an agreement between France and the papacy (the Concordat of 1802), the Catholic church was reorganized and re-integrated into French society. Religion as such was by no means excluded from schools; according to the Decree of 17 March 1808 (Titre V, art. 38), which established the *université*, it was required of all schools comprised therein that the precepts of the Catholic religion should form part of the curriculum. Yet the church, by the terms of the Concordat, was placed in a position of subservience to the state, its paymaster, the clergy now being salaried state officials. Even then, Napoleon still felt that organized religion, in its internationalism, could present a danger to his régime. From this deliberate exclusion of the church from secondary and higher education, and the church's unwillingness to accept it, was to come a reaction against the state's 'monopoly', claiming freedom of education, freedom here meaning not only the right of the private individual, but also of the church, to have their own schools.

In spite of the inherent anti-clericalism of Napoleon and of the system which he established, the church was not in fact excluded as much as he would have wished.[19] This situation also applied during the Bourbon restoration to an even more marked degree; the same system was maintained with some modifications, whilst the church was permitted to infiltrate it. This close alliance between throne and altar, redolent of the *Ancien Régime*, raised such feeling that when the restoration fell, the church, its strong supporter, found itself politically compromised.

The July Monarchy saw the first innovation in terms of primary education with the *Loi Guizot* of 1833, which also changed relations between church and state in this area. The change lay in the fact that state primary schools were to be established. Yet private individuals also were allowed to open primary schools if they could prove that they were suitably qualified and of good conduct and morality. This law is of interest, for, while on the one hand it represents an inroad of the state into primary education, hitherto always regarded as a prerogative of the church, it also marked a departure from the principle of state monopoly into the beginnings of dualism, with the co-existence of private and state schools. However in all primary education, a marked emphasis was put on religious and moral instruction, which, in the legislator's view was of great importance. 'Par l'instruction morale et religieuse, il pourvoit déjà à un autre ordre de besoins tout aussi réels que les autres, et que la Providence a mis dans le coeur du pauvre, comme dans celui des heureux de ce monde, pour la dignité de la vie humaine et la protection de l'ordre social' (Guizot, *Moniteur universel*, 3 January 1833). Religion, and hence the church, still had a part to play in the maintenance of social stability, and the co-operation of the *curé* was necessary for this. The law stated that he or the local protestant *pasteur* should be a member of the *comité de surveillance* of the local state primary school, which would give him some influence in its affairs, and, it was hoped, prevent him from setting up his own school in opposition. In reality, the *instituteur* (primary school teacher) tended to be very much at the beck and call of the *curé* (see G. Duveau, *Les Instituteurs*, Paris, Seuil, 1961). This compromise did not please the catholics, who had to accept that even at primary level, children could not be forced to receive religious instruction against their parents' wishes. Morality also was no longer wholly the domain of the church, since a form of philosophy, known as 'eclecticism' was also taught, which admitted the existence of God, but arrived at this concept by reasoning, and not by an acceptance of revealed truth; it also professed a number of fundamental truths taken from various currents of philosophic thought. Catholics, who considered such teaching to be atheistic, objected to it. Nor was this their only grievance: although they had gained their 'freedom' in primary education by virtue of the *Loi Guizot*, secondary education remained out of reach, since it changed little during the July Monarchy.

The freedom sought by Catholics did not come to secondary education until after the 1848 revolution. It then became clear to the governing classes that the church provided an excellent means of keeping the masses in check, and was therefore a useful ally. The outcome was the *Loi Falloux* of 1850; by its terms, the freedom provided at primary level by the *Loi Guizot* was extended to secondary education, which gave Catholics their chance. In other ways too, this law provided for greater Catholic influence via academic councils at departmental and national level. During the first decade of the Second Empire this legislation permitted a substantial expansion in Catholic education.[20] Although in the second decade it was thought advisable to curb this, French education was split in two ways as a result of the *Loi Falloux*, a consequence which was to have its effect later in the century.

Yet it cannot be asserted that this legislation was universally acceptable to Catholic opinion.[21] For the most extreme, it did not go far enough, since it did not reinstate Catholic education to the exclusion of all else, nor did it allow freedom in higher education. This last was not achieved until the law of 12 July 1875 was passed – the final triumph of the nineteenth-century dualist system.

Thus, during the nineteenth century the church was viewed as an element of social and political conservation, even if its motives were sometimes distrusted. Although Catholic opinion contained some liberal elements, it was mainly conservative (whether moderate or extreme) and consequently tended to support conservative governments. The Third Republic, in its earlier years, had to face an unreconciled church which would have favoured a return to a form of monarchy -- more likely, in its views, to favour Catholic interests. An education system, of which a large part was Catholic, represented therefore a *political* threat to the republic, which was already weakened by the ideological split fostered by the effects of the *Loi Falloux*. The legislation undertaken by Jules Ferry in the 1880s was the logical answer to the republic's problems. This made primary education secular, obligatory from age six to thirteen, and free of charge. If parents wished their children to receive religious instruction, it was for them to arrange this out of school hours, although moral instruction still was a high priority on the curriculum. The secular principle (*laïcité*) was thus assured in state education, although teaching orders wishing to continue their work in France were required to obtain authorization in 1886. Relations between church and state did not improve up to the beginning of this century, when, between 1901 and 1904 all teaching orders were banned, and in 1905, the separation of church and state was enacted. This simply did away with Napoleon's Concordat (apart from Alsace-Lorraine, which, as a German territory in 1905 was not subject to French legislation, and to this day is still under the *régime concordataire*). The French state was now totally neutral as between one religion and another, its only duty being to ensure freedom of conscience. The clergy were no longer state salaried officials, nor was the choice of bishops in any way the state's concern; church buildings reverted to the state but could still be used for religious worship. This legislation was hotly contested by Catholic opinion, and by the papacy itself, although in the long run it was of benefit to the church, and the issue ceased to be politically explosive.

The issue of Catholic education however remained controversial during the inter-war period, with the Vatican solemnly denouncing the neutral or secular school as irreligious in the encyclical *Divini Illius Magistri* of 1929. During the Second World War, the Vichy régime clearly indicated its support for the church in 1940 by re-introducing optional religious instruction in state schools, by lifting the ban (hitherto more honoured in its breach than in its observance) on the religious teaching orders, and by the provision of state aid for private schools, either via the communes or via grants to pupils from private or state schools. The Catholic church's involvement, particularly that of the hierarchy, with Vichy[22] was to prove an embarrassment after the liberation, since it yet again made the adherence of the church to the principle of republicanism suspect, in so far as the church seemed once more to have given way to an instinctive predilection for authoritarian régimes. However, the precedents set by Vichy in state aid to private schools were to have a second birth during the Fourth Republic, and were to be politically very divisive. The *Loi Marie* and the *Loi Barangé* of September 1951 provided respectively credits for the education minister to award to the most deserving pupils attending either state or private secondary schools, with priority for the former, and allocated a special amount at the treasury for parents with children attending state or private school (1,000 old francs per child per term). This legislation was opposed by communists, socialists and some Radicals and was supported by Gaullists, some Radicals and the MRP. The *Loi Barangé* in particular aroused great hostility, and an attempt was made to repeal it in 1956, which failed by only nine votes. By 1958, over one and a half million pupils were attending private schools, of which the substantial majority were Catholic.[23]

The Fifth Republic went further towards a dualist system with the *Loi Debré* of 1959 which offered to private schools a number of alternatives, in which aid would be made available (or not) according to the choice made. A school could opt:

(a) for complete integration into the state system – becoming thus a state school, and the teachers state employees;

(b) for the *contrat simple*, whereby the state not only approves the appointment of teachers, but pays their salaries (initially this alternative was conceived as a provisional one);

(c) for the *contrat d'association*, whereby the state pays teachers, and also contributes to the school's running costs, based on the number of pupils (*forfait d'externat*). A school opting for this arrangement had to accept directives about timetable, curriculum, etc., as well as supervision in teaching methods and finance from the administration;

(d) for total liberty, in which case no subsidy was provided.

The law caused much controversy, being opposed by the parties of the left and also by the *Comité national d'action laïque* (CNAL). However, de Gaulle threatened the dissolution of the *assemblée nationale* if the proposed legislation were not passed, and this was sufficient to get it through both houses with a substantial majority. In spite of secular opposition to it, there was something essentially ambiguous about the *Loi Debré*. On the one hand, it gave the state the chance to take over private schools; but on the other, it gave the private sector the opportunity to profit financially from state resources whilst still retaining its separate identity. In 1965 the *Loi Debré* paid out in teachers' salaries the sum of 1,035,800 NF — a sum far greater than that provided by earlier legislation.[24]

However, in 1971, G. Pompidou personally imposed a solution to the provisional nature of some aspects of the *Loi Debré*, not only on parliament, but on his prime minister, J. Chaban-Delmas, apparently more favourable to secularist views. The *contrat simple*, initially envisaged as a temporary measure, was made permanent for Catholic primary schools and the *contrat d'association* in the secondary schools. After 1979, the *contrat simple* was no longer to be permitted to the latter. The result of this was that by 1982 98 per cent of primary schools were under contract (78 per cent *contrat simple*, 21.5 per cent *contrat d'association*), whereas all secondary schools now have the *contrat d'association* (see C. Vial in *Le Monde*, 26 January 1982). It is equally worth noting that secular private schools have in the main chosen to remain independent. Consequently, when between 9 and 10 per cent of the 1984 budget (just over 18,188 million francs) is devoted to private education under a government committed to its absorption into the state system, it is almost exclusively Catholic education which benefits.

Although over ten million signed the CNAL petition against the *loi Debré* in 1960, a decrease in feeling against the law seemed to go hand in hand with a waning of church influence, particularly in the urban and industrial areas. Yet the parties of the left, the teaching unions in the FEN (*Fédération de l'éducation nationale*) and other pressure groups maintained a fairly consistent hostility to the Fifth Republic's subsidizing of private schools, with the promise of changes when the left came to power. 'Le bénéfice des lois laïques sera étendu à tout le territoire (y compris Alsace-Moselle). Dès la première législature, les établissement privés . . . percevant les fonds publics seront en règle générale nationalisés.'[25] However the left's hostility to private education has given rise, over the past eight years or so, to a good deal of political embarrassment.

The municipal elections of 1977 brought the left to power in many areas, and educational policies at local level were re-framed in consequence. In particular, the cutting off of credits required by law for private schools (see *Le Monde*, 17 June and 7 September 1977)[26] seemed ominously like the shape of things to come, in the event of a left-wing victory in 1978. There was also the added embarrassment of the so-called *Rapport Mexandeau*, proposed socialist policy on education, which had to be toned down, lest its views on the future of private education alienate both party members and the electorate at large. In September 1977, therefore, the PS issued a directive to all its municipal representatives not to cut off subsidies to private schools without negotiation.

With the left thus having to 'back-pedal', as it were, on the issue,

G. Guermeur, RPR deputy for Finistère, and president of the parliamentary association for freedom of education (APLE), seized his opportunity. The law of October 1977 (*Loi Guermeur*) provides for state loans at reduced interest for the building of private secondary schools and of workshops required by the *réforme Haby*; and improvement in the calculation of the *forfait d'externat*; financial aid from the state for the training of teachers, who would henceforth be the responsibility of the heads of private schools. The state would thus have less control than before, whilst paying substantially more. The cost of these measures was reckoned at the time to be in the order of 800 million francs.

In spite of the left's low profile on the issue at this time, the law was calculated to arouse hostility on the part of the parliamentary parties the FEN and the *Fédération des conseils de parents d'élèves des écoles publiques* (FCPE). Its then president, J. Cornec, took the view that the *loi Guermeur* was yet another stage in the long war waged by the Catholic hierarchy against France's national education (see J. Cornec, 'Libres opinions', *Le Monde*, 7 July 1977). Neither the FCPE nor the FEN have changed their views in the intervening years, in spite of a change of leadership,[27] and both, together with the CNAL and other pressure groups, clearly expected swift changes when the left gained power in 1981. However, there was clearly a determination on the part of the new government to take no precipitate action, since Mitterrand had expressed the wish to bring about a unification of the education system but only through negotiation. First of all, the expected choice of L. Mexandeau as education minister was not made. Instead the post went to A. Savary, regarded as more diplomatic.

Savary proceeded with caution; it was not until January 1982 that he instituted discussions with all the interested parties on the future of private education, with a view to bringing about its absorption. These consultations lasted about a year, during which there were not only public demonstrations both for and against private education but also much discussion in the press.

On 20 December 1982 Savary revealed his plan, composed of six main proposals. (1) The private schools wishing to receive continued subsidy must accept their own inclusion in the *carte scolaire*. This would mean that a subsidized private school could only in future be opened where there was a recognized need for one, and it would be the state who would make the appropriate decisions. Any school unwilling to accept these arrangements would have its contract annulled, and lose all subsidy. (2) Parents with children at state schools would no longer be subject to *sectorisation*, i.e. be compelled to send their children to the nearest one. There would thus be a choice for these parents also (enjoyed before only by parents with children at private schools) from amongst all the schools, both state and subsidized schools in a given area. (3) The

financial arrangements would be the same for both kind of school.
(4) The incorporated private schools would have an altered legal status,
becoming either singly or in groups, *établissements d'intérêt public* (EIP).
There would be a tripartite *conseil d'administration*, composed of representatives of the state, the local authority, and the association governing the private school. (5) There would be a measure of autonomy over
the plan to be drawn up on educational, cultural and religious matters.
(6) Teachers and some administrators in the private sector in a situation
not unlike their counterparts in the state system could be assimilated
into the state categories. This would give them benefits in terms of
pension and tenure; and both private and state teachers could teach in
these integrated private schools.

In many ways, this was not an illiberal set of proposals; it was also
intelligently engineered to appeal to parents on both sides of the argument, both of whom could benefit from the freedom of choice provided.
Yet there was too an element of compulsion, in the sense that schools
refusing Savary's offer would be bereft of the state help accorded to
them over the years. Thus it was clearly hoped that there was enough in
the proposals to appeal to both sides.

In fact they were satisfactory to very few. Whereas opponents of
private education felt that the plan, though a compromise one, was
worth discussing, the leaders of Catholic education, members of the
Comité national de l'enseignement catholique (CNEC), took the view
that the proposals did away with freedom in education, and would
endanger the *caractère propre* (individuality) of Catholic private education. In consequence, on 9 January 1983 they refused to negotiate
until further guarantees were provided on these points. Savary's response
to this was to put off negotiations (13 January 1983) for the time being,
presumably to allow time to let the dust settle before the municipal
elections to be held in March of that year.

There, to all appearances. the matter rested until October 1983, when,
after many private discussions, Savary tried again. On this occasion he
tried a different tack, drawing up a calendar of negotiations with three
groups of problems, the easiest to be dealt with first, the most difficult
to be left to the end. These problems, all to be resolved by 1986, were
to be negotiated on the basis of three principles: equality of educational
opportunity, freedom of conscience, and freedom of education. It was
also intended that any reforms arrived at should relate both to state and
private education, in an endeavour to bring about subsequent harmon-
ization. The Catholics grudgingly indicated their willingness to negotiate
on some of the points, but this time it was the turn of the *laïcs*, the
CNAL in the van, to refuse, since there was now no clear indication
that there would in the long run be total absorption, but, rather, a dualist
solution, and thus a climb-down on the part of the government.

Savary, however, who is known to have the support of Mitterrand in his reforming intentions (see C. Arditti in *Le Monde*, 20 December 1983) announced (21 December 1983) his intention of negotiating on concrete proposals most concerning those who were prepared to enter into negotiation with him. The fruit of these discussions is a draft bill approved by the council of ministers, 18 April 1984, and which will shortly be put to the *Assemblée nationale*. The proposed legislation resurects the concept of the EIP to which private schools must belong in order to have a *contrat d'association* (the *contrat simple* ceasing to exist) with the State. However there is explicit reference to the need for liberty of conscience to be respected, and provision is made for continued financial assistance, either by local authorities or the State. It can thus be said that the dualist system of education in France is maintained. Yet on the other hand, there is a possibility for private school teachers to become *fonctionnaires*, and for teachers from the State system to teach in private schools under contract. This matter is of great concern to the CNEC since there is a fear that if private school teachers are given tenure in this way, they will escape from the control of Catholic education, they will be replaced in due course by state teachers, and absorption, for being gradual, will be no less real. It is debatable, in spite of Savary's efforts, whether genuine compromise is possible. It should be remembered that the three principles on which Savary wished to base his negotiations of October 1983 can, if interpreted from the standpoint of Catholicism or from that of *laïcité*, be mutually exclusive. One thing is sure: those who, a few years ago, were sure that anti-clericalism was dying out have been proved painfully wrong.[28]

The question must be asked as to why this should be? If it is clear that Catholicism, as a religious force, is losing ground in France, and statistics seem to bear out this assertion,[29] what have the *laïcs* to fear?

A British reader, accustomed to debates on the relative merits of comprehensive or grammar schools, might be tempted to take the issue out of context, and view it simply as a conflict between the freedom of choosing a school, which it is alleged parents should have (freedom of education), and the need to avoid a system which maintains a privilege which only wealthy parents can exercise (social justice). This would partly explain the problem, although it has been asserted that in 1974 nearly 30 per cent of pupils in Catholic schools received grants, and in some areas the percentage was twice as high. In 1981-2 there were 195,243 pupils to whom grants were awarded (at secondary level) in private schools, out of a total of 1,427,926.[30] It is sometimes suggested that Catholic schools are merely the instruments of capitalism and reactionary employers, but the purpose of Catholic education, according to the Roman Catholic church, is totally different: 'contribuer à la construction d'une monde nouveau nettement opposé à une mentalité caractérisée par la recherche du plaisir, de l'obsession de l'efficacité et de la tyrannie de la consommation' (*Le Monde*, 7 July 1977).

It could also be said that, although a minority, regularly practising Catholics still represent 6 million people, which, when added to the 4 million who are less regular in attendance, makes up a large conservative minority, to be feared by the left. Yet it *is* in decline, and the left might well feel that time is on its side. In the short term, this 'party political' aspect may indeed have an effect here. It is possible that Catholic schools are more likely to produce, if not practising Catholics, then certainly right-wing supporters (see Table 6.2). In an opinion poll published in *Témoignage chrétien* (2 March 1978), it transpired that 59 per cent of ex-pupils from non-Catholic schools were pro-left and 57 per cent from Catholic schools were pro-right. This could in part account for the illiberal tendencies to be found on both sides.[31]

Table 6.2   Left-wing sympathy according to religion (percentages)

	1974	1977	Change
Catholic	45	48	+3
Regular churchgoer	19	19	0
Occasional churchgoer	36	41	+5
Non churchgoer	59	60	+1
Other religion	53	61	+8
No religion	83	79	−4

Source: C. Peyrefitte, 'Les Choix de 1981 − contrastes du catholicisme', *Faire*, December 1980, p. 48 (adapted)

There is one more factor, of a practical nature, which may help to envenom the issue, the fear felt by partisans of the state system that it may be losing custom to its rival. There has arisen an unflattering image of state education, which can lead even left-wing activists to sacrifice their principles by sending their children to private schools: 'Grèves trop fréquentes, discipline éclatée, violence, résultats aléatoires, et surtout nivellement par le bas: on généralise et on s'affole . . . Les parents soucieux d'assurer un bon 'ticket' à leur progéniture fuient la supposée chienlit du 'public' (D. Granet, 'Ecole: la revanche du privé', in *L 'Express* no. 1471, 22 September 1979). Yet the statistics do not wholly bear out this impression of a 'private take-over'. Since the passing of the *loi Debré*, the overall proportion of school population attending private school has declined. From 1958 up to 1976 the percentage of primary school pupils attending private school went down from 18.6 per cent to 15.9 per cent; and from 1979 to 1982–3 the numbers of pupils attending private nursery/primary school have gone down by 32,000. It is true that this is made up at secondary level: from 1979 to 1982–3, figures have gone up by 49,000; and for 1983–4 the figures for all types of private secondary education are up on the previous school year from

1,060,200 to 1,067,900 (see *Le Monde*, 8 June 1977, 8 September 1983).

Yet the fact remains that the government has a majority; why therefore does it hesitate to do what so many of its partisans urge upon it? The answer is that these same partisans, however strong their 'gut reaction'[32] are not representative of opinion in the country at large. A recent opinion poll conducted by IFOP (see *La Croix*, 14 December 1983) makes it clear that 71 per cent of the population is favourably disposed to private education, although 62 per cent think (contrary to the Catholic leaders) that it would be normal for private school teachers to be *fonctionnaires*. Whilst 58 per cent and 54 per cent respectively give credit to Mitterrand and Savary for trying to bring peace to education, only 29 per cent give the same credit to the CNAL. Yet of this same group, given the choice of a state or private school near their home, only 33 per cent would choose the private school. This appears to indicate that the French public is favourable to private schools only out of what it regards as practical necessity. It further suggests that if more choice is provided, and if the state system improves itself and its image, some of this support could well fall away.

In the meantime the government is in a difficult position. From the viewpoint of the British onlooker, it might well seem that the vast sums of money expended by the state on private education seem hardly fair, and that some kind of change is in order. Nevertheless since private schools enjoy a measure of national support, it could be thought that there are more urgent matters requiring the government's attention. Judging by the applause automatically evoked by every reference to *laïcité* at the PS congress held at Bourg-en-Bresse in October 1983 the government may find it easier to deal with the Catholics than with its own supporters. It is perhaps unfortunate that, of all the large unions, the government has closest links with the FEN, which has chosen this potentially dangerous issue as its prime consideration. The government could almost be said to be a prisoner of its most vociferous partisans who force it to make an absolute priority of an issue which cooler political calcualtion would undoubtedly put further down the scale.

(3) Primary and secondary education

In view of the centralized organization of the French education system, the activities of the state háve assumed, for well over a century, a primordial importance. The French Revolution may be said to have laid down the definitive principles for education in France; the subsequent 170-odd years can be viewed as a long, painful and often vain endeavour to put them into practice.

Initially, it may seem as if little attempt was made in this direction, since Napoleon, while adapting the concept of state education to his own requirements, neglected the more egalitarian aspects of the revolution's educational principles, and his example was followed, with some modification, by subsequent governments.

While it is a fact that the *Loi Guizot* of 1833 reduced illiteracy,[33] progress was slow because primary education was not obligatory; nor was it free of charge, except for the children of destitute parents. This law, apparently of democratic tendencies, was not conceived by its author for such a purpose. In his view, education had to be appropriate to the social classes; consequently, primary education was divided into two parts to suit different strata of society. The first level (*instruction primaire élémentaire*) was to be sufficient for the lower classes, but the second level (*instruction primaire supérieure*) was aimed at 'une partie très nombreuse de la nation, qui, sans jouir des avantages de la fortune, n'est pas non plus réduite à une gêne sévère' (Guizot, speech of 2 January 1833, *Archives parlementaires*, Paris, 1891, vol. 78, p. 465). Secondary education for these strata of society, was considered a positive danger, causing many to feel dissatisfied with their lot. Its task was to educate the middle classes for their role as leaders of society. 'C'est par l'instruction secondaire seulement que la classe moyenne peut se préparer aux professions libérales, aux industries scientifiques, aux travaux et aux fonctions de tout genre qui sont sa vocation naturelle' (Guizot, speech of 1 February 1836, *Archives parlementaires*, Paris, 1899, vol. 100, p. 85).

As long as education was viewed as a positive danger to the social order and a source of dissatisfaction, the question of free primary schooling was not likely to be a burning issue. The wealthier classes could afford to pay, and the poorer classes were not obliged to send their children to school. By the end of the Second Empire the idea of free education for all had become more widely accepted, and the legislation of 1881 was the last step in a series of advances from the 1860s onwards, when an increasing number of children attended school free of charge. This undoubted advance was assisted by the law of 1882, which made primary education obligatory for children of both sexes from the ages of six to thirteen. There is no doubt that the thinking behind these laws was essentially egalitarian, imbued with the desire to remove social inequalities by education, which had hitherto helped to maintain, rather than reduce, class differences. The task before the legislators of the 1880s was, in the words of Jules Ferry, the initiator of these reforms, to: 'faire disparaître la dernière, la plus redoutable des inégalités qui viennent de la naissance, l'inégalité d'éducation' (Jules Ferry, speech of 10 April 1870, quoted by A. Prost, *L'Enseignement en France, 1800-1967.*, p. 14). Ferry was very much alive to the political consequences of an education system which maintained inequalities since, in his opinion, a genuine equality, as opposed to a merely theoretical one, would never be attained without the benefit of an adequate education for all.

Yet the changes brought about by Ferry were not sufficient to redress the balance. First of all, while primary education was obligatory up to the age of thirteen, and no fees were charged in the state primary schools, the parents of any child who wished to continue studying and go on to a secondary school had to find the money for school fees, since secondary education in state schools was still not free of charge, and it was thus more difficult for children of poorer families to benefit from further study. The poorer classes were consequently still at a disadvantage, however much equality was thought to exist at the obligatory primary stage. Moreover, the two areas of education still remained distinct, complete in themselves. Each, for example, has its own version of the other; primary education had its own type of secondary level with the *écoles primaires supérieures* and the *cours complémentaires*, whereas secondary education had its own elementary classes — the *petites classes* of the *lycées*. It was not until after the First World War that any solution to these problems was envisaged. One was financial; between 1929 and 1933, all classes in secondary education ceased to be fee-paying. However, this, together with a population increase, augmented to such an extent the numbers of children wishing to enter secondary education that an entrance examination was imposed in 1933–4.

However, the solution which might have solved the problem of the separation of primary and secondary levels was the concept of the *école unique*, which proposed a much less rigid barrier between the two, either by prolonging the primary stage, or by creating schools at an intermediate stage to, as it were, fill the gap. Also, incorporated into the concept of the *école unique* was the idea of *orientation* (educational guidance) that a child would receive after primary schooling, and before going on to any definitive courses of study. Depending on aptitude, these would be studies in either a *lycée*, a technical school, or workshop. The idea behind these views was democratic enough: 'Faire en sorte que les distinctions d'origine sociale cèdent le pas au seul mérite, afin que chaque Français accède à la culture sans autre considération que celle de ses aptitudes.[34]

The man who came closest to implementing these views was Jean Zay, a Radical, who was minister of education from 1936 to 1939, in the government of the *Front Populaire* and in its successors. His proposed reform of 1937 provided for three elements of primary education:

(1) *enseignement primaire élémentaire*
(2) *enseignement primaire complémentaire*, for those not going on to secondary education

(3) *enseignement post-scolaire*, to be provided for those over fourteen years of age attending neither the complementary courses just mentioned, nor classes at secondary level.

The *certificat d'études primaires* (CEP), obtained after examination, and normally taken by children aged twelve-plus, could be taken a year earlier by those intending to continue their education at secondary school, for which it was obligatory. This hurdle overcome, the first year of secondary education (6e) was to be characterized by a *tronc commun* (a common syllabus), at the end of which pupils would be guided, according to their abilities and to parents' wishes, towards one of three courses of study: *classique, moderne* and *technique*. Since the reform also allowed pupils to switch from one section to another where this was considered advisable, all three sections had to run parallel to each other.

While the maintenance of the CEP meant that selection was applied, this proposed legislation tended to reduce the element of class discrimination which had hitherto existed. However, overall reform was never discussed in parliament, and Jean Zay was only able to bring elements of it into being on an experimental basis, notably the *classe d'orientation* at 6e.

These innovations had not been forgotten when René Capitant education minister in the provisional government at Algiers set up a commission to consider possible reforms in education. At that time, there was a serious preoccupation with the inadequacies of the education system as demonstrated not only by the collapse of France in 1940, but by subsequent collaboration.

> Il semble bien que, si les hommes du peuple, formés par l'école primaire se sont montrés . . . admirablement courageux et patients pendant la guerre ouverte et la guerre clandestine . . . les 'élites', compte tenu d'honorables exceptions individuelles, ont montré, elles, un manque lamentable de caractère . . . Ceux qui pouvaient se dire issus des sommets de notre enseignement sont ceux dont la lâcheté a été la plus éclatante (M. Durry, 'Rapport général sur les travaux de la commission pour la réforme de l'enseignement', *Bulletin officiel du ministère de l'éducation nationale*, 16 November 1944, p. 13).

The paradox of this state of affairs was thought to lie in the nature of French secondary education, 'enseignement de caste qui continuait à maintenir en France une féodalité de l'argent et des charges' (ibid.).

However, it is from the report of the Langevin–Wallon commission, set up by R. Capitant in November 1944, that the definitive plan for a renovated education system was to come. It proposed no more than two main sections: *second degré* (higher education) and *premier degré*, that is, compulsory school education from ages six to eighteen, divided

into four stages:
(a) nursery schooling (*école maternelle*);
(b) a first cycle for children aged six to eleven, with a *tronc commun*;
(c) a second cycle (*cycle d'orientation*) for eleven- to fifteen-year-olds, where part of the syllabus would be for all, and part more specialized, relating to individual abilities. There would be, in the later years, options leading to differing types of education provided in the following cycle;
(d) *cycle de détermination* (for fifteen- to eighteen-year-olds), subdivided into: *section pratique*, for those whose manual competence was greater than their intellectual abilities; *section professionnelle*, for those who were likely to form middle management and were less biased towards theoretical studies; and the *section théorique*, for those whose abilities were more specifically intellectual, whether scientific or literary, and who would take the *baccalauréat* or its equivalent.

However, it is perhaps less for its proposals which were fairly general, and were never implemented, than for its underlying ideology, that the Langevin–Wallon report is significant. Its views on the need for the democratization of education, based on social justice, have a strong affinity with those of Condorcet. Against the current prejudice in favour of intellectual pursuits, it also emphasized the equal importance of more practical types of work, including manual labour, in an endeavour to bring about a change of approach on this issue, thus going beyond the usual scope of educational reforms, in its desire to associate education and democracy.

> Le travail manuel, l'intelligence pratique sont encore trop souvent considérés comme de médiocre valeur. L'équité exige la reconnaissance de l'égale dignité de toutes les tâches sociales, de la haute valeur technique. Ce reclassement des valeurs réelles est indispensable dans une société démocratique moderne dont le progrès et la vie même sont subordonnés à l'exacte utilisation des compétences.
> (Commission ministérielle d'étude, *La Réforme de l'enseignement*, Paris, Ministère de l'éducation nationale, n.d., pp. 8-9.)

Perhaps the breadth of vision and the idealism shown by the commission account for the lasting prestige of the report amongst those wishing to see far-reaching changes in the education system.[35] Consequently, later reforms may be regarded as more or less successful attempts to implement some of the proposals of Langevin–Wallon.

There seems little reason to doubt the good will of the Fourth Republic in the realm of education, since several vain attempts were made to introduce measures of reform (those of E. Depreux in 1948, of Y. Delbos in 1949 and J. Berthoin in 1955). One cause for this

apparent stagnation was the inherent weakness of coalition government, which did not always give a minister sufficient time to work
out and propose effective measures. Other difficulties related more
to the opposition of teachers' unions, who felt their interests were
threatened by changes. This seems to have been in part the reason for
the failure of the reform bill proposed by René Billères, education
minister in the government of G. Mollet. The main aim of these
proposals was to deal with the class discrimination which obtained as
between primary and secondary education. This problem was clearly
indicated by the social origins of children entering secondary education of whatever kind. Billères estimated that 13 per cent of the
children of agricultural workers went on to secondary level, as opposed
to 21 per cent of industrial workers, 81 per cent management, 86 per
cent officials and 87 per cent from the liberal professions.[36] To meet
this flagrant inequality, he proposed to extend obligatory education up
to age sixteen, and perhaps more importantly, to institute middle
schools (*écoles moyennes*). The purpose of these was to do away with
the sharp line drawn between primary and secondary education, which
would permit a greater degree of social mobility in that secondary
education might become less of a purely middle-class prerogative.
Two years would be spent in these schools. During the first, the
programme would be common to all pupils; in the second, it would be
part common to all and part optional, depending on individual abilities.
The two-year period in the middle schools was designed to prepare
pupils for subsequent courses of study, whether practical, professional
or leading to higher education.

While these proposals might have gone a long way towards solving
the problem of the inequality in education, they were received with
hostility by the unions of secondary teachers who did not wish to see
any link between primary and secondary, where the latter might be
reduced, to the former's benefit. Such hostility from the unions made
it difficult for Radicals and socialists, and the government itself, to
give the proposals strong support, and they were shelved. Clearly any
attempt to bridge the gap between primary and secondary would have
to be less than profound, if it were to have any hope of success.

Such were undoubtedly the conclusions drawn, in the early days
of the Fifth Republic, by J. Berthoin, who introduced (significantly,
by decree) in January 1959 a modified version of Billères's proposals.
The school-leaving age was increased to sixteen, to come into effect
in 1967; and the CEP, giving admittance to the *lycée*, was suppressed.
The specially created *école moyenne* envisaged by Billères was rendered
down into a two-year period (*cycle d'observation*) of which one term
only had a teaching programme common to all pupils — to take place
in whatever school the pupils found themselves. This meant that the
erstwhile *école moyenne* could be included in secondary education if

the teaching took place in a *lycée*, or in primary if it took place in a *collège d'enseignement général*; yet it was indicated in the decree (article 8) that the courses of study during these two years should be as similar as possible. These provisions had the advantage of not upsetting the teaching unions, since there could be no suspicion either at primary or at secondary level that either side was poaching on the other's preserves. They equally had the disadvantage of rendering the 'bridging' quality of the genuine *école moyenne* null and void, since it now remained in one camp or the other.

Whatever the defects, 'the reform contained seeds of growth that could not be impeded'.[37] The fact that both primary and secondary teachers were involved in the *cycle d'observation* gave a greater possibility for primary teachers to move into the secondary level. as *professeurs d'enseignement général des collèges* (PEGC). The *certificat d'aptitude* (CAPCEG) is gained after a course lasting a maximum of three years, which qualifies the PEGC to teach in two disciplines of literature, language or science. Also the use of *conseils d'orientation*, originally proposed by Billères, added the counsellor to the school personnel. The greatest extension to the Berthoin reform was put into effect under the auspices of Christian Fouchet. In 1963, the two-year *cycle d'observation*, having been found inadequate, was extended to four years, and a new form of school was set up, the *collège d'enseignement secondaire* (CES) with three sections: Modern I (*lycée*-style course), Modern II (CEG-type course) and Transitional III, into which were placed those unable to cope with the more academic programmes.[38] The courses in the CES were to last four years – 6e to 3e – which thus constituted the first cycle of secondary education to be taken away from the *lycées*. The introduction of the CES met with mixed response. The minister claimed, with some justice, that it was an important step towards the democratization of education, 'puisque, pour la première fois dans l'histoire des institutions scolaires françaises, tous les élèves quittant l'école élémentaire se trouvent réunis dans un même établissement' (Ministère de l'éducation nationale, *La Réforme de l'enseignement, août 1963–juin 1966*, Paris, n.d., p. 2). At all events, this was the ideal goal to be reached, and the creation of CES throughout France proceeded apace (1968 – 1,500; 1972-3 – 2,426; 1975-6 – 3,040).

While the CES brought comprehensive education from primary to secondary level, it brought also confusion when changes were effected, and led ultimately to resentment on the part of both pupils and teachers. A further target of criticism was the existence of the differing sections in the CES, into which pupils were divided according to ability (streaming). It was felt that those who were not capable of academic study were down-graded in every sense, since they would in due course find themselves in a subordinate role *vis-à-vis* their more successful colleagues.

Guidance into these sectors could not therefore be viewed merely as an academic distinction, but one affecting the individual's place in society, and, as a corollary, the salary which he or she earns. In consequence, the democratic purpose of the CES was regarded by some as more apparent than real.

A further attempt to improve secondary education came during Joseph Fontanet's term of office as education minister. Although his reform proposals were nipped in the bud by Pompidou's death and his own consequent departure from the ministry, they are worth looking at, since they show areas where the Fouchet legislation required amendment. The system of three streams of ability in the first part of secondary education, although in theory permitting a pupil to pass from one to another, in fact allowed for very little mobility. To add to the rigid hierarchy system, the *lycée*-type stream (I) was taught only by *agrégés* and *certifiés*, and the other two streams by PEGC and *instituteurs* respectively. J. Fontanet's solution was to remove total streaming, and replace it by a compromise system: certain subjects would be taught in mixed ability classes, others in homogeneous or partly homogeneous classes, permitting pupils, however, to pass from one group to another, depending on progress. The teaching of the first part would, in due course, become the province of a specific type of teacher (*enseignement du premier cycle*) to which PEGC and *instituteurs* could accede; the *agrégés* and *certifiés* would in time teach only in the later cycle of secondary education. While remedial teaching could be provided where necessary, the practice of *redoublement*, i.e. the repeating of a whole year, would be done away with, requiring in turn a less rigid organization of classes and time-table. However, where it was thought that an extra year would be genuinely beneficial at the end of the first cycle, this would be allowed.

After the election of Giscard d'Estaing in 1974, it was the turn of René Haby to see how he could improve the system. It seems clear enough that the guiding principles of the legislation are to be found in the views of Giscard d'Estaing — views which Haby undoubtedly shares. In his *Démocratie française*,[39] the former states the importance of education in giving all children the opportunity to develop abilities to the full. 'La justice . . . est de faire en sorte que, quel que soit le milieu d'origine, les personnalités de nos enfants puissent se développer et trouver dans la vie sociale, à mérite égal des chances équivalentes. Une démocratie sincère doit fixer cet objectif au premier de ses ambitions.' In other words, social origins should not prove a handicap to genuine ability. In presenting his proposals, M. Haby spoke of the need to create genuine equality of opportunity and therefore to ensure that late development, often a result of cultural deprivation, was not penalized: 'déculpabiliser le retard' (see *Le Monde de l'éducation*, March 1975). The text of the law, as passed by the *assemblée nationale* on 11

July 1975, is, as befits a *loi cadre*, exceedingly vague; but it seems to be egalitarian in tendency. It provides for nursery education, which is not obligatory, but which any five-year-old child may attend if the family wishes. Nursery education is regarded as having a crucial role to play in the removal of disadvantages caused by class differences. 'Elle tend à prévenir les difficultés scolaires, à dépister les handicaps et à compenser les inégalités' (article 2). Primary education, with five successive levels, although the duration of the initial period may vary, remains as before, based on a common syllabus. After primary education, all children enter a *collège* (the distinction between CEG and CES having been removed) where a further four levels of common syllabus are taught; although in the two final levels, more vocational training may be comprised in the curriculum for those working towards this type of qualification. Further secondary education takes place in the *lycée*, and qualifications there obtained may lead on to higher education. The *filières* are dispensed with, and decisions taken as to the future are arrived at on the basis of observation and assessment, due heed being paid to the family's wishes, and with the possibility of appeal.

Alterations in the running of schools are also provided for by a measure of parent participation, with the election of parents' representatives to the *comité des parents* and the *conseil d'école* at nursery and primary level or to the *conseils d'établissement* at secondary level; parents' delegates also have the right to be present at the *conseil de classe*, one for each class of children.

With the total abolition of streaming, certain provisions were made, in favour of those who progress either more quickly or more slowly than the norm. Further study – *activités d'approfondissement* is provided for the quicker pupil, and remedial work for the pupil who finds it difficult to keep up.

At this stage, it may be appropriate to give an indication as to how the system should function for a child beginning in nursery education at the earliest age – two years old. After four years, he/she passes into primary school where, in five or six years, he/she passes through the stages of *cours préparatoire*, *élémentaire* and *moyen*. Without any sanction or selection, the child begins a four-year course in a *collège*. The first two years are based on a common syllabus; the latter two (4e and 3e) may comprise more vocational training, some of which may take place away from the *collège*. It is at the end of 3e where the final decision as to *orientation* must be taken; either to opt for *lycée*, *baccalauréat* and, subsequently, higher education if appropriate; or to opt for the *lycée d'enseignement professionnel* (formerly technical college) and prepare for the various vocational qualifications -- CEP (*certificat d'éducation professionnelle*), a one-year course without examination; or the more exacting BEP (*brevet d'études professionnelles*) and CAP (*certificat d'aptitude professionnelle*). This simplified description may make it possible to see that, in spite of the claims made for the *collège unique*, and a removal of *filières*, a measure of orientation inevitably takes place at 5e, and more decisively at 3e. Those who are either not considered suitable for the *lycée* cycle of secondary education, or who do not wish to enter it, begin some of their vocational training in their last two years of *collège*. It is, however, at 3e when many futures are settled; and it appears that it is on results gained in mathematics that they turn, since this leads to the *baccalauréat* C, which in turn provides greater chances of further success. 'Les mathématiques commandent l'entrée des grands concours, mais aussi des petits. Les mathématiques ouvrent les études de médecine, les carrières de l'Administration. Tous les métiers aux débouchés assurés . . .' (D. Granet, 'La gare de triage de la 3e', *L'Express*, 13–19 June 1977).

The Haby reforms have taken a number of years to bring into effect. The first secondary class – 6e – received its common syllabus in 1977, and this has been introduced successively to subsequent years since then. The *terminale*, the final year of the *baccalauréat* only received its modifications at the *rentrée* of 1983, so that the complete reform has only now regulated the education of one generation of secondary school children.

It might have been thought that such a reform, introducing a more genuine form of the *collège unique*, with a common programme up to 3e level, and *orientation* thereafter, would have been sympathetically received by the left, and by the teaching unions. Hostility was strong from the beginning; while Haby's purpose was to permit children to progress at their own speed, without penalty for late development, this purpose was considered to be no more and no less than a sham (see J. Chambaz, *Le Monde de l'éducation*, March 1975).

Such was the attitude of the left before the legislation was even voted; and union hostility has been maintained ever since, mainly on the grounds that selection is maintained even when, officially, it is being removed. The remedial help provided by the law was not thought to be sufficient (three hours per week) to be of any real assistance to backward children, and there is justification for such an opinion. Even as early as the *cours préparatoire* in primary school, the *rapport* (Laurent) *Schwartz* has pointed at the very least to a lack of progress in this respect:

> après une baisse jusqu'en 1977, les redoublements (repetition of a school year) recommencent à progresser. Le pourcentage des éleves en retard d'une année qui était de 14,6% en 1974–75 avant la mise en place de la réforme et qui était tombé à 12,7% en 1978–79 est remonté à 14% en 1980–81. Le total des élèves en retard qui était de 15% en 1978–79 est monté à16,4%. (Commission du bilan, *La France*

en mai 1981, vol. 4, *L'enseignement et le développement scientifique*, Documentation Française, Paris, 1982, p. 31).

The report further went on to state that a large proportion of pupils requiring remedial assistance (1 in 5 for French or Mathematics, 52.7 per cent for both subjects) came from the underprivileged classes. Selection, albeit unintentional, was still evidently present in the system, with the middle classes, employers, and capitalism in general being regarded as the main beneficiaries.

Yet it should not be assumed that all criticism attacked the élitism of the reforms. The independent union of *lycée* teachers, SNALC, take the view that the *réforme Haby* is a form of confidence trick, designed to lower the standard of education in France, on the part of a technocracy (recruited from the bourgeoisie and the aristocracy).

Pour pérénniser une puissance abusive et illégitime, la méthode la plus sûre ne consiste-t-elle pas à médiocriser l'enseignement destiné à la masse, sous couvert d'"égalité des chances"; à empêcher la promotion intellectuelle et sociale d'élites potentielles étrangères à l'intelligentsia? (G. Simon, *SNALC et la réforme de l'enseignement*, Paris, Livre Vert, 1976).[40]

It is evident that the Haby reforms suit neither the left nor elements of the right, and, paradoxically, this may help to explain the approach which the socialist government has adopted to school education since coming to power.

The Haby reform provided a reasonable framework for school education, if properly applied, it might be thought – in other words, if there were adequate financing, and hence enough teachers. (During the ministries of R. Haby and of his successor C. Beullac, there was constant union pressure for the creation of more teaching posts.) If this were done, then the government could put other educational matters higher on its list of priorities i.e. decentralization, private and higher education. If the successive education budgets of the left are looked at, it will be seen that it has made very substantial efforts in this direction alone, from very early in its tenure of office. 14,775 posts in primary and secondary education were created in the additional finance law to the previous government's budget for 1981 (the *collectif budgétaire* of July 1981 and in the 1982 budget, 16,828 more.[41] The total figure over this period, 28,625, represents one third of all posts created by the entire government in 1981–2. (For further details, see *Cahiers de l'Education nationale*, no. 1, January 1982, pp. 20–1.) The budget for 1983 provided, in a time of economic difficulty, for 8,368 posts, nearly one half of all those created by the government as a whole. Yet this had been achieved by abolishing extra teaching hours (*heures supplémentaires*) and cutting down on *stagiaires*, pupil-teachers who provided a certain amount of teaching and whose numbers had been substantially raised on the previous financial year. In consequence, the *real* rise in jobs was only 5,346. Yet another issue which had caused much ill-feeling during the Haby and Beullac era was that of the *auxiliariat*, teachers who were employed as the need arose, but who enjoyed no tenure, and were thus at the mercy of the rise or fall in pupil population for the maintenance or termination of their employment. 14,399 such employees gained tenure in the 1983 budget (see *Cahiers de l'Education nationale*, no. 11, January 1983, pp. 20-1). Again, in the 1984 budget, half the posts created in the *fonction publique* by all ministries were for education, and expenses for the salaries of all employees accounted for 87 per cent of the total budget (as opposed to 85.4 per cent in 1982, and 86.5 per cent in 1983). In fact there were to be 4,590 extra posts all told.[42]

Yet this is not to suggest that no further thought was given to other, more fundamental changes in French education. On coming to power, the socialist government established a *commission du bilan* to assess the overall situation of the country, and one of the domains under review was education. The *rapport Schwartz*, covering all aspects of education, was the result. Thereafter, several reports were commissioned, on more specific issues. Reference has already been made to the *rapport Soubré* on decentralization (see above, Section 1), and higher education will be discussed in the next section. In the context of school education, the two most significant reports are those presided over respectively by Louis Legrand on the *collège*, and by Antoine Prost on the *lycée*.

The title of the *rapport Legrand, Pour un collège démocratique* (published in 1983), makes its intentions abundantly clear, and its proposals bear them out. Changes are proposed, (1) *in the passage from primary to secondary education*. As a rule, all pupils leave primary school at the age of eleven. A *commission de passage*, comprising the *collège* head, the *inspecteur départemental, conseiller d'orientation*, educational psychologist, and, in equal number, primary and secondary teachers, and parents' representatives, would discuss all cases, and would recommend, where a pupil has difficulties in reading an extra year at primary school. However no pupil over the age of twelve might stay at primary school. (2) *Organization of classes*. There would no longer be any selection in 6e and 5e. Pupils would be placed in mixed groups of 106, to be sub-divided into groups of twenty-six. After one month's observation, it would be possible to establish homogeneous groups for French and for mathematics, and in the second term, for foreign language classes. At 5e, this same arrangement would operate from the beginning of the year. Once every three months, the teaching group (*équipe pédagogique*) together with the *conseiller d'orientation*, and the *conseiller d'information*, would forgather to discuss progress, and alter the composition of the groups where necessary. On the question of *orientation*, premature selection, hitherto regarded as a sign of failure, was to be phased out as soon as possible. Entry at the end of 5e into the LEP, and in particular into CPPN (*classe préprofessionnelle de niveau* – general education, plus technological initiation into specific areas of possible employment) would in future be on a voluntary basis only, and the CPPN would be abolished as soon as possible. (3) *Role of pupils and teachers.* It was felt that the foregoing changes would make it possible for the pupil to make a responsible choice about courses to follow, and to gain the habit of working on his/her own, and of self-assessment. The changes would be even greater for the teachers. Added to the usual duties would be *travail en équipe*, group working. Crucial in this domain would be the *projet d'action éducative*,[43] which is already regarded as an essential in the fight against scholastic failure; assessment of the teaching done would also be of importance. Yet the most radical change, in a French context, was the proposal to introduce the *tutorat*. Teachers, selected by the pupils themselves, would act as tutor to a maximum of fifteen pupils, giving both academic and personal advice. Legrand also proposed the abolition of differentiation of teaching hours as between categories of teachers. All would now have sixteen hours' teaching per week, plus three hours' *tutorat*, and another three hours to be spent in discussion and concerting of work with other teachers. Other suggestions related to more technological education, and institutional changes, along the lines proposed by the *rapport Soubré*.

Inevitably, the report provoked mixed reactions. Whilst the SNI-PEGC considered that the proposals were on the whole positive (see *L'Ecole libératrice*, no. 15, 22 January 1983, J.-C. Barbarant, 'Un rapport pour négocier',), other opinions were mixed or hostile. The SNC (*syndicat national des collèges*) was well-disposed to the idea of both *tutorat* and *concertation*; it did not like the decentralizing measures proposed by Legrand which merely repeated the 'deplorable' Soubré proposals (see *SNC-Bulletin*, February 1983, pp. 10–14). The SNALC inevitably took a hostile view, firstly because, in its opinion, the proposals interfered with the freedom of the individual teacher (it disliked the 'collectivist' approach), but also on the grounds that mixed ability classes – a recipe for disaster – were maintained (see *Quinzaine universitaire*, 15 February 1983). Yet it is probably the proposed unification of teaching hours which is most displeasing to the most highly qualified teachers, and which seems to have aroused the strongest protest (see Legrand's open letter to protesting teachers in *Quinzaine universitaire*, 15 October 1982, pp. 159–63).

However, this last proposal has not as yet been adopted wholesale by the minister. The three points which have been retained at present are: the *équipes pédagogiques*, the reorganization of classes into *groupes de niveau*, and the *tutorat*. These will be put into operation in volunteer *collèges*, and here, the PEGC will have their teaching hours reduced (*Le Monde*, 6 January 1984).

As for the *rapport Prost*, entitled *Les Lycées et leurs études au seuil du XXIe siècle*, no decision has as yet been taken on its findings. While in certain respects it was quite positive in its view of the instruction provided in the *lycées*, it also found causes for complaint: over-ambitious teaching, too heavy a syllabus, and therefore too heavy a time-table, too much information to be imparted, insufficient emphasis on techno-logical disciplines, and, inevitably, overmuch selection. To combat these shortcomings, practical proposals have been made, some of which mirror those of Legrand, such as the *équipes pédagogiques*. In an endeavour to encourage *lycéens* to work independently, either singly or in groups, it is proposed to organize the time-table on a weekly basis, spread over ten half-days, and over six days in the week, with more flexibility. Guidance and assessment of *lycéens* should be carried out on the basis of regular meetings with pupils, so as to have adequate infor-mation on their main interests and on what they have achieved. Other points relate to the relative facility with which a *lycéen* may pass from one section to another, the optimum size for *lycées* (600–700 pupils, and never more than 900), more emphasis on technological studies as an integral part of culture. On an institutional basis, reforms have been proposed to increase co-operation between *lycées*, and also between other areas of activity, (industry, administration, higher education, etc.), allowing greater linkage between *formation* and job opportunities. In this domain also, the need to combat geographical inequalities in edu-cational facilities and hence in educational opportunity was emphasized.

These considerations on aspects of secondary education have one point in common – namely the need for education less as a cultural necessity, and more as a specifically vocational training, which in turn means an emphasis on science and particularly, technology. This is not a new idea. E. Faure, in presenting his proposed reform of higher edu-cation in 1968, made the point that forms of education other than literature (i.e. scientific and technical) would assume larger proportions in primary and secondary. Such a renewal was desirable, given a society which was in a perpetual state of flux and which required an education more suited to modern life. 'Cette éducation nationale doit participer à la vie de toute la nation comme la nation tout entière doit contribuer à son devenir' (E. Faure, *L'Education nationale et la participation*, p. 19).

Since, in spite of criticisms, the *Loi d'Orientation* acquired such eminence that all ministers of education have had at the very least to pay lip-service to it, we may expect to find, in the decade since 1968, changes introduced in line with the spirit of Faure's reform. The legislation of 16 July 1971 (three separate laws) is concerned with the organization of vocational and technological education, apprentice-ship, and adult education (*formation continue*) for employed workers.

The first provides for an initiation into technology and economics from 4ᵉ and 3ᵉ onwards. It also requires that adequate information be provided on the differing branches of education, job possibilities and on 'les perspectives scientifiques, techniques et économiques dont dépend l'évolution de l'emploi' (article 3). The second, on apprenticeship, deals with its reorganization, in apprentice training centres, with training lasting from one to three years, and with the possibility of proceeding to further study and higher qualifications. These two laws clearly represent an attempt to induce a higher esteem on the part of the public for these areas of study, as well as an endeavour to provide appropriate training for work in a technological society. Yet it is perhaps the third law on *formation continue* which comes closest to the ideals of May 1968. This gives a worker in employment the right to have time off from work in order to pursue courses of study approved by the state, leading to further qualification. As a rule the maximum period of absence from work is either one year, or 1,200 hours, depending on the nature of the course. This is an innovation which seems to give education the possibility of achieving what many think of as its main task, the social (and consequently, financial) up-grading of the working classes. The socialist government in this area too has shown its willingness to improve the content of technical education, as well as the necessary equipment; to bring more young people into technical education, and to improve the allowances made to them (see *Cahiers de l'Education nationale*, no. 14, April 1983, 'Dossier: la rénovation technique').

Here, too, the increase in financing is very marked. In 1981, *formation continue* at secondary level cost the state 408.7 million francs, and at university level, nearly 9.6 million; private funding totalled 224 and 129 million respectively (see *Cahiers de l'Education nationale*, no. 9, November 1982, 'Dossier: la formation continue'). There seems little doubt that this is regarded not only as a long-term means to social advancement, but in the short-term, as a useful weapon against unemployment. This also could be said to mark a change in the left's attitude to education, as in the past, there has been perhaps less willingness to accept the propriety of gearing education to the needs of the economy, and hence of capitalism.

In spite of the financial generosity of the present government's policy in education, it would be unfair if this were portrayed as merely unthinking extravagance. On the contrary, a very serious endeavour is being made, to make funding available where it is most necessary via the *zone prioritaire* – a concept introduced as early as July 1981. This idea predates the arrival of the left to power (see B. Schwartz, *Une autre école*, Paris, Flammarion, 1977, pp. 111 ff.). It is a departure from the usual 'blanket' form of egalitarian measure, regardless of the relative prosperity or poverty of those whom it is proposed to assist. Basically, extra financing, and hence extra facilities for a limited period of time, would be concentrated in an area where there had been, for example, a particularly high rate of scholastic failure. If an area was deprived, the children living there would suffer in educational terms, and the only way to break out of the vicious circle was to remove the deprivation. While the criteria for judging an area to be deprived are flexible, some are regarded as particularly important. Thus it would be necessary to study the statistics relating to: numbers of children in nursery schools relation of pupil numbers at 3e to those at 6e, numbers attending CPPN and apprenticeship classes, numbers of non-French children in the area, and numbers of children quitting school without a qualification, together with the overall social and economic state of the area.

It is too early to tell how successful this programme will be, but it does show the willingness of the present government to translate precept into reasonable practice. Certainly the policy is now in very extensive operation (see Table 6.3, p. 300).

In general, it can be said that school education is facing some very profound changes in the desire of the government to achieve a greater measure of social equality. The long-term realization, if it is achievable, will only be effected by means of vast budgetary resources. When in opposition, the left regarded education as the number one priority, and it is now so treated. Yet even for the socialists, the public purse is not bottomless, and the government's well-wishers may well fear that too much is being done too quickly for financing to be adequate. The reason behind this haste is clear enough: if the reforms are to be successful there has to be a change in mentality, amongst teachers and in society at large, and the sooner that is set in motion, the better. But this solution is a political one: to achieve such changes in education, and hence in society, the left will need at least as long a period in power as the right enjoyed from 1958 to 1981.

(4) Higher education

As with education at school level, so has higher education also been the subject of much thought over the last thirty-odd years. This has led to reform, and attempts at reform, both before and since the events of May. If we look at the higher education system as it existed in the immediate post-war period, we find the following elements.

(a) *Qualifications*: a *baccalauréat* giving automatic access to higher education: a *licence* composed, in arts, of four or five *certificats* (in different subjects, with a separate examination for each); three *certificats* were required in science. The *licence en droit* was not split up in this way, and medical studies followed a different pattern again. There were also the *agrégation* – a competitive examination taken after the *licence*, giving to the successful candidate entrance into teaching in higher education or into *lycée* teaching — and the *doctorat*: either a *doctorat d'université* or a *doctorat d'état* — the ultimate qualification in higher education.

(b) *Institutions*: the teaching for the university qualifications was dispensed in the *facultés*. Another path into higher education was to prepare for entrance into the *grandes écoles*, autonomous educational establishments providing courses leading to a professional qualification of the most prestigious kind. These *classes préparatoires*, lasting several years and leading to competitive examinations for entry, were themselves selective. Graduates from the *grandes écoles* were expected to provide an élite of the highest calibre, whose training would enable them to take on duties in many areas of activity, but all possessed of considerable influence. Some of these institutions date back to the eighteenth century, even before the Revolution, but the tradition of providing an élite of administrators was continued by Napoleon and his successors.

This was, in general terms, the system as it existed at the end of the Second World War. The most substantial reforms in higher education have been introduced since the establishment of the Fifth Republic, but some piecemeal changes brought in during the life of the Fourth have not been without influence. As indicated earlier, secondary and higher education was not thought to have covered itself with glory during the Second World War, as a result of the activities of many who had passed through the system. It was inevitable therefore that changes would be proposed, not only in relation to qualifications as such, but also to the training of teachers.

Among the innovations put forward by the Langevin–Wallon report was a year of study — *enseignement propédeutique ou préuniversitaire*, to be undertaken by all *bacheliers*. It was to have a dual role: preparation for further study, and also to provide the necessary help and guidance for school-leavers starting a career. Ideally, it should have taken place neither in the *lycées* nor in the *facultés*. A move in this direction, instituted before the publication of this report, provided for a *propédeutique* year in the *facultés*, which was to prepare the hopeful student for higher education, by providing suitable advice and guidance as to the type of studies to be undertaken, consolidating the knowledge already acquired, and introducing students to methods of study appropriate at university level. However, an examination at the end of the course acted as a hurdle allowing the successful student to prepare for the *licence*, but preventing the unsuccessful candidate (who was left with the *baccalauréat* as sole qualification) from pursuing further study.

It should also be borne in mind that, in the main, perhaps even more in literary studies than in others, the function of higher education

Table 6.3 Extent of the zone prioritaire policy, 1982–3

Académies 1982–1983	Number of zones prioritaires in each académie	Nursery		Primary		Total		Colleges		LEP	
		% Schools	% Pupils	% Schools	% Pupils	% Schools	% Pupils	% Schools	% Pupils	% Schools	% Pupils
Aix-Marseille	29	19.8	18.0	15.3	18.1	16.9	18.1	30.0	25.0	33.3	27.0
Amiens	11	5.6	5.5	1.4	4.3	1.9	4.6	7.0	8.4	–	–
Besançon	18	10.4	10.7	6.1	13.1	6.9	12.3	15.5	19.3	12.1	10.7
Bordeaux	13	3.5	6.5	6.7	7.5	6.0	7.3	13.9	13.6	12.0	12.0
Caen	6	4.5	4.5	2.9	4.9	3.2	4.3	4.7	5.1	–	–
Clermont-Ferrand	11	6.4	8.5	5.2	5.2	5.3	6.0	6.3	7.5	6.3	8.5
Corse	18	–	–	17.6	51.5	15.0	38.0	42.0	33.0	100.0	100.0
Créteil	25	7.4	7.6	6.7	9.0	7.0	8.5	8.3	10.0	5.7	6.0
Dijon	15	10.6	12.0	6.9	9.3	7.7	10.0	10.6	9.2	7.5	7.8
Grenoble	13	6.0	7.0	4.0	6.0	4.0	7.0	9.0	8.5	6.0	8.0
Lille	39	7.5	8.5	6.0	7.4	6.5	7.7	14.4	12.1	–	*
Limoges	*	*	*	*	*	*	*	*	*	*	*
Lyon	22	–	–	–	–	8.7	11.8	11.1	12.7	17.2	16.5
Montpellier	14	13.1	11.6	17.7	13.2	16.5	13.0	22.2	14.8	17.6	14.2
Nancy-Metz	22	1.9	9.6	5.0	11.4	4.0	10.8	12.4	16.0	–	–
Nantes	7	11.4	9.0	5.9	8.3	7.3	8.6	3.1	3.0	–	–

Table 6.3 continued

Académies 1982–1983	Number of zones prioritaires in each académie	Schools						Colleges		LEP	
		Nursery		Primary		Total					
		% Schools	% Pupils	% Schools	% Pupils	% Schools	% Pupils	% Schools	% Pupils	% Schools	% Pupils
Nice	7	6.0	6.1	4.0	6.2	4.6	6.2	6.0	6.5	16.0	13.7
Orléans-Tours	5	4.7	5.3	2.8	5.2	3.3	5.2	5.0	4.8	–	–
Paris	6	18.0	17.8	17.5	19.8	17.8	19.0	13.8	13.4	18.0	18.5
Poitiers	9	7.0	6.0	2.0	7.0	3.0	6.0	6.0	8.0	12.0	10.0
Reims	11	7.0	9.5	5.3	8.7	5.7	9.0	9.6	11.1	11.1	14.6
Rennes	7	3.0	2.4	6.0	5.0	5.2	4.0	13.5	10.0	11.5	10.0
Rouen	18	11.0	10.0	4.0	7.8	6.0	8.6	22.4	21.7	9.3	12.5
Strasbourg	5	2.1	6.1	2.2	6.6	2.3	6.4	7.4	8.5	7.5	8.5
Toulouse	14	10.0	12.0	11.5	12.0	11.0	12.0	13.0	11.0	11.0	11.0
Versailles	11	–	–	–	–	4.3	6.1	5.0	5.7	–	–
Antilles-Guyane	7	13.3	9.0	12.0	10.4	12.3	10.0	8.7	6.0	14.3	12.0
Total	363	7.4	9.3	6.3	7.6	8.7	8.7	11.0	10.6	8.8	8.0

Source: Cahiers de l'Education nationale, no. 16, June 1983

Note: The *académie* of Limoges has no *zones prioritaires* as such, but rather, an entire *programme*, as the region is particularly underprivileged.

had traditionally been to provide teachers. The term *licence* originally meant precisely that: a licence to teach. While the *agrégés* were automatically appointed to teaching posts in *lycées*, the *certifiés* – that is, teachers with a licence – were normally expected to teach in *collèges*, although they too could take up posts in a *lycée*. With the increase in numbers of pupils, more and more of the latter obtained *lycée* posts, and to ensure a maintenance of standards, a further qualification was required; from 1952 onwards, a competitive examination gained for the successful candidate the *certificat d'aptitude à l'enseignement du second degré* (CAPES). This qualification, based on a competitive examination, may be said to typify in this respect much of higher education. The problem of numbers caused much of the system to seem more and more competitive. While every *bachelier* had the automatic right to a place in a *faculté* for the first year, the *propédeutique* examination was an obstacle in the path of further study. It could also be said with some justice, that while the preparation for certain *certificats* was not unduly onerous, the examination in other disciplines was neither more nor less than a competition, allowing success to a fraction of the total candidates who had to pass in both written and oral. It was possible to resit the examination, but this was time-consuming, and made what might have been a two-year course last between three and five years. The problem was exacerbated by the fact that although student numbers were on the increase, staff numbers were not, and it was virtually impossible for teachers in higher education to give individual guidance and help, or indeed to do more than rely on the *cours magistral* (lecture), without any kind of back-up in the form of small-group teaching. Many students also were unable to work full-time at their studies, since they needed to earn money in order to make ends meet. Some were teaching part-time in schools which undoubtedly provided useful experience for a future career, but postponed the time when they would be fully qualified. It was not only the inefficiency of the system which was criticized, but also the relevance of the studies which were pursued. The country needed people with technological qualifications, but the branches of education providing these were much less popular than the letters and law faculties; yet job opportunities were less immediate in these areas.

These were, overall, the problems facing C. Fouchet, when he became education minister in 1962. We have already seen his endeavours to increase the extent of the comprehensive principle at secondary level. This was to be crowned by a re-organization of the *baccalauréat*, which was to be divided up into five main sections. Although a *baccalauréat technique industriel* had existed since 1946 there would now be much less emphasis on literary studies, and a correspondingly greater one on science and technology. While Fouchet claimed that the aims of this reform were to preserve the role of secondary education as a provider of general culture, as well as to bring a more positive content to the concept of *orientation* by indicating precise possibilities to pupils in relation to their abilities, it provided one section for literary studies, one for social sciences, but two for science, and one for scientific and technical knowledge combined. This last provided for three *baccalauréats* of a more technical nature.

Another institution of higher education was established, the *institut universitaire de technologie* (IUT) to provide two-year courses for the training of highly qualified technicians: 'des cadres et techniciens supérieurs des activités industrielles et du secteur tertiaire, dont le rôle est de traduire dans le concret les conceptions abstraites ou les résultats des recherches théoriques. Ils doivent donc posséder une formation technique plus profonde et plus précise que celle des ingénieurs et, éventuellement, une vue générale des choses plus large que celle des simples techniciens' (Ministère de l'éducation nationale, *La Réforme de l'enseignement, août 1963–juin 1966*, Paris, n.d., p. 7). A qualification was obtained after the two-year course – the *diplôme universitaire de technologie* (DUT) – and instruction given not only by full-time teachers but also by people with practical experience in management.

The organization of the *baccalauréat* was further changed in that the examinations, instead of being staggered over two years, were in future to be taken at the end of the third year (*classes terminales*). However, the most important change was perhaps less in the *baccalauréat* itself than in the use which could be made of it. Traditionally the *baccalauréat* gave unrestricted entry into the *facultés*, according to the *bachelier*'s choice. Fouchet proposed to curtail this freedom by tying specific *baccalauréats* to specific university courses, and, by the same token, requiring prospective university candidates to make a firm decision as to their choice of discipline much earlier. This did not mean that it was wholly out of the question for a *bachelier* to consider pursuing a course to which his *baccalauréat* did not strictly entitle him; but in that case he would only be accepted by the *faculté* of his choice after consideration of his *dossier*, or after success in a special examination.

C. Fouchet also reorganized higher education, providing three cycles of study. Once the *bachelier* was duly admitted to a *faculté*, he would, instead of facing the *propédeutique* examination at the end of the first year, prepare for a qualification to be gained after a two-year course either in arts (*diplôme universitaire d'études littéraires* – DUEL), or in sciences (*diplôme universitaire d'études scientifiques* – DUES). Study for these diplomas was divided up into a number of sections, thought to be particularly appropriate for students preparing for a career in teaching. Once this initial qualification was obtained, the student could either seek employment or continue into the second cycle, in which one further year of study conferred the *licence* (still required as a qualification for teachers in secondary school), and two years further study after the DUEL or DUES led to the *maîtrise* (master's degree). The third cycle comprised the options of *agrégation* or *doctorat*.

The purpose behind the three-cycle system was to provide in the first cycle for the acquisition of basic knowledge, in the second for specialization, and in the third for research, or, in other words, to separate teaching from research work. Hitherto it had been possible to pass from teaching in secondary school to teaching and research in a *faculté*, but with the new system and the new qualification of the *maîtrise*, this flexibility would be less feasible, with secondary school teaching provided for by the *licence* and CAPES and higher education provided for by *maîtrise, agrégation* and *doctorat*. Such a change was welcome to scientists, but less so to teachers in the arts faculties.

A further criticism levelled at the reforms was that, although no selection existed in theory, in reality the creation of the IUT could well attract only the weaker *bacheliers*. The question of selection was, and still is, of vital importance. In Britain selection of university entrants, by a variety of means, is in the main accepted, if not wholly approved. Since for many years any *bachelier* had an automatic right to a place in a *faculté*, any curtailing of that right was inevitably viewed as a retrograde and reactionary step, contrary to the democratization of education. Unfortunately, the absence of selection at entry operated much more brutally, by failure, at the end of the first year. Fouchet's first cycle, DUEL and DUES, was an attempt to deal with that difficulty; but no attempt was made to deal with the underlying problem of a lack of selection, aggravated by the ever-increasing student numbers. At the *colloque de Caen* of 1966 one notable partisan of selection, M. Zamansky, then dean of the Paris science faculty, proposed a solution; namely to turn the *baccalauréat* into a genuine qualification of secondary education, which the large majority of pupils would obtain. Only then would any selection operate, not on the basis of failure, but on a positive approach to individual abilities. 'Au système actuel: vous êtes bon à ceci ou vous n'êtes bon à rien; il faut substituer le système, vous êtes bon à quelque chose et voici à quoi' (M. Zamansky in *colloque de Caen*). However, Fouchet had not felt it possible to adopt such a radical approach. It has been suggested that all the education reforms introduced by Fouchet were directly inspired by de Gaulle; yet in the matter of selection, the latter's influence did not prevail.[44]

These reforms were undoubtedly important, and attempted to provide for the French economy the greater number of scientific and technological experts which it needed for expansion. Yet the problem of numbers was not dealt with, save by the hasty construction of extra universities and overspill annexes, such as Nanterre, which within a few years were themselves overcrowded. The problems created by overcrowding were therefore permanent, and provided one of the causes of the dissatisfaction leading to the events of May 1968.

If the May events achieved no more, they forced the government to face up to the question of higher education and the radical views expressed as to the purpose of higher education, which could no longer be regarded either as the privileged domain of the upper classes, or as a high powered sausage-machine, geared to produce an appropriate number of managers, administrators, scientists, etc. as required by the state, the economy or the consumer society. Consequently other criteria had to be established with the participation of all those involved in higher education, whether as teachers, students or in some other capacity.

This was the task allotted to Edgar Faure in June 1968 – to produce a reform which would take into account the many views which had been expressed. His initial move was to intensify the arrangements made by his predecessor, F. Ortoli, by the use of *chargés de mission* to provide him with information, in co-operation with the *recteurs*, since many universities and faculties had produced proposals for reform.

His speech to the *assemblée nationale* of 24 July 1968 gave a clear enough indication of his reforming intentions. Society was in a state of constant change, and higher education had to keep pace with it, which it had hitherto signally failed to do. The old-style *université*, Napoleon's creation, was out-dated and all traces of it should be eradicated, whether in legislation, teaching methods, or relations between teachers, students and administration, whether central or local. One essential goal to aim for was (yet again) democratization of education from nursery school to university, whilst at the same time maintaining high cultural standards. In this context there would have to be, as well as financial assistance to poorer families, changes in the curriculum, in order that there should no longer be an in-built advantage to the culturally privileged classes.

To avoid the feeling of alienation experienced by many students at university, numbers should not be excessive. 'Les universités nouvelles doivent avoir une personnalité. Chacune d'elles . . . doit être à l'échelle humaine, c'est-à-dire accueillir dix mille ou douze mille étudiants.'[45] A limit of student numbers was also laid down for certain types of classes: small groups – 25 maximum; *travaux pratiques* (seminars) – 40 maximum; and no more than 250 students at the formal lecture.

With these very specific indications about suitable numbers in classes and in the ideal university it might have been expected that

Faure would have embraced selection as a solution to the problem of student numbers. Yet a decision was taken not to adopt a selective system, the reasons being that the right of *bacheliers* to enter the faculties had been long accepted, and that any selective system should not be adopted hastily, merely to deal with an immediate problem of numbers; on the contrary, it should be weighed up, and if introduced thereafter, very carefully organized. These reasons were doubtless important, but there was one other far more powerful: student reaction to selection was feared, and with some reason, since the proposal to introduce it had been made in April 1968, and had not been well received. No one in the government wished to see a recrudescence of the events of May, and, whatever else was to be reformed, the open-door policy could not be touched. In other words, Faure's task was to produce a law which would assist in the shoring-up of a régime which had come near to collapse, by radically reforming higher education and consequently obtaining support from those who felt reforms to be essential.[46] Concessions already made, whatever troubles they might have caused, would not be rescinded.

Some of the most important changes would have to come in the administration of education, so much criticized during May 1968 for its excessive centralization. To bring about these changes, Faure proposed, in general, the remedy of *participation* to all levels and in varying ways, in new units of higher education, with a wider range of subjects (*pluri-disciplinarité*) than that encompassed by the out-dated *faculté*.

After a summer of consultations with all interested parties (except the extreme right and the *groupuscules* of the extreme left), the law came before the *assemblée nationale* in September 1968, and was passed by it on 11 October and by the *sénat* a fortnight later.

The *Loi d'Orientation* provided for a complete structural reorganization of higher education, with the abolition of *facultés* and the introduction of the *unité d'enseignement et de recherche* (UER) as the basic unit of the *université*. The UER is governed by an elected council, and a director elected thereby for three years. In the same way the council of the *université* is elected, and in turn, elects the president for five years. In each case the councils comprise not only teachers, researchers and students, but also non-teaching staff and people from outside the academic world. In mixed councils, the proportion of teachers' representatives was to be at least equal to that of the students. Student representation was to be related to the number of voters. If the latter fell to less than 60 per cent of the total registered, then the number of representatives would be proportionately reduced.

The principle of autonomy was also not wholly neglected. While it was stated that the state provides finance for the *université*, the latter also may enjoy the use of other resources, i.e. donations, bequests, etc. The *université* votes on its budget, which, says the law, must balance. The organization of teaching and research, again, is a matter for each *université*, as is the assessment of students' work, by examination or continuous assessment. Yet in this area of what is called *autonomie pédagogique*, the awarding of degrees is still the prerogative of the ministry of education, for although qualifications from specific establishments do exist, they lack the standing of the nationally recognized degree or diploma. It also became clear, once university institutions began to attempt their reorganization in the light of the *Loi d'Orientation*, that there was only one acceptable interpretation — that of the minister. Furthermore, one crucial element of the centralized system — namely the administration — in no wise came within the competence of the law, so that while the new universities were re-organized on a supposedly decentralized and participatory basis, the administrative framework remained essentially as before.[47]

The concepts of participation and autonomy thus may be seen as less generous in scope than they seem at first glance. Centralization, or, at least, bureaucracy, could be suggested as being greater than before. The *Loi d'Orientation* provided for a *Conseil national de l'enseignement supérieur et de la recherche* (CNESER), to replace the previous CNES. This is presided over by the minister and has a total of ninety members, fifty-four elected university members including students, six from other establishments of higher education, and thirty representing national interests, i.e. politicians, union members, etc. It meets at least twice a year, but maintains a *section permanente*, whose members are elected by the whole council and a *commission scientifique permanente*, with the task of examining university research programmes, and teaching at the *troisième cycle* and *doctorat* level. The task of the CNESER seems to be essentially consultative; it is involved in the planning of higher education and research, in relation to the National Plan; it gives opinions as to university curricula, requests for credit, and the apportioning of budget resources, on national diplomas, and on decisions by an *recteur* to suspend the proceedings of the universities' councils within his *académie*. On a local level, regional councils have been set up, composed of elected representatives from universities and other institutions within the region, as well as representatives of regional activities. The task of these councils is to co-ordinate higher education and research in the region and, again, they have a consultative role on curricula and requests for credits from universities.

Doubtless this seems like an effort towards decentralization, but of a very cumbersome kind. 'Such an elaborate apparatus appears to be a heavy price to pay for participation',[48] particularly when the power to act, as opposed to the possibility of being consulted, seems so limited.

One further institution must be added to the list of bodies to which the *Loi d'Orientation* has, as it were, acted as midwife — namely the *conférence des présidents*, which was formally created by the decree of 24 February 1971. When the new universities came into being with their elected presidents, the need was felt to form a body on which every university would have a representative (which is not the case in the CNESER). During 1970 regular meetings were held. This body has, like the others, a consultative role, giving its opinion on matters submitted to it by the minister; yet it also has the right to study questions of interest to the universities and to put proposals and plans to the minister. With its regular meetings it is a powerful body wielding considerable influence.

E. Faure, in office for scarcely a year, had little time to devote to other aspects of higher education. Subsequent ministers have not done away with the provisions of the *Loi d'Orientation*, although these may not have been interpreted as widely as he would have wished. The two most important changes introduced since 1968 have been:

(1) the replacement of the DUEL and the DUES, and

(2) the reform of the second cycle.

In 1973 J. Fontanet, then minister of education, changed the first cycle of university studies by introducing, in place of Fouchet's DUEL and DUES, the *diplôme d'études universitaires générales*, for law, economics, economics and social administration, social sciences, letters and science, each discipline consisting of a number of sections. The courses were to be multi-disciplinary — the principle subject to be studied for 60 per cent of the course, and the other 40 per cent to be devoted to optional work. The qualification would be awarded partly on assessment of work, and partly on the result of examinations and would lead either to employment or to further study. The reasons behind this change were twofold: to deal with the problems created by the existing system, over-specialization, and also wastage, with a good half of the students failing and leaving university without a qualification.

It was also thought that the DEUG would indicate the attainment of a reputable standard which would be acceptable to employers. Neither of these hopes have as yet been wholly realized. The percentage of failure is still very high — in some disciplines, 50 per cent, in others more than this (see for details G. Herzlich, 'Les chances de succès dans chaque discipline', *Le Monde de l'éducation*, June 1978). Also the continual difficulties of graduates in obtaining suitable employment have meant that higher qualifications are demanded than would have been the case some years ago. The basic DEUG therefore is insufficient, and in many cases the DUT is more immediately attractive to the prospective employer.[49]

The second major change since the *Loi d'Orientation* was even more contoversial, the so-called *arrêté Soisson* of 16 January 1976, validated in June 1977 and signed in fact by J. P. Soisson's successor, A. Saunier-Seïté, the second occupant of the autonomous *secrétariat d'état aux universités*, since raised to a full ministry. This measure dealt with the *licence* and *maîtrise*, to take one year each after the DEUG. In general the second cycle was to provide 'une formation scientifique de haut niveau qui prépare les étudiants à la vie active et à l'exercice de responsabilités professionnelles' (Arrêté 16 January 1976, article 1). The various types of *licence* and *maîtrise* would be authorized as national diplomas by the secretary of state, after the consideration of detailed proposals by the various universities, by the *groupes d'étude technique* consisting not only of academics but also people from other professions. The idea behind this was to prevail upon universities to provide high-level courses with a bearing upon subsequent employment, that is, of a more technological nature. It seems hard to believe that there would have been any opposition to this, had it not been for the fact that as in theory all *licences* and *maîtrises* had to go before the *groupes d'étude* (which would inevitably have a bias towards the more vocational and less purely academic course), those teaching the more traditional courses felt their positions threatened if their second-cycle syllabus were not approved. Saunier-Seïté not only had to face opposition on the part of students but also that of the university presidents. In due course, concessions were made, in the sense that the *groupes d'étude technique* lost a good deal of its power, which the CNESER and the president's conference gained.

The opposition of the university presidents may not seem wholly surprising in view of the vested interests which required protection, in the shape of traditional courses of study, and also in view of some clashes of personality. The student position is, historically, possibly less consistent, particularly if we relate this problem to some of the ideas of May 1968. It will be remembered that one of the criticisms levelled by students at French higher education was that of the irrelevance of what was taught, since in many cases the qualifications gained led to teaching, and little else besides. While such a view might not commend itself to those who feel that a country's (or a civilization's) cultural heritage ought to be protected, cherished, and passed on from one generation to another, the unemployed graduate cannot as a rule take such an elevated stand on the issue. It might therefore have been supposed that changes along these lines would have met with some approval; instead they met with hostility, violence and prolonged strikes. That being said, it should be borne in mind that eight years had passed since May 1968, the students were consequently of another generation. Equally, the views expressed then had not been quite consistent since, while on the one hand higher education had been criticized for turning out unemployable graduates, it was also criticized for its tendency to assist in the maintenance of a capitalist, consumer society, by training the leaders and managers for it.

Since 1976, however, attitudes have changed again. While it might be suggested that the very emphasis put on technological studies has itself brought about a gradually less Olympian approach on the part of students towards the purpose of study, economic circumstances have played an even greater part. The fear of graduate unemployment, so much greater even than in 1976, must be the prime factor,[50] and as will appear, even a left-wing government would not be able, or indeed willing, to avoid the issue.

Any student entering upon higher education at this point in time would begin with the first cycle, the two-year DEUG. If successful, he could then continue his studies into the second cycle, with the *licence* and *maîtrise* as a rule for those intending to enter the teaching profession. However, with the advent of the *arrêté Soisson*, he would also have the possibility of studying for more vocational *maîtrises*, in three categories: (a) *maîtrise de sciences et techniques* (MST), (b) *maîtrise d'informatique appliquée à la gestion* (MIAGE), or (c) *maîtrise de sciences de gestion* (MSG). On completion of the *maîtrise* he could enter the third cycle, where three possibilities present themselves: either to prepare for a *diplôme d'études supérieures spécialisées* (DESS), which, lasting only for a year, would prepare for some form of employment, with, as part of the training, vocational experience. If on the other hand our graduate was of more academic persuasions, he could prepare for a *doctorat de troisième cycle* (roughly M.Phil.), a three-year course at most, with a qualification at the end of the first year — the *diplôme d'études approfondies* — with initiation into research work and, as necessary, laboratory experience. The final stage is still the *doctorat d'état*, no longer of limitless duration, but to be completed in five years, unless any extension is granted. This qualification by thesis is still the most prestigious of the purely academic qualifications.

Yet if we look at the figures of degrees awarded in 1981, at the level of the DEUG, it can be seen that the greatest number still come from the arts and social sciences (17,627) as opposed to, for example, law (9,502) or science (9,441). The same picture is to be found at the *licence* level: law, 9,156; science, 8,371; arts and social sciences, 18,569. (*L'Education nationale en chiffres*, op. cit., p. 35). The trend here shows little sign of shifting, and the literary imbalance is far from being seriously corrected. This situation could stem from two factors, one that arts subjects, possibly easier, or considered so, attracted members of the poorer classes who had had more of a struggle to enter higher education, or that the prejudice in favour of literary studies has not yet died, and that another generation of school teachers may have to pass before a change in attitude comes about.

One element which is solidly entrenched in the French education system is that of competition, whether by marked selection in the DEUG or more openly in the *concours*. This is particularly harsh in the competitive examinations for the *agrégation* and the CAPES. For the former, in 1982, out of 12,727 who sat the exam (17,430 registered) 1,251 were successful; for the latter, 29,174 registered for the examinations, with 3,161 posts available (see *Note d'information*, no. 83-11, 21 March 1983). Since government policy overall provides for greater availability of teaching posts, the ratio of posts to entrants is more favourable than it was, but there is still great wastage of energy and resources in a system where many will try repeatedly before succeeding. Yet this is a system which many French academics find perfectly normal, and indeed desirable.[51]

The starkest competition is that which obtains the *classes pré-paratoires*, and the entrance examination into one of the *grandes écoles*. Only those with excellent results at the *baccalauréat* are admitted to these classes, with prepare for three categories: (a) scientific establishments such as the *école des mines* or *polytechnique*, (b) literary, essentially the *écoles normales supérieures*, such as Sèvres or Saint-Cloud, or the *école des chartes*; (c) commercial, the most prestigious being the *hautes études commerciales*. The newest addition to these is the *école nationale d'administration*, founded in 1945. In this case only, the *classes préparatoires* take place, not as for the others, in the fifty most important *lycées* in Paris and the provinces, but at the *institut d'études politiques*, and many graduates from other *grandes écoles* proceed from there to ENA.

Even those candidates who fail to enter a *grande école* after the *classes préparatoires* invariably benefit when they enter the universities, from the training received there. While the standard achieved in the *grandes écoles* is exceedingly high, and those who come out at the top of the examination list at the end of the course have a choice to enter directly into, for example, the *inspectorat de finances* (as often happens with graduates of ENA), nevertheless the system 'creams off' the best brains and guides them away from the universities and a possible career in research, and into what are extremely high-powered vocational courses. This means that, however democratic the rest of the system may become, the process will never be complete while the *grandes écoles* maintain their system of selection and, it must be admitted, their high standard, and while they keep themselves totally separate from the rest of higher education. They still may be said to fulfil the role for which they were created, to supply the state with its leaders, both political and administrative, with results at once beneficial perhaps to the planning of the economy, but also harmful to the democratic process.[52] However, the government has made a beginning here to attempt a greater democratization in one *grande école* – the

ENA, where the two decrees (82–819, 27 September 1982, and 83–229, 22 March 1983) provide for an additional *concours interne* for the admission of people aged forty-one (initially thirty-six) who have spent five years as a *fonctionnaire* either for the state, or for a local authority, or some other public body. Yet this can be regarded at present as little more than a gesture of good will, until the degree of viability becomes apparent.

The reign of A. Saunier-Seïté could in certain respects be regarded as a clear indication of the suspicion with which *Loi d'Orientation* was regarded by the right. This suspicion is clearly evidenced in relation to two matters which were both institutional and specifically political. In the first instance, the *Loi Sauvage* (21 July 1980) required an alteration in the *conseils d'université*, so that they had to have, in their representation, 50 per cent of *professeurs titulaires de chaires*, even although this senior category only made up 24 per cent of the university teaching staff. By giving this preponderance to senior academics, it was suggested, the pre-Faure *facultés* were virtually restored in fact (as they still existed by name). Yet the main purpose of the *loi Sauvage* was, in the minister's view, to reduce the degree of marxist influence in the universities. The second problem related to the *Conseil supérieur des corps universitaires* (CSCU) to which A. Saunier-Seïté (decree 15 August 1979) entrusted the task of selecting, via competition (*concours*), those teachers who were to enter a career in higher education. There were many criticisms of this procedure. It was alleged that it failed to select the best candidates, as the use of the *concours* ought to have ensured. It was also felt that new disciplines and new methods were disadvantaged. However, one even graver allegation, that of political bias, was made. Candidates of known leftist sympathies were thought to suffer in terms of their career. It is therefore scarcely surprising that many appeals were made for the suppression of the CSCU.

One other controversial decision taken by the minister concerned Paris VIII – Vincennes, which accepts candidates who are not *bacheliers* but who are at least twenty years old, having been in employment and paid social security contributions for at least two years. If the candidate is over twenty-four, no conditions of entry are made. The idea behind Vincennes, a creation of E. Faure, was to make higher education available to the working classes, who are still underprivileged in this respect (see Table 6.4), with the liberal professions and higher management still taking the lion's share of university places. It had been understood that Vincennes could only occupy its then buildings until 1978 at the latest. Initially, Marne-la-Vallée was to be Paris VIII's new home, but it was thought to be too distant for students in employment. During its Parisian phase, Vincennes was always controversial, for reasons which A. Saunier-Seïté found highly displeasing.

Table 6.4 Evolution of French student population, 1977–81, according to socio-professional category of parents

Catégories socio-professionnelles des parents	1977–8		1978–9		1979–80		1980–1	
	Effectifs	%	Effectifs	%	Effectifs	%	Effectifs	%
Agriculteurs exploitants	36,664	5.1	37,325	5.1	36,619	4.9	35,912	4.8
Salariés agricoles	2,806	0.4	2,692	0.4	2,603	0.4	2,612	0.4
Patrons du commerce et de l'industrie	73,261	10.1	72,735	9.9	71,259	9.6	69,352	9.3
Professions libérales et cadres supérieurs	226,660	31.3	229,075	31.1	232,058	31.3	231,901	31.0
Cadres moyens	117,706	16.3	121,706	16.5	121,638	16.4	124,345	16.6
Employés	61,117	8.4	61,929	8.4	62,431	8.4	61,097	8.2
Ouvriers	86,559	12.0	90,075	12.2	92,132	12.4	91,236	12.2
Personnel de service	5,973	0.8	6,714	0.9	6,769	0.9	7,170	1.0
Autres catégories	43,123	6.0	42,825	5.8	42,061	5.7	46,149	6.2
Sans profession – rentiers	18,612	2.6	19,297	2.6	19,491	2.6	23,488	3.1
Indéterminés	50,396	7.0	52,488	7.1	54,876	7.4	54,060	7.2
Total	722,877	100.0	736,861	100.0	741,937	100.0	742,322	100.0

Source: Commission du Bilan: *la France en Mai 1981*, vol. 4, *l'Enseignement et le développement scientifique*, p. 317

Le nom de Vincennes était associé à tant de faits divers. Dans cette 'cité interdite', le trafic et la consommation de la drogue, les travaux practique de 'sexualité de group', les étudiants illettrés, un diplôme délivré à un cheval, régulièrement inscrit par des farceurs sous le nom qu'il portait sur les champs de course, coexistaient avec des enseignements souvent sérieux et même parfois brilliants. Ils défrayaient la chronique, scandalisant les esprits dits rétrogrades, et émerveillant les esprits supérieurs de Saint-Germain-des-Prés. (A. Saunier-Seïté, *En première ligne*, p. 146, Plon 1982)

On its move to Saint-Denis (Creteil *académie*) Vincennes had to face a reduction of its numbers and a loss of its experiemental role and unconventionality. The numbers (27,000 in 1983) are still less than at the time of removal (32,000); conditions of entry still apply but Vincennes is now much less in the public eye.

These changes, and the spirit in which they were made, have given the impression of a departure from the general line of policy adopted by earlier ministers, from 1968 to 1976.

Elle a rompu, peut-être sans en avoir conscience, avec l'orientation libérale commune à ses prédécesseurs. Plutôt que de prendre appui sur la confiance réciproque entre le ministre et les Universités, elle a préféré recourir à des démonstrations d'autorité . . . Sous sa férule le retour a été rapide à des pratiques peu compatibles avec l'autonomie et fort étrangères à l'inspiration libérale qui avait prévalu depuis 1968. (R. Rémond, *La règle et le consentement*, p. 434)

Since this was the opinion of an undoubted moderate, it was clear that A. Saunier-Seïté's policies would appeal even less to the left. The question was, would the left when in power consider it sufficient to return to the *status quo ante*, or would further reforms be thought desirable? In some specific respects it could be suggested that the present government has endeavoured to return to the spirit, if not the letter of the 1968 legislation. The abrogation of the *loi Sauvage*, together with the abolition of the student quorum (already reduced again to 25 per cent in 1980) show clearly the direction of the government's intentions. The new arrangements to replace the CSCU provide another example. As already mentioned, there had been many requests for its removal, and this was done on 24 August 1982 (decree no. 82–738) when the CSCU was replaced by a *conseil supérieur provisoire des universités*, and subsequently by the CSU (*conseil supérieur des universités*). This body is comprised of a number of sections and sub-sections relating to disciplines, whose members are elected. The task of these sections or sub-sections is essentially to pronounce on candidatures for posts, for which a jury is selected. The jury selects approved candidates and submits these to the appropriate (sub-)section. The *dossiers* of approved candidates are then passed for consideration to a *commission d'établissement et de spécialistes* (CES), who would take into account the views of the *conseil scientifique* and of the candidate's own UER council, before arriving at a decision.

However, if no further steps had been taken by a government committed to a policy of democratization of education, it might be thought that the government was only tinkering with the system. As already mentioned, A. Savary took the view that the *Loi d'Orientation* had not given entire satisfaction. It was therefore proposed to bring in legislation which would revise the *Loi d'Orientation* in the autumn of 1982. Savary set up a commission under the presidency of C. Jeantet to prepare a text. This was not put before the *assemblée nationale* until April 1983, after eighteen months of enquiry and discussion with all interested parties (see *Cahiers de l'éducation nationale* no. 15, May 1983, 'Dossier: Le projet de réforme des enseignements supérieurs, pp. 3 ff.). The bill emphasized the principal concepts underlying Faure's legislation, pluridisciplinarity, participation, and autonomy. The proposal that aroused the greatest controversy however was undoubtedly that of selection. While the desire of the government was to increase the number of students (*bacheliers*) entering university for the DEUG (to be retained in a modified form much more geared to *orientation*), there were some reservations: (1) If the course were specifically vocational (i.e. *classes préparatoires*, IUTs etc.), then selection would be permitted; (2) at the second cycle, the size of the institution and the possibility of jobs at the end of training could affect selection.

Selection is not a thing easily introduced in France, where its supposed absence in the university system ends in the most brutal of all – selection by failure. Since 1968, it has existed in two main forms: (a) the type of *baccalaureat* obtained, category C (mainly scientific) being the one which, overall, is most advantageous for future success in higher education, and (b) the system adopted for a time whereby Parisian universities could only take in the same number of students as they had been allowed in the previous year. The result in 1977 and 1978 was what was caustically, but aptly, named 'la sélection par le sprint'. This was the ultimate absurdity: the government, rather than face up to a political taboo, obliged the Parisian universities to take the first applicants who presented themselves, regardless of suitability, and provincial universities to operate the 'open door' system.

It thus seemed as if Savary were prepared to resolve this problem once and for all. Yet this solution was not satisfactory for the SNESup as it was 'le maintien de procédures de sélection autoritaire', at the second cycle, and the union asked for its rejection (see SNESup document, *Loi sur l'enseignement supérieur*, s.l.n.d., p.iv). For others, notably L. Schwartz, it is the indispensable ingredient which has made, for example, the IUTs so successful (see L. Schwartz, *Pour sauver l'Université*, Seuil, 1983, pp. 46-8). Selection still appears in the text of the final law, but given the hostility it arouses, it is doubtful whether it will be put into effect.

Concern was also felt about the structural organization of decision-making. There was a fear that the unions would take over these structures, particularly in cases where unions imposed voting discipline on their members. Senior academics obviously feared that their voice would be swamped by their younger, more politicized colleagues. (See *Libération*, 8 December 1983; *Point*, 19 December 1983, 'Loi Savary: deux universitaires s'expliquent', pp. 34–5.) (There was undoubtedly also displeasure at the phasing out – in due course – of the prestigious *doctorat d'Etat*, and the maintenance of the *doctorat de troisième cycle*.)

In terms of curriculum too, there were worries about the uniformity required by the bill. Teachers of law felt that their courses could not fit well into the proposed uniform structures. Students too feared for the lowering of their professional qualifications; there were protests, demonstrations, strikes and, in Paris, violence which immediately caused the old fears about May 1968 to rise again. Savary for a time seemed very isolated in his position, but in due course his legislation received its two rather hasty readings form Parliament, has been approved in the main by the *Conseil Constitutionnel*, and has formally been law since 27 January 1984.

The organization of the new universities and UFR are not unlike the Faure structures. The university will be governed by an elected president, with a five-year non-renewable mandate. He, with the aid of his *bureau*, would preside over three elective bodies: (1) *Conseil d'administration* (composed of 40–45 per cent teachers and researchers, 20–30 per cent external personalities, 20–25 per cent students representatives, 10–15 per cent non-academic staff) to decide on university policy, and to vote the budget; (2) *Conseil scientifique*, 50–70 per cent teachers/researchers, 7.5–12.5 per cent students of the *3e cycle*, 10–30 per cent external personalities (who may come from other universities), to attend to matters of research, allocation of money for research etc.; (3) *Conseil des études et de la vie universitaire*, 75–80 per cent researchers and teachers, and students (including *formation continue*) in equal proportions, 10–15 per cent external personalities, with responsibility for *formation continue*, organization and apportioning of teaching courses, and student activities. At UFR level, a similar structure, with an elected director and council, of which 20–50 per cent may be from outside.

In many ways therefore, the mixture is as before, except that the greater emphasis on *formation*, *formation continue* and inter-disciplinarity could be regarded as a possible advance on Faure. Yet the emphasis on vocational training can go too far, and if it is too narrowly oriented, then it will be no more helpful in solving the problem of unemployment than more academic forms of study. There is also a danger that those universities who are prepared to go along with the idea of close co-operation with outside bodies in business and industry (see art. 43) may themselves lose their own identity and run the risk, as now seems to be happening in some British universities, of becoming obsessed by the profit motive over and above longer-term considerations.

If however any success is to be achieved, then further changes (sacrifices might be a better word) will certainly be required of the university academic staff. Some changes are already being implemented, which will be regarded with relative favour or with hostility depending on age, seniority or union affiliation (see *Le Monde*, 1 July 1983). The idea of a single *corps* of teachers has been rejected, probably on grounds of expense, yet in other directions, attempts are being introduced to render the differences between junior and senior less blatant. One such relates to hours of work: *all* teachers, whatever their status, will undertake, in a thirty-two week academic year, 128 lectures or 192 seminars, or 288 hours' practical work, and they have to be spread out over a working week. This bears hardest on the professors, who in the past were required to do three hours' teaching per week in a twenty-five week year. As with many proposals of this kind, it does not take into account the fact that in some disciplines, a seminar may take more preparation and use up more energy than a formal lecture, and it also presupposes that professors will accept the ruling, and not stipulate for what they regard as their prerogative of *cours magistraux*.

The other ruling is closely related to the first, and it concerns residence near the university where a teacher works. There will now be a requirement for university teachers to live within reasonable distance from their place of work. This is a very necessary proviso, if students' work is in the future to be more vocational and if there is to be more guidance for them. It is presumably also intended to deal with that perennial phenomenon, the 'turbo-prof' who, in its most exaggerated form, arrives from Paris at a provincial university early one day, does the required load of teaching in that day, and is not seen again on the premises until the following week. Of course, *dérogations* (exceptions) are allowed, but if *orientation* is to function effectively, then this regulation will have to be strictly applied.

One serious question remains to be raised. If the left is determined to see many more young people attending university, with more contact between staff and students than has hitherto been the case, one of two things must happen: either all teachers will have to be prepared for a much heavier workload, which is doubtful, or the government will have to provide more staff, and more financing; and in view of the ever-increasing budget, it is difficult to see how much farther it can go. Yet if one of these two things is not achieved, the *Loi Savary* could be as unsuccessful as the left consider the *Loi d'Orientation* to have been.

Anything resembling a conclusion in present circumstances is a virtual absurdity. In almost every area of education, reforms are being considered, voted on, or put into practice. From the ideological view-point of the socialist party, some are much more urgent than others. The almost indecent haste with which all this is being done might make the British onlooker forget that M. Mitterrand is in power until 1988! There seems little doubt of the government's sincerity[53] in endeavouring to carry out policies of democratization, decentralization, and autonomy. The motivation for the precipitousness with which it is acting does need more consideration. On the one hand, the government is going through an unpopular period, and if the recession does not right itself, the unpopularity will remain. The danger here for M. Mitterrand and his government is that the *assemblée nationale* will be less co-operative after 1988, in which case all radical policies should be in position by then, and since they have their own logic and cohesion, it might be difficult for an incoming right-wing majority to eradicate them.

Another, more long-term motivation could be the need, as far as possible, not merely to change policies, but to transform attitudes, mentalities and values to fit them. Some of these changes in attitude will, it is hoped, come about by the practice of more participation, responsibility, and democracy in school. Yet added to this there is also to be an ideological, though not a spiritual, content.

The onlooker cannot but be struck with the degree of confidence that this matter has been taken up with by the present government. Under the last administration there seemed to be no confidence as to how the question of values should be treated.[54] It would clearly be naive to assume that because the left won the 1981 election, certainty has returned to society. It could probably be alleged that modern society still has no more than a consensus of uncertainty. Yet the government does seem to have a clear picture of the values it would like society to adopt (see, for example, *Note de service* 26 May 1983, *Sensibilisation des élèves aux problèmes du Tiers-Monde*).

Yet it is not just a question of internationalism which is relevant here. Under the auspices of the *réforme Haby*, geography and history were to be taught together, but also with *instruction civique* added in. Since the implementation of the *réforme Haby*, chronological history has been out of fashion, and it has been replaced by a kind of historical sociology based on the *Annales* school of history. The consequence of this has been that the ignorance of pupils as to 'what happened when' in their own national history is very substantial (see *Le Quotidien de Paris*, 12 November 1983, *IFRES-Sondage*). There were misgivings when this *pédagogie de reveil* was first introduced, and these were voiced more forcefully by eminent historians at a debate organized by *Historia* in May 1980. There were calls for a return to *l'histoire événe-mentielle* from P. Goubert, E. Leroy Ladurie, J. Tulard (see *Historia*, May 1980, pp. 6–9). These misgivings received support from the highest source, the president himself, who proclaimed himself 'scandalisé et angoissé par la perte de la mémoire collective des nouvelles générations' (*Quotidien de Paris*, 31 August 1983). The findings of the *rapport Girault* indicated that one in three *instituteurs* never teach history at primary school, and that in the *collèges* many of the teachers are not trained to teach it at primary level. Therefore, it is suggested that there should be a return to basic knowledge of national and regional history, and that the *collège* is the place where knowledge of other cultures should begin. The *lycée* should help to form an analytical mentality, and extra hours should be given to history in LEP and LT. Teachers should also receive an appropriate training.

This alarm and distress about the teaching of history does have its positive side, in the sense that it has permitted the government to make clear its priorities in the matter. There can be little solidarity amongst citizens if they do not realize why they belong together, and a knowledge of this is indispensable.

Yet there is a darker side to this question, specifically raised by Leroy Ladurie, namely the danger of politicization. The abolition of neutrality within educational establishments has led to politicization, to violence, but also to an impossibility of consensus. There has been of late a disquieting tendency for teachers to give way to partisan feelings at the expense of historical accuracy. The matter came to the fore in 1983 when a number of school textbooks were published for the *terminale* year covering the period 1945–1982. The most flagrant was that produced under the auspices of the PCF by Editions Sociales, entitled *L'Histoire du temps présent, 1939–1982*. Yet in the opinion of J.-F. Revel, more dangerous are the texts which give no indication of their allegiances. Revel concludes 'L'aliénation idéologique d'une grande partie du corps enseignant provoque une décadence de la conscience professionnelle', unthinkable in the 1950s and 1960s, and modern periods of history should not be the object of such textbooks, since there is no consensus on the very recent past (*Midi-Libre*, 29 September 1983 J.-F. Revel, 'Ecole: le nouveau cléricalisme').

It is undoubtedly healthy that these issues have been raised, and it is to be hoped that republican values rather than politicization will prevail. Otherwise, instead of the republicanism of J. Ferry, France will suffer that of *le petit père Combes*, and consensus will be further away than ever.

Notes

Chapter 1

1 Marshall Aid was in effect money transferred by the US government to west European governments, so as to finance the recovery of the western European economies after the war. As such it also served to check the spread of communist and socialist influence in that area.
2 M. Parodi, *L'Economie et la société française de 1945 à 1970*, p. 149.
3 G. Wright, *Rural Revolution in France*, Stanford University Press, 1964, p. 115.
4 The whole episode of collaboration/resistance is equivocal and complex. Many collaborators were executed at the liberation — thirty to forty thousand, according to Robert Aron (*Histoire de la libération*, Fayard, 1959, p. 655). Many others were imprisoned or barred from public life for several years. Some of these were, however, almost certainly innocent; and on the other side of the coin, many whose responsibilities in the crimes of the occupation were undoubtedly great escaped with impunity, sometimes without even having to leave France. As regards the resistance, while the bravery and fortitude of many thousands of authentic resisters is well documented, it is also true that many people only joined in by 1943 or later, when it was fairly clear who was going to win the war and equally plain that a good resistance record would be vital as a passport to success in politics or any other field, once hostilities were over. As can be imagined, this whole episode aroused strong passions and indeed continues to do so — logically enough, given that many of the resistance generation still occupy important positions in French society. No study of life in postwar France can ignore the long-term effects of this phenomenon.
5 Laos and Cambodia were 'associated states', not colonies, which would make it slightly easier for the French to concede independence in 1953. Today's Vietnam was divided into three: Tonkin in the north and Cochin–China in the south were colonies, and Annam was a protectorate.
6 The best overall description and analysis of French politics in this period is P. Viansson-Ponté, *Histoire de la république gaullienne*, 2 vols, 1970, 1971.
7 A good analysis of the politics of the Algerian crisis is D. Pickles, *Algeria and France*, pp. 60–120; for texts of policy statements and

320

documents relating to the Algerian crisis, see the relevant annual volumes of *L'Année politique*, Paris, PUF.

8   A good account of election and referendum campaigns and their results is in P.M. Williams, *French Politicians and Elections, 1951–69*, pp. 94–225; details of all referendum and election campaigns and results are in relevant annual volumes of *L'Année politique*.

9   A good description and analysis of French foreign and defence policies under de Gaulle is in G. de Carmoy, *Les Politiques étrangères de la France, 1944–67*, Paris, La Table Ronde, 1967, pp. 251–503. The English translation, *The Foreign Policies of France, 1944–68*, Chicago University Press, 1970, has the one distinct advantage that it takes the study up to 1968; texts of treaties, policy statements and press conferences referred to in this section on foreign affairs can be found in the relevant annual volumes of *L'Année politique*.

10   A good account of economic affairs in this period is in Parodi, op. cit., pp. 52–78; another brief but perceptive analysis is in J. Sheahan, *An Introduction to the French Economy*, Columbus, Merrill, 1969.

11   For a description of its inadequacies, see P. Seale and M. McConville, *French Revolution, 1968*, pp. 25–6.

12   A. Touraine, *Le Mouvement de mai ou le communisme utopique*, p. 103.

13   Daniel Cohn-Bendit is reported as having castigated the minister over his unwillingness to consider the sexual problems of young people. Missoffe's answer was to advise a cold dip in the swimming-pool. 'C'est une réponse fasciste' was the student reaction. This exchange of amenities made him a 'personality' on the campus.

14   In many accounts of the May events, it is stated that six students from Nanterre were required to appear before the disciplinary council. However the fullest and most authoritative account, L. Rioux and R. Backmann, *L'Explosion de mai*, points out emphatically that eight students and not six were convoked (see p. 91 and p. 94 n.).

15   B.E. Brown suggests that the student revolutionaries had agreed to have their papers checked at the local police stations and were taken away in police vans for that purpose. The bystanders outside the Sorbonne, unaware of this agreement, assumed that the students were being arrested, and the violence began as a result of the apparent provocation (see B.E. Brown, *Protest in Paris: the Anatomy of a Revolt*, p. 9). The then *préfet de police*, M. Grimaud, has stated that this verification of identity at police stations was common police practice (and presumably no one ought to have been surprised by it). See M. Grimaud, *En Mai, fais ce qu'il te plaît*, pp. 15 and 18.

16   On the question of police violence, see the letter from Maurice Grimaud sent to all members of the police force, dated 29 May 1968, in P. Labro *et al.*, *Mai–juin '68: ce n'est qu'un début*. See also Grimaud, op.cit., pp. 200–2, and letters to the editor of *Le Monde*, 7 and 9 May 1968. On the state of mind of the police

during the events of May, see Rioux and Backmann, op.cit., pp. 371–2.

17   See A. Kastler's account in Labro *et al.*, pp. 80–4.
18   Op.cit., p. 156.
19   There also had to be some negotiations with the police, against whom the demonstration was being held. For example, M. Grimaud, in discussions with M. Herzberg, representative of SNESup, prevailed upon the organizers not to have the demonstration pass in front of the Hôtel de Ville, which has always been the traditional goal in every French revolution. Curiously enough, the police were also asked if loud-hailers and the like could be provided for the *service d'ordre*. See Grimaud, op.cit., p. 181.
20   Seale and McConville, op.cit., p. 106.
21   The number of workers on strike during May and June 1968 is difficult to assess. According to J. Gretton, *Students and Workers*, p. 181, the accepted figure is ten million out of a total working population of fourteen million. However, a more likely figure appears to be around six or seven and a half million at the most. See G. Adam, 'Etude statistique des grèves de mai–juin 1968' *Revue française de science politique*, vol. 20, no. 1, February 1970.
22   Gretton (op.cit., p. 194) suggests that not only was the rally at the Charléty stadium much less significant politically than was thought at the time, but also that the presence of Mendès-France made it seem as if the rally was to be used to make political propaganda for him and his party. An expression of this view – a resentful one – can be found in D. Bensaid and H. Weber, *Mai 1968: une répétition générale*, p. 184, where it is further stated that Mendès-France's reception was in fact a very modest one.
23   Figures taken from A. Prost, *L'Enseignement en France, 1800–1967*, Paris, Colin, 1968, p. 461, and *L'Education nationale en chiffres*, Paris, Institut Pédagogique National, 1969, p. 29.
24   Figures taken from D. Singer, *Prelude to Revolution*, p. 52.
25   E. Cahm, *Politics and Society in Contemporary France, 1789–1971*, p. 460.
26   See also the bi-monthly periodical *Dialogue – Groupe Français d'Education nouvelle*.
27   Op. cit., pp. 105–7.
28   See R. Aron, *La Révolution introuvable*.
29   In a poll conducted for the monthly *Lire*, Gallup-Faits et Opinions asked 1006 people aged eighteen or over for their views on May '68. 51 per cent regarded the events as important, 29 per cent as very important, 11 per cent as of little importance, and 3 per cent as of none; 6 per cent had no views. Relations between teachers and pupils were considered as having been greatly influenced by May '68 (76 per cent yes, 13 per cent no, 11 per cent no answer), were relations between parents and children (67 per cent yes, 22 per cent no, 11 per cent no answer), employers and workers (65 per cent yes, 23 per cent no, 12 per cent no answer), State and citizens (59 per cent yes, no 25 per cent, 15 per cent no answer). Opinion

was more equally divided about the influence of May '68 on relations between intellectuals and workers, and between men and women.

30 V. Wright, *The Government and Politics of France*, 2nd edn, London, Hutchinson, 1983, chapters 1-3.

31 Le Monde, *L'Election présidentielle 26 avril-10 mai 1981*, Paris 1981, pp. 3-36.

32 ibid., p. 15.

33 D. Green, 'Economic policy and the governing coalition' in P. Cerny (ed.), *French Politics and Public Policy*, London, Pinter, 1980, pp. 158-76, and 'Individualism versus collectivism: economic choices in France', *West European Politics*, October 1978, pp. 81-96.

34 *Le Monde*, 14 May 1983.

35 The law reduced judges' autonomy by stipulating minimum sentences and forbidding the early release of certain types of offender; it gave increased advantage to the prosecution against the accused by speeding up the early stages of a trial. For a critique see J. Léauté, *Nouvel Observateur*, 21 May 1980.

36 J. Frears, *France in the Giscard Presidency*, London, Allen & Unwin, 1980, chapter 11.

37 *Le Monde, L'Election présidentielle, 26 avril-10 mai 1981*, Paris, 1981, p. 27. Pensioners were in fact subjected to a special tax in 1980 – a gesture which may have cost Giscard dear in 1981.

38 J. Frears, op. cit. p. 157 ff.

39 P. Crisol and Y. Lhomeau, *La Machine RPR*, Paris, Intervalle Fayolle, 1978, p. 43.

40 For the run-in to the campaign see *Projet*, December 1980 and February 1981; *Pouvoirs* 14, 1981, 'Elire un Président'. The results and their aftermath are analysed in *Pouvoirs* 21, 1982, 'La Gauche au pouvoir'; *La Revue politique et parlementaire* 892, mai-juin 1981; *Le Monde, L'Election présidentielle*, op. cit. and *Les Elections législatives de juin 1981; Journal of Area Studies* 4, 1981 and *Projet*, sept. 1981.

41 O. Duhamel and J.-L. Parodi, 'L'évolution des intentions de vote', *Pouvoirs* 18, 1981, pp. 169-84.

42 A. Vernholes, *Le Monde*, 12 May 1983.

43 For a concise account of the nationalizations see J.-P. Gilly, 'Nationalisations: un bilan en demi-teinte', *Projet* 178, oct. 1983, pp. 815-27.

44 M. Duverger, *Le Monde*, 20 July 1981.

45 During this time the deutschmark rose by 25 per cent and the dollar 38 per cent against the franc.

46 P. Petit, 'Defining the new French industrial policy', in S. Williams (ed.) *Socialism in France from Jaurès to Mitterrand*, London, Pinter, 1983, pp. 81-91.

47 F. Bardos, 'Les Fonctionnaires et le pouvoir politique', *Pouvoirs* 21, 1982, pp. 101-14.

48 M. Noblecourt, 'Le pouvoir syndical depuis le 10 mai 1981', *Pouvoirs* 26, 1983, pp. 101-8.

49 P. Avril, 'Le président, le parti et le groupe', *Pouvoirs* 21, 1981, pp. 115–26.

50 M. Beaud in two fine articles (*Le Monde* 30 and 31 December 1982) brings out the difficult context of the socialist experiment: abroad the depressive effects of monetarism, coupled with France's increasing dpenendence on foreign trade, and at home the fact that even modest reforms do tend to secrete corporate and sectional jealousies, even among those who are only slightly better-off than the poorest (e.g. the reactions of skilled manual workers when their pay differentials are squeezed).

Chapter 2

1 The best historical introduction to the French economy is T. Kemp, *Economic Forces in French History*.

2 INSEE, *Tableaux de l'économie française, 1982*, pp. 138 ff.

3 C.P. Kindleberger, 'The French Economy' in S. Hoffmann (ed.), *In Search of France*, pp. 118–59.

4 R.O. Paxton, *Vichy France: Old Guard and New Order*, Barrie & Jenkins, 1972, pp. 330–52.

5 M. Parodi, *L'Economie et la société française de 1945 à 1970*, Colin, 1971, pp. 41 ff.

6 The PME are firms employing from 11 to 249 employees (in commerce) or 11 to 499 employees (in industry). Firms with 10 employees or fewer are usually counted as artisanal – see below.

7 *Fortune*, 10 August 1981, pp. 206 ff.

8 *Nouvel Economiste* 408, 10 October 1983.

9 In December 1977 Giscard d'Estaing announced his objective of a 20 milliard franc surplus for agriculture within France's balance of payments. At the same time he spoke of the 'modernization' necessary to achieve such a result. It is hard to imagine the small farmer fitting readily into such a grand design (*Le Monde*, 18–19 December 1977).

10 Value added is the base of the VAT. It is equivalent to the difference in price between the costs that have gone into the making of a product or service and the sales price of the latter. The GDP of a country could thus be said to be the sum of the value added by the work of its population.

11 Commissariat du Plan, *Emploi dans les services (8e. Plan)*, Paris, Documentation française, 1980.

12 *L'Expansion*, 4–17 December 1983.

13 For readable accounts of the world economy in the 1980s see D. Clerc *et al.*, *La Crise*, Paris, Syros, 1983; B. Sutcliffe, *Hard Times – The World Economy in Turmoil*, London, Pluto, 1983.

14 A census was in fact taken in 1982 but no suitable figures were available at time of writing.

15 The half million artisans in France are of course direct producers of commodities, but own their means of production; hence they can-

not be considered as part of the working class. Their class-situation is closest to that of the small independent peasantry.

16 A medium-sized firm, it will be recalled, employs up to 500 workers.

17 F. Morin, *La Structure financière du capitalisme français*, Paris, Calmann-Lévy, 1974, pp. 92–3.

18 A girl in a typing pool or on a supermarket checkout, for instance, performs a very arduous kind of manual labour. But would either necessarily see herself as part of a 'proletariat' or working class?

19 For a short critique of this type of statistic see A. Wolfelsperger, 'Regard sceptique sur la mesure des inégalités du revenu en France', *Problèmes économiques* 1706, January 1981, pp. 23–7.

20 These figures apply to the mid-1970s, but in the absence of extensive fiscal reform they are unlikely to have altered significantly. They were based on the earnings of male workers only.

21 G. Mathieu, in *L'Année économique et sociale: 1977, la langueur*, Paris, *Le Monde*, 'Dossiers et documents', 1978, p. 120.

22 A. Vernholes, *Le Monde*, 11 December 1972. The proportion of receipts taken in indirect tax in 1981 was still 60 per cent.

23 Mathieu, op.cit., p. 125.

24 F. Parkin, *Class, Inequality and Political Order*, London, Granada, 1972, p. 56.

25 X. Debonneuil and M. Gollac, 'Structure sociale des villes', *Economie et statistique*, 98, March 1978, pp. 51–66.

26 J. Marceau, *Class and Status in France*, Oxford University Press, 1977, p. 62.

27 Ideology: a system of beliefs and values, common to a class or group, which enables it to identify itself and situate itself in relation to other segments of society.

28 *Notable*: during the July Monarchy the term designated the few thousand property-holders who formed the political class. They had a strong local base, plus influence in Paris. Nowadays the term refers more loosely to anyone well placed in local affairs (mayor, *conseiller général*, etc.) or in a party machine.

29 Problematic: a *series* of questions, some of them apparently disparate, but in fact linked by an underlying (and implicit) set of assumptions. This determines the way in which the questions are put.

30 V. Wright, *The Government and Politics of France*, London, Hutchinson, 1978, pp. 173–212; H. Machin, *The Prefect in French Public Administration*, London, Croom Helm, 1977.

31 S. Hoffmann, 'Paradoxes of the French Political Community' in *In Search of France*.

32 M. Crozier, *Société bloquée*.

Chapter 3

1 It could also be asserted that the régime of Marshal Pétain fitted likewise into the authoritarian tradition of France. However, the

influence of the fascist dictatorships also had a role to play here; furthermore, there was no pretence at any kind of popular consultation.

2   Jean Casimir–Périer in 1895; Alexandre Millerand in 1924.

3   Vincent Wright, *The Government and Politics of France*, London, Hutchinson, 2nd edn, 1983, p. 129.

4   The uproar over this decision stemmed from the fact that there was an article (no. 89) which provided for constitutional reforms. It stated that a proposed revision should be passed in identical terms by the two legislative bodies, and only thereafter put to referendum. Another method required that the two houses of parliament in a congress should vote on proposed changes, when a three-fifths majority was necessary for the reform to become law. No referendum was necessary in this case. The proposed election of the president of the republic by universal suffrage was put to referendum according to article 11 of the constitution, which allowed a referendum to be called on 'tout projet de loi portant sur l'organisation des pouvoirs publics'. It must be admitted that this interpretation of article 11 is not wholly unjustifiable, but in that case article 89 seems to be totally superfluous. At all events, the *conseil constitutionnel*, when asked to pronounce on the constitutional propriety of de Gaulle's decision, alleged that it was not competent to do so.

5   During his electoral campaign of 1974, V. Giscard d'Estaing announced that he would endeavour to change the regulations concerning *suppléants*, so that representatives should have the right to take up their seats on leaving the ministry if they so desired. The two attempts made in this direction have met with no success, the last one having been quashed by the *conseil constitutionnel* (see *Le Monde* of 27–28 May, 16 June and 7 July 1977).

6   M. Debré and J.-L. Debré, *Le Pouvoir politique*, pp. 30–1.

7   See the following editions of *Le Monde* for these exchanges: Debré–de Gaulle, 12 July 1962; Pompidou–de Gaulle, 12 July 1968; Chaban-Delmas–Pompidou, 7 July 1972; Chirac–Giscard d'Estaing, 27 August 1976.

8   P. Mendès-France, interviewed by I. Allier and J. Julliard in *Nouvel Observateur*, no. 695, 4 March 1978.

9   See J.-L. Debré, *La Constitution de la Ve République*, pp. 17–19.

10 R. Pleven described the narrow interpretation of article 40 as 'talmudique'. He cited an example where a proposal inviting the government to ratify an international convention (on the increased repression of prostitution) was deemed unacceptable, on the grounds that it would have brought about an increase in police expenditure! See *Journal officiel*, Débats, 29 May 1959.

11 The Chirac government contained 24.32 per cent of ministers without a previous career in parliament, and 75.67 per cent of ministers who were deputies or senators at the time of their appointment. This compares with the overall percentage from January 1959 to June 1974: 23.5 per cent non-parliamentarians, 76.5 per cent parliamentarians. For further details and statistics, see P.

Antoni and J.-D. Antoni, *Les Ministres de la Ve République.*
Pierre Mauroy continued this tradition by including in his first two
ministries well over 25 per cent of non-parliamentarians, some in
very influential posts. See J. Hayward, *Governing France: the one
and indivisible Republic*, 2nd edn, 1983, London, Weidenfeld &
Nicholson, p. 112; P. Avril and J. Gicquel, *Chroniques constitution-
nelles françaises 1976-1982*, Paris, PUF, pp. 302-3.

12 See F. Giroud, *La Comédie du pouvoir*, Paris, Fayard, 1977,
pp. 25-34.

13 J. Hayward, op. cit., p. 175.

14 See J. Chevallier, *La Radio — télévision entre deux réformes*, Paris
LGDJ, 1973, p. 319.

15 J. Whale, *The Politics of the Media*, Glasgow, Fontana, 1977, p. 122.

16 A good guide to local finances is in *Pouvoirs* 23, 1982, 'L'Impôt'.

17 P. Richard and M. Cotten, *Les Communes françaises d'aujourd'hui*,
Paris, PUF, 1983, p. 81.

18 Cf. K. Newton, *Balancing the Books*, London, Sage, 1980.

19 J.-L. Parodi, *Le Monde*, 3-4 April, 1983.

20 Full coverage of the municipal elections is in *Le Monde, Les
Elections municipales de mars 1983*, Paris, 1983, where the full
complexities of the electoral law are amply illustrated. See also
D. Bell and B. Criddle, 'The French municipal elections of March
1983', *Parliamentary Affairs* 36,3, Summer 1983, pp. 146-57.

21 J. Hayward, *Governing France: The One and Indivisible Republic*,
London, Weidenfeld & Nicholson, 1983, p. 21.

22 Y. Mény, 'Crises, régions et modernisation de l'Etat', *Pouvoirs* 19,
1981, pp. 6-18.

23 J. Hayward, 'Incorporer la périphérie: l'essor et la chute de la
régionalisation fonctionnelle en France', ibid. pp. 103-18.

24 P. Sadran, 'Les Socialistes et la région', ibid. pp. 139-49.

25 *Cumul des mandats* is holding local and national office simultaneously (e.g. *député-maire* or *sénateur-conseiller général*, to name
two of the simpler combinations); guaranteeing access to important
people in Paris as it does it is plainly a key element in the power of
notables. The Debarge report of 1982 suggested some modest
limitations to this practice; see D. Ashford, 'Reconstructing the
French Etat — the Progress of the Loi Defferre', *West European
Politics*, Summer 1983, pp. 203-10.

26 V. Wright, 'Questions d'un jacobin anglias', *Pouvoirs*, op. cit.
pp. 119-30.

27 On Corsica see *Le Monde*, 12-13 June 1983, and P. Hainsworth,
'Corsica: the Regional Assembly Elections of 1982', *West European Politics* VI, 2, April 1983, pp. 15-17.

Chapter 4

1 C. Ysmal, 'La résistible ascension du RPR', *Projet* 178, September
1983, pp. 105-14. The membership statistics are in *Le Monde*,
8 November 1983.

2   P. Crisol and Y. Lhomeau, *La Macine RPR*, p. 187.
3   C. Ysmal, op cit.
4   J.-P. Soisson (ed.), *Le Parti républicain*, p. 31
5   C. Ysmal, 'Le chemin difficile du PR', *Projet* 118, September–October 1977.
6   A. Campana, *L'Argent secret: le financement des partis politiques*, p. 60.
7   *Le Matin, Dossier des législatives 1978*, Paris, 1978, pp. 32–3.
8   Y. Roucaute, *Le Parti socialiste*, Paris, Bruno Huisman, 1983, pp. 132 ff.
9   H. Portelli, 'La présidentialisation des partis français', *Pouvoirs* 14, 1980, pp. 97–106.
10 P. Hardouin, 'Les caractéristiques sociologiques du PS', *Revue française de science politique*, XXVIII, 2, April 1978, pp. 220–56.
11 N. Nugent and D. Lowe, *The Left in France*, London, Macmillan, 1981, pp. 139–40.
12 A. Rollat, *Le Monde*, 7 and 8 October 1983.
13 Though they may sometimes be party members; some leaders of GRECE (*Groupe de recherches et d'études sur la civilisation européenne*) are in RPR. On new right ideology see M. Vaughan, 'Nouvelle Droite: cultural power and political influence' in D. Bell (ed.), *Contemporary French Political Parties*, London, Croom Helm, 1981.
14 *récupéré* (lit. 'salvaged'): term used to describe the process whereby concepts are taken over from ther originators, losing their radical quality.
15 J. Howorth, 'The French CP and class alliances' in D. Bell (ed.), op. cit., pp. 89–108.
16 G. Lavau, *A quoi sert le PCF?*, Paris, Fayard, 1981, pp. 414 ff.
17 V. Wright, *The Government and Politics of France*, London, Hutchinson 1983, 2nd edn, pp. 219 ff.
18 *Le Matin*, 4–5 September 1983; *Intersocial* 86, December 1982.
19 P. Martin, 'Les élections prudhomales de décembre 1982', *Pouvoirs* 26, 1983, pp. 125–32.
20 G. Ross, *Workers and Communists*, Berkeley, California University Press, 1982.
21 B. Brizay, *Le Patronat*, Seuil, 1975, pp. 243–4.
22 *Intersocial* 83, August–September 1982.
23 P. Pineau, 'Les artisans-commerçants et la nouvelle politique', *Eglise aujourd'hui* 433, December 1981, pp. 585–97.
24 F. Gresle, 'Les petits patrons et la tentation activiste' in G. Lavau *et al.* (eds), *L'Univers politique des classes moyennes*, Paris, FNSP, 1983, pp. 293–308.
25 R. Mouriaux, 'La résistance à l'éclatement: le cas de la CGC', in *L'Univers politique*, op. cit. pp. 313–25.
26 J. Keeler, 'Corporatism and official hegemony: the case of French agricultural syndicalism' in S. Berger (ed.), *Organizing Interests in Western Europe*, Cambridge University Press, 1981, pp. 185–208.
27 *Nouvel Economiste* 302, 14 September 1981.

Chapter 5

1 When asked in November 1981 where they wished to stand in East-West relations, French preferences were 30 per cent for US, 3 per cent for USSR, and 58 per cent for neutrality (corresponding British figures were 43 per cent, 1 per cent and 46 per cent) *Gallup Report 1982*, p. 107; when asked in October 1980 how much they trusted various nationalities, French respondents ranked peoples thus: French 81 per cent, Belgians 75 per cent, Swiss and Luxemburgers 65 per cent, Germans 60 per cent, British 53 per cent, Americans 52 per cent, Greeks 44 per cent, Italians 43 per cent, Japanese 38 per cent, Chinese 33 per cent, Russians 21 per cent (corresponding British ranking was: British 85 per cent, Swiss 72 per cent, Dutch 71 per cent, Americans 70 per cent, Danes 66 per cent, Germans 60 per cent, Belgians 55 per cent, Chinese and Japanese 41 per cent, Italians 39 per cent, Greeks 37 per cent, French 32 per cent, Russians 18 per cent) *Gallup Report 1981*, p.90; these are interesting indicators of French and British differences in East-West commitment, national confidence and mutual antagonism.
2 ibid., vol. 1, p. 1.
3 The various aspects of independence, and interpretations of French policy, are discussed in N. Waites, 'French foreign policy: external influences on the quest for independence', *Review of International Studies*, vol. 9, no. 4, October 1983, pp. 251–64.
4 De Gaulle, op. cit., vol. 1, p. 1.
5 Televised broadcast by de Gaulle, 27 April 1965, printed in *L'Année politique, 1965*, pp. 431–2.
6 K.J. Holsti, *International Politics: a framework for analysis*, pp. 83–96; see also J. Frankel, *National Interest*, London, Macmillan, 1970, pp. 70–1.
7 R. Aron, *Paix et guerre entre les nations*, Paris, Calmann-Lévy, 1962, pp. 730–4; and *La République impériale*, Paris, Calmann-Lévy, 1973, pp. 323–8.
8 R.O. Keohane and J.S. Nye, *Power and Interdependence*, Boston, Little, Brown, 1977, pp. 140–3.
9 K. N. Waltz, *Theory of International Politics* (Reading, USA, 1979) p. 149–50; it has been argued that de Gaulle's policy was so clearly utopian that it was really intended for domestic impact, to create a political consensus on a moral role in the world and thereby to strengthen support for Gaullism in France, P. G. Cerny, *The Politics of Grandeur* (Cambridge, 1980) pp. 89–90.
10 I. Wallerstein, *The Capitalist World Economy* (Cambridge, 1979); the probability of a redistribution of power is also discussed in J.-B. Duroselle, *Tout empire périra* (Publications de la Sorbonne, 1981) pp. 340–8.
11 An analysis of the evoltuion of attitudes to the EEC on the French left (and interesting comparison with the British left) is in M. Newman, *Socialism and European Unity* (Junction Books, 1983).
12 The structure of French aid changed from 60.5 per cent public and

39.5 per cent private in 1966 to 45 per cent public and 55 per cent private by 1976, and the private aid consisted by then of 51 per cent export credits, 39 per cent banking loans and only 8.3 per cent direct investment, *Le Monde diplomatique*, November 1978.

13　G. de Carmoy, 'The last year of de Gaulle's foreign policy', *International Affairs*, vol. 45, no. 3, July 1969, pp. 424–35.

14　These interpretations are based on the following: G. M. Lyons, 'Expanding the study of international relations: the French connection', in *World Politics*, October 1982, pp. 135–49; M. Merle, 'Sur la "problématique" de l'étude des relations internationales en France', in *La Revue française de sciences politiques*, June 1983, pp. 403–27; S. D. Krasner, 'Third World vulnerabilities and global negotiations', in *Review of International Studies*, October 1983, pp. 235–49; Wallerstein, op. cit.

15　G. Pompidou, press conference in Paris 2 July 1970, taken from P.-B. Cousté and F. Visine, *Pompidou et l'Europe*, Paris, Librairies techniques, 1974, pp. 108–12.

16　G. Pompidou, press conference 27 September 1973, *L'Année politique 1973*.

17　V. Giscard d'Estaing, television interview printed in *Le Monde*, 22–3 December 1974, providing perhaps the best indication of the philosophy of *mondialisme*; see also J. François-Poncet, 'Diplomatie française: quel cadre conceptuel?', in *Politique internationale*, no. 6, 1980.

18　'Le Commerce extérieur de la France', *Le Monde*, dossiers et documents no. 101, May 1983; H. Bourguinat noted that France's foreign debt stood at 53 billion dollars at the beginning of 1984 and it represented over 10 per cent of GNP, probably requiring net repayments of 8 billion dollars per annum over four years and smaller sums for many more years; other economists noted that the trade balance was favourable from August 1983 and good prospects for 1984 might make debt repayments easier, *Le Monde*, 17 January 1984, pp. 17–20.

19　Mitterrand's views are in his book *Ici et maintenant*, Fayard, 1980, pp. 234 ff., and in his television interview 16 November 1983, *Le Monde*, 18 November 1983, pp. 7–8; Cheysson's views are in *Politique internationale*, Summer, 1983, and Club de la presse, Europe I, 9 October 1983.

20　M.-C. Smouts, 'The external policy of François Mitterrand', in *International Affairs*, Spring 1983, pp. 155–67.

21　For PS views see P.-M. de La Gorce, 'Les Socialistes français et les choix de politique extérieure', in *Le Monde Diplomatique*, October 1983, pp. 10–11; analysis of the PS-PC accord is in *Le Monde*, 1 and 2 December 1983; analysis of opposition views is in *Le Monde*, 7–12 December 1983; Chirac's visit to Germany is recorded in *Le Monde*, 19–21, 28 October 1983.

22　Barre had first-hand appreciation of the extent of French interests to be defended through visits to his residence in Réunion.

23　A useful analogy is with football where the role of the 'sweeper' is not integrated and can be combined with that of a 'libero' to turn defence into attack.

24 S. Cohen, 'Les hommes de l'Elysée', in *Pouvoirs*, no. 20, 1981, pp. 87–100; S. Cohen, 'Prospective et politique étrangère: le Centre d'Analyse et de Prévision du ministère des relations extérieures', in *Revue française de science politique*, December 1982, pp. 1055–76; Z. Steiner (ed.), *The Times Survey of Foreign Ministries of the World*, London, Times Books, 1982, pp. 203–23; the difficulty of assessing influences on policy is illustrated by this last work where Georges Dethan from the Quai d'Orsay includes the *Centre d'Analyse et de Prévision* on his organigram but excludes it from his text, whereas Cohen ascribes significant influence to it.

25 The British had particular difficulties over this, when trying for example to account for Mitterrand's rejection of EEC proposals in Brussels in March 1982 and in Athens in December 1983 after his ministers had apparently given their approval.

26 *Journal officiel, débats parlementaires, assemblée nationale*, séance du Lundi 16 Mai 1983, pp. 1074–1125; see also discussion in *Le Monde*, 13–14 September 1981, and interview with Hernu in *Le Monde*, 22 April 1983, pp. 1, 6–7.

27 These and subsequent details of French forces are taken mainly from *The Military Balance, 1983–4*, London, International Institute for Strategic Studies, 1983, pp. 31–4.

28 *Rapport fait au nom de la Commission de la Défense Nationale et des Forces Armées sur . . . la programmation militaire . . . 1984–8*, par L. Tinseau, Assemblée Nationale, no. 1485, 18 May 1983, Première Partie, pp. 5–28; F. de Rose, 'La Politique de défense du Président Giscard d'Estaing', Colloque sur la Politique extérieure de Valery Giscard d'Estaing, Fondation nationale des sciences politiques, 26–7 May 1983, (forthcoming publication 1984).

29 *Rapport*, op. cit., p. 16.

30 J. Klein, 'Commerce des armes et politique: le cas français', in *Politique étrangère*, no. 6, 1976, pp. 563–85; E. A. Kolodziej, 'French arms trade: the economic determinants', in *SIPRI Yearbook 1983*, pp. 371–90; further indications are given by J. Isnard in *Le Monde*, 13 October 1983, pp. 1, 6.

31 R. Aron, *The Great Debate: theories of nuclear strategy*, pp. 135–43; cf. also W.L. Kohl, *French Nuclear Diplomacy*, pp. 169–77; also L. Ruehl, *La Politique militaire de la Ve République*, pp. 158–89.

32 For Communist views see Y. Roucaute, *Le PCF et l'armée*, PUF, 1983; also N. Gnesotto, 'Le PCF et les euromissiles', in *Politique étrangère*, no. 3, 1983; for the evolution of Socialist views see C. Hernu, *Soldat-Citoyen* and P. Krop, *Les Socialistes et l'armée*, PUF, 1983; for Giscardian views see M. Tatu, 'Giscard d'Estaing et la détente', Colloque, 26–7 May 1983, Fondation nationale des sciences politiques; for Gaullist views see F. Valentin, *Une Politique de défense pour la France*, Calmann-Lévy, 1980.

33 Mitterrand visited Germany 19 July 1983, and Chirac went 17 October 1983; for analyses of the euromissile crisis see H. C. d'Encausse and F. de Rose (eds) *Après la détente*, Hachette,

Collection pluriel, 1982; P. Lellouche, *Pacifisme et dissuasion*, Institut Français de Relations Internationales, 1983; P. Chilton and J. Howorth (eds), *Defence and Dissent in France* (Croom Helm, 1984).

34 F. Lewis, article in *International Herald Tribune*, 25 February 1978; cf. also *Le Monde* article, 18 July 1978.

35 L. Mandeville, J.-L. Loubet del Bayle and A. Picard, 'Les forces de maintien de l'ordre en France', *Défense nationale*, July 1977, pp. 59–76.

36 *Le Monde*, 6, 7, 12–27, 29, 30–1 October, 2 November 1983; for a useful account of the French secret service, see *Middle East*, August 1981, pp. 32–6, and February 1982, pp. 11–12.

37 The text of the memorandum was published, not at the time but long after de Gaulle's death, in *Espoir* (review of the *Institut Charles de Gaulle*), no. 15, June 1976, together with a commentary by Couve de Murville, the French foreign minister in 1958.

38 See J. Newhouse, *De Gaulle and the Anglo-Saxons*, p. 129.

39 F.C. Bergsten and L.B. Krause (eds), *World Politics and International Economics*, Washington DC, Brookings Institution, 1975, pp. 50–51, 184, 192.

40 R.O. Keohane and J.S. Nye, *Power and Interdependence*, pp. 84–6.

41 Details of the agreement were meant to be secret, but the West German chancellor, Schmidt, leaked them to American journalists on 16 July. See *L'Année politique, 1976*, pp. 234–5.

42 This interpretation is discussed by C. Zorgbibe, 'François Mitterrand, champion de l'Occident ou dissident virtuel?', in *Politique internationale*, Autumn 1981; but a different view is taken by M.-C. Smouts, op. cit., *International Affairs*, Spring 1983.

43 For the economic co-operation agreement with the Soviet Union see *Financial Times*, 4 February 1984, p. 2.

44 Report in *Guardian*, 31 October 1978, p. 7.

45 L. Dollot, *Les Relations culturelles internationales*, Paris, PUF, 1968, pp. 36–60.

46 M. McQueen, *Britain, the EEC and the Developing World*, London, Heinemann, 1977, pp. 48–54.

47 M. Sauldie, 'France's military intervention in Africa', *Africa*, no. 77, January 1978, pp. 43–9.

48 Général Méry, Conférence à l'Institut des Hautes Etudes de Défense Nationale et au Centre des Hautes Etudes de l'Armement, 3 April 1978, printed in *Défense nationale*, June 1978, pp. 17–42.

49 See J.-P. Cot, 'La France et l'Afrique: quel changement?', in *Politique internationale*, no. 18, Winter 1982–83, pp. 9–21, S. Turquié, 'Les Objectifs de la politique française dans la crise du Liban', in *Le Monde Diplomatique*, January 1979, pp. 9–10.

Chapter 6

1 *Education, Culture and Politics in Modern France*, Oxford, Pergamon, 1976, p. vii.

Notes to pages 258-63 333

2 For more detailed statistics, see A. Trognon, *L'Equipement des ménages en biens durables au début de 1977*, Paris, INSEE, coll. M61, 1978, pp. 28–29 and Ministère de la culture et de l'environnement, *Annuaire statistique de la culture: données de 1970 à 1974*, Paris, Documentation française, 1977, pp. 62–4, also Ministère de la culture – Service des études et des recherches, *Pratiques culturelles des Français, Description socio-démographique – Evolution 1973-1981*, Paris, Dalloz, 1982, pp. 13, 35–7.

3 See C. Baudelot and R. Establet, *L'Ecole capitaliste en France*.

4 See P. Bourdieu and J.-C. Passeron, *La Réproduction*.

5 Article 4 of the decree of 17 March 1808 stated that there should be as many *académies* as there were *cours d'appel*, i.e. twenty-nine. Yet the list of *académies* in the text of the decree mentions twenty-seven in all.

6 The limitations of this 'liberalizing measure' are clearly illustrated by the references made to the financing of faculty library facilities: 'La bibliothèque universitaire est et reste un service commun par excellence. Elle n'est pas plus la bibliothèque de telle Faculté que de telle autre. Elle est la bibliothèque du corps universitaire. Mais, si elle a en soi une individualité incontestable, elle n'a pas la personnalité civile. Il était donc impossible de lui constituer, comme à chaque Faculté prise à part, un budget particulier . . .', *Bulletin administratif du ministère de l'instruction publique*, vol. 47, Paris, Imprimerie Nationale, 1890, p. 246.

7 Here too the same type of limitation prevails; article 4 indicates very precisely what financial resources come to the universities and what the latter may do with them. 'A dater du 1er janvier 1898, il sera fait recette, au budget de chaque Université, des droits d'études, d'inscription, de bibliothèque et de travaux pratiques acquittés par les étudiants conformément aux règlements. Les ressources provenant de ces recettes ne pourront être affectées qu'aux objets suivants: dépenses des laboratoires, bibliothèques et collections; construction et entretien des bâtiments; création de nouveaux enseignements; œuvres dans l'intérêt des étudiants. Les droits d'examen, de certificat d'aptitude, de diplôme ou de visa acquittés par les aspirants aux grades et titres prévus par les lois, ainsi que les droits de dispense et d'équivalence, continueront d'être perçus au profit du Trésor' (A. de Beauchamp, *Lois et règlements sur l'enseignement supérieur* (5 vols), Paris, Delalain frères, 1880–98, vol. 5, p. 591).

8 G. Vedel, 'Les exigences du service public' in AUPEL, *Pour que l'Université ne meure*, Paris, Le Centurion, 1977, p. 31.

9 P. Seale and M. McConville, *French Revolution, 1968*, Penguin, 1968, p. 27.

10 See P. Bourdieu and J.-C. Passeron, *Les Héritiers*, pp. 48–58.

11 E. Faure, *L'éducation nationale et la participation*, p. 18.

12 R. Drago however suggests that a separate ministry for higher education 'restera la solution la plus intéressante et la plus efficace pour résoudre les problèmes administratifs de l'enseignement au niveau central'. See his contribution 'L'Administration de l'enseignement de 1945 à 1980', in the collective work by P. Bousquet and

others, *Histoire de l'administration de l'enseignement en France 1789–1981*, Paris and Geneva, Champion and Droz, 1983, p. 141.

13 Although the 1944 Education Act gave to the British minister of education wide powers which are apparently increasing (see W.O. Lester-Smith, *Government of Education* (rev. ed.), Penguin, 1971, pp. 133–7), these are limited by comparison with those of the French minister. For a description of the British education minister's powers see Edward Boyle and Anthony Crosland in conversation with M. Kogan, *The Politics of Education*, Penguin, 1974, pp. 124–8, 159–60.

14 In the two liberalizing reports on the *collèges* (Legrand), and on the *lycées* (Prost), a fixed number of classes per week is still proposed (although with greater room for manoeuvre).

15 The hours per week required of teachers are as follows: fifteen for *agrégés*, eighteen for *certifiés*, twenty-one for PEGC (see below). For *instituteurs*, the *Rapport Legrand* (p. 121) states the figure to be twenty-four hours, but in answer to a query made at the *centre de documentation* of the education ministry, the writer was told that *instituteurs* should not undertake more than thirty hours per week, and that the customary workload is at least twenty-seven hours.

16 The SNI-PEGC showed hostility to the proposal made by J.-M. Schléret, president of the parents association PEEP (*Fédération des parents d'élèves de l'enseignement public*), that school textbooks should in future be selected by the *conseils d'école*. This suggestion was regarded by the union as gross interference, and as a slight on the professional competence of teachers. It seems here as if paranoia is not far below the surface: while the SNI-PEGC claims to be in favour of genuine *ouverture*, it is opposed to the extension of the powers of the *conseils d'école* as organized by R. Haby and his successor C. Beullac, either of whom 'remettait en cause la responsabilité de l'enseignant'.

17 There are undoubtedly still a number of *universitaires* who would prefer a centralized university system. One distinguished example is that of the historian R. Mousnier. See his article 'Les universités de demain' in *Le Figaro*, 10 January 1984. There are also others, who by dint of having lived under the pre-1968 centralized system, still unconsciously yearn for it. See R. Rémond, *La Règle et le consentement*, Paris, Fayard, 1979, p. 187.

18 ed. A. Dansette, Paris, Flammarion, 1969.

19 See J. Godechot, *Les Institutions de la France sous la révolution et l'empire* (2nd ed.), Paris, PUF, 1968, pp. 735–6.

20 The following statistics are given by R.D. Anderson, in *Education in France, 1848–70*, Oxford, OUP, 1975, p. 112. In 1850, the Catholic teaching orders ran a total of 10,312 primary schools (public and private); by 1863, this had risen to 17,206. In 1850, the teaching orders taught at primary level 15 per cent of all boys, 45 per cent of all girls; in 1863, 22 and 54 per cent respectively. Over all, 1,600,000 pupils attended Catholic schools in 1863 (see

E. Cahm, *Politics and Society in Contemporary France*, London, Harrap, 1972, p. 521).

21 See A. Prost, *L'Enseignement en France, 1808–1967*, pp. 172–89.

22 See on this question, A. Werth, *France, 1940–1955*, London, Robert Hale, 1956, pp. 57–65.

23 For greater detail, see W.R. Fraser, *Reforms and Restraints in Modern French Education*, London, Routledge & Kegan Paul, 1971, p. 63.

24 See Fraser, op.cit., p. 69.

25 *Programme commun de gouvernement* (préf. G. Marchais), Paris, 1973, p. 77.

26 This is a practice which has reappeared since 1981 – doubtless in the hope of changes to come. Since the passing of the legislation of 1982–3 on decentralization, there appears to be a doubt as to whether local authorities can be required by law to pay subsidies to private schools. See: *Le Monde*, 18 February and 3 March 1982; 25 and 30 August 1983; *Libération*, 12 December 1983, *Le Figaro*, 26 December 1983.

27 J. Andrieu has taken over the leadership of the FCPE from J. Cornec; J. Pommatau is now *secrétaire-général* of the FEN, replacing A. Henry, for a time *ministre du Temps libre*.

28 Even in 1977, R. Rémond dissented from this view. See his article 'L'anti-cléricalisme n'est pas mort', *Projet*, September-October 1977. Such an opinion seemed borne out by the hostility of observations made on the presence of Giscard d'Estaing, the government, and the presidents of the houses of Parliament at a religous service held on 11 November 1977, to commemorate France's war dead. See P. Avril and J. Gicquel, 'Chronique constitutionnelle française', in *Pouvoirs*, no. 4, 1978.

29 In 1958, 36 per cent of the French attended mass each Sunday, by 1968 the figure was down to 26 per cent, and in 1977 to 17 per cent. See C. Peyrefitte, 'Les Choix de 1981 – Contrastes du catholicisme', in *Faire*, no. 62, December 1981, pp. 47–51.

30 See *L'Education nationale en chiffres – année scolaire 1981–1982*, SIGES, Paris, October 1983, p. 7.

31 The party political undertones of this issue may account for the illiberal tendencies displayed at times by both sides, who each claim to speak in the name of freedom of thought. In fairness it should be said that there is an ambiguity in the French political tradition, since the republic is *laïque* (see Constitution, article 2), and the *Déclaration des droits de l'homme et du citoyen* states (article 10) that 'nul ne doit être inquiété pour ses opinions, même religieuses'. See on this point P. Arrighi, 'A l'université, les élections et l'avenir de l'école libre', *Revue des deux mondes*, March 1978, pp. 662–3.

There is no doubt that the left would be happy to see the end of private education as such; the CPG of 1972 refers to the absorption of subsidized and, eventually, unsubsidized schools into the national system (*Programme commun de gouvernement*, p. 77).

It is also the case that at least some partisans of Catholic education are equally happy to prevent the existence of state schools where possible. An example of this is the small town of Plogonnec (Finistère), where a state primary school was opened only in 1976 in the face of strong Catholic opposition, including apparently, G. Guermeur himself. See *Le Nouvel Observateur*, no. 620, 27 September–3 October 1976.

32   No apology is made for using this term, which is exemplified by the violence of sentiment expressed by J. Andrieu (at present leader not only of FCPE but also of CNAL) in his opposition to Savary's proposals of October 1983. 'Décidément, tout porte à croire qu'on n'est jamais *trahi* [my italics] que par les siens.' *Pour l'Enfant . . . vers l'Homme*, November–December 1983. One slightly ridiculous example is that of A. Laignel, *maire* and PS deputy of Issoudun, who is insisting on putting up in the town warning signs *Attention Ecole Privée* (instead of the more usual *Attention Ecole*). (See *Le Quotidien de Paris*, 26 December 1983).

33   See Anderson, op. cit., p. 31.

34   M. Chavardès, *Un Ministre éducateur: Jean Zay*, Paris, SEVPEN, 1965, p. 43.

35   The FEN has always accorded great respect to the report, and has reprinted it four times, the latest impression being included in the supplement *L'Ecole de l'éducation permanente* to *FEN-Informations* of 16 February 1977. A. Prost (op. cit., p. 420) writes of the 'référence liturgique' constituted by the report for supporters for a more democratic education system, and of its 'prestige quasi sacral'.

36   See R. Billères, 'Exposé des motifs' in the supplement to *L'Education nationale*, no. 35, 13 December 1956, p. 135.

37   Fraser, op. cit., p. 127.

38   Initially there was one other section – classical (*lycée*-type) – which no longer obtains.

39   Paris, Fayard, 1976, pp. 65–6.

40   Criticisms of the present education system do not have to be of a specifically political nature, and in many ways, they are far more convincing when they are not. See M. T. Maschino, *Vos Enfants ne m'intéressent plus*, Hachette, Paris, 1983.

41   The difficulty for any education minister ever to satisfy the teaching unions, particularly in hard times, and even when the education budget continues to be the first budget of the state, is exemplified by the article of G. Dessieux in *FEN-Informations*, no. 24, November 1982, 'Education: *des efforts*, peut mieux faire'.

42   See *Le Monde*, 5 October 1983, and Ministère de l'éducation nationale, *Projet de Loi de Finances pour 1984 . . . "budget de programmes"*, Paris, Imprimerie nationale, 1983, p. 12.

43   These can be essentially of three kinds: (1) multi-disciplinary activities to make class work less abstract, and more practical, using a range of teaching methods as well as local resources; (2) cultural and educational activities out of school hours, such as the establish-

ing and running of clubs, which could take place in the school or elsewhere; (3) proposals made by the pupils themselves of improvements which they could make in the conditions of school work, on a practical level.

44 O. Guichard, *Un chemin tranquille*, Paris, Flammanon, 1975, p. 137.

45 Faure, op.cit., p. 29.

46 There is little doubt that E. Faure's radical intentions provoked some alarm among the more conservative Gaullists, and that his reform might never have been realized but for de Gaulle's continued support. As a sop to conservative opinion, a Gaullist deputy was appointed *secrétaire d'état*, but during his term of office was allowed virtually no areas of responsibility which had not previously been approved by Faure himself.

47 It also explains the comment made by Savary in his speech of 17 September 1981, which, taken out of context, might be interpreted as implying that the radical changes attempted by the *Loi d'Orientation* had failed completely: 'Le centralisme autoritaire doit maintenant faire place à l'autonomie et à la démocratie' (*Principales déclarations de M. Alain Savary*, p. 23).

48 Halls, op. cit., p. 211.

49 Apart from the fact that the vocational training provided in the DUT may seem more immediately usable than the DEUG, which tends to be regarded as a mere half-way stage in terms of academic qualification, there is another factor to be taken into account. The DUT benefits from its recognition by *conventions collectives* between the *patronat* and the *syndicats*. The DUT thus has an immediate value on the job market, which the DEUG does not enjoy.

50 See *Les Dossiers de l'étudiant*, June 1983. B. Prot, in his editorial, 'Les vrais enjeux', quotes a poll taken amongst students: 21 per cent of those asked did not expect to find employment at the end of their studies, 55 per cent thought they would manage to find work, but with great difficulty, as opposed to 24 per cent who expected to find work easily or very easily. See also, in the same number, 'Les Palmarès des Universités', pp. 49-64, where students were asked to evaluate the universities according to certain criteria. Paris IX-Dauphine, very much concerned with vocational studies, came high on the list on several counts, and in particular has succeeded in making itself very well known in business circles. See also R. Rémond's article in *Débat*, May 1983, 'L'Université: une loi en trop' where he points to the paradox of the left's change of heart on this issue.

51 See the *rapport Schwartz* for an example of this attitude (p. 180), where, in the midst of his very adverse comments of PEGC training, is a reference to the fact that the internal PEGC examination those who pass it number over 80 per cent — which he tends to view as proof of laxism.

52 See M. Vaughan, 'The *grandes écoles*: selection, legitimation, perpetuation', A. Stevens, 'The contribution of the *Ecole nationale*

d'administration to French political life', in J. Howorth and P. Cerny, *Elites in France* (Frances Pinter, 1981).

53 There has however been the odd demagogic act on the part of the education ministry, for example, the removal of all *mentions* from the *baccalauréat* (Decree 83-369, 4 May 1983 – a measure later rescinded at presidential insistence).

54 For an example see the publication introduced by C. Beullac, entitled *Enseignement et valeurs morales* (Documentation Française, 1981), where the whole book is redolent of extreme timidity and uncertainty.

Bibliographical essay

Books in English are published in London and books in French are published in Paris, unless otherwise stated.
Books asterisked thus * contain particularly useful hints on further reading.

Chapter 1

1944–58: The best general history of the period is **G. Dupeux**, *La France de 1945 à 1965* (3rd ed., Colin, 1972). **A. Werth**, *France 1940–55* (Hale, 1956) is more impressionistic, but full of insights. **P.-M. de la Gorce**, *L'Après-guerre* (Grasset, 1978) is very detailed.

On social and economic change, the best introduction is **M. Parodi**, *L'Economie et la société française depuis 1945** (Colin, 1981) which is excellently documented and goes much deeper than a mere introduction, **J. Ardagh**, *France in the Eighties* (Penguin, 1982) is full of information but is rather eclectic and apolitical. **J. Lecerf**, *La Percée de l'économie française* (Arthaud, 1963) evokes well the 'technocratic' nature of post-war growth. The reactions of victims of change are clinically analysed in **S. Hoffmann** (ed.), *Le Mouvement Poujade* (Colin, 1956) and in a more general study by **D. Borne**, *Petits Bourgeois en révolte – le mouvement Poujade* (Flammarion, 1977). **L. Wylie**, *Village in the Vaucluse* (Cambridge, Harvard University Press, 1957) catches the change in lifestyle at grass-roots level.

On the politics of the Fourth Republic, no one has surpassed **P. Williams**, *Crisis and Compromise** (Longmans, 1964) which is exhaustive and very readable. **D. MacRae jun.**, *Parliament, Parties and Society in France, 1946–58* (New York, St Martin's Press, 1967) uses much more abstract political science techniques. **J. Fauvet**, *La Quatrième République* (Fayard, 1959) concentrates particularly on the parliamentary scene. **G. Elgey**, *La République des illusions, 1945–51* (Fayard, 1965) is massively detailed, as is its companion *La République des contradictions, 1951–4* (Fayard, 1968). Defences of 'the system' are put up by **J. Barsalou**, *La Mal-Aimée* (Plon, 1964) and, more discursively by **F. Fontvielle-Alquier**, *Plaidoyer pour la IVᵉ République* (Laffont, 1976). A critical socialist account is **J. Julliard**, *La IVᵉ République* (Calmann-Lévy, 1968). **N. Leites**, *On the Game of Politics in France* (Stanford UP, 1959) is good on the psychology of the professional politician.

An extrmely thorough recent study is **J.-P. Rioux**, *La France de la Quatrième République,** 2 vols, (Seuil, 1980–2). General accounts of foreign policy are given in the notes to chapter 5. On colonial matters, **R.E.M. Irving**, *The First Indo-China War* (Croom Helm, 1975) is concise and well written, to be supplemented by a lengthier study, **D. Lancaster**, *The Emancipation of French Indo-China* (New York, Octagon, 1975). As for Algeria, **G. Andrews**, *French Politics and Algeria* (New York, Appleton, 1962) is a concise account of the impact of the war on domestic politics. The role of the army in politics has been studied illuminatingly by **J.S. Ambler**, *The French Army in Politics, 1945–62* (Ohio State UP, 1966). See also **G. Kelley**, *Lost Soldiers: the French Army and Empire in Crisis, 1947–62* (MIT Press, 1965); **R. Girardet**, *La Crise militaire française, 1945–62* (Colin, 1964). The general work by **H. Grimal**, *La Décolonisation, 1919–63* (Colin, 1965; translated as *Decolonization*, Routledge & Kegan Paul, 1978) fits French policy into the international context.

1958–68: As with other periods, a very useful brief narrative in English supported by documents in French is provided in **E. Cahm**, *Politics and Society in Contemporary France, 1789–1971* (Harrap, 1972). Otherwise the best full narrative and analysis of the period is **P. Viansson-Ponté**, *Histoire de la république gaullienne* (2 vols, Fayard, 1970, 1971) which is eminently readable and reliable partly because of its size. On the Algerian war the same point applies, and to understand a complex period the best work is **Y. Courrière**, *La Guerre d'Algérie* (4 vols. Fayard, 1970–2); the most recent work is **A. Horne**, *A Savage War of Peace: Algeria 1954–62* (Macmillan, 1977) which is more descriptive than analytical; the most clear-cut guide to the political implications at each stage of the war is still provided by **D. Pickles**, *Algeria and France* (Methuen, 1963). For description and analysis of developments in France particularly after the war ended, the best work is **P.M. Williams** and **M. Harrison**, *Politics and Society in de Gaulle's Republic* available in paperback (New York, Doubleday, 1973), to be supplemented by **P.M. Williams**, *French Politicians and Elections, 1951–69* (Cambridge UP, 1970) which is particularly useful for insight into electoral campaign issues as well as the results. For an understanding of the socio-economic structures of France under de Gaulle the indispensable work is **M. Parodi**, *L'Economie et la société française de 1945 à 1970* (Colin, 1971).

The events of May 1968: The most detailed and authoritative account is undoubtedly **L. Rioux** and **R. Backmann**, *L'Explosion de mai* (Laffont, 1968), but a fairly extensive description may also be found in **P. Labro** *et al., Mai–juin '68: ce n'est qu'un début* (Denoël, 1968). For a more specifically Trotskyist approach, see **D. Bensaid** and **H. Weber**, *Mai 1968: une répétition générale* (Maspéro, 1968). Among books in English on the subject, the following may be consulted with profit: **P. Seale** and **M. McConville**, *French Revolution, 1968* (Penguin, 1968), lively, with some vivid descriptions, if at times a little gushing; **D. Singer**, *Prelude to Revolution* (Cape, 1970) – a sympathetic account; **B.E. Brown**, *Protest in Paris: the Anatomy of a Revolt* (Morristown, NJ, General Learning

Press, 1974), for a more conservative approach to the events; **J. Gretton**, *Students and Workers* (MacDonald, 1969) possibly the best work on the subject in English. For the events of May and their effect on the political parties of the left, see **A. Barjonet**, *La Révolution trahie de 1968* (John Didier, 1968), explaining in doctrinal terms the reasons for the failure of the communist party to back up the student revolt; **R. Johnson**, *The French Communist Party versus the Students* (Yale UP, 1972); **J. Poperen**, *L'Unité de la gauche, 1965-73* (Fayard, 1975), particularly parts 2 and 3. There seems to be little available on the *lycéens*, but a collection of their views and proposals has been published: Comités d'action lycéens, *Les Lycéens gardent la parole* (Seuil, 1968).

The political aspects are adequately covered in **P. Viansson-Ponté**, *Histoire de la république gaullienne*, vol. 2 (Fayard, 1971) which is particularly good on de Gaulle's 'disappearance'. One recent book which well repays study is that of **M. Grimaud**, *En Mai, fais ce qu'il te plaît* (Stock, 1977), which looks at the events from the standpoint of the *préfet de police*. There have been a number of reflections and analyses of the events: **E. Morin** *et al.*, *Mai 1968: la brèche* (Fayard, 1968), sympathetic to the student revolt, with **R. Aron**, *La Révolution introuvable* (Fayard, 1968), profoundly hostile. A more sustained interpretation is that of **A. Touraine**, *Le Mouvement de mai ou le communisme utopique* (Seuil, 1968), while a useful summing-up of the main interpretations is provided by **P. Beneton** and **J. Touchard**, 'Les interprétations de la crise de mai–juin 1968', *Revue française de science politique*, vol. 20, June 1970). **V.-C. Fisera** (ed.), *Writing on the Wall – May 1968, A Documentary Anthology* * (Allison & Busby, 1978) shows well the diversity and complexity of the movement. Finally, there is a valuable collection of documents, tracts, posters, etc. produced during May 1968 in *Le Mouvement social* (July–September 1968) entitled 'La Sorbonne par elle-même'.

1969 to the present: **P. Alexandre**, *Le Duel de Gaulle–Pompidou* (Grasset, 1970) deals especially with the politics of Pompidou's accession to power. **J.-D. Bredin**, *La République de Monsieur Pompidou* (Fayard, 1974) is a polemical view from a leading left-Radical. **G. Martinet**, *Le Système Pompidou* (Seuil, 1973) is a brilliant and hostile account of his presidency. **C. Debbasch**, *La France de Pompidou* (PUF, 1974) is more of a socio-economic cross-section of France than anything else.

On the Giscard years there is an overview by **A. Duhamel**, *La République giscardienne* (Grassot, 1980) and an enthusiastic account by **J. Frears**, *France in the Giscard Presidency* * (Allen & Unwin, 1981). **V. Wright** (ed.) *Conflict and Consensus in France* (Cass, 1979) is useful.

Even early on, the Mitterrand septennate attracts analysts. A quick introduction is **A. Duhamel**, *La République de M. Mitterrand* (Grasset, 1981). **D. MacShane**, *François Mitterrand – a Political Odyssey* (Quartet, 1982) reflects a Labour left viewpoint. **M. Beaud**, *Le Mirage de la croissance* (Syros, 1983) shows the difficulties of economic voluntarism, as does, from a slightly different angle, **Les Gracques**, *Pour réussir à gauche* (Syros, 1983). **J. Mandrin**, *Le Socialisme et la France* (Sycomore, 1983) attacks Mitterrand from a CERES standpoint. The president's own hopes are usefully summarized in his **F. Mitterrand**, *Ici et maintenant* (Fayard, 1980). Finally two very handy articles analyse socialist economics: **J. Story**, 'Capital in France: the changing pattern of patrimony?', *West European Politics*, VI, 2, April 1983; **P. Cerny**, 'Democratic socialism and the tests of power', *ibid*. VI, 3, July 1983, pp. 197–215.

General books on the politics of the Fifth Republic abound. **F. Goguel** and **A. Grosser**, *La Politique en France* (5th ed., Colin, 1975) is well written. There are two very clear American works: **H. Ehrmann**, *Politics in France* (4th ed., Boston, Little, Brown, 1983) and the earlier **J.S. Ambler**, *The Government and Politics of France* (Boston, Houghton Mifflin, 1971). **P. Williams** and **M. Harrison**, *Politics and Society in de Gaulle's Republic* (Longman, 1971) is very informative.

D. Pickles, *The Government and Politics of France* (2 vols, Methuen, 1973) marshals many examples to support a rather pro-Gaullist analysis. There are useful essays in her *Problems of Contemporary French Politics* (Methuen, 1982) and in **P. Cerny** and **M. Schain** (eds), *French Politics and Public Policy* (Methuen, 1982). **D. Ashford**, *Policy and Politics in France** (Philadelphia, Temple UP, 1982) is well documented and shows well the Gaullist effort at modernization. A recent comprehensive survey is **W. Andrews** and **S. Hoffmann** (eds), *The Fifth Republic at Twenty* (Albany, State University of New York, 1981).

The most recent British works are **V. Wright**, *The Government and Politics of France** (Hutchinson, 1983) which stresses well the nature of presidential decision-making and **J. Hayward**, *Governing France: The One and Indivisible French Republic** (Weidenfeld & Nicholson, 1983) which is more critical and harder to read; both books are very good on the relationship between politics and administration.

Of French textbooks, **S. Sur**, *La Vie politique en France sous la Cinquième République* (Monchrestien, 1982) is workmanlike, and **J.-L. Quermonne**, *Le Gouvernment de la France sous la Ve. République*, 2nd ed, (Dalloz, 1983) ranges beyond a 'droit public' approach. To keep up with the rapid movement of French politics it is important to become familiar with the political press. Any selection of this is likely to be arbitrary, so at the risk of disappointing some readers, the following are suggested: *Le Monde* (daily) is distinguished for the perspicacity of its political analyses. It publishes documentary specials on all major elections, and also periodic selections of relevant articles in its *Dossiers et documents* series. *Le Matin* (daily) is pro-socialist and readable. *La Croix* is well informed and not so partisan as its title suggests. Among the weeklies, *Le Nouvel Observateur* caters for the more intellectual socialist reader, whereas *L'Express* and *Le Point* are of liberal persuasion; *L'Expansion* is aimed at *cadres* and is invaluable for its reporting of the social and economic conjuncture. *Le Nouvel Economiste* is similarly useful. Annual summaries of developments in the major areas of French society come in *L'Année politique, économique, sociale et diplomatique*, edited by **E. Bonnefous** and **J.B. Duroselle** and published by PUF and Editions du Grand Siècle. Of the main French reviews dealing with contemporary politics and society *Pouvoirs* (each number devoted to one theme) and *Projet* are both penetrating and concise. *Revue française* *de science politique* is more diffuse and academic. In English, *West European Politics* is usually interesting. The best source of rapid information on new publications on contemporary France is the *Review* of the *Association for the Study of Modern and Contemporary France*, an interdisciplinary grouping welcoming all who are interested in modern France. Details from Dr P. Morris, Politics Dept., Nottingham University.

Chapter 2

Economy: The best historical introductions are **T. Kemp**, *Economic Forces in French History* (Dobson, 1971) and *The French Economy, 1913–39* (Longmans, 1972). See also the clear study of **C. Kindleberger**, *Economic Growth in France and Britain* (Harvard UP, 1964). On postwar growth, **B. Guibert**, *La Mutation industrielle de la France* (2 vols, INSEE, 1976), is wide-ranging and well-documented. **J.-J. Carré, P. Dubois** and **E. Malinvaud**, *French Economic Growth* (Stanford UP, 1976) is a more technical discussion. **J. Fourastié**, *Les trente glorieuses* (Fayard, 1979) is an enthusiastic account, and **R. Kuisel**, *Capitalism and the State in Modern France* (CUP, 1981) takes a long-term view. Recent analyses of the economy include **A. Cotta**, *La France et l'impératif mondial* (PUF, 1978) and a wide-ranging series of essays on policy in **S. Cohen** and **P. Gourevitch** (eds), *France in the Troubled World Economy* (Butterworth, 1982).

On introductions to contemporary economic structures, **P. Maillet**, *La Structure économique de la France* (PUF, 1975) is brief; **J. Sheahan**, *Introduction to the French Economy* (Columbus, Merrill, 1969) brings a more political analysis. **J. Albertini**, *L'Economie française – initiation* (Editions Ouvrières, 1978) presents the topic in a novel and provocative way. **J. Hough**, *The French Economy* (Croom Helm, 1982) is a concise introduction. Basic information on industry is in **Ministère de l'Industrie**, *Traits fondamentaux du système industriel français* (1983). **B. Bellon**, *L'Industrie en France* (Flammarion, 1983) is very detailed.

On agriculture an invaluable introduction is **J. Klatzmann**, *L'Agriculture française* (PUF, 1978).

The relationship between economy and state has received much treatment, most of it centring on the theme of planning. **P. Bauchet**, *La Planification française* (5th ed., Seuil, 1966) seems aware of the political dimension of planning, as does **J. Sheahan**, *Promotion and Control of Industry in Post-war France* (Harvard UP, 1963). Of accounts by planners, **Y. Ullmo**, *La Planification en France* (Dalloz, 1975) is readable. **J. McArthur** and **B. Scott**, *Industrial Planning in France* (Harvard UP, 1969) shows the structural limits to intervention, while **J. Zysman**, *Political Strategies for Industrial Order – State, Market and Industry in France* (University of California Press, 1977) builds up its theory from a detailed study. For international comparisons see **J. Hayward** and **M. Watson** (eds), *Planning, Politics and Public Policy* (Cambridge UP, 1975) and **J. Hayward** and **O. Narkiewicz** (eds), *Planning in Europe* (Croom Helm, 1978).

As regards left-orientated critiques of contemporary structures, **F. Morin**, *La Structure financière du capitalisme français* (Calmann–Lévy, 1974) is a sophisticated neo-marxist analysis. The PCF view is in **P. Boccara** (ed.), *Études sur le capitalisme monopoliste d'état, sa crise et son issue* (Editions Sociales, 1973). Cf. also PCF, *Le Capitalisme monopoliste d'état* (2nd ed., Editions Sociales, 1976). **A. Gauron**, *Histoire économique et sociale de la Ve. République** (Maspéro, 1983) is a readable left critique of recent developments.

Invaluable instruments for keeping up with developments in all fields of the economy are the ongoing INSEE collections, with a wealth of documentation and analyses that are more accessible to non-specialists than might be supposed. The main series are D – Démographie; E – Entreprises; C – Comptabilité; M – Ménages and R – Régions. The yearly *Tableaux de l'Economie française* (INSEE) is a very handy condensed source of information.

Social stratification: The best historical introduction is **G. Dupeux**, *French Society, 1789-1970* (Methuen, 1976). There are interesting documents, but a rather shallow presentation, in a work dealing with the contemporary period: **G. Vincent**, *Les Français, 1945-75: chronique et structures d'une société* (Masson, 1977). **C. Quin**, *Classes sociales et union du peuple de France* (Editions Sociales, 1976) gives the PCF line. **A. Granou**, *La Bourgeoisie financière au pouvoir* (Maspéro, 1977) is from a more leftist viewpoint. **J. Marceau**, *Class and Status in France** (Oxford UP, 1977) is vastly informative and rather eclectic in its leftish approach.

On particular classes or fractions **P. Birnbaum** *et al.*, *La Classe dirigeante française* (PUF, 1978) tries to demonstrate empirically the nature of the ruling class. Cf. also here his *Sommets de l'état* (Seuil, 1977). **C. Baudelot**, **R. Establet** and **J. Malemort**, *La Petite Bourgeoisie en France* (Maspéro, 1974) is a provocative study, hostile to its subject. **M. Roy**, *Les Commerçants: entre la révolte et la modernisation* (Seuil, 1971) pinpoints with no great sympathy the plight of the *petit commerçant*. **J.P. Bachy**, *Les Cadres en France* (Colin, 1971) has concise analysis and documents. **M. Faure**, *Les Paysans dans la société française** (Colin, 1966) is a good introduction. **B. Lambert**, *Les Paysans dans la lutte des classes* (Seuil, 1970) presents the articulate view of a leftist farmer and union leader. The new middle class is studied subtly in **R. Mouriaux** and **G. Grunberg**, *L'Univers politique et syndical des cadres** (FNSP, 1979) and set alongside the old in **G. Lavau** *et al.*, *L'Univers politique des classes moyennes* (FNSP, 1983).

On élites generally **M. Vaughan**, *Social Change in France* (Robertson, 1980) is clear. Especially illuminating is the work of **E. Suleiman**, notably *Elites in French Society* (Princeton UP, 1978) and *Politics, Power and Bureaucracy* (idem, 1974). A wide range of themes are studied in **J. Howorth** and **P. Cerny** (eds), *Elites in French Society* (Pinter, 1982).

On the working class **P. Gavi**, *Les Ouvriers* (Mercure de France, 1970) is an impressionistic, leftist view, very much inspired by 1968. A more sober scientific analysis comes in **G. Adam** *et al.*, *L'Ouvrier* *français en 1970* (Colin, 1970). Access to the debate about the changing nature of the working class can be had through the writings of **S. Mallet**, notably *La Nouvelle Classe ouvrière* (4th ed., Seuil, 1969) and **A. Touraine**, *La Société post-industrielle* (Denoël, 1969). There is valuable work by **D. Gallie**, *In Search of the New Working Class* (CUP, 1978) and a useful survey-based study in **R. De Angelis**, *Blue Collar Workers and Politics – A French Paradox* (Croom Helm, 1982)

Political culture: Most of the general works on the Fifth Republic listed in chapter 1 have some pages on this, but book-length studies are rare. The best start is **S. Hoffmann** (ed.), *In Search of France** (Harper & Row, 1963), especially Hoffmann's own essay on 'Paradoxes of the French Political Community'. Hoffmann has further developed his ideas in *Decline or Renewal? France since the 1930s* (New York, Viking, 1974). Other studies include **E. Deutsch, D. Lindon** and **P. Weil**, *Les Familles politiques* (Editions de Minuit, 1966), brief, but brings out ideological cleavages, and the provocative, pro-Gaullist view of **C. Morazé**, *Les Français et la république* (Colin, 1956), written at the apogee of the Fourth Republic and catching well the attitudes of the day. **P. Fougey-rollas**, *La Conscience politique dans la France contemporaine* (Denoël, 1963) insists on the tension between national consensus and partisan values. **H. Waterman**, *Political Change in Contemporary France* (Columbus, Merrill, 1969) sees political culture with an 'end of ideology' problematic and thus produces a very ideological, transatlantic view. **P. Avril**, *Politics in France* (Penguin, 1969) has some lucid insights from this Mendesist analyst.

On relations between state and citizen, the most authoritative work is by **M. Crozier**, notably his *Société bloquée* (Seuil, 1970) and *Le Phénomène bureaucratique* (Seuil, 1963). On religious cleavages there is both sharp analysis and plentiful documentation in **A. Coutrot** and **F.-G. Dreyfus**, *Les Forces religieuses dans la société française** (Colin, 1965) and **R. Rémond** (ed.), *Forces religieuses et attitudes politiques dans la France contemporaine** (Colin, 1965). A special tradition is historically studied in depth in **Rémond's** *L'Anticléricalisme en France: de 1815 à nos jours* (Fayard, 1976).

Chapter 3

Central government: works listed above on the Fifth Republic all contain useful accounts of the topic dealt with in this chapter, to which should be added an indispensable work of reference: **D. Maus**, *Textes et documents sur la pratique des institutions de la Ve République*, 2nd edition, (Documentation française, 1982). The periodicals *Projet*, particularly the articles entitled 'La conjoncture politique', and *Pouvoirs* may always be consulted with profit; in the latter, the 'Chronique institutionnelle' of **P. Avril** and **J. Gicquel** is a goldmine of information. The *chroniques* for 1976–1982 have just been issued in book form, PUF, 1983, and may be more easily consulted there. An excellent analysis is provided in **F. de Baecque**, *Qui gouverne la France?* (PUF,

1976), which contains a selection of key documents up to the early years of Giscard's presidency. The Gaullist view of the constitution is typified by **M. Debré** and **J.-L. Debré**, *Le Pouvoir politique* (Seghers, 1976) and **J.-L. Debré**, *La Constitution de la Ve République* (PUF, 1975). Among the many works of **M. Duverger**, see in particular *La Ve République* (5th ed., PUF, 1974); see also informative study by **L. Hamon**, *Une République présidentielle* (2 vols, Bordas, 1975, 1977).

On the role of the president of the republic, a useful introduction is provided by **J. Baguenard, J.-Ch. Maout** and **R. Muzellec**, *Le Président de la Ve République** (Colin, 1970). **J. Massot**, *La Présidence de la république en France* (Documentation française, 1977) situates the presidency in its historical context. **B. Tricot** *et al.*, *De Gaulle et le service de l'état* (Plon, 1977) give a fascinating, if discreet, account of the General's presidency; see also, **S. Cohen**, *Les Conseillers du Président de la République de Charles de Gaulle à Valéry Giscard d'Estaing* (PUF, 1980).

On the role of the prime minister, see **J. Massot**, *Le Chef du gouvernement en France* (Documentation française, 1979) for an historical approach, and for the services of the prime minister's office, see **M. Long**, *Les services du Premier ministre* (Presses universitaires d'Aix-Marseille, 1981).

For basic introductions on the role of parliament, see **J.-Ch. Maout** and **R. Muzellec**, *Le Parlement sous la Ve République* (Colin, 1971) and *Documents d'études*, no. 14, *Le Contrôle parlementaire* (Documentation française, 1970). The role of the deputy and the various constraints put upon his/her liberty is well described by **J.-C. Masclet**, *Un député, pourquoi faire?* (PUF, 1982).

The constitutional vicissitudes of de Gaulle's republic are covered by **Ph. Braud**, *Les Crises politiques de la Ve République* (Colin, 1970).

For an introduction to a study of the *conseil constitutionnel* see **G. Dupuis, J. Georgel** and **J. Moreau**, *Le Conseil constitutionnel* (Colin, 1970), **L. Favoreu** and **L. Philip**, *Le Conseil constitutionnel* (PUF, 1978); a more detailed study by the same authors, *Les Grandes Décisions du conseil constitutionnel* (Sirey, 1975) makes clear the political implications of the *conseil's* activities. The monstrously expensive *Recueil des décisions du conseil constitutionnel*, (Imprimerie nationale) published annually, is worth consulting as a work of reference. On the *conseil d'état*, the most up-to-date study in English is that of **M. Rendel**, *The Administrative Functions of the French Conseil d'Etat* (Weidenfeld & Nicolson, 1970). A collective historical study, **A. Parodi** (ed.), *Le Conseil d'état, 1799–1974* (CNRS, 1974) provides a clear account of its controversial decisions. See also, **M.-C. Kessler**, *Le Conseil d'état* (Colin, 1968) and **P. Escoube**, *Les Grands Corps de l'état* (2nd ed., PUF, 1977).

On the central administration (ministries, etc.), the clearest (and best set out) introduction is **L. François**, *Les Institutions politiques et administratives de la France* (Hachette, 1976). At a higher level, see **B. Gournay** *et al.*, *Administration publique** (PUF, 1967), **G. Belorgey**, *Le Gouvernement et l'administration de la France** (2nd ed., Colin,

1970). **F. de Baecque**, *L'Administration centrale de la France* (Colin, 1973) is a highly technical study. On the finance ministry see **X. Beauchamps**, *Un Etat dans l'état? le ministère de l'économie et des finances* (Bordas, 1976). *Les Notices de la documentation française: Finances publiques* (Documentation française, 1974). For a brilliant essay on the governing élites, see **P. Birnbaum**, *Les Sommets de l'état* (Seuil, 1977); see also **P. Antoni** and **J.-D. Antoni**, *Les Ministres de la Ve République* (PUF, 1976) for a detailed sociological study of the Fifth Republic's political class.

On the media, a useful account is to be found in **J. Ardagh**, *France in the 1980s* (Penguin, 1982). A highly technical and comprehensive exposition of the problems, the legal situation and the main theories of communication is provided by **F. Balle**, *Institutions et publics des moyens d'information* (Montchrestien, 1973). See also **R. Cayrol**, *La Presse écrite et audiovisuelle* (PUF, 1973). On radio and television, see **G. Dupuis** and **J. Raux**, *l'ORTF** (Colin, 1970) for a good introduction to the ORTF **J. Chevallier**, *La Radio-télévision entre deux réformes** (LGDJ, 1973) and **R. Thomas**, *Broadcasting and Democracy in France** (Bradford UP, 1976) for an excellent analysis of the political dimensions of the subject.

On the press see **J. L. Lepigeon** and **D. Wolton**, *L'Information demain*, 2nd edition (Documentation française, 1983) and **P. Albert**, *La Presse française** (Documentation française, 1978); but **B. Voyenne**, *La Presse dans la société contemporaine* (Colin, 1970) is still very well worth reading, together with his *L'Information en France* (McGraw-Hill-France, 1972).

Local government: There are good introductory works in English, notably **F. Ridley** and **J. Blondel**, *Public Administration in France** (Routledge & Kegan Paul, 1969). Two older works which are still of interest are **B..Chapman**, *Introduction to French Local Government* (Allen & Unwin, 1953) and *The Prefects and Provincial France* (Allen & Unwin, 1955), the latter to be supplemented with a well-researched and clear study, **H. Machin**, *The Prefect in French Public Administration* (Croom Helm, 1977). **M. Kesselman**, *The Ambiguous Consensus* (New York, Knopf, 1967) shows up the realities of small communes, while **J. Lagroye**, *Société et politique: J. Chaban-Delmas à Bordeaux* (Pedone, 1973) is an excellent study of a large town. *Pouvoirs* 24 (1983) 'Le Maire' has both theoretical analysis and practical examples. Useful primers are **P. Richard** and **M. Cotten**, *Les Communes françaises d'aujourd'hui* (PUF, 1983) and **J. Auby**, *Le Commissaire de la République*, (PUF, 1983). See also **P. Bernard**, *L'Etat et la décentralisation – du préfet au commissaire de la République* (Documentation française, 1983).

There is an invaluable collection prepared by the ADELS (a group of local government specialists close to the PS), aimed mainly at activists, but short and easy to read. All are published by Syros. Cf. especially **G. Gontcharoff** and **S. Milano**, *La Décentralisation* (1982); **R. Beaunez** and **J.-P. Muret**, *La Commune – nouvelles compétences, gestion et démocratie locale* (1982) and also *Les municipales – lois nouvelles*, *éléctions, organisation communale* (1982); P. **Barge** *et al., L'Intervention économique de la commune* (1983). P. **Gourevitch**, *Paris and the Provinces − The Politics of Local Government Reform in France* (Allen & Unwin, 1980) is a readable overview, to be followed by the more theoretical P. **Grémion**, *Le Pouvoir périphérique* (Seuil, 1976). An excellent overview is Y. **Mény**, *Centralisation et décentralisation dans le débat politique français 1945–69* (LGDJ, 1974).

Inevitably, in the logic of centralization, there are many works on public administration which have substantial sections on local (subaltern) government. C. **Debbasch**, *L'Administration au pouvoir* (Calmann-Lévy, 1969) is brief but telling. B. **Gournay** *et al., Administration publique** (PUF, 1967) is a thorough textbook, as is G. **Belorgey**, *Le Gouvernement et l'administration de la France** (2nd ed., Colin, 1970), which brings out well the weight of centralization. For useful comparative treatments see J. **Lagroye** and V. **Wright** (eds), *Local Government in Britain and France* (Allen & Unwin, 1979); S. **Tarrow**, *Between Center and Periphery − Grassroots Politicians in Italy and France* (Yale UP, 1977) and D. **Ashford**, *British Dogmatism and French Pragmatism,** (Allen & Unwin, 1982).

On regions, one needs to approach the problem from an economic as well as from a political angle; much pioneer work was done by J.-F. **Gravier**, notably *L'Aménagement du territoire et l'avenir des régions françaises* (Flammarion, 1964). There is a readable general study by an economic geographer: I. **Thompson**, *Modern France: a Social and Economic Geography* (Butterworth, 1970). N. **Hansen**, *French Regional Planning* (Edinburgh UP, 1968) is written from a planner's point of view, but is rewarding if at times fairly technical. On a more polemical level, J.-J. **Servan-Schreiber**, *Le Pouvoir régional* (Grasset, 1970) presents a reformist view; a socialist-cum-autonomist viewpoint is developed in a series of works by R. **Lafont**, notably *Autonomie: de la région a l'autogestion* (Gallimard, 1976). *Pouvoirs* 19 (1981)* 'Régions' is a fascinating survey of the problems involved in the new laws. M. **Philipponneau**, *La grande Affaire − décentralisation et régionalisation* (Calmann-Lévy, 1981) gives a militant view, and a sceptical one is found in J. **Vié**, *La décentralisation sans illusion* (PUF, 1982). On particular regions, R. **Dulong**, *La Question bretonne* (FNSP, 1975) is a sophisticated marxist treatment.

On Corsica a short introduction is J. **Renucci**, *La Corse* (PUF, 1982) while R. **Ramsay**, *The Corsican Time Bomb* (Manchester UP, 1982) is a more topical treatment.

Chapter 4

The most useful introductions to French parties are F. **Borella**, *Les Partis politiques** (2nd ed., Seuil, 1975) which is lucid and critical, and J. **Frears**, *Political Parties and Elections in the Fifth French Republic** (Hurst, 1978) which is well documented but less incisive. More up to date works are F. **Wilson**, *French Political Parties under the Fifth*

Republic (New York Praeger, 1982) and **D. Bell** (ed.), *Contemporary French Political Parties* (Croom Helm, 1981). **P. Campbell**, *French Electoral Systems and Elections since 1789* (Faber, 1966) is a concise outline. It can be supplemented by **F. Bon**, *Les Elections en France* (Seuil, 1978) and the handy reference book **C. Leleu**, *Géographie des élections françaises* (PUF, 1971). A classic study of electoral behaviour is **G. Michelat** and **M. Simon**, *Classe, réligion et comportement politique* (FNSP, 1977). Recent trends in the electorate are revealed in **J. Capdevielle** (ed.), *France de gauche, vote a droite* (FNSP, 1981). On women and politics **J. Mossuz-Lavau** and **M. Sineau**, *Enquête sur les femmes et la politique en France** (PUF, 1983) breaks new ground. Election results are analysed in detail in the Dossiers et Documents series of *Le Monde*, and there are further studies in the series of books edited by **H. Penniman** and published by the American Enterprise Institute of Washington: *The Presidential Elections of 1974* (1975) and *The French National Assembly Elections of 1978* (1980).

The most important recent party publications, which state theoretical and current policy stances, are: Rassemblement pour la République, *Atout France* Roudil, 1980); Parti Républicain, *Le Projet républicain* (Flammarion, 1978); Centre des démocrates sociaux, *L'Autre Solution* (Editions Sociales, 1976); Parti socialiste, *Projet socialiste* (Flammarion, 1980). There is a handy version of the CPG introduced by **G. Marchais**: Parti communiste français, *Programme commun de gouvernement* (Editions Sociales, 1972).

The right: An essential introduction is **R. Rémond**, *The French Right Wing from 1815 to de Gaulle* (Pennsylvania UP, 1969), which is absolutely lucid and should be followed by **M. Anderson**, *Conservative Politics in France* (Allen & Unwin, 1973).

On Gaullism the most authoritative work is that of **J. Charlot**, notably *Le Gaullisme* (Colin, 1970) and *The Gaullist Phenomenon* (Allen & Unwin, 1971). **A. Hartley**, *Gaullism* (Routledge & Kegan Paul, 1972) offers a sympathetic view. Earlier works, of a more introductory character but still worth looking at, are: **P. Avril**, *UDR et Gaullistes* (PUF, 1971) and **P. Viansson-Ponté**, *Les Gaullistes* (Seuil, 1963). **J. Touchard**, *Le Gaullisme, 1940–69* (Seuil, 1978) sets Gaullism, approvingly, in the context of French nationalism. An early PCF view is in **H. Claude**, *Gaullisme et grand capital* (Editions Sociales, 1961). A Trotskyist viewpoint is in **J.-M. Brohm** *et al.*, *Le Gaullisme et après: état fort et fascisation* (Maspéro, 1974). **P. Crisol** and **Y. Lhomeau**, *La Machine RPR* (Intervalle Fayolle, 1978) has much up-to-date and solid information on Gaullism under Chirac. Charlot's *Le Gaullisme d'opposition* (Fayard, 1983) illuminates the earlier phase of the movement. *Pouvoirs* 28 (1984) is devoted to the RPR. There is an informative biography of its leader in **T. Desjardins**, *Un inconnu nommé Chirac* (Table Ronde, 1983).

On Giscardism, literature is beginning to grow. **J.-C. Colliard**, *Les Républicains indépendants* (PUF, 1971) is a thorough early study, to be supplemented by a brilliant sociological interpretation of the differences within the right, **P. Birnbaum**, *Les Sommets de l'état* (Seuil, 1977). **V. Giscard d'Estaing** defines his own position in *Démocratie française*

(Fayard, 1976). **B. Lecomte** and **C. Sauvage**, *Les Giscardiens* (Albin Michel, 1978) has much up-to-date information. **R.E.M. Irving**, *Christian Democracy in France* (Allen & Unwin, 1973) is clear and thorough. Essays on various aspects are in the special number of *Pouvoirs* 9 (1979) and in **V. Wright** (ed.), *Continuity and Change in France* (Allen & Unwin, 1984). **J.-C. Petitfils**, *La démocratie giscardienne* (PUF, 1981), covers doctrine and organization.

Radicalism has had several studies, starting with the brief introduction by a supporter: **C. Nicolet**, *Le Radicalisme* (PUF, 1974). **J.-T. Nordmann**, *Histoire des Radicaux, 1820–1973* (Table Ronde, 1974) is by a collaborator of **J.-J. Servan-Schreiber**, whose own *Le Manifeste* (Firmin-Didot, 1977) is a concise statement of current positions. Mendesism is discussed in the special number of *Pouvoirs* 27 (1983) and in **J. Lacouture**, *Mendès-France* (Seuil, 1981). MRG positions are found in **M. Crépeau**, *L'Avenir en face* (Seuil, 1981).

The left: **G. Lefranc**, *Les Gauches en France, 1789–1972* (Payot, 1973) is a long-term study. Studies covering more recent time-spans include **J. Touchard**, *La Gauche en France depuis 1900* (Seuil, 1977), with its vast grasp of detail and lack of sympathy; **F.-G. Dreyfus**, *Histoire des Gauches en France, 1940–74* (Grasset, 1975) from a hostile, fairly pro-Gaullist viewpoint, and two works by socialists: **J. Poperen**, *L'Unité de la gauche, 1965–73* (Fayard, 1975), a work of meticulous detail and **R. Verdier**, *PS–PC: une lutte pour l'entente** (Seghers, 1976). **J. Charlot** (ed.), *Quand la Gauche peut gagner* (Moreau, 1973) is vital to the understanding of the dynamics of left unity. A clear, well-documented study is **N. Nugent** and **D. Lowe**, *The Left in France* (MacMillan, 1982) and a briefer one is **D. Bell** and **E. Shaw** (eds), *The Left in France – Towards a Socialist Republic* (Spokesman, 1983). The recent wrangling is wryly recorded in **R. Johnson**, *The Long March of the French Left* Macmillan, 1981), while **O. Duhamel**, *La Gauche et la Cinquième République** (PUF 1980), shows at length how the left came round to presidentialism. *Pouvoirs* 20 (1982) assesses its performance in office.

On socialism, it is useful to start with an historical account of the SFIO. **G. Lefranc**, *Le Mouvement socialiste sous la Troisième République* (Payot, 1963) is a sound study by an SFIO and trade-union activist. **R. Quilliot**, *La SFIO et l'exercice du pouvoir* (Fayard, 1972) by a socialist senator is essential for understanding the party's decay after 1945. The dilemmas of the 1960s are studied in detail by two US scholars: **F. Wilson**, *The French Democratic Left, 1963–9* (Stanford UP, 1971) and **H. Simmons**, *French Socialists in Search of a Role, 1956–67* (Cornell UP, 1970). The structures and leaders of the PS are studied briefly, but penetratively, by **T. Pfister**, *Les Socialistes* (Albin Michel, 1977) and more discursively by **J.-F. Bizot**, *Au Parti des socialistes* (Grasset, 1975). **F.-O. Giesbert's** biography *François Mitterrand ou la tentation de l'histoire* (Seuil, 1977) is full of insight into the development of the post-war left. Recent PS success has led to more studies of it (often by professionals from within its ranks). The sharpest is **H. Portelli**, *Le Socialisme français tel qu'il est* (PUF, 1981) which makes short shrift of the party's ideological maximalism. Sociological approaches come from **J. Kergoat**, *Le PS* (Sycomore, 1983) and from the study of party élites by **P. Bacot**, *Les Dirigeants du PS* (Presses universitaires de Lyon, 1979), which reproduces Poperenite certainties with boring earnestness. American scholars see the party as a modernizing vehicle, cf. **G. Codding** and **W. Safran**, *Ideology and Politics — the Socialist Party of France* (Boulder, Colorado, Westview Press, 1979) and the more interesting **B. Brown**, *Socialism of a Different Kind* (Greenwood Press, 1982). The ex-communist **Y. Roucaute** gives a CERES line in his *Le PS* (Bruno Huisman, 1983). A wide range of topics is covered in **S. Williams** (ed.), *Socialism in France from Jaurès to Mitterrand* (Frances Pinter, 1983). On the differrent fractions, the CERES group present their views in a resolute and readable analysis by **M. Charzat, J.-P. Chevènement** and **G. Toutain**, *Le CERES, un combat pour le socialisme** (Calmann-Lévy, 1975). **Chevènement** has also produced *Le Vieux, la crise, le neuf* (Flammarion, 1974) and *Les Communistes, les socialistes et les autres* (Aubier-Montaigne, 1977). In English there is an introduction to CERES in **D. Hanley**'s chapter in **Bell** and **Shaw**, *The French Left*, op. cit. Poperenism is explained by a loyalist in **G. Pudlowski**, *Jean Poperen et l'UCGS* (Editions St. Germain des Prés, 1975). The Rocardians are best approached through **M. Rocard**, *Parler vrai* (Seuil, 1979) and more theoretically through **P. Rosanvallon** and **P. Viveret**, *Pour une nouvelle culture politique* (Seuil, 1977). They are attacked from a Trotskyist angle in **D. Bensaid**, *L'anti-Rocard* (La Brèche, 1980).

The PCF has several historical studies devoted to it, the most penetrating being **J. Fauvet**, *Histoire du parti communiste** (2nd ed., Fayard, 1977). **R. Tiersky**, *French Communism, 1920–72** (Columbia UP, 1974) is very clear. On party structures the work of **A. Kriegel**, especially *Les Communistes* (Seuil, 1970) is very well informed, and hostile — not unsurprisingly, perhaps, for an ex-communist. There are essays on varied aspects of party activity in **F. Bon** (ed.), *Le Communisme en France* (Colin, 1969) and **D. Blackmer** and **S. Tarrow**, *Communism in Italy and France* (Princeton UP, 1975). A brief study by **A. Stiefbold**, *The French Communist Party in Transition* (Praeger, 1977) situates the PCF with regard to the Soviet Union.

The leadership's view is given in the writings of **G. Marchais**, notably *Le Défi démocratique* (Grasset, 1973) and *Parlons franchement* (Grasset, 1977). **J. Elleinstein**, *Le PC* (Grasset, 1976) is by the 'official liberal' of the party, now expelled; a more oblique and prudent line of dissent comes in **G. Molina** and **Y. Varga**, *Dialogue à l'intérieur du parti communiste français* (Maspéro, 1978). Of recent works **D. Buffin** and **P. Gerbaud**, *Les Communistes* (Seuil, 1981) is a very clear introduction. A wide range of issues is discussed in **O. Duhamel** and **H. Weber**, *Changer le PC?* (PUF, 1979). Two hostile views come from ex-member **P. Robrieux** in his *Histoire intérieure du PC*, 3 vols, (Seuil, 1980–2) and **J.-J. Becker**, *Le PC veut-il prendre le pouvoir?* (Seuil, 1981). The most sober assessment is **G. Lavau**, *A quoi sert le PCF?* (Seuil, 1981). Little-known aspects of party life emerge in **R. Pronier**, *Les Municipalités communistes* (Balland, 1983) and **D. Lacorne**, *Les Notables rouges* (FNSP, 1980). A good example of recent intra-party dissent is **F. Hincker**, *Le PC au carrefour* (Albin Michel, 1981).

On fringe parties, **B. Brigouleix**, *L'Extrême Droite en France* (Intervalle-Fayolle, 1977) is well-informed and clear. There is a good guide to the theoretical foundations of much French leftism in **R. Gombin**, *Les Origines du gauchisme* (Seuil, 1971) and **T. Pfister**, *Le Gauchisme* (Filippachi, 1972). **Y. Craipeau**, *Le Mouvement trotskiste en France* (Syros, 1971) by a veteran Trotskyite, traces the movement in its fissiparousness down to 1968. On the PSU, **M. Rocard**, *Le PSU et l'avenir de la France* (Seuil, 1969) is still readable, if slightly dated. On the PSU the best informed work in English is by **V.-C. Fisera**, to be found in **S. Williams**, *Socialism in France* and **D. Bell**, *Contemporary French Parties*, op. cit. A useful survey-based study is **C. Hauss**, *The New Left in France* (Greenwood Press, 1978). Useful introductions to ecologism are **M.-C. Vadrot**, *L'écologie, histoire d'une subversion* (Syros, 1978) and **D. Simonnet**, *L'Ecologisme* (PUF, 1981).

Interest groups: A good start, in terms of a general approach to the problem, is **J. Meynaud**, *Nouvelles Etudes sur les groupes de pression en France* (Colin, 1962). On unions, **J.-D. Reynaud**, *Les Syndicats en France** (2 vols, Seuil, 1975) is an excellent textbook with many documents. **G. Caire**, *Les Syndicats ouvriers** (PUF, 1971) is very detailed and informative. **G. Lefranc** is sound on trade-union history, see notably his brief *Le Syndicalisme en France* (8th ed, PUF, 1973) and the two-volume *Le Mouvement syndical* (Payot, 1969) which goes up to 1968. A handy documentary introduction is **J. Capdevielle** and **R. Mouriaux**, *Les Syndicats ouvriers en France** (Colin, 1970). **R. Mouriaux**, *Les Syndicats et la société française* (FNSP, 1983) is probably the most complete textbook. **G. Adam**, *Le pouvoir syndical* (Dunod, 1983) is a well-documented introduction. *Pouvoirs* 26 (1983) 'Le pouvoir syndical' covers many aspects. The new Auroux laws are handily summarized in **Le Monde**, *Les nouveaux Droits des travailleurs* (Maspéro, 1983). Pro-CGT views are expressed in **J. Bruhat** and **M. Piolo**, *Esquisse d'une histoire de la CGT* (CGT, 1966). A critical view, from a communist disillusioned by 1968, is **A. Barjonet**, *La CGT* (Seuil, 1969). **G. Ross** analyses the relative autonomy of union and party in *Workers and Communists** (California UP, 1982). A general introduction to CGT is **R. Mouriaux**, *La CGT* (Seuil, 1983) and an unsympathetic one is **C. Harmel**, *La CGT* (PUF, 1982).

The CFDT presents its views in *La CFDT* (Seuil, 1971) and in the committed work by **E. Maire** and **J. Julliard**, *La CFDT aujourd'hui* (Seuil, 1975). **H. Hamon** and **P. Rotman** set CFDT in the context of the anti-statist, 'alternative' left in *La Deuxième Gauche* (Ramsay, 1982).

On FO, **A. Bergounioux**, *Force ouvrière* (PUF, 1982) is a critical left-socialist view. **A. Bergeron**, *FO* (Force ouvrière, 1973) gives an official view.

On the CNPF, **H. Ehrmann**, *Organized Business in France* (Princeton UP, 1957) is a thorough history, to be brought up to date by the well-informed **B. Brizay**, *Le Patronat** (Seuil, 1975). A brief introduction is **J.-M. Martin**, *Le CNPF* (PUF, 1983).

On farmers' groups **G. Wright**, *Rural Revolution in France** (Stanford UP, 1964) is an admirable historical introduction. **Y. Tavernier**, *Le Syndicalisme paysan – FNSEA: CNJA** (Colin, 1969) is an excellent study of the structures of farmers' organizations. His *Univers politique des paysans** (FNSP, 1972) is both deep and wide-ranging. There are perceptive articles by **J. Keeler** in **S. Berger**, *Organizing Interests*, op. cit., and by **S. Sokoloff** in **P. Cerny** (ed.), *French Politics and Public Policy* (Methuen, 1980).

CIDUNATI has attracted little book-length study, but its ideology comes across clearly in the autobiographical **G. Nicoud**, *Au Risque de déplaire* (Bourg de Péage, L'Objectif, 1977). A sober and concise assessment of the movement is **A. Bonnet**, 'Un nouveau groupe de pression', *Revue politique et parlementaire*, no. 843, June–July 1973, pp. 44–61.

There is much information in **G. Lavau** et al., *L'Univers politique des classes moyennes** (FNSP, 1983) and **S. Berger** has an essay in her *Organizing Interests in Western Europe* (Cambridge UP, 1981), pp. 83–102. Peripheral groups are studied in **P. Cerny** (ed.), *Social Movements and Protest in France* (Pinter, 1982).

The FEN has two historical studies: **J. Clark**, *Teachers and Politics in France: a Pressure-group Study of the FEN* (Syracuse UP, 1967) and a more recent and more pro-FEN view **R. Chéramy**, *La Fédération de l'éducation nationale: 25 ans d'unité syndicale* (Epi, 1974).

Chapter 5

Values, purposes and organisation: For influences of tradition and political culture on foreign policy the best work is still **J.-B. Duroselle** (ed.), *La Politique étrangère et ses fondements* (Colin, 1954). Discussions of various internal and external influences on foreign policy are in **W. Wallace**, *Foreign Policy and the Political Process* (Macmillan, 1971), applied to France in his chapter in **P.G. Cerny** and **M.A. Schain** (eds), *French Politics and Public Policy* (Methuen, 1980), and in a fuller theoretical framework provided by **K.J. Holsti**, *International Politics* (Prentice-Hall, 1974), the best French equivalents being **C. Zorgbibe**, *Les Relations internationales* (PUF, 2nd edn, 1978) and **J.-B. Duroselle**, *Tout empire périra* (Sorbonne, 1981); but see works listed in notes 9 and 10 to appreciate diverse interpretations. More empirical approaches are in **R.C. Macridis**, *Foreign Policy in World Politics* (Prentice Hall, 1976) and **F.S. Northedge** (ed.), *Foreign Policies of the Powers* (Free Press, 1975). For discussions of French independent motivations and their limitations see **S. Hoffmann**, *Decline or Renewal? France since the 1930s* (New York, Viking, 1974), **D. Colard**, 'La Conception française de l'indépendance', *Studia Diplomatica*, no. 1, 1975, **P.G. Cerny**, *The Politics of Grandeur* (Cambridge, 1980), **A. Grosser**, *French Foreign Policy under de Gaulle* (1965, transl. Little, Brown, Boston, 1967), and a theoretical analysis in **N.H. Waites**, 'French Foreign Policy: external influences on the quest for independence', *Review of International Studies*, no. 4, 1983. For French purposes since de Gaulle see **E.A.**

Kolodziej, *French International Policy under de Gaulle and Pompidou* (Ithaca, 1974), **P.-B. Cousté** and **F. Visine,** *Pompidou et l'Europe* (Librairies techniques, 1974), **J.-C. Petitfils,** *La Démocratie giscardienne* (PUF, 1981), a subject treated critically in **C. Zorgbibe,** 'La Diplomatie giscardienne', *Le Monde diplomatique,* mars 1978, p. 3, and in the substantial if not definitive work *La Politique extérieure de Valéry Giscard d'Estaing* (Colloque 26–7 mai 1983, published by Fondation nationale des sciences politiques, 1984), and for socialist policy **Cl. Manceron** et **B. Pingaud,** *François Mitterrand* (Flammarion, 1981), **C. Zorgbibe,** 'François Mitterrand: champion de l'occident ou dissident virtuel', *Politique internationale,* no. 3, 1981, **M.-C. Smouts,** 'The external policy of François Mitterrand', *International Affairs,* no. 2, 1983, and for the ambitious early period before austerity **N.H. Waites,** 'Fance under Mitterrand: external relations', *The World Today,* June 1982, and **D. Moisi,** 'France's new foreign policy', *Foreign Affairs,* winter 1981–2.

To situate French policy broadly see **G. de Carmoy,** *The Foreign Policies of France* (Chicago UP, 1970), **C. Zorgbibe,** *Les Politiques étrangères des grandes puissances* (PUF, Que sais-je? 2160, 1984), **J.-M. Le Breton,** *Les Relations internationales depuis 1968* (Nathan, 1983), and in English there is **P. Calvocoressi,** *World Politics Since 1945* (Longmans, 4th edn, 1983).

For organisation see **J. Chazelle,** *La Diplomatie* (PUF, Que sais-je?, 1968), **Z. Steiner** (ed.), *The Times Survey of Foreign Ministries of the World* (Times Books, 1982), **J. Massot,** *La Présidence de la République* (Documentation française, 1977) and *Le Chef du gouvernement* (Documentation française, 1979) supplemented by **M. Long,** *Les Services du Premier Ministre* (P.U. d'Aix-Marseille, 1981) but see also works by **S. Cohen** listed in note 24, and the critique by **A. Kriegel,** 'François Mitterrand diplomate', *Politique internationale,* no. 16, 1982.

Defence: For a penetrating discussion of the nature of security see **B. Buzan,** *People, States and Fear* (Wheatsheaf, 1983), and for the alliances seeking to provide it, **R. Hunter,** *Security in Europe* (Elek, 1972). French military arrangements are in **L. Ruehl,** *La Politique militaire de la Ve République* (Fondation nationale des sciences politiques, 1976), and briefly summarised in **H. Haenel,** *La Défense nationale* (PUF, Que sais-je? 2028, 1982). A comprehensive analysis of change in the armed forces is **M.L. Martin,** *Warriors to Managers: the French Military Establishment since 1945* (North Carolina UP, 1981), while early nuclear developments are analysed in **W.L. Kohl,** *French Nuclear Diplomacy* (Princeton UP, 1971) and a participant's account is **B. Goldschmidt,** *Les Rivalités atomiques* (Fayard, 1967). The controversial issues involved in the conscript system are discussed in **M.L. Martin,** 'Le Déclin de l'armée de masse en France', *Revue française de sociologie,* jan–mars 1981, while those involved in arms sales are discussed in **A.J. Pierre,** 'Arms sales: the new diplomacy', *Foreign Affairs,* winter 1981–2, and in **E.A. Kolodziej,** 'French arms trade: the economic determinants', *SIPRI Yearbook 1983,* the most recent discussion being **F. Varrenne,** 'Exportations d'armements', *Projet,* 174 & 177, avril et juillet-août 1983.

French military strategy and relations with the Atlantic alliance are discussed in **M.M. Harrison**, *The Reluctant Ally: France and Atlantic Security* (John Hopkins UP, 1981). For debate the most recent Gaullist view is in **F. Valentin**, *Une politique de défense pour la France* (Calmann-Lévy, 1980), while a Centrist view is in **F. de Rose**, *Contre une stratégie des curiaces* (Julliard, 1982) summarised in an article in *Foreign Affairs*, Fall 1982, and socialist views are in articles by **P. Dabézies, C. Mellon, J.-C. Romer** and **J. Klein** in *Projet*, juillet-août 1982. **J. Klein** discusses French disarmament policy in *Politique étrangère* no. 2, 1979, and **N. Gnesotto** discusses PCF policy on euromissiles in the same periodical, no. 3, 1983. The political debate can be pursued through sources in notes 32 and 33, and is summarized in **P.-M. de La Gorce**, 'La France et la défense de l'Europe', *Le Monde diplomatique*, jan. 1984. Official statements of policy can be found regularly in *Défense nationale*, and controversies relating to the 1984–8 loi-programme are discussed in *Le Point*, 19 sept. 1983 and in **J. Marcus** and **B. George**, 'The ambiguous consensus: French defence policy under Mitterrand', *The World Today*, Oct. 1983. Finally, internal security is discussed by **L. Mandeville, J.-L. Loubet del Bayle** et **A. Picard**, 'Les Forces de maintien de l'ordre en France', *Défense nationale*, juillet 1977, and sources in note 36.

Directions of foreign policy: Super-power relations and the French role are analysed expertly in **A. Grosser**, *The Western Alliance* (transl. Macmillan, 1980). A useful discussion of the de Gaulle period is in **J. Newhouse**, *De Gaulle and the Anglo-Saxons* (Deutsch, 1970), while the Pompidou period is treated by **M.-C. Smouts** in **A. Grosser**, *Les Politiques extérieures européennes dans la crise* (Fondation nationale des sciences politiques, 1976), that of Giscard by **M. Tatu** in the 1983 Sciences Po. colloque, *La Politique extérieure de Valéry Giscard d'Estaing* (1984), and socialist policy is discussed in **M.-F. Toinet**, 'La France socialiste et les Etats-Unis', *Le Monde diplomatique*, déc. 1981. The nature of French relations with the Soviet Union has been analysed in **R. Legvold**, 'Franco-Soviet rapprochement after de Gaulle', *Survey*, autumn 1974, a subject he has brought up to date in *Atlantic Quarterly*, spring 1983; also very useful is **T. Schreiber**, 'Les Relations de la France avec les pays de l'Est 1944–1980', *Notes et études documentaires*, no. 4569–70, Documentation française, 30 avril 1980 brought up to date in nos. 4737–8, 27 Oct. 1983. Insight into French persuasive approaches to the US is provided by **R. Putnam** and **N. Bayne**, *Western Summitry* (forthcoming, 1984) but points of economic friction are discussed in **R. Parboni**, *The Dollar and its Rivals* (New Left Books, 1982), and in **J.-M. Baer**, 'L'Europe des Dix sous les assauts de la puissance américaine', *Le Monde diplomatique*, juin 1981, though more positive analysis is provided by **S. Hoffmann**, 'L'Europe et les Etats-Unis entre le discorde et l'harmonie', *Politique étrangère*, sept. 1981.

For French relations with European neighbours the fundamental work is **J. Rideau** *et al.*, *La France et les Communautés européennes* (Librairie Génerale de Droit et de Jurisprudence, 1975); for successive periods the most useful works are **F.R. Willis**, *France, Germany and the New Europe 1945–63* (Stanford UP, 1965), **E. Jouve**, *Le Général de*

Gaulle et la construction de l'Europe (LGDJ, 2 vols, 1967–9), **P.-B. Cousté** et **F. Visine**, *Pompidou et l'Europe* (Librairies techniques, 1974), **D.M. Pickles**, *Problems in Contemporary French Politics* (Methuen, 1982), and **F. de La Serre**, 'La Politique européenne de la France: New Look ou New Deal', *Politique étrangère*, no. 1, 1982. Analyses of Mitterrand's plans for the EEC are in *Economist*, 17 Oct. 1981 and in *Financial Times*, 8 Feb. 1984. The fundamental work on relations with Germany is **R. Poidevin** and **J. Bariéty**, *Les Relations franco-allemands 1815–1975* (Colin, 2e edn, 1979), and the chapter by **H. Menudier** in *La Politique extérieure de Valéry Giscard d'Estaing* (1984), but see also the expert writings by **A. Grosser** and his interview in *Politique internationale*, hiver 1982–3. For relations with Britain there is **N.H. Waites** (ed.), *Troubled Neighbours: Franco-British Relations in the 20th Century* (Weidenfeld & Nicolson, 1971) updated by his 'Britain and France: towards a stable relationship', *The World Today*, Dec. 1976. Controversies regarding political cooperation are discussed in **K.J. Twitchett** (ed.), *European Cooperation Today* (Europa, 1980) and in **C. Hill** (ed.), *National Foreign Policies and European Political Cooperation* (Allen & Unwin, 1983). For the debate within France see **M.-C. Smouts**, 'French Foreign Policy: the domestic debate', *International Affairs*, Jan. 1977, **S. Serfaty** (ed.), *The Foreign Policies of the French Left* (Westview Press, 1979), and an invaluable study of a perennially sensitive topic, **M. Newman**, *Socialism and European Unity* (Junction Books, 1983).

For French relations with the 'third world' a very useful start is **W.H. Morris-Jones** and **G. Fischer**, *Decolonisation and After* (Cass, 1980) and more up to date is **P. Cadénat**, 'La France et le tiers monde', *Notes et études documentaires* no. 4701–2, Documentation française, 14 jan. 1983. French policy in Africa gets fair analysis from **R. Bourgi**, *Le Général de Gaulle et l'Afrique noire* (LGDJ, 1980) and *La Politique française de coopération en Afrique: le cas du Sénégal* (LGDJ, 1979), then analysis is provided by **P. Dabezies**, 'Le rôle de la France chez ses protégés africains', *Le Monde diplomatique*, avril 1980; also **J. Maspéro** (ed.), *La France contre l'Afrique*, Tricontinental, 1981,1, Paris, Maspéro, and the special problems of Chad are discussed by **E. Rouleau** in the same periodical in Sept. 1983; socialist policy is discussed by a man initially in office, **J.-P. Cot**, 'La France et l'Afrique; quel changement?', *Politique internationale*, hiver 1982–3. The same issue of that periodical carries articles on French relations with the Middle East; then there is **T.F. von Munchhausen**, 'France's relations with the Arab World', *Aussenpolitik*, no. 4, 1981, while penetrating analyses of French handling of the Lebanon are **S. Turquié**, 'Les objectifs de la politique française dans la crise du Liban', *Le Monde diplomatique*, jan. 1979, **J.-L. Schlegel**, 'Le Liban, Israel et la France', *Projet* Nov. 1982, and French interests in the Indian Ocean are assessed in *Projet* avril 1982, and in *Regards sur l'actualité*, Documentation française, mai 1983. For French relations with Latin America there is **M. Tatu**, 'La position francaise: les difficultés d'être un bon "latino"', *Politique étrangère*, juin 1982. Finally, French policy in the United Nations has been practised by **A. Bérard**, *Un Ambassadeur se souvient* (3 vols, Plon,

1975-9) and analysed by **M.-C. Smouts**, *La France à l'ONU* (Fondation nationale des sciences politiques, 1979). To draw conclusions one may usefully consult **E. Jouve**, *Le Tiers Monde dans la vie internationale* (Berger-Levrault, 1983).

Chapter 6

The daily and periodical press indicated above will provide information on this subject. *Le Monde de l'éducation*, which goes into greater detail, is indispensable. Since January 1982, the education ministry has brought out a new monthly publication (much improved on the old *Courrier*), entitled *Cahiers de l'éducation nationale*. This contains a great deal of information presented in an approachable form, and it also has the advantage of being relatively inexpensive (at the time of writing, 70 francs per year, for ten numbers). *Autrement* often has perceptive insights to offer on the problems of present-day education, which are generally made the theme of a single number.

Statistics are published in the frequent *Notes d'information*, published by SEIS. There is also a collection of these statistics, hitherto published annually, the *Tableaux des enseignements et de la formation*, the most recent edition being for the academic year 1980-1, published by SIGES in 1982. However this convenient format is due to be changed, and in future a shorter, less detailed version will be produced. For the details formerly contained in the *Tableaux*, the reader will have to consult the periodical *Statistiques des enseignements*, also published by SIGES. To cover the gap, a shorter collection of statistics, *L'Education nationale en chiffres, année scolaire 1981-1982*, was published by SIGES in October 1983.

Periodicals of the teaching unions and of parents' associations are always worth consulting, not only for the information which they contain, but also for the insight which they give into the mentality and ideology of these bodies. The FEN publishes two periodicals, *FEN-Informations*, and *L'Enseignement public*, the latter giving much more detailed information. See also *L'Ecole libératrice*, organ of the SNI-PEGC, *SNC-Bulletin* (*Syndicat national des collèges*), and *Quinzaine universitaire*, for a conservative approach. For the mainstream views of higher education unions, see *Syndicalisme universitaire* (SU) of the SGEN-CFDT, and *le Snesup* (*Syndicat national de l'enseignement supérieur-FEN*), both appearing twice monthly. *Pour l'enfant . . . vers l'homme*, the organ of the FCPE, is a very revealing, especially on the private education issue, whereas *la Voix des Parents* (PEEP) indicates its more moderate stance.

There is now a four-volume history of education in France, *Histoire générale de l'enseignement en France*, (dir. **L.-H. Parias**, published by Nouvelle Librairie de France, 1981). The third and fourth volumes are relevant to a study of modern French education: 3, **F. Mayeur**, *De la Révolution à l'école républicaine*, 4 **A. Prost**, *L'Ecole et la famille dans une société en mutation*. A useful and accessible work of reference is **D. Demnard** and **D. Fourment**, *Dictionnaire d'histoire de l'enseignement*

(J.-P. Delarge, 1981). The best of the more accessible histories is undoubtedly that of **A. Prost**, *L'Enseignement en France, 1800-1967* (2nd ed., Colin, 1970) while further information is provided by **F. Ponteil**, *Histoire de l'enseignement en France, 1789-1964* (Sirey, 1965), **P. Chevallier** *et al.*, *L'Enseignement français de la Révolution à nos jours* (2 vols, Mouton, 1968-71).

Since so many changes are in perspective in French education, the reports commissioned by the education minister on various aspects are worth consulting, in spite of their not being the most accessible of reading matter. The most significant reports so far published are: **B. Schwartz**, *L'insertion professionnelle et sociale des jeunes*, (Documentation Française, September 1981) **Commission du bilan**, *La France en mai 1981*, vol. 4, *L'Enseignement et le développement scientifique*, (*rapport L. Schwartz*), (Documentation Française, December 1981); **A. de Peretti**, *La Formation des personnels de l'Education nationale* (Documentation Française, 1982); **L. Soubré**, *Décentralisation et démocratisation des institutions scolaires* (CNDP, May 1982); **L. Legrand**, *Pour un collège démocratique* (Documentation Française, December 1982); also author of *Pour une politique démocratique de l'éducation* (PUF, 1977), and *L'école unique: à quelles conditions?* (Scarabée, 1981); **R. Girault**, *L'Histoire et la géographie en question* (CNDP, 1983); **A. Prost**, *Les Lycées et leur études au seuil du XXIe siècle* (CNDP, 1984).

Most accounts of French education contain more than fleeting references to the administrative system in its more traditional form. One overall account is Cahiers de documentation, *L'Organisation de l'enseignement en France* (INRDP, 1976). A more exhaustive study is **J.-L. Crémieux-Brilhac**, *L'Education nationale* (PUF, 1965). For a more recent, and excellent account, see **J. Minot**, *L'Education nationale*, (Berger-Levrault, 1979).

On higher education, **C. Fourrier**, *Les Institutions universitaires* (PUF, 1971) gives good basic guidance; for a fuller description, see **I. Boussard**, **M.-J. Guédon** and **D. Wolf**, *Les Institutions universitaires françaises* (Documentation française, 1977). The *Cahiers de l'INAS* have published some useful information with the relevant texts on aspects of university structures; *Conférence des présidents d'universités*, 1975; *Conseil national de l'enseignement supérieur et de la recherche*, 1975.

On the issue of Catholic education, a short history of the church/state problem is provided by **B. Mégrine**, *La Question scolaire en France* (PUF, 1963), see also **A. Coutrot** and **F.-G. Dreyfus**, *Les Forces religieuses dans la société française* (Colin, 1965), **R. Rémond** (ed.), *Forces religieuses et attitudes politiques dans la France contemporaine* (Colin, 1965) and **R. Rémond**, *L'Anticléricalisme en France de 1815 à nos jours* (Fayard, 1976). For a particularly vivid insight into the anti-clerical mentality, see **J. Cornec**, *Pour l'Ecole libre* (Laffont, 1977). His successor, **J. Andrieu**, adopts a more sophisticated, although equally exclusive attitude. For an example of this see his *Vous avez dit 'laïque'?* (pref. **J. Cornec**) Editions Rupture, 1980), which is part autobiography, part *profession de foi*. There is a fairly ample literature on private education: see **E. Dreyfus**, *Libres écoles? Enquête sur l'enseignement privé* (Le Centurion 1982) for a good overview and discussion;*L'Enseignement catholique* (Fayard, 1982), for a specifically pro-Catholic *plaidoyer*; see also **N. Fontaine**, *L'Ecole libre et l'Etat* (Unapec, 1982) and for more detail her longer work of reference, *Guide juridique de l'enseignement privé associé à l'Etat part contrat: la liberté d'enseignement*, 3rd edn (Unapec, 1980). On the question of parental choice, see **R. Ballion's** thought-provoking work, *Les Consommateurs d'école: stratégie des familles* (Stock, 1982); similar ideas are contained in his article, 'L'enseignement privé, une "école sur mesure"?' in the *Revue française de sociologie*, April–June 1980.

There are some good general studies on French education, notably **W.D. Halls**, *Education, Culture and Politics in modern France** (Oxford, Pergamon, 1976); **W.R. Fraser**, *Reforms and Restraints in Modern French Education** (Routledge & Kegan Paul, 1971) and **J. Majault**, *L'Enseignement en France* (McGraw-Hill, 1973) are well worth study, in spite of their less recent date of publication.

Books by teachers, containing accounts of their experiences, give considerable insight into the workings (effective or otherwise) of the education system, e.g., **J. Roussel**, *Etre institutrice* (Cerf, 1973); **R. Bréchon**, *La Fin des lycées* (Grasset, 1970) gives a perceptive account of life in a school in the immediate post-1968 period; **N. Delanoë**, *La Faute à Voltaire* (Seuil, 1972) deals with some of the same problems, but from a more specifically leftist approach. **S. Citron**, *L'Ecole bloquée* (Bordas, 1971) concentrates more on the extent to which the education system is unadapted to educational needs; examples of this are **C. Duneton**, *Je suis comme une Truie qui doute* (Seuil, 1976) and for a grimmer picture, **M.T. Maschino**, *Vos enfants ne m'intéressent plus* (Hachette, 1983). See also **V. Cachilles**, *Un petit collège très ordinaire* (Scarabée, 1982) and **P. Boumard**, *Un conseil de class très ordinaire* (Stock, 1978) for a critical view of that institution. Other useful studies include: **G. Langoulet** *et al.*, *Questions-résponses sur les collèges* (Editions ESF, 1980) (there is a whole series of *Questions-résponses* including books on the *lycée, école maternelle* etc.,); **D. Paty**, *12 Collèges en France* (Documentation Française, 1981) an enquiry into the organization and functioning of twelve very different schools, with a consideration of the social categories of children which they receive. *Expérimentation d'une pédagogie de soutien dans sept académies, 1976–1980* (Ministère de l'éducation nationale, August 1981) gives a detailed picture of the problems involved in remedial teaching; **J. Ferraz** and **P. Scalabre**, *Le Collège: Guide pratique de gestion* (Berger-Levrault, 1982) contains an historical account of the important texts from the Berthoin reforms, via the Haby reforms, to the directives of Savary. The special number of *Paradoxes* (no. 48–49) entitled *L'éducation en question* (automne 1982) well repays study, as it contains articles of over forty people closely concerned with education from all sides of the political spectrum. One other important contribution to the debate on education is **B. Schwartz**, *Une autre école* (Flammarion, 1977).

A mine of information on primary education is the *Code Soleil* (52nd ed., Sudel, 1982). See also, Intensive Study Visits–France, *Aspects of the*

French Education System seen through British eyes (Central Bureau for Educational Visits and Exchanges, n.d.). E. **Faure**, *L'Education nationale et la participation* (Plon, 1968) is clearly a key text in any consideration of the *Loi d'orientation*. J. de **Chalendar**, *Une Loi pour l'université* (Desclée de Brouwer, 1970) gives an interesting account of the preparation of the law. On the workings of the Faure law in one specific university — Nanterre — see R. **Rémond**'s revealing and fascinating account of his university presidency, *La Règle et le consentement — Gouverner une société* (Fayard, 1979). Two books of interest in a consideration of higher education are **AUPEL**, *Pour que l'Université ne meure* (Le Centurion, 1977) — a moderate view — and M. **Duffour**, D. **Monteux**, and Y. **Schwartz**, *L'Université de la crise au changement* (Editions Sociales, 1978) for a PCF view of higher education. For the proposed changes by Savary, see the minister's collected speeches, *Principales déclarations de M. Alain Savary, ministre de l'éducation nationale juin 1981–mai 1982* (Service de l'Information, CNDP, n.d.); see also L. **Schwartz**'s *Pour sauver l'Université* (Seuil, 1983) — a spirited and convincing science-oriented defence of selection in higher education. On the IUTs, see M. **Domenc** and J.-P. **Gilly**, *Les IUT, ouverture et idéologie* (Cerf, 1977) — a left-wing view — and on Vincennes M. **Debeauvais**, *L'Université ouverte: les dossiers de Vincennes* (PUF de Grenoble, 1976) — a committed approach.

On the possibilities of *éducation permanente*, see D. **Chevrolet**, *L'Université et la formation permanente* (Brussels, Casterman, 1977) and on the position today, P. **Besnard** and B. **Lietard**, *La Formation continue* (PUF, 1976).

On the purposes of education, C. **Baudelot** and R. **Establet**, *L'Ecole capitaliste en France* (Maspéro, 1971) giving a marxist viewpoint, attacks the education system as a means of reproducing social class-structures. P. **Bourdieu** and J.-C. **Passeron**, *La Réproduction* (Editions de Minuit, 1970) considers a similar problem, that of the continuing social and cultural dominance exercised by the upper classes.

Other works considering related problems are: R. **Boudon**, *L'Inégalité des chances* (Colin, 1973); J.-M. **Berthelot**, *Le Piège scolaire* (PUF, 1983). See also J. **Fournier**, *Politique de l'éducation* (Seuil, 1971); J. **Capelle**, *Education et politique* (PUF, 1974) and, as a corrective, J. **Wilson**, *Fantasy and Common sense in Education* (Martin Robertson, 1979). An account of the realization of experimental approaches to education is given in R. **Gloton** (ed.), *L'Etablissement scolaire: unité éducative* (Brussels, Casterman, 1977).

The class structure of higher education is well illustrated by P. **Bourdieu** and J.-C. **Passeron**, *Les Héritiers* (Editions de Minuit, 1964).

Finally, for reference, B. **Lemennicier** *et al.*, *L'Aide aux étudiants en France* (CNRS, 1977) and more recently, P. **Gerbod**, 'Note sur la condition matérielle et morale de l'étudiant français', in *Revue française de sociologie*, April–June 1980. One book, which unfortunately is now virtually unobtainable, but a godsend to the student wandering through the jungle of education initials, is C. and R. **Guy**, *Abbréviations et sigles enseignement* (Casteilla, 1975). It is hoped that an updated version will soon be published.

Index

361

364   *Index*